The Freudian Exodus: Psychoanalysis and the Mosaic Legacy

Contemporary Psychoanalytic Studies

VOLUME 32

The titles published in this series are listed at *brill.com/cps*

The Freudian Exodus: Psychoanalysis and the Mosaic Legacy

By

Andrew Barnaby

BRILL

LEIDEN | BOSTON

Cover illustration: *Journey* (1991) by Samuel Bak. Image courtesy of Pucker Gallery.

Library of Congress Cataloging-in-Publication Data

Names: Barnaby, Andrew Thomas, author.
Title: The Freudian exodus : psychoanalysis and the mosaic legacy / by Andrew Barnaby.
Description: Leiden : Brill, [2025] | Series: Contemporary psychoanalytic studies, 1571-4977 ; vol.32 | Includes bibliographical references and index. | Summary: "The Freudian Exodus redefines the traumatic experience that Freud argued was the origin of Judaic monotheism, the murder of Moses. Focusing instead on the Babylonian Exile, the study explores a series of topics understood as the aftershocks of that cultural trauma. Among these are the nature of anti-Semitism, Christianity's vexed relationship to Judaism, the fantasmatic status of subjectivity, the cultural function of Torah, and Freud's escape at the end of his life from Nazi controlled Austria. The in-depth analysis of these topics aims for a new understanding of psychoanalysis, conceived more as a philosophy than as a mode of therapy"– Provided by publisher.
Identifiers: LCCN 2024030801 (print) | LCCN 2024030802 (ebook) | ISBN 9789004701083 (hardback) | ISBN 9789004701663 (ebook)
Subjects: LCSH: Freud, Sigmund, 1856-1939. Mann Moses und die monotheistische Religion. | Moses (Biblical leader) | Monotheism. | Psychology, Religious.
Classification: LCC BS580.M6 B255 2025 (print) | LCC BS580.M6 (ebook) | DDC 211/.34–dc23/eng/20240826
LC record available at https://lccn.loc.gov/2024030801
LC ebook record available at https://lccn.loc.gov/2024030802

Typeface for the Latin, Greek, and Cyrillic scripts: "Brill". See and download: brill.com/brill-typeface.

ISSN 1571-4977
ISBN 978-90-04-70108-3 (hardback)
ISBN 978-90-04-70166-3 (e-book)
DOI 10.1163/9789004701663

This book is printed on acid-free paper and produced in a sustainable manner.

To Mary O'Connor and Gabriel Moyal, for everything

It is not enough for the psychoanalyst to rely on the resources of his science, nor on the support of myth. He must also become a philosopher.

—JEAN LAPLANCHE and JEAN-BERTRAND PONTALIS,
"Fantasy and the Origins of Sexuality"

Contents

Acknowledgements

Text is reprinted from the following sources:

A portion of Coda 1 (The Murder of Moses and the Temporality of Trauma) was originally published in "The Psychoanalytic Origins of Literary Trauma Studies," in *Trauma and Literature*, ed. Roger Kurz. © Cambridge University Press, 2018. Reproduced by permission of Cambridge University Press through PLSclear.

A portion of Chapter 2 ("How can we sing a song of the LORD?": The Compulsions of the Postexilic Unconscious) was originally published under the same title in *Psychoanalytische Perspectieven*, 42.1 (2024): 71–94.

Portions of Chapter 3 (Torah and / as Tradition) and Chapter 4 ("Stored like fragments in an ark": Freud, Hamlet, and Filial Exodus) were originally published in chapter 6 of *Coming Too Late: Reflections on Freud and Belatedness*. © SUNY Press 2017.

A portion of Chapter 4 was originally published in "Tell My Story: Freud, Hamlet, and the Burdens of Self-Authorship," *Mosaic: An Interdisciplinary Critical Journal*, 52.4 (2019): 21–36.

I want to thank the Humanities Center at the University of Vermont for funding in support of the publication of this book. I would also like to thank the University of Vermont's Department of English and the College of Arts and Sciences for other forms of support.

Note on Citations from Major Primary Works

1 Freud

1. With the exception of those from *Moses and Monotheism*, most of the citations of Freud's writings will be from *The Standard Edition of the Complete Psychological Works of Sigmund Freud*, ed. and trans. James Strachey et al. 24 vols. London, 1953–74. With the individual work identified as necessary, citations from the *Standard Edition* will be given by volume and page number(s) following the abbreviation SE.
2. Citations of some of Freud's earliest writings will be from *The Origins of Psycho-Analysis: Letters to Wilhelm Fliess, Drafts and Notes, 1887–1902*, ed. Marie Bonaparte, et al; trans. Eric Mosbacher and James Strachey, New York, 1954. Citations will be given by page number(s) following *Origins*.
3. Citations of Freud's *Moses and Monotheism* will be from Katherine Jones' translation, New York, 1954. Citations will be given by page number(s). I will at times also provide the alternative translation from the *Standard Edition*.
4. Unless otherwise noted, citations from the original German texts, identified as necessary, will be from *Gesammelte Werke*, 18 vol., ed. Marie Bonaparte, et al. Frankfurt am Main, 1968–78. Citations will be given by volume and page number(s).

2 Bible

2.1 *Hebrew Bible*

Citations, by chapter and verse number(s), will be from *Tanakh: A New Translation of the Holy Scriptures According to the Traditional Hebrew Text*, New York, 1985.

2.2 *New Testament*

Citations, by chapter and verse number(s), will follow the NRSV.

Introduction

> [After] "the German invasion, … in the certainty of persecution—now not only because of my work, but also because of my "race"—I left, with many friends, the city which from early child, through seventy-eight years, had been a home to me. I found the kindliest welcome in beautiful, free, generous England. Here I live now, a welcome guest, relieved from that oppression and happy that I may again speak and write—I almost said "think"—as I want or have to.
>
> —FREUD, *Moses and Monotheism*

•••

> Philosophy begins in loss, in finding yourself at a loss.
>
> —STANLEY CAVELL, *This New Yet Unapproachable America*

∵

At various points in *Moses and Monotheism*, Freud distinguishes between what he calls "material truth" (*die materielle Warheit*) and "historical truth" (*die historische Warheit*). In a section of Part III labeled "*Die historische Warheit*" (German text: 16:236–40), for example, Freud remarks about the truth-status of religious belief—here, specifically, the commitment to "the conception of an Only God"—that the believer's own "solution" to the question of *why this belief?* ("because it is part of eternal truth which, hidden for so long, has at last come to light") does "contain … truth." In a way that the believer does not fully grasp, however, Freud adds that this truth "is not … the material truth, but a historical truth" (*Moses and Monotheism*, 165–66). The difference in these two types of truth appears to rest on the distinction between what we consciously experience (think of this as the portion of our lived reality or even of history more broadly that is visible to us, like the portion of an iceberg that we can see above its surrounding water) and the much larger but invisible foundation of lived reality or history (the bulk of the iceberg below the waterline). Freud, we might say, is imposing on the very idea of lived reality or history his core distinction between conscious and unconscious aspects of psychical life. What we experience or understand (here, of our own religious faith) is true, but it is only a small part (the "material" portion) of the fuller "historical" truth, that

 | DOI:10.1163/9789004701663_002

which lies submerged (repressed) and, as Freud's study aims to document, can only become visible through the lens of psychoanalysis.

If then, for Freud, material truth is that part of our lived reality or history that is available to conscious understanding while historical truth is its motivating or driving (typically unconscious) force, historical truth is thus also more fully explanatory: to reconstruct history within the framework of psychoanalytic theory and practice would be to show the causal connections underlying what happens in cultural experience. To take just one example of what Freud means, towards the close of *Moses and Monotheism* he remarks that "the emergence of the conception of one great God ... must be recognized as a memory—a distorted one, it is true, but nevertheless a memory." And if, "as far as its distortion goes, it may be called a delusion," to the extent the concept "brings to light something from the past, it must be called a truth" (167). Freud's point is that, as memory, distortion, or delusion, "the conception of one great God," consciously understood as a faith-doctrine—the very core of monotheism—would more properly mark the material truth of the matter and not the historical truth.

But in what sense is there a psychoanalytic method of *historical* investigation? Reflecting earlier in *Moses and Monotheism* on the notion of the return of the repressed, Freud writes:

> It is specially worthy of note that every memory returning from the forgotten past does so with great force, produces an incomparably strong influence on the mass of mankind, and puts forward an irresistible claim to be believed, against which all logical objections remain powerless ... This strange characteristic can only be understood by comparison with the delusions in a psychotic case. It has long been recognized that delusions contain a piece of forgotten truth, which had at its return to put up with being distorted and misunderstood, and the compulsive conviction appertaining to the delusion emanates from this core of truth and spreads to the errors that enshroud it. Such a kernel of truth—which we might call *historical* truth—must also be conceded to the doctrines of various religions. (107–08)

The historical truth is the "kernel of truth" or "piece of forgotten truth" that remains from the past but is available to us only in distorted or misunderstood form. The material truth—the truth of the past to which we consciously adhere—can at once reveal and conceal the forgotten and, because forgotten, more foundational truth. In other words, the historical truth is an originary event or incident that, precisely by being denied or otherwise psychically defended against, becomes all the more potent because *not* consciously recognized. That is what Freud means by saying that "every memory returning from the forgotten past does so with great force, produces an incomparably strong influence ..., and puts forward an irresistible claim to be believed." It is in that context that he can write earlier: "I have never doubted that religious phenomena are to be understood on the model of the neurotic symptoms of the individual ... as a return of long-forgotten important happenings in the primeval history of the human family, [and] that *they owe their obsessive character to that very origin and therefore derive their effect on mankind from the historical truth they contain.* (71; my emphasis). Later he will write that "the ... conviction issues from this [pattern of forgetting and return in distorted form] and extends to the whole delusional fabrication surrounding it" (166). Understood on the model of neurotic symptomology, the "conviction" and the corresponding "delusional fabrication surrounding it" together function as the interpretive foundation of historical investigation precisely to the extent they are understood as what Melford Spiro has called a "culturally constituted defense mechanism."[1] In short, while Freud concedes that "it is not easy ... to introduce the conception of the unconscious into mass psychology" (163), he believes that, especially in the context of the study of religious phenomena, he can employ a psychoanalytic method of historical investigation precisely to the extent there is a functional analogy that "bridge[s] the gap between individual and mass psychology" (128).[2]

It is from this interpretive vantage that Freud's chief goal of answering "the question of the origin of monotheism among the Jews" (81) takes as one of its critical starting points the hypothesis that, at the very beginning of their collective life, "the people [who would become the nation of Israel] passed through what may properly be termed a traumatic experience" (65). To unpack that trauma—to undistort and to understand what has been distorted and misunderstood (purposefully if unconsciously so)—is thus at the very heart of Freud's project because the trauma is both the origin and the unresolved driver of Jewish history. And if it is less immediately visible than that history's material truth, this historical truth as conceived in Freud's terms has, as noted

1 "Religious Systems as Culturally Constituted Defense Mechanisms," in *Culture and Human Nature: Theoretical Papers of Melford E. Spiro*, ed. Benjamin Kilborne and L. L. Langness (Chicago: University of Chicago Press, 1987), 145–60.

2 As Freud had remarked earlier, "the analogy is met with in psychopathology, in the genesis of human neurosis: that is to say, in a discipline belonging to individual psychology, whereas religious phenomena must of course be regarded as a part of mass psychology. We shall see that this analogy is not so startling as it appears at first sight; indeed, it is rather in the nature of an axiom" (91).

above, more explanatory force: unearthing the Jewish trauma of the ancient past—the chief goal of *Moses and Monotheism*—not only promises, as Freud writes in his final paragraph, to shed "light on the question how the Jewish people acquired the qualities that characterize it" but also to solve "the problem how they could survive until today as an entity" (176).

As a pathway into Freud's effort to explicate this foundational cultural trauma especially in relation to how the Jewish people were in the past and continue to be in the present mysteriously sustained in the very experience of surviving it, I would like to reflect briefly on the cover art for my study, a painting by the Lithuanian-born Samuel Bak who, like Freud himself (though as a boy rather than as an old man), managed to survive the Nazi invasion of his homeland and the post-invasion genocide.[3] If Freud grounds the thesis of *Moses and Monotheism* in a collective trauma he locates in the Jewish past, Bak grounds his art in a collective trauma of the Jewish present (the Holocaust), a present that was just beginning as Freud was completing his study in 1938. At the same time, even as Freud's focus on the past yet aims to solve a "problem" in the present—"how ... could [the Jewish people] *survive until today* as an entity"—Bak's focus on the present leads him towards a painful reckoning with the Jewish past: nothing less than how the biblical narrative in broad terms and particularly the Exodus account at the heart of Torah lay at the origin and subsequent (hi)story of God's chosen people, a (hi)story that, drawn forward to the twentieth century, must then grapple with the perverse mutation of what is primarily a celebration of ancestral freedom into modern genocide.

The painting in question, "Journey" (1991), was included in Bak's justly acclaimed series *Landscapes of Jewish Experience*. Of the series in general, Lawrence Langer has commented that "we cannot look at the monumental paintings ... without feeling the tension that slowly mounts as we grope to interpret their images. The shapes and spaces on the canvases first unite with each other, creating a fragile balance between substance and ruin. Then they leap forth to challenge us with the dual appeal of chaos and form ... Among other possibilities, these paintings are dramatic bulwarks against amnesia. They

3 Bak was born in 1933 Vilna (modern Vilnius), which, though now the capital of Lithuania, was part of Poland during in the interwar period. One of the great centers of Yiddish culture, Vilna was occupied by the Soviet Union in 1940 and then invaded by Germany the following year. Of the 60,000 or so Jewish inhabitants at that time, only a few thousand (at most) lived to see the Soviet return in 1944. Most of Bak's family did not survive the Nazi terror—his father was shot just a few days before the Soviets retook the city. Along with his mother, Bak moved to central Poland and then to a displaced-persons camp in Germany where they lived from 1945 to 1948. They immigrated to Israel in 1948.

are reminders of a sacred past, criminally besieged, crowded with emblems of a ravaged civilization." Substance and ruin, chaos and form, presence and absence, the sacred and the desecrated: these are some of the key figurative and, we might say, rhetorical pairings by which, as Langer adds, Bak creates "a giant jigsaw puzzle ... that burden[s] viewers with the task of retrieving its missing pieces, while leaving them wondering whether those pieces may have been lost forever."[4]

In "Journey," we find several of Bak's most evocative and consistently used images of those pairings, expressed here as elsewhere in the series in what Langer calls "relics of ruin" in "a wasteland of Jewish tradition struggling out of its disarray."[5] On the painting's horizontal or diagonal axis defined by the side of a mostly visible ship, we see a Star of David, faded and not fully whole (wounded, we might say), and the side of the ship itself is a stone wall that clearly aims to recall the Western Wall in Jerusalem's Old City and, by extension, the Roman act of destruction that in 70 CE reduced the foundation of the Second Temple to a memorial of national loss. Still along that axis but on the ship itself, we see what remains of the Jewish ghetto of Bak's youth, collapsed now under the weight of Nazi atrocities, and then a small-scale repetition of the ghetto that appears on two otherwise empty stone structures in the shape of the Tablets of the Law that Moses received from God as the first record of the Decalogue. Still on the ship but creating a separate vertical axis, we see a building with two smokestacks, one of the deathcamp crematoria serving here as a synecdoche of systematic annihilation of European Jewry. And atop the smokestacks, the drifting smoke telling us that this crematorium is still at work (if perhaps also, bizarrely, providing the power to move the ship forward) is a chilling marker of the form the Final Solution ultimately took: an oblique if still terrifying explanation of why in a painting called "Journey" there are no human figures.

The images individually and as part of the various interconnections comprising the painting's puzzle-like quality merit further comment. We might start with the wall visible on the side of the ship and the replicas of the Mosaic tablets because, as Langer notes, "the Kotel" (the Western or Wailing Wall in Jerusalem) and "the shattered fragments of the original Commandments" are

4 *Landscapes of Jewish Experience: Paintings by Samuel Bak* (essay and commentary by Lawrence L. Langer) (Boston: Pucker Gallery in association with Brandeis University Press, 1997), 2. As Langer writes in a way that helps us understand the title of the series, "Bak's paintings comprise a visual testimony to the disaster, a profusion of images that admit us to an event many considerable unimaginable" (3).

5 *Landscapes of Jewish Experience*, 3.

"the most sacred 'Ur-ruin[s]' of the Jewish imagination."[6] Bak's rendering, while purposefully recalling the sacred, emphasizes the ruin, even the impossibility of sustaining the very meaning of the sacred in the wake of the Holocaust. As noted above, the wall that makes up the side of the ship is at once an image of Jerusalem's Western Wall and a memorial of the lost Second Temple (not restored in almost 2000 years); but that very memorial harkens back to the destruction of the First Temple, razed by the Babylonians in 586 BCE. The imagistic transformation of what we would expect to be a material more suitable for a ship (e.g. wood) into that specific stone wall thus suggests that any journey forward in space and / or time for the Jewish people is weighted down with unforgotten and unredeemed losses. More to the point, recollected here in the stone wall, the pain of that past and in particular God's inexplicable failure to sustain the terms of the covenant might cause the overheavy ship to sink. The image of the stone tablets (the very locus of God's physical presence in the world as described in Exodus 31:18) is now empty of the original divine words (the link between God and his chosen people as mediated through the gift of Torah). Bak has replaced the missing words with an image of the primary site of legal observance (the Jewish home), but these two slight structures are effectively overwhelmed by the distorted and falling houses of the ghetto positioned immediately to the left. Addressing us with what Langer aptly calls "a language of tainted familiarity," whatever meaning the Law might once have had now "echoes with a hollow solemnity in a universe just awakening from the slaying of the people it was designed to enlighten." Commenting on a similar use of this image in the painting "Shema Yisrael," Langer adds that, while "the blank tablets ... [are] waiting to be engraved anew, presumably by a Divine Hand[,] ... the Chosen People are nowhere to be seen, their absence raising the unsettling question of how the effort to exterminate them has disrupted the ancient narrative of Genesis and Exodus."[7]

The image of the smoke above the crematorium chimney is even more unsettling. Here as in other paintings in the series the billowing smoke from the chimneys has a majesty to it that suggests a divine power and presence. But if the most appropriate biblical association is what is described in Exodus 19:18—"Now Mount Sinai was all in smoke, for the LORD had come down upon it in fire; the smoke rose like the smoke of a kiln, and the whole mountain trembled violently"—then, as Langer remarks in a related context, Bak

6 *Landscapes of Jewish Experience*, 9.

7 *Landscapes of Jewish Experience*, 5, 8. In a related comment on "From Aleph to X," Langer finds Bak posing the fundamental question: "If faith is to endure, must the Torah be 'rewritten' to include the legacy of Auschwitz?" (5).

appears to be playing on how this verse uncannily "forecasts ... the unforeseen fate of the Jewish people at the hands of the Germans."[8] More daringly (or bitterly), Bak also appears to be proposing that the miraculous transformation during the Sinai theophany through which the divine smoke initiating the revelation of the covenant (Exodus 19) will fully solidify in the stone Tablets of the Law (Exodus 31) has itself been transformed: after the Holocaust all that is left are the floating wisps of the millions of bodies consumed by fire hovering with a perverse density above the very means of their disposal. And the divine presence that once promised to sustain the covenantal people—a covenant that, in a terrible irony, included the law "You shall not murder"—is just as absent from the scene as the people themselves.

What, finally, are we to make of Bak's choice of title? What sort of journey is he asking us to imagine? We might start with a simpler question: is the boat moving or stationary? In his commentary on the painting, Langer assumes that it is "moored in a proper harbor." But even if that is the case, what precisely constitutes "proper" is not entirely clear. And if the ship is in harbor, has it arrived at its destination or is it awaiting departure (and is the departure imminent)? If the ship has reached its destination, the painting presents a truly terrifying spectacle: those "relics of ruin" Langer speaks of (here, the Western Wall, the Star of David, the Tablets of the Law, the Jewish ghetto, the smoke revealing the divine call to the covenant) would then point to how the end of the journey is effectively the end of the Jewish people; there is simply no place left to go. And the absence of the covenantal people would tell us that no one has survived to carry on anyway—the collapse of the ghetto homes and the smoke from the crematorium's chimneys say all that need to be said). Even God has disappeared.

But we might look at the painting in another way. The beckoning openness and brightness of the vista in the upper-left corner of the painting and the calm waters promising smooth sailing might be meant to show that the ship is headed in that direction even if it has not yet left the harbor. In other words, this may not be the end of the journey; this may not be the end of the (hi)story of the Jewish people. Other details might encourage us to believe that the ship is already on the move. If the shape of the surrounding land might permit us to imagine a natural harbor, we can see no anchor or rope to secure the ship and no pier, wharf, or marina where it might be docked. The smoke that drifts slightly to the right could be intended to show that the ship is moving to the left, and the proximity of the side of ship to large rocks is less suggestive of a

---

8 *Landscapes of Jewish Experience*, 71.

safe arrival than of the immediate problem of navigating in dangerous waters. The eddies near the rocks point to some motion, though this could simply be the result of natural currents and not the result of the ship's forward movement. If the ship is moving, it is moving slowly, a hint that the voyage is just beginning: the fact that we can see rocks points to fairly shallow waters.

Whether it is moving or not, it makes most sense to conclude that the ship is pointed in the direction of, even guided by, the Star of David as though that were an insignia painted on side of the ship close to the bow. If the very idea of the journey might then suggest another Exodus, we might infer that the Star of David, especially in tandem with the synecdochic reminder of the Jerusalem Temple, refers at once to the ancient kingdom whose capital was the city of David and to the modern state of Israel, where Bak and his mother moved in 1948. We might then wonder if Bak wants us to imagine that another Exodus (or just an exodus, a departure) holds out the hope of another Promised Land (or at least a someplace else). That optimistic reading, of course, might be as wrong as the pessimistic reading offered above; or, to think of this another way, the optimistic and pessimistic readings might be in conceptual dialogue because the product of Bak's own ambivalence: he and his mother might have survived, but six million of his fellow Jews did not. Whatever living future awaits, it cannot forget a deadly past. And even if as part of this journey the Star of David and the Western Wall could somehow be returned to Israel as their true place of origin, they would do so in such diminished form that they could only ever speak of what has been lost: a people, a nation, a culture, an everlasting bond with the God who chose them. Reflecting on the "character trait[s] of the Jews" as he knew them especially from his life in Vienna, Freud observed with real admiration that "they are animated by a special trust in life, such as it is bestowed by the secret possession of a precious gift; it is a kind of optimism. Religious people would call it trust in God" (*Moses and Monotheism*, 134). Painting "Journey" some fifty years later, Bak knew things that Freud did not. From that vantage, the deathcamps that would only come to light after Freud's death may have destroyed any notion that the people were in "secret possession of a precious gift" or that it was wise to trust in a God whose promises could not be trusted.[9]

9 While Freud died before the full scope of the Nazi terror was revealed to the world, he yet understood that subjection to repeated persecution was the cost paid by the Jewish people for holding onto their cultural identity. He writes in the next-to-last paragraph of *Moses and Monotheism*, "only a part of the Jewish people accepted the new doctrine [Christianity]. Those who refused to do so are still called Jews. Through this decision they are still more sharply separated from the rest of the world than they were before.... They have been made to suffer severely for it" (176).

Langer remarks that "one of the many atrocious consequences of the Holocaust, in addition the slaughter of millions of men, women, and children, was the ravaging of their roots, of the social and cultural traditions that they have passed from generation to generation." Despite that ravaging, however, or perhaps because of it, "Journey" and many of the other paintings in *Landscapes of Jewish Experience* portray the Jewish people's endurance, their resilience in the face of catastrophe. Without knowing the full extent of the terror to come, Freud had made a similar observation; as part of a broader reflection on the root-causes of anti-Semitism, he points to a "peculiarity" of the Jewish people: "they defy oppression, ... even the most cruel persecutions have not succeeded in exterminating them" (*Moses and Monotheism*, 116). If there is a painful if unintended irony here—the Nazis were even then planning crueler persecutions precisely with extermination as their goal—Freud's statement in the closing paragraph of *Moses and Monotheism* that, historically speaking, the survival of the Jewish people is an "enigma" (176; German: *Rätsel* [16:246]) might apply even after the Holocaust. For while six million Jews were murdered, the Jewish people live on, and their "social and cultural traditions" continue to be "passed from generation to generation." If from the perspective of Samuel Bak, who spent most of his life in the Holocaust's shadow, a survivor had a moral duty to bear witness to the "wasteland of Jewish tradition" created by unspeakable violence, Bak's own act of bearing witness also, as Langer points out, press on the paintings' viewers the task "to determine from this turmoil how much of a chance for renewal remains." Langer concludes that what Bak finally portrays, however, is "less a miracle of renewal than a stubborn resolve to stay alive."[10] Such resolve, for Bak, can no longer be based on "trust in God"; it appears, rather, to be based on the Jewish will to survive—and to survive as Jewish—despite the people's long history of suffering.

Langer points out that "a favorite term in Nazideutsch—a special language devised by the Germans to conceal and express their plans for the Final Solution—was *ausrotten*, to uproot or extirpate, and by association exterminate." He adds that "'uprooting' ... is part of the history of the Jewish people, and Bak exploits this dual usage to inspect the experience of past and present." In the paintings "Family Tree" and "Destinies," for example, "the central motif ... is a tree severed from its trunk or ripped from the earth, but in neither instance has this violation of nature led to its total death.... [T]he continued survival of the Jewish people is confirmed in the small shoots that spring from

10 *Landscapes of Jewish Experience*, 3, 18–19. Langer adds that "if [Bak] can be said to celebrate anything in this series, it is the stamina of the spirit of Jewish memory, affected and even afflicted by the powers of darkness, but never entirely annulled" (4).

the base of the trees even as the upper trunks are sheared away."[11] "Journey" and other paintings in the series that portray a voyage of some kind imagine the cultural uprooting in a different, though no less resonant, way. If, as Langer suggest, "the search for the final locale of Jewish identity is another recurrent theme" in Bak's series, the very concept of "home is an inconclusive credential for a people known through legend and history for their wandering—to and from native terrain, or transient place of exile, or more recently, the sites of their murder." But even as "the wish of Jews to settle down in a place called home has been disrupted by repeated efforts of others to settle them elsewhere" (to uproot them), Bak might be said to be turning the tables on those "others" by reimagining what Langer calls "the loneliness and wandering that has long been part of [the Jewish people's] historical pilgrimage" into a source of their strength, an extension of the biblical narrative's regular idealization of nomadism as an alternative to permanent settlement.[12] It may also be that, as "Journey's" very ambiguity hints at, the "*search for* the finale locale" is more important to Jewish identity than the finality of the location precisely because things that can be easily transported—words, texts, rituals, laws, the very concept of a people bound together in myriad ways, including a shared history of uprooting and a god whose presence among them was fixed in a traveling tabernacle centuries before a Temple was built—are more central to the Jewish idea of nationhood than any specified Promised Land. As is suggested by the first epigraph above and as we shall see in detail in Coda 4, Freud's completion of *Moses and Monotheism* itself depended on a disruptive uprooting (his flight to England in the wake of the *Anschluss*) that, whatever sense of loss it evoked in him, was more properly experienced in the words of Shakespeare's Rosalind from *As You Like It*: "Now go we in content // To liberty, and not to banishment."[13]

Freud's final journey from Austria to England will be just one of the several points of consideration through which, inspired in part by the rhetorical complexity of Bak's *Landscapes of Jewish Experience*, I explore the title I have chosen for this study: "The Freudian Exodus." In broadest terms, the four chapters with their corresponding codas offer a series of reflections on Freud's reconstruction in *Moses and Monotheism* of what he understands as the *historical* truth of the Moses-Exodus story. More specifically, I will give primary

11 *Landscapes of Jewish Experience*, 18–19.

12 Langer, 54. For discussion of the ambivalent depiction of nomadism in the Hebrew Bible, see Regina M. Schwartz, *The Curse of Cain: The Violent Legacy of Monotheism* (Chicago: University of Chicago Press, 1997), 42–55.

13 *As You Like* (1.2.137–38), in *The Riverside Shakespeare*, 2nd ed., ed. G. Blakemore Evans et al. (Boston: Houghton Mifflin, 1997), 410.

emphasis to Freud's understanding of this historical truth—a truth grounded, as noted above, in a collective "traumatic experience"—as it establishes the foundation myth of Jewish culture. In Freudian terms, manifested through and indeed functioning as the prime causal force of Jewish history—and, through that history, even of modern Jewish identity—this truth must be read in its relation to the material (consciously understood) truth of Judaic (and at times Judeo-Christian) faith. If the essence of that faith, for Judaism at least, was, as Freud thought, the monotheistic idea, it was not simply in the form of what Freud calls the "the *conception* of one great God" (167) that monotheism was essential. Freud's point was that Judaic monotheism was always more than an idea within Jewish culture. More fundamentally, it functioned at the heart of the obsession that defined the culture. And as what Eric Santner has called Judaism's "demonic core," monotheism was inseparable from other ideas, themselves inseparable from the unconscious attachment or collective drive that sustained Jewish identity in the face of the people's constant hardships.[14] Among these other ideas we should certainly give special privilege to the conviction that the people of Israel were God's chosen people and the interrelationship between covenantal election and the required adherence to Mosaic law that would become the chief expression of the covenant. (Freud would see this adherence as one of the primary markers of the "obsessive quality" [167] sustaining Judaism.) We shall take up these topics and a series of related ones precisely because, while they often need to be examined separately, they are interlocked parts of a greater whole.

That said, the aim of what follows is not to produce a grand unified theory of Judaism and Jewish culture as reconstructed through the lens of psychoanalysis. While I will at times pull the various competing strands of my own narrative into conceptual harmony and while the four chapters and their accompanying codas are designed to be read in the order in which they appear, each chapter / coda pairing is discrete in the sense of addressing a different aspect of the Freudian framework. What truly unites the four pairings is that they always start from, and grapple with, Freud's own claims. But they also frequently and necessarily revise those claims—at times making modest adjustments, at other times reconceptualizing them in much more radical ways. These revisions do not simply reject Freud's thought outright, for even his interpretive failures often register powerful insights. It would be more accurate to say that in what follows I seek to reclaim what Freud himself lost sight by recognizing that many of his best ideas are buried under the weight of

14 Santner, *On the Psychotheology of Everyday Life: Reflections on Freud and Rosenzweig* (Chicago: University of Chicago Press, 2001), 97.

the oedipal apparatus he could never completely dispense with even when its terms did not apply. I thus want to restore many of those *missed* ideas by working from the inside, through what, following Elizabeth Bellamy, we might call the method of "immanent critique, or a critique from within, conducted on the terms Freud laid down himself."[15] So conceived, the goal throughout will be to provide a more complete account of what is at stake in, and what finally can be learned from, the psychoanalytic approach to the biblical story of the Exodus and its aftermath.

A Final Note

While for obvious reasons Freud's notion of the material truth of Jewish history is of less importance to him than its historical truth, his own truth-seeking in *Moses and Monotheism* is yet dependent on the material truth because, as with the symptoms of one of his patients, it is often the only point of access to the truth that lies buried under the surface. Precisely because it serves that function (a point of necessary access to a deeper truth, one buried beneath the more visible aspects of history), in the Appendix I will give extended attention to Freud's understanding of what at one point he calls "the fateful content of the religious history of the Jews" (57). I will focus there on how Freud came to formulate the material truth of Jewish religious history and how we might situate that formulation in relation to current scholarly consensus. At times this consensus is at odds with Freud's claims and so offers necessary correctives; at other times, it can be taken as offering various levels of confirmation of those claims and in fact often demonstrates what an informed and astute reader of the Bible and of Jewish history Freud actually was. For any reader who lacks a basic knowledge of Israelite / Judaean / Jewish history as presented in the biblical narrative, the Appendix might serve as an appropriate starting point.

---

15 Elizabeth Bellamy, "From Ficino to Freud: Egyptian / Greek / Jew in Cultural History," in *Repossessions: Psychoanalysis and the Phantasms of Early Modern Culture*, ed. Timothy Murray and Alan K. Smith (Minneapolis: University of Minnesota Press, 1998), 24.

CHAPTER 1

A Father Religion and a Son Religion: Judaism, (Pauline) Christianity, and the Return of the Repressed

> The great deed and misdeed of primeval times, the murder of the father, was brought home to the Jews, for fate decreed that they should repeat it on the person of Moses, an eminent father-substitute.
>
> —FREUD, *Moses and Monotheism*

1

In a letter dated December 12, 1934, Freud explained to Arnold Zweig that, while "Moses being an Egyptian" was the "starting point" of his researches that would eventually take the form of *Moses and Monotheism*, it was "not the essential point."[1] Because he did not go on to state what the essential point was, we must look for clarification elsewhere. We find it in an earlier letter to Zweig—this one dated September 30, 1934—but in a form that also suggests a very different beginning of the project: "The starting point of my work is familiar to you … Faced with the new persecutions, one asks oneself again how the Jews have come to be what they are and why they have attracted this undying hatred."[2] This statement points to the escalating anti-Semitism of the early 1930s ("the new persecutions") as the proper context for understanding Freud's decision to write a book about Moses. In Part III of *Moses and Monotheism* Freud will explicitly refer to this context on two separate occasions. What is particularly curious about the phrasing in his letter to Zweig is that the study's actual "essential point" appears to sidestep a psychoanalytic perspective on the anti-Semitic haters (and perhaps on the nature of toxic bigotry more broadly) in favor of

1 *Letters of Sigmund Freud and Arnold Zweig*, ed. Ernst L. Freud, trans. Elaine Robson-Scott and William Robson-Scott (New York: Harcourt, Brace & World, 1970), 98.

2 *Letters of Sigmund Freud and Arnold Zweig*, 91.

 | DOI:10.1163/9789004701663_003

examining the origin of this hatred in Jewish experience itself—"how the Jews have come to be what *they are*" so as to attract the hatred.[3] Still, it is in relation to that particular focus that we can more fully credit Freud's observation that "Moses being an Egyptian" was "not the essential point" of *Moses and Monotheism.* For in the end the study is less concerned with Freud's assertion of the basic fact of Moses' Egyptian identity (though this idea is at the heart of the argument in Part I and the first half of Part II) than with what in the opening section of Part III Freud more broadly refers to as "the question of the origin of monotheism among the Jews" (80–81). Because for Freud monotheistic faith and Jewishness are inseparable, to explore the origin of monotheism is thus also to explore "how the Jews have come to be what they are."

That said, precisely what Freud means by "the origin of monotheism" is itself open to interpretation. One of the central claims of *Moses and Monotheism* is that Judaic monotheism originated in the Atonism established as the Egyptian state religion during the brief reign of Amenhotep IV (Akhenaten or Ikhnaton); in the wake of Akhenaten's death and the reversion to traditional forms of Egyptian religious doctrine and practice, a disenchanted Moses subsequently brought Atonism to the Jews living in Egypt who, after leaving Egypt under Moses' leadership, became the foundation of the people of Israel.[4] But Freud understands the evolution of monotheism among the Jews as the work of many centuries. Among the Israelite polytheists of the pre-monarchical and monarchical periods (not much different from their Canaanite neighbors), Judaic monotheism first took root in the cult of Yahweh that emerged among the Temple priesthood and priests at other cultic sites as well as among many of the preexilic prophets. While most of the preexilic kings continued to recognize the many gods of the Canaanite pantheon (Freud twice refers to this collective as the "Baalim" [87, 159] in reference to the Canaanite storm-god Ba'al) and even at times the gods of other nations—see, for example, the harshly negative assessments of Solomon in 1 Kings 11, Ahab in 1 Kings 18, and Manasseh in 2 Kings 21—a select few (notably Hezekiah as reported in 2 Kings 18 and Josiah as reported in 2 Kings 23) practiced a form of monolatry in their adherence to Yahweh alone. The period of the exile then saw the emergence of universal monotheism as Yahweh was reconceptualized as the one and only god, as determinative of events in Babylon, Egypt, and Persia (and everywhere else) as

3 At one point in *Moses and Monotheism,* Freud does offer an extended reflection on the hidden motives that drive anti-Semitism, material we shall consider in section 5 below.

4 For a full discussion of Freud's understanding of Jewish history, including the Egyptian origins of Judaic monotheism, see the Appendix.

he was in the Promised Land.[5] The full development of Mosaic monotheism in the form of the covenantal law came next as the first edition of Torah entered the Persian province of Yehud Medinata with the priest Ezra sometime in the mid- to late-fifth century BCE. And while Torah-based monotheism initially gave primary attention to the rituals of Temple worship in Jerusalem, it also had to find ways to accommodate developing faith traditions that emerged outside of Judaea, primarily in newly established synagogues both in areas that had in the past been part of Israel and in other areas (Egypt and Persia initially, eventually throughout the Greek and Roman Empires) where Jews had settled after political control of their homeland had been lost to foreigners. Finally, in the wake of the Roman destruction of the Second Temple, Pharisaic-rabbinical Judaism spread through the network of synagogues. With the Temple gone, the rabbinical emphasis on non-Temple ritual and moral law made possible the development of diasporic covenantal communities. In that context, the God of Israel could truly become the god of all nations because he was present wherever his chosen people had settled.

Freud certainly knew this basic historical trajectory. That knowledge also shaped his understanding of how and why Jews of his own day—even non-observant Jews like himself—were still bound to the traditions (including the biblical writings) of an ancient time and to a land most of them had never seen. That very condition of boundedness, moreover, pointed Freud toward a different perspective on the origin, the origin both of Judaic monotheism, the ostensible topic of his study, and of his own impulse to write about it from a psychoanalytic perspective. For if "the origin of monotheism among the Jews" was simply the point of entry into what he had earlier called "the fateful content" of their "religious history" (57), that was because the full historical development of Judaic monotheism mysteriously carried with it or within it an aspect that one could almost describe by the word "fate": something determined, something imposed by a seemingly external force, something no Jew could easily refuse except by a concerted exertion of will and intellect.[6] Viewed in that context, Freud's fascination with "how the Jews have come to be what they are"—the real starting point of *Moses and Monotheism*—was inseparable from his interest in the psychological dimensions of Judaic tradition which was

5 For broad discussion of the various forms of monotheistic discourse, with special attention to the differences between Egyptian and Israelite-biblical versions, see Jan Assmann, *Of God and Gods: Egypt, Israel, and the Rise of Monotheism* (Madison, WI: University of Wisconsin Press, 2008).

6 For a rich discussion of this issue, see Yosef Hayim Yerushalmi, *Freud's Moses: Judaism Terminable and Interminable* (New Haven: Yale University Press, 1991).

inseparable, in turn, from what Freud understood as the psychical condition itself, especially what possesses us and at times dispossesses us.[7] And having in Parts I and II already reconstructed the Jewish past from the patriarchal period all the way to the destruction of the Second Temple (with primary focus on the period of the Exodus and the wandering in the desert prior to the conquest of Canaan), Part III of *Moses and Monotheism* retold that history in terms of its affective quality or, in the vocabulary of psychoanalysis, as a neurotic compulsion: what over almost two millennia had kept Jews who they were even in the face of ceaseless hostility.

Freud had first broached this subject in *Totem and Taboo* (1913) where he had asked "what are the ways and means employed by one generation in order to hand on its mental states to the next one?" (*SE*, 13:158). He would return to and clarify the problem in *Moses and Monotheism*: "A tradition based only on oral communication [of ideas] could not produce the *obsessive character which appertains to religious phenomena*" (130; my emphasis).[8] Freud then wants to draw on his own psychoanalytic theories to understand "in what exactly consists the ... nature of a tradition, and in what resides its peculiar power, ... [and] from what sources certain ideas, especially religious ones, derive the power to subjugate individuals and peoples." It is within the conceptual framework of the "nature of a tradition" and "its peculiar power to subjugate individuals and peoples" that Freud takes up the "particular case of Jewish history" (65). For this case—what he says "may be properly termed a traumatic experience" (65)—exemplifies for him how a religious tradition becomes a burden on a people, how it "take[s] ... hold" of them with an "irresistible claim to be believed, against which all logical objections become powerless" (107–08). It is in that

7 Despite his own proudly secular outlook, Freud acknowledged the difficulty of separating himself completely from his Jewish heritage: see, for example, his preface to the 1930 Hebrew translation of *Totem and Taboo*, *SE*, 13:xv. Two years later in a letter to Zweig, who had just returned from British Palestine, Freud puzzled over the emotional tug of the Jewish legacy for Europeans like himself:

"[H]ow strange this tragically mad land you have visited must have seemed to you. Just think, this strip of our mother earth is connected with no other progress, no discovery or invention ... Palestine has never produced anything but religions, sacred frenzies, presumptuous attempts to overcome the outer world of appearance by means of the inner world of wishful thinking. And we hail from there (though one of us considers himself a German as well; the other does not); our forbearers lived there for perhaps half or perhaps a whole millennium ... and it is impossible to say what heritage from this land we have taken over into our blood and nerves ... Oh, life could be very interesting if we only knew and understood more about it." (*Letters of Sigmund Freud and Arnold Zweig*, 40)

8 *Moses and Monotheism* makes several direct references to *Totem and Taboo*, e.g. 65, 68, 71, 102–08, 167–69, 171–72.

context, as Yosef Hayim Yerushalmi has argued, that the "true axis" of *Moses and Monotheism* became the "problem of [Jewish] tradition" conceived first and foremost in terms of its "dynamics": how the experience of passing on the monotheistic tradition from one generation to the next was constituted less by the unfolding history of its core ideas and the corresponding cultural and religious practices than by the emergence of a largely unconscious attachment.[9]

But how does such an unconscious attachment take root among a people in the first place? In regard to the origin of religious sensibility broadly understood, Freud had argued in the *Psychopathology of Everyday Life* (1901) that "a large part of the mythological view of the world, which extends a long way into the most modern religions, *is nothing but psychology projected into the external world*." He would add that "the obscure recognition ... of psychical forces and relations in the unconscious is mirrored—it is difficult to express it in other terms, and here the analogy with paranoia must come to our aid—in the construction of *supernatural reality*, which is destined to be changed back once more by science into the *psychology of the unconscious*" (*SE*, 6:258). He would go on to address religious psychology in more specific terms first in *Totem and Taboo* and subsequently in *Moses and Monotheism*. In both texts, Freud depicts religion as a social-psychological neurosis deriving primarily from and in turn fueling the filial ambivalence—the tension between identification and hostility—at the heart of the son's (or sons') vexed relationship to his (their) father. In Part III of *Moses and Monotheism*, Freud offers this aphoristic summary of his conclusion on the topic: "After these considerations I have no qualms in saying that men have always known ... that once upon a time they had a primeval father and killed him" (129). As Freud outlines the fuller process both in *Totem and Taboo* and then again in *Moses and Monotheism*, the killing of the primeval father fuels a guilt that, under the force of repression (and so disguising a continuing hostility), subsequently returns in the highly distorted form of a collective neurosis. This return of the repressed in what Freud calls "mass psychology" then creates a range of religious beliefs and practices that mark the "father deity" as a "restoration of the [slain] primeval father" (106, 109).

With some slight modifications, that is the general framework within which *Moses and Monotheism* locates the "historical" (as opposed to the "material") origin of Judaic monotheism. Having given "the religion that Egypt disdained" (the Aton religion) to the Jews living in Egypt, Moses dreamed that his new people would "be a better substitute for the Egyptians he left behind.... He wished

9 Yerushalmi, *Freud's Moses*, 29.

to make them a 'holy nation'" (32, 33–34). Moses' own version of Atonism may have been, as Freud speculates, "more uncompromising than that of his master," Akhenaten, precisely because "he had no need to retain any connection with the religion of the sun-god since the school of On would have had no importance for his alien people" (18, 57–58). In any event, in opposition to the rigor of the new religion as well as to Moses' particularly uncompromising personality, the newly constituted people constantly rebelled against Moses' leadership (as represented, for example, in the story of the Golden Calf and the various uprisings against Moses and Aaron as recounted throughout the books of Exodus and Numbers) until they finally overthrew him and killed him.[10]

For Freud, it is this event that, as the founding moment of Jewish history, explains the compulsive aspect of Judaic monotheism, especially as distinct from the earlier Egyptian rejection of Akhenaten's reforms.[11] Drawing again on the earlier account he had offered in *Totem and Taboo* on the prehistoric origins of human religion, he argues that the slaying of Moses reawakened in the people of the Exodus archaic memories of the hordic sons' murder of the primeval father and with these memories the same remorse the sons had experienced in its aftermath. Within those primitive tribal groups remorse would turn eventually to guilt, longing and, finally, denial only to give rise in turn to the creation of the totemic system to commemorate the slaying: at once an act of appeasement of the slain father and a ritualized expression of continuing

10 Freud begins *Moses and Monotheism* with two key working assumptions, though ones he feels compelled to qualify even as he states them: "Although the decision lacks final historical certainty, the great majority of historians have expressed the opinion that Moses did live and the exodus from Egypt, led by him, did in fact take place. It has been maintained with good reason that the later history of Israel could not be understood if this were not admitted" (4). There are two factual assertions here: "Moses *did live*" and "the exodus from Egypt, led by him, *did in fact take place*." At the same time, "the decision" as to whether we should actually credit these two assertions "lacks ... certainty" in part because the very factness in question is no more than the expression of the "opinion" of (the great majority of but certainly not all) historians. As Donald Redford notes, "the event [of the Exodus] is supposed to have taken place in Egypt, yet Egyptian sources know it not.... The effect on Egypt must have been cataclysmic—the loss of servile population, pillaging of gold and silver ..., destruction of an army—yet at no point in the history of the country during the New Kingdom is there the slightest hint of the traumatic impact such an event would have had on economics or society." Yet "despite the ... unreliability of the story in Exodus, no one can deny that the tradition of Israel's coming out of Egypt was one of long standing. It is found in early poetry (e.g. Exod. 15) and is constantly alluded to by the prophets": *Egypt, Canaan, and Israel in Ancient Times* (Princeton: Princeton University Press, 1992), 408, 412.

11 In Part III, Freud refers both to Judaism's "obsessive character" (71, 130) and to the "compulsive conviction" (108) it imposes on its adherents.

hostility to his authority—in short, another manifestation of the original filial ambivalence though now in highly distorted form of religious practice (*Moses and Monotheism*, 103–07, 164–70). And just so the guilt-ridden Jews would deny their deed—"There came a time when the people regretted the murder of Moses and tried to forget it.... [T]he painful fact of his violent removal was ... successfully denied" (58–59)—only to return to the scene of the crime after a centuries-long process of transformation. Their slain founder (leader, lawgiver, educator) would thus be reborn as the father-god by a fusing of the barely remembered Mosaic doctrines, laws, and rituals with the volcano-god, Yahweh, which the wandering Jews had appropriated from tribal groups living somewhere south of Canaan (for Freud, biblical Midian).

Taking the long-view, Freud's remarks that "the religion of Moses did not achieve its effects immediately, but in a strangely indirect manner.... It took a long time, many centuries, to do so." For, after the "Jewish people shook off the religion of Moses," the Mosaic tradition existed only as "a sort of memory"; it "survived, obscured and distorted" (159). Earlier, he had generalized to say that "recent events [may] produce impressions or experiences which are so much like the repressed material that they have the power to awaken it. Thus the recent material gets strengthened by the latent energy of the repressed, and the repressed material produces its effect behind the recent material and with its help" (121). He then applied this model to Jewish tradition following the murder of Moses. As he summarized the evolution of his own thinking on the topic,

> That conviction I acquired a quarter of a century ago, when I wrote my *Totem and Taboo* (in 1912), and it has only become stronger since. From then on I have never doubted that religious phenomenon are to be understood on the model of neurotic symptoms of the individual, which are so familiar to us, as a return of long-forgotten important happenings in the primeval history of the human family, that they owe their obsessive character to that very origin and therefore derive their effect on mankind from the historical truth they contain. My uncertainty begins only at the point when I ask myself the question whether I have succeeded in proving this for the example of Jewish monotheism chosen here. (71)

In the final paragraph of *Moses and Monotheism* Freud writes that, in investigating "the question of how the Jewish people acquired the qualities that characterize it," the related "problem how they could survive until today as an entity has not proved so easy to solve" (176). The very completion of the book was meant as his solution, a declaration of having "succeeded in proving" the applicability of the broader theory to "the example of Jewish monotheism."

We might, then, sum up Freud's theory both of "the origin of monotheism among the Jews" and of Judaic monotheism's continuing viability and vitality (what enabled the very survival of the Jewish people "until today as an entity") as follows. The compulsory force that Freud finds so particular to Jewish monotheism (a monotheism "treasured by them as their most precious possession" [108]) derived from a double experience of the return of the repressed. First, the overthrow of Moses awakens repressed memories regarding the slaying of the primeval father: murderous hostility toward followed by the guilt for actually killing him. Second, the new repression of the guilt following the slaying of Moses repeats and in that way intensifies the original primeval forgetting. This repetition at once transfers the deeply repressed filial ambivalence of archaic man to the father-founder Moses and over time, through the process of distortion that at once reveals and obscures the continuing repression, opens the door to a new return of the repressed in the beliefs and practices associated with the father-god, Yahweh. Or, as Freud succinctly puts it, in the person of the father-founder Moses "the figure of the great man [grew] into a divine one" (141). The "Father religion" (111) as Freud calls Judaism would thereafter become an expression, though a necessarily distorted one, of the longing for the slain father. And submission to the deified father (now in the form of the god Yahweh) through obedience to the Law and adherence to tradition more generally would ever after fuel even as they would be fueled by collective repression and its attendant neurosis. Raised now to a cultural force through "mass psychology" (163), the ambivalence that in his view "belongs to the essence of the father-son relationship" (172) provides the psychoanalytical explanation for the peculiarly and mysteriously compulsory force of Judaic faith and indeed of Jewish identity itself.

2

By early in Part III of *Moses and Monotheism*, Freud feels confident enough in the relation he has asserted between the psychopathology of the neurotic individual and the mass psychological qualities of religious experience to say that the "analogy ... approximating to identity ... is rather in the nature of an axiom" (90–91). By itself, however, the axiom is not a firm predicter of subsequent developments. And so, in this last section of the study, Freud varies his critical focus: at times he continues his analysis of the origins of Judaic monotheism (a "Father religion" [111]), and at other times he shifts his attention to the origins of Christian counter-monotheism (a "Son religion"). Even as it presents both from a psychoanalytically-oriented perspective, the study ends by tracing two very different evolutionary paths for the two religions which themselves reveal paired but otherwise opposed motive forces at the heart of their respective obsessive attachments.

While neither religion *consciously* understands the original traumatizing episode—the "savage Semites" (58) killing of their Aton-worshipping leader, Moses—Freud argues that Judaism was more successful at keeping the repressed material anchored in the Unconscious: in contrast to its Christian counterpart, the Jewish psyche more tenaciously blocked the return of "the murder of the father" precisely because in Mosaic times "it was a case of acting instead of remembering.... They responded to the doctrine of Moses—which should have been a stimulus to their memory—by denying their act ... [and thus] did not progress beyond the recognition of the great father" (113). That deeper repression is, as Freud wants to make clear with a sort of ancestral pride, productive of moral and spiritual excellence. While, as previously noted, he accepts as a general axiom that ambivalence "belongs to the essence of the father-son relationship,"

> in the religion of Moses ... there was no room for direct expression of the murderous father-hate. Only a powerful reaction to it could make its appearance: the consciousness of guilt because of that hostility, the bad conscience because one had sinned against God and continued so to sin. This feeling of guiltiness ... soon became an integral part of the religious system ... If they wished to keep happiness, then the consciousness of guilt because they themselves were such sinners offered a welcome excuse for God's severity. They deserved nothing better than to be punished by him, because they did not observe the laws; the need for satisfying this feeling of guilt, which, coming from a much deeper source, was insatiable, made them render their religious precepts ever and ever more strict ... In a new transport of moral asceticism the Jews imposed on themselves constantly increasing instinctual renunciation, and thereby reached—at least in doctrine and precepts—ethical heights that had remained inaccessible to the other peoples of antiquity. (172–73)

We might take special note here of how Freud's claim for the achievement of greater "ethical heights" among the Jewish people (what he had earlier referred to as their unique "progress in spirituality" [109]) depends on an orientation toward "moral asceticism" that itself produces "constantly increasing instinctual renunciation." Understood strictly in ethical terms, what we might deem a culturally-inflected inclination towards a kind of inner austerity could very well lead to ever more instinctual renunciation if by renunciation we do not mean simply a rejection or repudiation but also, and more properly, a relinquishing of one's own needs out of a commitment to higher principles (for Freud always truth and justice). In that context, moral asceticism—expressed perhaps through the habit of denial of immediate self-gratification—could serve as the foundation of an ethics of humility, selflessness (taking satisfaction in not demanding on behalf of oneself), rational tolerance, and a realistic acceptance of the way the world truly is (an outlook that the scientist in Freud cannot help but admire).[12]

More in line with Freud's own psychoanalytic theories, however, it makes more sense to reverse the temporal order and thus the causal relation between asceticism and renunciation: moral asceticism does not lead to (increasing) instinctual renunciation; rather, instinctual renunciation—where the word "instinctual" (*Trieb*) points to a response not immediately accessible to consciousness—leads to moral asceticism. As Freud understands the process, what is renounced at the heart of Judaic monotheism is not the filial guilt for the slaying of the primeval father, for it is precisely the "*consciousness* of guilt" that drives moral ascetism. Rather, what is renounced—where renunciation takes on a different meaning: an act of refusal, a disowning, or a disavowal of some kind—is the memory of the killing itself. As Freud puts it in the lengthy passage just quoted, "in the religion of Moses itself there was *no room for direct expression* of the murderous father-hate" (my emphasis). The murderous father-hate—the hate that became murder and so the murder itself—is so hidden away in Jewish (un)consciousness that only its residue remains: a guilty conscience.

To put this another way, the object of renunciation (the killing of the father-imago, Moses) is so deeply repressed that the renouncing act itself is all that is left. As the remnant of what has been denied (not admitted into consciousness), this lingering renunciation is then reassigned by being attached to a metonymic substitution: the forgotten murder of Moses becomes Mosaic law. And it is the renouncing of the Law in the sense of a refusal to abide by its terms that is all that is retained within the Jewish psyche as a conscious thought: "... the *consciousness of guilt* ... offered a welcome excuse for God's severity. They deserved nothing better than to be punished by him, *because they did not observe the laws*" (173; my emphases). In other words, what is left after the memory of the killing is renounced by being buried in the Unconscious is

12 For related comments on what Freud elsewhere calls the "higher spirituality" and the "special psychical fitness" of the Jewish people, see 19, 80, 108–09, 112, 142, and 147.

the "consciousness of guilt" that drives moral asceticism as a kind of collective masochism: the "happiness" that comes from being deservedly punished by God.

This shift in what is consciously remembered aids in the repression-renunciation because the substitution (one violation, the disobeying of Mosaic law, now stands in for another violation, the killing of Moses) is close enough to what it replaces to provide an effective screen: it conceals the original object of renunciation in the very act of revealing it. Commenting near the close of *Moses and Monotheism* on "the mechanisms that lead to a neurosis," Freud outlines just such a process, one that develops "as a consequence of a certain experience" from which "there arises an instinctual demand which claims satisfaction." (In the case of the murder of Moses, this is the satisfaction not just of killing the hated and dreaded father-imago but also of remembering the killing, where both act and recollection are filled with and fueled by deep ambivalence.) He continues:

> The Ego foregoes this satisfaction ... because it is paralyzed by the excessiveness of the demand ... [and so] guards against this danger by repression.... [T]he incitement, with the observations and perceptions belonging to it, is forgotten. This, however, does not bring the process to an end; either the instinct has kept its strength, or it will regain it, or it is reawakened by a new situation. It renews its claim and—since the way to normal satisfaction is barred by what we may call the scar tissue of repression—it gains at some weak point new access to a so-called substitutive satisfaction which now appears as a symptom, without the acquiescence and also without the comprehension of the Ego. (163–64)

If, following his model of the neurotic patient, we might say that what Freud calls the "obsessional neurosis" (173) of the Jewish people finds a "substitutive satisfaction," this is because the guilt that should derive from the now repressed original crime is transformed into a symptom: what is forgotten or repressed—the people's breaking of the law by murdering their leader, Moses—becomes the *consciousness of guilt* incurred for violating what the victim of the forgotten murder left behind: "they did not observe the [Mosaic] laws." And in what Freud himself might have called a secondary or corollary distortion (where distortion means "to put in another place" [52]), tradition reimagines and so remembers the true lawgiver not as Moses but as God, a father-imago who, precisely because divine, cannot be killed and so permits the people to deny in yet another way their actual killing of the first father and real lawgiver. If, as Freud suggests, the father-god Yahweh forever after stands in the place of the slain Moses, then, following Freud's apt phrasing, Yahweh might be conceived as the "scar tissue" of Moses: the living God both reminds the people of the slain father and repudiates the criminal act that led to his death: because the slain father is not truly dead (he lives on in God), then the people could not have killed him.[13] The primal father is with them, among them, always, whether they like it or not. Forever subjected to his implacable severity, the people are happy because, by being punished, they know that they are loved and good: loved because the chosen, the first-born and favorite child, and good because willing to renounce their own immediate needs and desires for something greater than themselves, a higher calling, a spiritual principle, a national destiny that promises one day to bring blessings on the whole world.[14]

3

Even among the very people Moses created (the people of Israel), however, it would not always be so. For, as Freud comments, "the other parts of the prehistoric tragedy also clamored for recognition," a clamoring that set the stage for a different "return of the repressed material." Here Freud introduces "Paul, a Roman Jew from Tarsus, [who] seized upon this feeling of guilt and correctly traced it back to its primeval source." That said, even as Paul conceptualized an originary uprising against authority (the primeval source of the guilt), he had no story to tell of a human murder. Rather, as Freud writes, "he called it original sin ... a crime against God" (*Moses and Monotheism*, 109). Thus, while Freud concedes that, in one respect, "Christianity marked a progress in the history of religion: that is to say, in regard to the return of the repressed" (113), to the extent this progress depended on return—some sort of acknowledgement of what had happened in the past—the phrase "*correctly* traced it back" (German:

13 In this context, the biblical tradition's way of memorializing the death of Moses (Deuteronomy 34:1–8) is particularly noteworthy. No one sees him die; no one knows where he is buried; even if he is dead, the people did not kill him; if anyone is responsible for Moses' death, other than Moses himself who had earned the divine lawgiver's wrath, it is the lawgiver God; if the true lawgiver condemned Moses, the people could not have murdered him.

14 Thus it is, Freud writes, that, though in the highly distorted form caused by continuing repression, "the restoration to the primeval father of his historical rights marked a great progress" for the Jewish people. For "it formed their character for good through the disdaining of magic and mysticism and encouraging them to progress in spirituality and sublimations. The people, happy in their conviction of possessing truth, overcome by the consciousness of being the chosen, come to value highly all intellectual and spiritual achievements" (109).

"… *und führte es richtig auf seine urgeschichtliche Quelle zurück*" [16:192) is misleading. For if, as Freud continues, "dark traces of the past lay in his soul, ready to break through into the regions of consciousness," Paul's way of returning to the starting point of Jewish guilt was just another distortion because, just as with his fellow Jews, "the murderous deed itself … was not remembered (109–10).[15]

In one sense, because the murder was still lost to consciousness, what emerged from Paul's return of the repressed could be nothing more than a variation of the consciousness of guilt Freud associated with Mosaic Judaism. That said, in Pauline Christianity, as Freud viewed it, not only was this consciousness—an awareness of a primal sin or condition (a crime against God)—much more openly admitted (114–115), but, more to the point, the very acknowledgement aimed to assuage the guilt (to "la[y] the ghost of the feeling of guilt" [112]): paradoxically, the hyper-consciousness of guilt was the pathway to explicitly renouncing it. Just as important, the Pauline disavowing of guilt (the impossibility of which was, for Freud, the lifeblood of Judaism's progress in spirituality) was possible precisely to the extent the new theology included the recognition that those who had sinned against God could do nothing to redeem themselves (as Paul would say, by works of the law); so Freud summarizes Paul's view:

> Death had come into the world through original sin. In reality, this crime, deserving of death, had been the murder of the Father who was later deified. The murderous deed itself, however, was not remembered; in its place stood the phantasy of expiation, and that is why this phantasy could be welcomed in the form of a gospel of salvation … A Son of God, innocent himself, had sacrificed himself, and had thereby taken over the guilt of the world. (109–10)

15 In the final section of *Moses and Monotheism*, Freud observes that Paul's "perception" that a primal guilt had come upon the Jewish people through the murder of Moses could only be understood by hiding Moses behind the figure of "God the Father." And even "in this formulation the murder of God was … not mentioned." Even more to the point, as Freud adds, Paul could only "grasp this [distorted] truth … in *the delusional guise* of the glad tidings": it was not the guilt itself but only its expiation that permitted any awareness that a murder of a human being (the great father of the Jews) had set the process in motion" (174; my emphasis). In Freud's own terms, it is, at most, only as an intuition that Paul *correctly* traces the concept of guilt, itself deriving from an "original sin," to the primal murder.

Freud sees this "phantasy of expiation" (Paul's doctrine of atonement: see especially his Letter to the Romans, 3:21–16) as just another "tendentious distortion," for "how could a man who was innocent assume the guilt of the murderer by allowing himself to be killed?" (110).

Following Freud's own interpretation of Jewish progress in spirituality as grounded in an ethics of renunciation, we might say that, by his own terms, there is a particular Jewishness to the Pauline notion that Christ's sacrificial death could "take over" and so atone for "the guilt of the world." It's not just that Paul is adapting a concept already central to the Law (the ritual of atonement as detailed in Leviticus 16); rather, Christ's saving action can atone precisely to the extent it takes to its logical conclusion Freud's idea that the Jewish triumph of moral asceticism is inseparable from a uniquely Jewish capacity for the "renunciation of instinctual gratification" (104). For the Jewish Paul, because of who Christ was, there could be no greater act of renunciation: in surrendering completely to God's will, Christ renounced the most powerful of all instinctual gratifications, the instinct to continue living. And so Paul writes in a famous passage from his Letter to the Philippians, that although Christ

> 6 … was in the form of God,
> [he] did not regard equality with God
> as something to be exploited,
> 7 but emptied himself,
> taking the form of a slave,
> being born in human likeness.
> And being found in human form,
> 8 he humbled himself
> and became obedient to the point of death—
> even death on a cross. (Philippians 2:6–8)

"Obedient to the point of death," Christ's perfection of radical selflessness makes him an exemplar of what Freud finds at the core of Jewish piety: a welcoming of divine severity, an insatiable hunger for ever stricter demands, a constant increase in instinctual renunciation leading finally to "ethical heights that had remained inaccessible to the other peoples of antiquity" (159).

In two very specific ways, Pauline Jewish-Christians (and later just Christians) would still, by Freud's reasoning, have distorted the truth in the same way Jews had since their very origin as a people: they still did "not remember" the murder of the founder, Moses—or rather, they repressed the memory of the "murderous deed"—and they maintained in displaced form a lingering (hyper-)awareness of guilt (sin) for which atonement or reconciliation with the offended deity was required. In both Judaism and Jewish-Christianity (from Paul's perspective, messianic Judaism), the very notion that the crime had been committed against God was a key aspect of the continuing distortion: it sustained the feeling of guiltiness but translated the source of the guilt from the actual murder of Moses into the failure to obey the laws of the father-god. The "original sin" was now understood as having been committed against God who conceptually stood in the place of the true lawgiver who was also the murder victim.

Nevertheless, as Freud is right to point out, the Pauline version of the Jewish return of the repressed had crucial differences. First, Pauline Christians would be were permitted (or would permit themselves) to absolve themselves of the very guilt of which they were so obsessively aware. They could do so not simply because, as Freud thought, they openly admitted their guilt; after all, that acknowledgement was a central element of the annual ritual of atonement described in Leviticus 16. Rather they could renounce guilt by declaring the ritual of atonement to have reached its perfect and never-to-be-repeated form in the singular act of the crucifixion. Because the crucified one was the sinless Christ (who prior to the Incarnation existed in "the form of God"), his death not only rendered superfluous any merely human attempt to effect reconciliation with God (in Leviticus, of course, the scapegoat is an actual goat, or two goats) but also removed once-and-for-all the burden of guilt.[16]

Moreover, precisely because Christ's purifying sacrifice, as a perfect one-time event, could never be repeated, in renouncing the burden of guilt the Jewish-Christians were also rejecting the need for the Law that, as Paul interpreted it, was the anchor of that burden. As he claimed in his Letter to the Romans, "through the law we become conscious of our sin" (3:20); and again, "where there is no law there is no transgression" (4:15); and again, "but law came in, with the result that the trespass multiplied" (5:20); and again, "sinful passions [are] aroused by the law" (7:5); and again, "I would not have known what sin was had it not been for the law ... For apart from the law, sin was dead.... [W]hen the commandment came, sin sprang to life" (7:7–9); and again, "for sin, seizing the opportunity in the commandment, deceived me and

16 As Freud says, in Paul's fantasy of expiation, Christ "had thereby taken over the guilt of the world" (110). So Paul writes in his Letter to the Romans that "a single act of righteousness [Christ's sacrifice] leads to acquittal and life for all men" (5:18); see also Romans 6:4–9 and 1 Corinthians 15:22. For the full doctrinal theory of Christ's sacrificial death as the fulfillment of the concept of atonement under the Law, see the (non-Pauline) Letter to the Hebrews 9:11–28.

through it killed me" (7:11).[17] For Paul, in other words, not only did the singular quality of Christ's atonement render any subsequent observance of the Law beside the point, but, even worse, that very observance would be counterproductive because, as Paul claimed, the Law itself simply put us in mind of the very guilt from which the crucifixion had freed humankind.

Alain Badiou's notion of the "event" or "truth procedure"—and particularly his concomitant understanding that Paul's proclamation of the resurrection of the crucified Christ should be understood as one of the most important examples in world history—is especially relevant in this context. Badiou writes in general terms that, "on the one hand, every truth procedure breaks with the axiomatic principle that governs the situation and organizes its repetitive series. A truth procedure interrupts repetition.... But, on the other hand, neither can a truth procedure take root in the element of identity. For if it is true that every truth erupts as singular, its singularity is immediately universalizable."[18] In terms of his view of Christ's singular atonement in opposition to (but also as the fulfillment of) the Law in which atonement was an *annual* ritual (and thus an instance of repetition interrupted by an event), what then does Paul seek by his doctrine of the resurrection? Badiou continues:

> Probably to drag the Good News ... out from the rigid enclosure with which its restriction to the Jewish community would confine it.... Paul's general procedure is the following: if there has been an event, and if truth consists in declaring it and then being faithful to this declaration, two consequences ensue. First, since truth is evental, or of the order of what occurs, it is singular. It is neither structural, nor axiomatic, nor legal. No available generality can account for it, nor structure the subject who claims to follow in its wake. Consequently, there cannot be a law of truth.... Truth is diagonal relative to every communitarian [e.g. Jewish / covenantal] subset; it neither claims authority from, nor ... constitutes any identity. It is offered to all, or addressed to everyone, with a condition

17 Paul expresses similar sentiments elsewhere. In his Letter to the Galatians, for example, he refers to the "curse of the law" (3:13). Later in Romans, he writes that "Christ is the end of the law" (10:4).

18 *Saint Paul: The Foundation of Universalism*, trans. Ray Brassier (Stanford: Stanford University Press, 2003), 11. For the broader theoretical framework, see *Being and Event*, trans. Oliver Feltham (London: Bloomsbury Academic, 2013). In broadest terms, an "event" is a moment of rupture within a paradigmatic closed system of some kind (in politics, science, art, or even in matters of the heart) that creates such a profound disturbance in that system so as to fundamentally overturn it by exposing the system as a limit on or reduction of truth.

> of belonging being able to limit this offer, or this address.... Thus every subsumption of its becoming under a law will be argued against. It will be necessary to proceed ... via a radical critique of Jewish law, which [as Paul sees it] has become obsolete and harmful.

And so, as Badiou remarks subsequently, the whole of Pauline thought comes to rest upon a key question: "What is the exact relation between the supposed universality of the postevental truth (that is, what is inferred from Christ's resurrection) and the evental site, which is, indubitably, the nation bound together by the Old Testament?"[19]

By way of introduction to his analysis, Badiou writes that, "for Paul, it is a matter of investigating which law is capable of structuring a subject void of all identity and suspended to an event whose only 'proof' lies precisely in its having been declared by a subject." Within that interpretive framework, the Christ-event cannot by definition be bound by Jewish tradition especially as that tradition is codified in Mosaic law. By contrast, for Paul's contemporary rivals (Jerusalem-based and so law-observing Jewish-Christians led by Peter, John, and Jesus' brother, James) "it is not a question of denying the power of the event. It is a question of asserting that its novelty conserves and sublates the traditional site of [Jewish] faith ... The Christ-event accomplishes the Law; it does not terminate it." And so against Paul's view, "Judeo-Christians of strict observance maintain the practice of distinguishing between degrees of belonging and find it genuinely scandalous that individuals possessing neither the markings nor the ritual practices of the community can be considered as equals. People who, in a word, have neither the slightest knowledge of, nor respect for the Law."[20]

As we have seen, though, in Freud's reconstruction of the origins of Christianity as a reaction against Judaic monotheism, having "no respect for the Law" is more foundationally an act of renunciation of the burden of guilt imposed by the Law. In that sense, paradoxically, it was Christ who first showed no respect for the Law—a position depicted in terms of the lived experience of Jesus of Nazareth time and again throughout the Gospels—because, in taking on the guilt of the world through his sacrifice of atonement, he made it possible for a

19 *Saint Paul*, 13–15, 22. As part of a fuller discussion of Paul's opposition to the Law, Badiou observes that "what is at issue here is nothing less than the problem of the unconscious (Paul calls it the involuntary, what I do not want ..."). Later, Badiou remarks that Paul appears to understand Torah's legal prescriptions to "arouse the infinity of desire through the transgression of the prohibition" (79, 89).

20 *Saint Paul*, 5, 22–23.

Jew like Paul and his (mostly gentile) Christian followers still to be conscious of guilt and to disavow its effect, to be guilty and not-guilty simultaneously. Where belief in the efficacy of Christ's sacrificial act—the final and perfect atonement—replaced the efficacy of covenantal obligations (the works of the law) as the path to at-one-ment with God, there would be no reason either to think much about the Law or to feel any special obligation to the lawgiver, Moses.[21]

In Freudian terms, then, Pauline theology took the distortion of the memory of Moses to its final form: the forgetting not just of the murder itself—an act that Freud believed gave compulsory force to Judaic Law—but of the very existence of the murder-victim. Thus we see that, as part of Paul's discussion of atonement in his Letter to the Romans, Moses' name effectively disappears (he is recollected primarily through Paul's dismissive term "the law" or sometimes "works of the law" [e.g. Galatians 2:16, 3:13]). Just as important, he is replaced in the providential narrative by the Jew before the Jews, the great patriarchal father, Abraham:

> [W]hat does the scripture say? "Abraham believed God, and it was reckoned to him as righteousness" [Gen 15:6].... How then was it reckoned to him? Was it before or after he was circumcised? It was not after, but before he was circumcised. He received the sign of circumcision as a seal of the righteousness he had by faith while he was still uncircumcised.... For the promise that he would inherit the world did not come to Abraham or to his descendants through the law but through the righteousness of faith ... Abraham [not Moses] ... is the father of all of us. (Romans 4:3, 10–11, 16)[22]

---

21 If the flipside of observance of the law (where observance itself is the work [*ergon*] of the law [*nomos*]) is faith, this is so because faith is a kind of unwork. (That said, for Paul there is a *law* of faith: Romans 3:27.) The very lack of work in faith may be related to Paul's sense, inseparable from his concept of Christ's atonement or reconciliation (itself imagined as a kind of work on our behalf), that sinful human beings are powerless to effect their own redemption. In that context, Badiou remarks, "sin is not so much a fault as living thought's inability to prescribe action. Under the effect of the law, thought disintegrates into powerlessness and endless cogitation, because the subject (the dead Self) is disconnected from a limitless power.... Sin is nothing but the permutation of the places of life and death under the effect of the law, which is precisely why Paul, dispensing with a need for a sophisticated doctrine of original sin, can simply say: we *are* in sin" (83–84).

22 It would be incorrect to say that Paul never uses Moses' name: there are nine such uses in the authentic letters (four in Romans, two in 1 Corinthians, and three in 2 Corinthians). Four of these explicitly link Moses to the limitations of the Law as a pathway to a new covenant with God. 2 Corinthians 3:7–8 occupy a sort of middle ground. At first, Moses

Where on some hierarchy of spiritual experience the Law comes a distant second to a much privileged belief or faith or trust (Hebrew: *emunah* / Greek: *pistis*), then the giver of the Law merits little attention. And if the lawgiver does not matter in the larger scheme of things, then precisely how he had died (was he murdered in the desert between Egypt and Canaan?) would also cease to matter. Freud observes that, with Paul, "the murderous deed itself … was not remembered; in its place stood … phantasy." But this wasn't just a fantasy of expiation (Christ had taken away our guilt), which was already a distortion. Rather, Paul promoted the fantasy in its most fundamental sense: the neurotic drive to reclaim what one never had to begin with.[23] The fantasy of Pauline Christianity was that one could have Judaic faith without Moses and thus without the murder of Moses. No murder of Moses, no guilt; no guilt, no need for the Law of Moses which itself maintained the murder but only as traumatic memory—at once revealing and concealing it via repression. As Freud would say so pithily, "Paul, by developing the Jewish religion further, became its destroyer" (*Moses and Monotheism*, 111). And what he destroyed most of all was the need for remembering Moses.

4

It is worth observing how, in the verses from Romans 4 just cited, Paul's championing of Abraham (faith before law) is formulated specifically in terms of circumcision. Badiou notes that for observant followers of Jesus (members of the Jerusalem Church most prominently), "the marks inherited from tradition (circumcision, for example) are still necessary." For Paul, by contrast, "the event renders prior markings obsolete, and the new universality bears no privileged relation to the Jewish community"; thus, "Paul considers all converts as fully

---

is alluded to only by the metonymic reference to the giving of the Law at Sinai, which is itself recalled in the synecdochic phrase "engraved in letters on stone." This phrase draws out the meaning of the contrast between killing "letter" and life-giving "spirit" of verse 6. But the limitation of the Law as a path to communion with God is then contrasted to a full experience of divine glory as anticipated in Moses' own special communion with God: "the Israelites could not look steadily at the face of Moses because of its glory, transitory though it was … the ministry of the Spirit will be even more glorious."

23 Although he does not here use the word fantasy, Slavoj Žižek effectively lays the groundwork for its emergence in his concept of "symbolic castration," which he defines as "the loss of something that one never possessed, that is to say, the object-cause of desire in an object that emerges through the very gesture of its loss / withdrawal" (*The Puppet and the Dwarf: The Perverse Core of Christianity* [Cambridge, MA: MIT Press, 2003], 51).

practicing followers, whatever their background and regardless of whether they are circumcised."[24] But, as we shall explore here and again in Chapter 4, circumcision is more than simply an example of "the marks inherited from tradition." For Paul at least and indeed for many observant Jews of his day, circumcision functioned as a synecdoche for Mosaic law—the very "sign of the covenant" (Genesis 17:11)—and thus as a metonymy for the Mosaic legacy more broadly. This is because circumcision literally rendered visible on the (male) body the distinction that is central to Jewish (male) identity. Understood in these terms, circumcision takes on an outsized role in Paul's thinking (see, for example, 1 Corinthians 7:17–20 and Galatians 2:6–10) because, for him, it is such a clear marker of the conceptual gap between the evental aspect of Pauline messianic Judaism (centered on Christ's crucifixion and resurrection) and mere tradition. To the extent the Mosaic legacy (the Law itself) is central to Jewish tradition, circumcision as a mark of ethnic distinction necessarily stands against truth—as Paul sees it as a "revelation" or apocalypse: the Christ-event is universal precisely because it refuses the distinctions of the Law for which circumcision is the most visible sign. Badiou thus interprets the heart of Paul's universalism as the refusal of the exclusions of the Law in favor of the sort of transcendent egalitarianism, tolerance, and inclusivity we find in Galatians 3:28: "There is neither Jew nor Greek, there is neither slave nor free, there is neither male nor female, for you are all one in Christ Jesus."[25]

Following Freud's line of inquiry more closely, though, we might say, *pace* Badiou, that Paul's universalism is based less on an act of inclusion than on an act of renunciation. Badiou is certainly right to say that, for Paul, in the wake of the Christ-event the freedom from bondage (to sin, to death) puts the very question of the Law at the center of doctrinal discourse. Badiou goes on to argue, moreover, that Paul's insistent championing of freedom as it derives from life "in Christ" is itself premised on a rejection of the notion that, within the terms of the Law (life in Moses, we might say), "every subject [is] configured in the form of legal subjection."[26] But what precisely is this "subjection" from which the Christ-event frees us? For Freud, it is not, as Badiou might have

---

24 *Saint Paul*, 22–23.

25 It is worth noting that the immediately following verse imagines this universality in terms of Abraham's role as founding-father: "And if you belong to Christ, then you are Abraham's offspring, heirs according to the promise" (Galatians 3:29). Žižek remarks that, for Paul, "it is the Christians who are the true 'children of Abraham.' … Thus we have a kind of *"transubstantiation" of the chosen people*: God kept his promise of redemption to the Jewish people, but, in the process itself, he changed the identity of the chosen people. (130)

26 *Saint Paul*, 25. For discussion of Paul's notion of living *in Christ*, see Marcus Borg and John Dominic Crossan, *The First Paul: Reclaiming the Radical Visionary Behind the Church's*

it, freedom from the sectarian- or enclave-identity of Jewish ethnicity in the spirit of inclusive universalism.[27] Rather, Paul's desire for freedom (his need for it, his obsession with it) is more properly understood as the desire to live free(d) from guilt, a guilt created and sustained precisely by observance of and thus *subjection to* Mosaic law.[28] Freud effectively captures this matrix of ideas in remarking that Paul's effort to lay to rest "the ghost of the feeling of guilt" was inseparable from "his giving up the idea of the chosen people *and its visible sign—circumcision*" (112; my emphasis). Giving up circumcision as the ritual at very heart of Jewish covenantal identity is tantamount to giving up the Mosaic law in its entirety. As for as Paul is concerned, achieving true freedom comes from renouncing an identity bound up with an inescapable awareness of, and subjection to, guilt. Without circumcision that is at once a synecdoche of the Law and a metonymy for Moses himself, there is no need to feel guilt for (or even to notice) the death of Moses, a murder that, for Freud, is the origin of that guilt.

Paul's decision to make his stand for a new Judaism (messianic or son-based Judaism) on the denial of the efficacy of circumcision—"For in Christ Jesus neither circumcision or uncircumcision counts for anything" (Galatians 5:6; see also Galatians 6:15 and Acts of the Apostles 15:1–11)—must be understood then as the lynchpin of his entire attack on the Law precisely to the extent his attack aimed to eliminate the need to remember Moses or, conversely, aimed to forget that the figure of Moses stood at the origin of Judaic faith. If, as Badiou comments, "in the final analysis" Paul is focused on "the relation between law and subject," this is because, as previously noted, he aims to challenge the idea that, under the terms of the Law, "every subject [is] configured in the form of legal subjection." For Freud, that subjection might be *consciously* understood first, as the imperative to obey the Mosaic law (what is demanded in return for covenantal election) and second, as the guilt that accrues from the awareness of failing to observe it. But *unconsciously*, subjection to the Law (the very creation of the subject as "under the law") reveals even in the process of concealing a

---

Conservative Icon (New York: HarperOne, 2009), ch. 7; for Paul's own wording, see, for example, 1 Corinthians 15:22, 2 Corinthians 1:19, Romans 6:4–11, and Galatians 2:26–29.

27 See Badiou, *St. Paul*, 56–57.

28 We might note that Badiou does occasionally show a firmer grasp of this different kind of universalism in Paul. Reflecting on Paul's understanding of the Christ-event, Badiou remarks that, for Paul, "Christ is, in himself and for himself, *what happens to us*. And what is it that happens to us? We are relieved of the law." But what does relief from the law mean? Going on to observe that "misery for Paul always consist[s] in a subjection to the law," Badiou adds that "it is only by being relieved of the law that one truly becomes a son" on the model of Christ (*Saint Paul*, 48–49).

more primal condition, the forgotten (repressed) murder that derived from the dispossessing uneasiness of submission to the father's priority and authority.[29] First and foremost symbolized in his renunciation of circumcision (one of the very first things a Jewish father imposes on a Jewish son under the terms of the Law), Paul's universalism, in short, marks an unconscious desire emerging from within Judaic tradition itself to escape perpetual filial servitude by killing off the father-imago, Moses, a second time.

It is precisely in this context that, as Freud muses, "Christianity marked a progress in the history of religion: that is to say, in regard to the return of the repressed" (*Moses and Monotheism*, 113). For while "the murderous deed itself ... was not remembered," under Paul's influence early Christians had a clearer understanding that the "crime against God" had in reality "been the murder of the Father." This greater awareness led them to formulate the doctrine of atonement explicitly in terms of "a Son of God," who "had sacrificed himself." "It had to be a Son," Freud adds, "for the sin had been the murder of the Father." That is what Freud means by adding that "dark traces of the past lay in [Paul's] soul, ready to break through into the regions of consciousness" (109–10). "Ready to break through into ... consciousness" is not the same thing as full consciousness, of course. Indeed, even as "progress," the Pauline return of the repressed was still a distortion of the truth that recollected the original crime only in the most shadowy of ways.[30]

We might even say that, in Freud's reconstruction, what early Christianity more fully recollected through the return of the repressed past was less the patricide itself than the original filial ambivalence prompting it, the love for the primal father balanced by dread and even hatred. Freud writes of the Christian notion of "the Redeemer [who] sacrificed himself as an innocent man" that, "in historical reality ... the 'redeemer' could be no one else but he who was most guilty, the leader of the brother horde who had overpowered the father." This

29 Building on Freud's statement in *Totem and Taboo* that "the dead father became stronger than the living one had been" (*SE*, 13:143; cf. 13:148, 150), Jacob Taubes aptly observes of Freud's position that "the son is murderously ambivalent about the father. And that he becomes even more deeply entangled in guilt not by way of the living father whom he wants to kill, but by way of the dead father, who has a much more powerful effect on him.... Freud, who is involved with the basic experience of guilt, is a direct descendent of Paul" (*The Political Theology of Paul*, trans. Dana Hollander [Stanford: Stanford University Press, 2004], 89).

30 Freud had ventured earlier versions of this theory that the Christian notion of atonement was a symbolic expression of expiation for the primal patricide: see *Totem and Taboo*, *SE*, 13:154, "Thoughts for the Times on War and Death," *SE*, 14:292–93, and *Civilization and Its Discontents*, *SE*, 21:136.

leader stood in for horde collectively in the sense that "each member ... had the wish to do the deed by himself and thus to create for himself a unique position as a substitute" (*Moses and Monotheism*, 110). The death of the "guilty" son (symbolically, all who longed to assume the place of the father) thus atoned for the collective guilt incurred through that desire: the murder of the father was a crime, and its subsequent recollection (in the form of the totem feast, for example, during which the repentant sons symbolically incorporated the father's body) marked, "in a tender and adoring sense," (111) a symbolic restoration of the father—the murdered father who was now "deified" (109)—by demonstrating how each of the sons submitted to paternal authority by identifying with it.[31] But Freud had earlier noted that the primitive totem system that emerged in the wake of the murder "retained the original ambivalency of feeling toward the father. The totem was, on the one hand, the corporeal ancestor and protecting spirit of the clan; he was to be revered and protected. On the other hand, a festival was instituted on which day the same fate was meted out to him [the totem animal] as the primeval father encountered. He was killed and eaten by all the brothers together ... This great day was in reality a feast of triumph to celebrate the victory of the united sons over the father" (104–05). And, as Freud sees it, so too for the Christian doctrine of the Son's atoning sacrifice: if, on the one hand, that sacrifice was an act of filial submission to the will of the divine father—an ethic of humility Paul sees as a model for all Christians (e.g. Philippians 2:3–5)—on the other hand, the entire scenario through which, as Paul recognized, the Son's obedience to the point of death led to his exaltation must be understood as part of the primal "wish-phantasy" (110) in which the oppressed son finally triumphed over the father.

Thus, Freud writes that "the ambivalency dominating the father-son relationship shows clearly ... in the final result of the religious innovation" we know as Pauline Christianity. For

> meant to propitiate the Father deity, it ends by his being dethroned and set aside. The Mosaic religion [with its more complete repression] had been a Father religion; Christianity [with the return of the repressed correspondingly more insistent] became a Son religion. The old God, the Father, took second place; Christ, the Son, stood in his stead.... [T]he guilt attached to the murder of Moses may have been the stimulus

31 For Freud's summary, see *Moses and Monotheism*, 102–03. Freud later notes "the close resemblance between the rite of Christian Communion—where the believer symbolically incorporates the blood and flesh of his God—and the totem feast, whose inner meaning it reproduces" (106).

> for the wish-phantasy of the Messiah, who was to return and give to his people salvation and the promised sovereignty of the world. If Moses was the first Messiah, Christ became his substitute and successor.... Then also there is some historical truth in the rebirth of Christ, for he was the resurrected Moses and the returned primeval father of the primitive horde as well—only transfigured, and as *a Son in the place of his Father*. (111, 114; my emphasis)

If in one sense, then, the crucified Christ represents the guilty son whose defiance of the father must be admitted and atoned for, he is also, as previously noted, "the leader of the brother horde who had overpowered the father." As sacrificial victim, the Christ of the crucifixion serves the father out of love and so honors (or at least defers to) the father's priority. The glorified Christ of the resurrection, by contrast, renounces nothing (he refuses even to truly die) and, instead, reasserts all his rebellious instincts in defiance of that priority, an act of dispossession of the very father who had first dared to dispossess him.

For Freud, the Christian resurgence of suppressed filial antagonism was akin to the revenge of the Egyptian priests of Amon-Re after the death of Akhenaten.[32] (The historical backdrop here is treated in detail in the Appendix.) And, like that restored Egyptian religion of the late-fourteenth century BCE, Christianity was marked by a form of polytheistic worship after its rejection of the moral and spiritual austerity of monotheism. There was, first and foremost, the restoration of multiple gods: the one universal god of Judaism became the father to a divine son (a Zeus to a Dionysius, who, like Christ, was the son of a mortal mother); the addition of the Holy Spirit then made a divine triad (the Trinity). The later tradition of venerating saints, the cult of the Blessed Virgin most extensively, created a vast if unofficial pantheon, gods and even goddesses everywhere and for all occasions.[33] Beyond that, there was the insistence on anthropomorphic depictions of god in human form as well as a reopening to what Freud would call "the penetration of superstitions ... and mystical elements" (112). Jesus' miracles, culminating in his bodily resurrection, would be the most oft-cited examples, of course, but, more broadly, the belief in the efficacy of prayer and the intercession of saints effectively

32 So Freud writes: "The triumph of Christianity was a renewed victory of the Ammon [sic] priests over the God of Ikhnaton [Akhenaten] after an interval of a millennium and a half" (112–13).

33 So Freud writes: "The Christian religion ... was no longer strictly monotheistic; it took over from the surrounding peoples numerous symbolical rites, re-established the great mother goddess, and found room for many deities of polytheism in an easily recognizable disguise, though in subordinate positions" (112).

restored the idea that the miraculous was part of the order of nature (certainly a not unexpected occurrence). Freud thought of belief in miracles as a subset of primitive notions of magic, and he found in the central Christian ritual of the Eucharist, with its defining moment of transubstantiation, both a shamanistic ceremony and a version of the primeval, cannibalistic totem feast. Finally, the Christian obsession with an afterlife was, for Freud, the most non-Jewish of all the Christian reversions: Christians sought by the notion of salvation to replace a this-world reality with an otherworldly fantasy—eternal existence in a place without suffering or sin (a heaven, a second paradise, a deified earth).

Echoing Freud's position in his passing comment that Christianity fundamentally marks a "regression to paganism," Slavoj Žižek suggests that, among its other distinguishing characteristics, paganism includes, if it cannot be limited to, a "'cosmic feeling' of oneness with the universe."[34] We might get a better perspective on what this distinction means by briefly considering how the emerging monotheism of the ancient Israelites articulated itself against the surrounding pagan world. In regard to the latter, Karen Armstrong summarizes a key moment in the Babylonian creation epic, the *Enuma Elish,* and speculates on its broader implications:

> Finally, … Marduk created humanity.… The first man [was] … created from the substance of a god [Kingu, the consort of Tiamat]; he therefore shared the divine nature, in however limited a way. There was no gulf between human beings and the gods. The natural world, men and women and the gods themselves all shared the same nature and derived from the same divine substance. The pagan vision was holistic. The gods were not shut off from the human race in a separate ontological sphere: divinity was not essentially different from humanity.[35]

The inverse of Armstrong's claim is that Hebrew monotheism, slowly developing as it was and, in its earliest phases, not always distinct from paganism, was not holistic. Hebrew monotheism, that is, *did* see a gulf between human beings and God (or even the gods—Yahweh and El or Elohim) and so viewed divinity as "essentially different from humanity." Robert Alter argues for this very different vision as central to what he calls the "monotheistic revolution" in observing that "the whole spectrum of biblical thought presupposes an absolute cleavage between man and God, man cannot become God and God (in contrast to

---

34 *Puppet and the Dwarf,* 119.

35 *A History of God: The 4000-Year Old Quest of Judaism, Christianity, and Islam* (New York: Ballantine Books, 1993), 9.

later Christian development) does not become man."[36] While it is not clear that the "*whole* spectrum of biblical thought presupposes" such an "absolute cleavage"—for example, King David and his royal heirs are understood to be "sons" of God in some texts—we might yet accept the notion that a conceptual cleavage in the human-divine relationship is precisely what Judaic-monotheistic discourse sought both to invent and to invest with authority. And it was compelled to do so because God's status as father to his creature-sons meant that some part of creation was, mysteriously, at once god and not-god, at once separate and inseparable from what, in the terms set out in John's Gospel at least, was there from "the beginning." If then "paganism is," as Žižek suggests, "the ultimate Christian dream," this is so, in part at least, because it seeks to overcome the gap that exists between humankind and god, to return, that is, to paganism's holistic vision: god did not come *before* humankind in either sense of priority (temporal or ontological).[37]

Although addressing the issue in a different context, Badiou is quite right to say that the effect of the Christ event is that humankind "shall cease to be separated from God." God paradoxically a*ffiliates* himself with humankind through the process that begins with the Incarnation and ends with resurrection, a process that seeks not just "an equality with God" in the broader pagan sense but, more importantly, an equality that derives from no longer being "bound to the legality of"—which is inseparable from the subjection to—"the Father." Badiou thus concludes that Pauline universality is about freedom from subjection in imitation of the son who claims equality with the father or might even dispense with the father's authority altogether.[38] From Freud's perspective, of course, such filial self-assertion is not just a Christian fantasy—the effort to reclaim what never truly existed—but, more to the point, expresses and even enacts a loss of something infinitely more valuable. In concluding that Christianity was "a cultural regression as compared with the older Jewish religion," Freud meant especially that it "did not keep to the lofty heights of spirituality to which the Jewish religion had soared" (*Moses and Monotheism*, 112) precisely because it had lost touch with what marked Judaism's special progress in spirituality, its commitment to living an ethical life in the world as it is and not as the mind wants it to be. Instead, Christianity went backward to an instinct

36 *The Art of Biblical Narrative* (New York: Basic Books, 1981), 154, 157.

37 *Puppet and the Dwarf*, 48. Žižek later rhetorically asks, "Is this not what Christianity it about," the "assertion of the direct identity of God and man?" (123). Drawing out the implications of Paul's claim that we are "reconciled to [God] by the death of his Son" (Romans 5:10), Badiou flips this idea around to venture that "through Christ's death, God renounces his transcendent separation; he unseparates himself through filiation" (70).

38 *Saint Paul*, 69, 49.

for childish gratification of hopes and dreams—it renounced Judaism's own "renunciation of instinctual gratification" (104)—and so returned to what in *Totem and Taboo* Freud had dismissively referred to as the primitive inclination to "the omnipotence of thoughts." As part of what can only be understood as an endorsement of Jewish culture's resistance to indulging in such flights of fancy, Freud notes his own continuing astonishment regarding the biblical narrative—and there is real admiration in this—"that the Jewish religion did not speak of anything beyond the grave" (29). And where there is no afterlife there is no futile hope of self-apotheosis, for Freud the epitome of the omnipotence of thoughts he finds typical of pagan-polytheistic traditions.

5

Judaism's reward for trying to be the adult in the room was to be despised and hated. In a very general way, Freud is not surprised for, as he remarks, cultural regression "happens regularly when a new mass of people of a lower cultural life effects an invasion of or is admitted to an older culture" (*Moses and Monotheism*, 112). What he wants to understand, though, is why cultural regression took the form of such virulent aggression, what he calls the "phenomenon of such intensity and lasting strength as the popular hatred of the Jews" (115). While Freud notes that "a whole series of reasons can be divined[,] ... the deeper motives of anti-Semitism have their roots in times long past." The first of these deeper motives (ones that "spring from secret"—which is to say, unconscious—"sources") is, Freud ventures, "the jealousy which the Jews evoked in other peoples by maintaining that they were the first-born, favorite child of God the Father," a jealousy "not yet ... overcome by those others, just as if the latter had given credence to the assumption" (116). This jealousy might make some sense when combined with what Freud sees as more overt reasons for the hostility: "Jews mostly live as a minority among other peoples" (and that status "invites suppression") and "in many respects, they are 'different' from their 'hosts' ... although," as he adds, "sometimes it is hard to define in what respects" (115–16).[39] That said, the Romans whose violence "in times long past" caused the final diaspora were unlikely to have felt any jealousy towards the Jews under their authority and would have been amused by the Jewish claim to be the "favorite child of God" since the great father-god, Jupiter, had clearly chosen the Romans to be his special people, a fact borne out by the fact that

39 Freud adds that "the feeling of solidarity of the masses, in order to be complete, has need of an animosity against an outside minority" (115).

Judaea was but a minor imperial province. The second reason Freud offers is the custom of circumcision, which makes "a disagreeable, uncanny impression on others" as a reminder of "the dreaded castration idea." Though obviously drawing on his broader theory of the oedipal economy, this reason is even less convincing historically since circumcision was and is practiced by non-Jewish individuals and entire cultures without provoking the same kind of extreme "racial intolerance" (116).

Freud's final reason is the most intriguing in that it depends on the idea that the most intense reactions against an identified Other derive from the need to deny (and thus to project externally) what cannot be tolerated in oneself (whether the self is an individual or a culture). This reason also makes more sense in that it specifies the locus of anti-Semitism as (European) Christian culture. Freud refers to this as "the most recent motive of the series":

> We must not forget that all the peoples who now excel in the practice of anti-Semitism became Christians only in relatively recent times, sometimes forced to it by bloody compulsion. One might say that they all are "badly christened"; under the thin veneer of Christianity they have remained what their ancestors were, barbarically polytheistic. They have not yet overcome their grudge against the new religion which was forced on them, and they have projected it on to the source from which Christianity came to them. The facts that the Gospels tell a story which is enacted among the Jews, and in truth treats only of Jews, has facilitated such a projection. The hatred of Judaism is at bottom a hatred of Christianity. (116–17)

Freud does not say here what it is about Christianity (or Judaism for that matter) that the still "barbarically polytheistic" converts so despised in the form of a grudge "against the ... religion which was forced on them." We might then try to understand this (self-)loathing both by analogy to Paul's own (Jewish-Christian) antagonism to Mosaic Judaism and by tracing that antagonism back to its source at the very origins of Judaic monotheism.[40]

---

40 Freud (114–15) actually cites as the first among the causes of anti-Semitism the traditional charge of deicide. At the close of *Moses and Monotheism* he returns to this idea: precisely because they did not "accept ... the new [Christian] doctrine," the Jews "had to suffer the reproach from the new religious community ... that they had murdered God" (176). It is worth noting that Paul himself never makes this accusation. We do find early expressions of the deicide accusation in other New Testament writings: e.g. Acts of the Apostles 3:11–26 (especially vv. 14–15).

If we interpret a certain kind of hostility as deriving from the return of the repressed, Pauline Christianity, we might say, hated in itself an element revealed in its own Judaic origins that it wanted to continue to conceal (keep repressed). Even though Paul's theology explicitly absolved all people, Jews and Gentiles alike, of guilt through the efficacy of Christ's atonement, Judaism reminded Christians that this guilt still lingered. More precisely, in struggling to renounce the guilt for some unnamable crime against God, Christians grappled with their deep ambivalence toward the very notion of an inescapable subservience to God, the deified projection of the murdered father whose primacy continued to haunt them. *Pace* Freud, then, Christians were not jealous of the chosenness of the Jews; rather, they were unconsciously repelled by what the very concept of chosenness meant. For chosenness was inseparable from submissiveness: being the favorite son still entailed (both in the sense of including and bequeathing, though here as the gift of an inheritance that is simultaneously a burden) the sense of being under subjection to paternal authority. And when that authority was the province of a deity, such submission would never end.

In describing the resistance to Moses among his first followers, Freud imagines in terms that almost exactly match his description of the motive force of the anti-Semitic reaction to Judaism just how much resistance to imposed authority was at the heart of Jewish beginnings: "those who felt themselves kept in tutelage, or who felt dispossessed, revolted, and threw off *the burden of a religion that had been forced on them*" (58; my emphasis). While Freud argues that the burden came from the particulars of the Aton-now-Mosaic religion (its special discipline and rigor) as well as from the violent and authoritarian nature of Moses' personality, I now venture that the burden of dispossession derived from the very experience of having been chosen and created through that very choice.[41] In short, the burden of being originated in the act of another ("from outside, from a great stranger" [63]) became the foundational crisis of Jewish consciousness. Freud will call the founding experience "traumatic" (65), a trauma focused especially, as we have seen, in the repressed memories of the very uprising in which the great father was murdered. But I would counter with the observation that, even if Moses had been murdered by the people of the Exodus, the motive for that killing, psychoanalytically speaking, was the crisis of the origin itself and the experience of dispossession that came

41 Freud remarks that "the rules the man Moses imposed on his Jews were even harder than those of his master and teacher Ikhnaton [Akhenaten]" (74). Freud imagines Moses to have been particularly "jealous, stern, and implacable" (37), "masterful, hot-tempered, even violent" (49), and "uncompromising" (57). He was, quite simply, a "tyrant" (58).

from his followers' recognition of their absence from the scene of their own creation: the great father had created them, and they could never escape the shadow of that dispossession. This moment was experienced as a burden precisely because what was absent at the scene of the origin was the people's own choice to exist.[42]

Although anti-Semitism is not his interest here, Badiou's comments on the Jerusalem conference as reported in Paul's Letter to the Galatians (chapter 2) and in Luke's Acts of the Apostles (chapter 15) are particularly illuminating as a way of understanding how this burden was passed on to Christianity and, in that new location, fueled hostility for the parent faith. Of the conference, where it was agreed that Peter would lead the mission among the Jews (the circumcised) and Paul would lead the mission among the Gentiles (the uncircumcised), Badiou writes that it, while it

> ultimately prevents Christianity from becoming a Jewish sect ... in curbing the zeal of those Gentile-Christians hostile to Judaism, and perhaps that of Paul himself, it [also] prevented Christianity from being merely a new illuminism, one just as precarious because devoid of all basis in historical Judaism. The Jerusalem conference is genuinely foundational, because it endows Christianity with a two-fold principle of opening and historicity. It thereby holds tight to the thread of the event as initiation of a truth procedure. That the event is new should never let us forget that it is such only with respect to a determinate situation [Jewish tradition].[43]

Badiou's "never let us forget" could be applied to Gentile-Christians themselves (and later just to Christianity as a whole, at least in its Pauline form): because of the compromise reached at the conference, they were never permitted to forget the Judaism that served as the "determinate situation" of their new religion. Thus, rather than saying that Judaism "endowed" Christianity with something, it would be more accurate to observe that, through the Jerusalem conference, followers of Jesus still committed to the Law *burdened* Gentile-Christianity with an origin it could never throw off. In this context we might return to Badiou's remark, cited earlier, that Paul's thought is founded on a key question: "What is the exact relation between the supposed universality of the postevental truth (that is, what is inferred from Christ's resurrection) and the evental

42 In line with his earlier assertion that Moses "chose [certain Semitic Neo-Egyptian tribes] to be his new people" (*Moses and Monotheism*, 32), Freud concludes that the Jews are not, in fact, God's chosen people; they were, rather, Moses' chosen people (54–55).

43 *Saint Paul*, 25.

site, which is, indubitably, the nation bound together by the Old Testament?"[44] One of the prime motivations for anti-Semitism, then, might be understood as the result of the inescapability of Judaism within Christianity—a relationship through which a terrible longing to be free from paternal authority is expressed. Following this logic, we might also return to Badiou's remark that, in grasping how "freedom puts into play the question of the law," Paul is also critiquing the Jewish notion that, under the Law, "every subject [is] configured in the form of legal subjection." Anti-Semitism, in short, is partly the result of Christianity's rebellion against the extension of such subjection into its very self-identity, a subjection that creates a self-loathing it then projects onto the parent religion.

While, as we've seen, Freud argued that Christians had never "overcome their grudge against the new religion which was forced on them," we might now amend that claim: the grudge was not against the religion itself so much as against the fact that it was forced on them; or, perhaps more accurately, at their very beginning they were subjected to an origin they did not choose. In retaliation, Christians "projected" their resentment "on to the source from which" their own religion "came to them," Judaism. Reading this conflict through the lens of psychoanalytic practice, we might say that Judaism stood where Freud himself might have in relation to one of his own neurotic patients. In an act of transference, Judaism functioned as the paternal site onto which its belated son, Christianity, attempted to work through its deep-seeded ambivalence toward the authority of what came before it. Christian anti-Semites hated Jews because in claiming the mantle of chosenness the latter reminded the former that they could never escape from the condition of filial submission, the situation of the son of prehistoric times forced to concede to the father's primacy within the clan. Freud is right, then, to imagine something very primitive in anti-Semitism, a tribal (un)consciousness that could not quite keep itself in a repressed state. For Christianity hated in Judaism what it hated first and foremost in itself: a desire to murder the primeval father that could find no other expression than in hatred for the religion that had come first, the Father religion that had figuratively sired the Son religion.

In projecting onto Judaism what it hated (and so tried to deny) in itself, Christianity officially celebrated the opposite: the exaltation of the Son. Thus, while, on the one hand, in Paul's theology of expiation the burden of guilt for a crime he could not even remember was simply transferred to the redeemer Son—"it had to be a Son," Freud notes, "for the sin had been the murder of the Father"—one the other hand, as Freud also reminds us, "the final result

44 *Saint Paul*, 22.

of the religious innovation ... meant to propitiate the Father Deity ... ends by his being dethroned and set aside" (*Moses and Monotheism*, 110–11). In other words, Paul's willingness to absolve himself and any other believer of the guilt of patricide by placing it all on the submissive Son was inseparable from a reversal: the Son deified by his very submission "becom[es] God himself beside the Father and in truth *in place of the Father*" (175; my emphasis).

In this context, we might note Robert Paul's observation that, as a "salvation religion," Christianity specifically "defines what people need to be saved from as *a fault inherent in Judaism*." To the extent "Christianity first has to convince them that they need to be saved, ... it teaches them the 'old testament' so that they too will find themselves in the state from which Christianity, by its design, is supposed to save them. What for the Jews has been the support for an ongoing social system has been reinterpreted through the lens of the Christian myth as *an intolerable condition one from which a person self-evidently needs to be rescued*."[45] The question, of course, is how Christianity perceives this intolerable condition and why, from the perspective of anti-Semitism in particular, it locates this condition in Judaism, its own parent faith.

This very location strongly suggests that what Christianity finds intolerable in Judaism is precisely that Judaism *is* the parent faith. Thus, while Pauline Christianity focuses explicitly on the need to be redeemed from a state of sin or guilt before the Law, I would suggest that what Paul unconsciously aims at is freedom from subservience itself, a condition that Judaism marked for Pauline Christians precisely to the extent that they understood themselves, to borrow a term from Jean Laplanche, in a position of temporal and ontological afterwardsness.[46] Anti-Semitism, in short, was a response to Christianity's self-perceived belatedness relative to Judaism, and its hostility to Judaism was a way of signaling that, if it were to be a Son religion in relation to the Father religion, its status would be akin to the Christ's relation to God-the-father: it would dethrone what claimed priority because it came before as a father comes before the son. Pauline Christianity aimed to reject guilt, but guilt itself derived not from sin but from what Freud calls "repressed hostility to God" (*Moses and Monotheism*, 173). This hostility derived, in turn, from filial ambivalence in the face of paternal imposition, the very imposition that created an intolerable gap between human and divine. To be saved from sin by

45 *Moses and Civilization: The Meaning Behind Freud's Myth* (New Haven: Yale University Press, 1996), 194; my emphases; original italics deleted.

46 "Afterwards" or "afterwardness" is Laplanche's suggested translation of Freud's *Nachträglichkeit*, more typically translated as "deferred action" (*Essays on Otherness*, ed. John Fletcher [New York: Routledge, 1999], 263).

the triumphant Son is to be removed from the very possibility of guilt and thus also from an originary filial ambivalence by assuming the place of the Father and so eliminating the distinction that permits the imposition of paternal law.

It is worth observing in this context that the concept of subservience to God as it is linked to the ongoing awareness of guilt is, for Paul, effectively eliminated in Christ's atoning sacrifice (Romans 3:25). A spiritual clean slate is possible not simply because the sacrificial death of the innocent Christ substitutes (atones) for the death we owe God due to our sinful condition but also because as part of exchange inhering in this substitutive process God bestows "his grace as a gift" (Romans 3:24). Observing that the "implication is that grace is in some sense opposed to law," Robert Paul adds that "the gift of grace" as Paul imagines it "expects no return, flowing from a bounteous source that never needs to be replenished or repaid."[47] To put this in somewhat more defiant terms, in the wake of the atonement, we owe God nothing: we escape from his demands, his laws, his insistent presence, his control. In the Acts of the Apostles, Paul is depicted declaring at Antioch that the particular form of this new freedom is our awareness that we are no longer bound to the dictates of Torah: "by this Jesus everyone who believes is set free from all those sins from which you could not be freed by the law of Moses" (13:39). What we see here is how Paul's version of messianic Judaism offers redemption from the burdens of Mosaic Judaism as Mosaic Judaism itself imposes upon its adherents the perpetual debt—manifested as sin, guilt, death, damnation—to an implacable God. But to be freed from guilt and thus discharged from the debt we owe because of it is to experience liberation from our ontological inferiority.[48] For Paul, we might say, Mosaic Judaism, which accepts eternal subservience to God as the price of chosenness, separates humankind from its own natural divinity. If as a faith-practice Christianity might be understood, then, as a defense mechanism against existential humiliation before the creator father-god, anti-Semitism is a secondary defense: a displacement of hostility from the father-god onto his favorite and all too compliant child. If, as Freud ventures, as a "Son religion" Christianity could not escape "the fate of having to displace the Father" (*Moses and Monotheism*, 175), in simpler terms it actively sought out and embraced this fate as its own. For, as Badiou puts in, within Pauline Christianity (the Son religion) the Christ-event functions as "the means to equality with God himself."[49]

---

47 *Moses and Civilization*, 200.

48 Robert Paul remarks that in the "pleasurable and exhilarating experience of liberation from guilt and obligation ... lies some of the intoxicating appeal of the 'good news'" (212).

49 *Saint Paul*, 69.

In sum, what Paul's return of the repressed unconsciously acknowledged was that the "savage Semites" (58) as Freud calls them—as "stubborn and unruly towards their lawgiver and leader" (74) as their ancestors, the brother horde, had been toward their father—were right to have killed Moses. Paul's own act of patricide could only be symbolic, of course: he would kill traditional Judaism (at least fatally injure it) by killing Moses a second time; he would, that is, rid his new Judaism of Mosaic Law and thus of Moses himself. In this way, Judaism "returned" in Pauline Christianity as a fantasy that the Son would claim the privilege of the Father and so would no longer be dispossessed by paternal priority (both as preeminence and as a coming before).

In venturing that "in their relationship to God the Father, Judaism and Christianity are both son-religions," Yerushalmi argues that Christianity's hostility toward Judaism is less a manifestation of the filial hostility (the Oedipus complex) than one of sibling rivalry taken to the extreme of fratricide. He goes on to suggest that this rivalry (akin to that between Esau and Jacob) has less to do with the father than with the mother (they are each more interested in Rebekah than in Isaac). And he then asks: "Who, then, at the juncture we have reached, is the mother?" His answer is Torah: "it is over possession of her that Christianity, the younger son, came to challenge, not so much the Father as Judaism, the elder son."[50] Yerushalmi's revision of the Freudian narrative might derive in large part from his own investment in Torah and in particular in the stories of Genesis which, starting with Genesis 4, are so captured by the ceaseless struggle between brothers. (We might think of Luke's parable of the prodigal son as a Christianized example of the stories of Genesis.) While it makes more sense to understand Christianity as a "son" displacing its hostility toward the father-god onto a father-substitute (the father-religion Judaism as the parent-religion to Christianity), even in Yerushalmi's terms the tension-point is not as he imagines it: the brothers' competition for possession of the mother's primary affection (that is, to be the mother-Torah's favorite child). To think of this situation in terms of Luke's parable, there is no mother in the parable (so no competition for her affection), and what the younger son initially wants is not the attention of the father but to be free from the father: to leave the father's estate and make his way in the world on his own terms. (In Luke's telling, he fails spectacularly in this endeavor, which doesn't change the fact that freedom is what he seeks.) And to the extent that the father's attention is explicitly what the older son craves (not to be free of the father but to be acknowledged by him), we might imagine that the very reason the younger son

50 *Freud's Moses*, 92.

wants to strike out on his own is precisely because of the obsequiousness he observes in his brother. That is, the elder brother shows to the younger brother what any relation to the father will necessarily entail: never-ending subservience that yet longs for, even if it is constantly denied, the master-father's "love." To translate this scenario into the terms Freud uses to theorize the cause of anti-Semitism, we might then say that Christianity hates in Judaism what it hates in itself: its awareness of its own foundational secondariness in relation to paternal priority. This is why Paul's obsession with the risen Christ is a way of imagining a kind of self-apotheosis under the show of submission: once he has been glorified, he will no longer merely serve the father because, like the Son, he will be equal to the father.

As he turned from his study's main focus on the origin of Judaic monotheism to its (d)evolution into Christianity, Freud argued that the actual murder that started it all (the murder of the primeval father, an act then repeated in the murder of Moses) was no longer so traumatic for Christians because no longer as repressed: the Christians admitted what had been done—even admitted they themselves "had murdered God"—and so could declare themselves "purified" (*Moses and Monotheism*, 115). Of course, even by Freud's own logic, they had admitted no such thing: "the murderous deed" that sat at the origin "was not remembered," and the aim of Pauline theology was to lay to rest the guilt for the crime (even as that guilt was acknowledged) by displacing it onto a scapegoat, the innocent Christ. If, then, the originary moment was still distorted ("suppressed and abnegated in material hidden away" [52]), it would make more sense to say that what was more clearly drawn into the open—those "dark traces of the past ... ready to break through into the regions of consciousness" (109–10)—was the filial ambivalence that had always been embedded in and expressed through the primal murder. But in this renewal of what Freud saw as the demands of narcissistic self-gratification, Christians with and after Paul thereby also renounced what Freud saw as Judaism's greatest blessing, its capacity for instinctual renunciation, a surrender to an authority that would always be greater.[51] Repudiating the Judaic genius for renunciation, Christians

---

51 Freud yet sees a powerful element of infantilization underlying Jewish renunciation. If "a transport of devotion to God is ... the first response to the return of the Great Father,"

"the first effect of the reunion with what men had long been missed and yearned for was overwhelming and exactly as the tradition of the law-giving on Mount Sinai depicts it. There was admiration, awe, and gratitude that the people had found favor in his eyes; the religion of Moses knows only of these positive feelings towards the Father God. The conviction that his power was irresistible, the subjection to his will, could not have been more absolute with the helpless, intimidated son of the father of the horde than they were here." (172)

with and after Paul became deluded with the omnipotence of thoughts in its most extreme form, the dream of godhead. As instinctual renunciation once again became instinctual gratification, the pagan-polytheistic elements that had always promoted fantasy over reality—the desire for immortality most of all—would return with a vengeance worthy of the priesthood of Amon-Re. Freud thus writes close to the end of *Moses and Monotheism*: "After the Christian doctrine had burst the confines of Judaism, it absorbed constituents from many other sources, renounced many features of pure monotheism, and adopted in many particulars the ritual of other Mediterranean peoples. It was as if Egypt had come to wreak her vengeance on the heirs of Ikhnaton [Akhenaten]" (175).

Freud had earlier written in *Civilization and Its Discontents* (1930) that "a considerable amount of aggressiveness must be developed in the child against the authority who prevents him from having his first, but nonetheless his most important, satisfactions ... But he is obliged to renounce the satisfaction of the revengeful aggressiveness" (*SE*, 21:129). If Judaism might be understood as the exemplar of such renunciation in terms of a religious tradition, Christianity could then be understood as undoing the Judaic superego in its quest to restore the child's fantasy of (self-)omnipotence. Even earlier in his career in his "Contributions to the Psychology of Love" (1910), Freud has described what we might consider the extreme limit of this fantasy at least from the perspective of the oedipal son: a son's ambivalence towards his father "make[s] him say: 'I want nothing from my father.' ... All his instincts ... find satisfaction in the single wish *to be his own father*" (*SE*, 11:172–73). For Christians, that satisfaction comes precisely from the transformation of the crucified Jesus into the resurrected Christ, a transformation that makes it possible for all ambivalent sons through a kind of participatory atonement (at-one-ment with God) to fulfill the childish wish to be their own fathers.

CODA 1

The Murder of Moses and the Temporality of Trauma

> [I]n the history of the Jewish religion there is a long period, after the breaking away from the Moses religion, during which no trace can be found of the monotheistic idea ... [W]e are prepared for the possibility that the solution to our problem is to be sought in a special psychological situation.
>
> —FREUD, *Moses and Monotheism*

∴

As a way of laying the conceptual and historical foundation for the central topic of Chapters 2 and 3, I want revisit Freud's claim that, whatever the importance of Egyptian Atonism as an essential precursor, it was the murder of Moses that stands as the true origin of Judaic monotheism. As Freud puts in Part III of *Moses and Monotheism*, "the murder of Moses by his people" is an "indispensable part of [his] reasoning," the critical "link between the forgotten deed of primeval times"—the slaying of the father of the prehistoric horde—"and its subsequent reappearance in the form of monotheistic religions" with their devotion to the universal father-god (114). That said, to the extent Freud aims to show that the murder was less important in itself than was the people's response to it—they "passed through what may properly be termed a traumatic experience" (65)—this Coda tries to demonstrate how and why Freud's description fails to adequately account for how a foundational trauma took root in, and so came to define, Jewish culture. In short, something is missing from Freud's presentation of the traumatic etiology that, in his interpretation, is the answer to the question he had posed to Arnold Zweig in 1934: how [have] the Jews ... come to be what they are[?]"[1] But to understand Freud's (mis)representation, we must first consider how he had previously conceptualized the etiology of traumatic neurosis at the level of the individual. In what

1 *Letters of Sigmund Freud and Arnold Zweig*, ed. Ernst L. Freud, trans. Elaine Robson-Scott and William Robson-Scott (New York, 1970), 91.

 | DOI:10.1163/9789004701663_004

follows, then, I will examine how Freud developed his notion of the etiology of neurosis in the case of a traumatized individual (with special attention to trauma understood as a multifaceted temporal sequence). I will then take up his attempt in *Moses and Monotheism* to apply that model by way of analogy to the mass-psychological phenomenon he sees as inextricably linked to what he calls "the fateful content of the religious history of the Jews" (57).

1

Summarizing a metapsychological position first staked out in *Beyond the Pleasure Principle*, Freud writes in *Inhibitions, Symptoms and Anxiety* that "in the experiences which lead to a traumatic neurosis the protective shield against stimuli is broken through and excessive amounts of excitation impinge on the mental apparatus" (*SE*, 20:130). As befits a medical-scientific statement about trauma—or, more precisely, a neurosis brought on by trauma—there is, as we would expect, something decidedly technical about Freud's description here: "protective shield against stimuli," "excessive amounts of excitation." The latter phrase particularly underscores Freud's broadly economic approach to the workings of the mind, the notion that psychical processes determine even as they are constituted by the production, maintenance, and distribution of instinctual energy. Jean Laplanche and Jean-Bertrand Pontalis observe, for example, that the "economic point of view consists in taking into consideration the cathexes—their movement, the variations of their intensity, [and] the antagonisms that arise between them."[2] We might also follow Laplanche in understanding trauma as the near-total "disqualification of normal defenses and a triggering of a virtually atopical kind of reaction on the part of the ego."[3] From this perspective, in line with the original Greek meaning of the word, a trauma is best understood as a wounding of the mind in the sense that the psychical grasp of selfhood is injured to the point where that identity emerging through and dependent upon the complex interworkings of the various psychical processes and states is put at risk. In "Mourning and Melancholia" Freud

2 *The Language of Psycho-analysis*, trans. Donald Nicholson-Smith (New York: Norton, 1974), 27. Ten years before the publication of *Inhibitions, Symptoms and Anxiety*, Freud had explicitly positioned trauma within this diagnostic framework: "the term 'traumatic' has no other sense than an economic one" (*Introductory Lectures*, *SE*, 16:275).

3 *Life and Death in Psychoanalysis*, trans. Jeffrey Mehlman (Baltimore: Johns Hopkins University Press, 1976), 130.

would refer to such a scenario as "the impoverishment of the ego on a grand scale" (*SE*, 14:253).

Freud at times used the word trauma and its variants in an almost generic sense. At one point in his pre-psychoanalytic treatise *Project for a Scientific Psychology* (1895), for example, he refers to trauma simply as "an "experience of pain" or, in somewhat more Freudian terms, "a release of unpleasure" (*Origins*, 416). In other words, trauma can simply mean for Freud any psychically undesirable experience.[4] Three decades later in *Inhibitions, Symptoms and Anxiety* he will conceptually locate trauma in relation to a vaguely defined "situation of danger," which "consists in the subject's estimation of his own strength compared to the magnitude of the danger and in his admission of helplessness in the face of it … Let us call a situation of helplessness of this kind that has been actually experienced a *traumatic situation*" (*SE*, 20:166).[5]

Even in the early *Project*, though, Freud aimed at describing the "release of unpleasure" in the context of mental processes—particularly the complex relationship between troubling memories (often just psychical impressions) and various kinds of defense mechanisms organized against these—and, more broadly, the status of the ego relative to other competing components of the psyche as these were meshed into the processes of identity formation. At the point in *Project* previously alluded to, Freud distinguishes normal traumas that are effectively reined in by the ego through the creation of "lateral cathexes" that, over time, dissipate the force of the trauma from other sorts of trauma (e.g., ones producing a hysterical reaction) that are not "on the occasion of the *first* release of unpleasure" accompanied by "an inhibition by the ego." Particularly virulent or pathological traumas "escape the ego" and so create (and then are experienced as) what Freud refers to as a "'posthumous' primary affective experience." The word "posthumous" here points to a situation in which, though psychically retained, the impression of the original experience, not at first excessively troubling, "only become[s] a trauma *after the event*" (*Origins*, 416, 413).

The *Standard Edition's* rendering of that final italicized phrase—"by *deferred action*" (1:356)—is undoubtedly the more widely recognized translation of

4 For related comments, see *Studies in Hysteria*, *SE*, 2:5–6.

5 In *Moses and Monotheism*, Freud comments almost in passing that "all depends on what is defined as traumatic. If we may assume that an experience acquires its traumatic character only in consequence of a quantitative element—that is to say, that if the experience evokes unusual pathological reactions, the fault lies in its having made too many demands on the personality—then we can formulate the conclusion that with one constitution something produces a trauma whereas with another it does not" (92).

Freud's own *nachträglich*.[6] In their encyclopedia of psychoanalytic terms, Laplanche and Pontalis remark that "although he never offered a definition, much less a general theory, of the notion of deferred action, it was indisputably looked on by Freud as part of his conceptual equipment."[7] At a very early stage in his thinking on the subject (specifically in the context of the etiology of hysteria), Freud offers this description of the psychical processes at work in such deferral, that temporal delay effectively constituting trauma as always and necessarily "after the event":

> If a cathexis which releases unpleasure were able to escape attention, the *ego's intervention would come too late*. And this is precisely what happens in the case of hysterical *proton pseudos* [first lie or distortion]. Attention is focused on perceptions, which are the normal occasions for the release of unpleasure. But here it is not a perception but a memory-trace which unexpectedly releases unpleasure, and *the ego discovers this too late*. It has permitted a primary process [e.g. displacement of the original experience] because it did not expect one. (*Origins*, 415–16; my emphases)

To align the ego's disorienting belatedness (the "too late") with the previously mentioned notion of impoverishment, we might tentatively infer that a key element in trauma's capacity to render the ego problematic to itself is that there is something missing or misplaced in an experience that, while not necessarily traumatic in its original form, will only later, by some activity of retrospection, become the focal point of mental disruption. Laplanche and Pontalis observe in this context that a deferred response to a past experience acts on "whatever has been impossible in the first instance to incorporate fully into a meaningful context. The traumatic event is the epitome of such unassimilated experience."[8]

What it means to say that an experience is unassimilated is one of the central questions of trauma theory and indeed of psychoanalysis as a whole. While over the course of his career, Freud will offer an array of possibilities, his first extended foray into the subject comes in his analysis of his patient, Emma, in the 1895 *Project*. Here is part of his initial description of the case:

6 *Aus den Anfängen der Psychoanalyse: Briefe an Wilhelm Fliess, Abhandlungen und Notizen aus den Jahren 1887–1902* (London: Imago Publishing, 1950), 435.

7 *The Language of Psycho-analysis*, 111.

8 *The Language of Psycho-analysis*, 112. This position has been developed in some detail by Cathy Caruth in *Unclaimed Experience: Trauma, Narrative, and History* (Baltimore: Johns Hopkins University Press, 1996).

> On two occasions, when she was a child of eight, she had gone into a shop to buy some sweets and the shopkeeper had grabbed at her genitals through her clothes. In spite of this first experience she had gone to the shop a second time, after which she stopped away. Afterwards she reproached herself for having gone a second time ... And in fact a "bad conscience" by which she was oppressed could be traced back to this experience. (*Origins*, 411)

The experience with the shopkeeper had effectively been psychically displaced (unassimilated) and, in deferred form, had come be to be symbolized in relation to a second encounter four years later, an encounter with which her conscious memory then associated a hysterical response:

> Emma is at the present time under a compulsion not to go into shops *alone*. She explained this by a memory dating from the age of twelve (shortly before her puberty). She went into a shop to buy something, saw the two shop-assistants ... laughing together, and rushed out in some kind of *fright*. In this connection it was possible to elicit the idea that the two men had been laughing at her clothes and that one of them had attracted her sexually. (*Origins*, 410)

Freud literally sketches out the process by which the original experience, which didn't even properly exist in Emma's memory (at most a "memory-trace"), is mnemonically (re)triggered by the second event. The second event then becomes the psychical expression of what in the first event was never consciously registered because it came before any conscious awareness of sexuality. In short, in the context of an experience to which we might apply the term "traumatic," there is an initial situation from which some element appears to be missing or unassimilated and that then can only be (re)experienced in such a vexed way that the ego must erect defenses against it. Freud thus writes that, for Emma, "the recollection aroused ... anxiety[:] ... she was afraid the shop-assistants might repeat the assault, and ran away" (*Origins*, 411).

Although these will be subject to subsequent modification, two elements of Freud's account of Emma's case merit special emphasis. First, despite the oft-rendered critique of psychoanalysis for its deterministic understanding of the past (in the economic model, for example, the storing up of psychical energy that is only discharged at a later date), Freud is clear in this early discussion—and, while his description of the psychical mechanism will change, he never truly waivers from this point—that the origin of a traumatic neurosis does not simply reside in an initial event; rather, the neurosis is constituted as a relationship between two events. Just as important, in this first formulation of the concept at least, neither of the events is deemed traumatic in itself. As Laplanche and Pontalis observe of Freud's initial "schema" for the etiology of traumatic neurosis,

> in the first scene, called "seduction scene," the child is subject to a sexual approach from the adult ..., without arousing any sexual excitation in himself [or herself:] ... there is neither an afflux of external excitation nor an overflow of defenses. If it can be described as sexual, it is only from the point of view of the external agent, the adult. But the child has neither the somatic requisites of excitation nor the representations to enable him [or her] to integrate the event: although sexual in terms of objectivity, it has no sexual connotation for the subject, it is "pre-sexually sexual" ... As for the second scene, which occurs after puberty, it is, one might say, even less traumatic than the first: being non-violent, and apparently of no particular significance, its only power lies in being able to evoke the first event, retroactively by means of association. It is then the recall of the first scene which sets off the upsurge of sexual excitation, catching the ego in reverse, and leaving it disarmed, incapable of using the normally outward directed defenses, and thus falling back on a pathological defense, or "posthumous primary process"; the recollection is repressed.[9]

In terms of the etiology of her trauma, while Emma's experience started with an actual assault (or a "seduction" as Freud more typically calls it), at the time the assault occurred she could not understand the experience in those terms; it is only as retroactively prompted by a second and otherwise unrelated event that the unassimilated residue of the original event—the shopkeeper's groping—truly becomes the foundation if not precisely the origin of the neurosis. In short, in this initial formulation Freud theorizes a particular temporal structure to trauma: something in an original event (something that had truly happened) cannot be integrated into conscious thought and memory, and it is only by means of a retrospective—and unconscious—conferral of significance upon the original event as triggered by a second unrelated event that a traumatic neurosis emerges through pathological defense: in Emma's

9 "Fantasy and the Origins of Sexuality," *The International Journal of Psycho-analysis* 49 (1968): 4. For elaboration of trauma's double time-frame, see Ruth Leys, *Trauma: A Genealogy* (Chicago: University of Chicago Press, 2000), 18–22.

case, repression of the original event that manifests as anxiety.[10] Freud will generalize this relationship of past and present in an 1896 letter to Wilhelm Fliess: "I am working on the assumption that our psychical mechanism has come about by a process of stratification: the material present in the shape of memory-traces is from time to time subjected to a rearrangement in accordance with fresh circumstances—is, as it were, transcribed" (*Origins*, 173). In the more particular context of the etiology of traumatic neurosis, Laplanche and Pontalis remark that in situations where "the subject revises past events at a later date ... it is this revision which invests them with significance and *even with efficacity or pathogenic force.*"[11]

The second element of this analysis that merits special emphasis is that, extrapolating from the details of Emma's case, Freud is drawn to the notion that the sexual experiences of childhood are particularly susceptible to initial nonassimilation. This is so because of the peculiarly human delay in full sexual maturation. Freud thus moves from the specifics of Emma's situation—"Here we have an instance of a memory exciting an affect which it had not excited as an experience, because in the meantime *the changes produced by puberty* had made possible a new understanding of what was remembered"—to the formulation of a general principle: "Although it is unusual for a memory to arouse an affect which the actual experience has not produced, this is nevertheless what quite ordinarily happens in the case of sexual ideas, precisely *because the retardation of puberty is a general characteristic of the organization*" (*Origins*, 413; my emphases). Laplanche and Pontalis observe that, as this stage in the evolution of his thinking "Freud was concerned theoretically to justify the connection he had discovered between sexuality, trauma, and defense: to

10 Drawing on Freud's statement in Draft K (1896) that "here ... we have the one possibility of a memory subsequently producing a more powerful release than that produced in the first instance by the corresponding experience itself" (*Origins*, 147), Laplanche and Pontalis add regarding "the repartition of the trauma into two stages" that "the psychological trauma can only be conceived as arising from [something already there,] the reminiscence of the first scene.... [E]ach scene acquires sexual quality solely through the evocation of an earlier scene without which it would have no meaning for the subject" ("Fantasy and the Origins of Sexuality," 5).

11 *The Language of Psycho-analysis*, 112; my emphasis added. Because the significance of the original event could not be grasped at the time of the time of its occurrence, Laplanche is no doubt correct in his observation that the "psychical status of the memory of the first scene" (the assault) is not really a memory at all and therefore not originally in a state that could be repressed: "it would seem that for Freud [the recollection of the assault] persists neither in a conscious state nor, properly speaking, in a repressed state; it remains there, waiting in a kind of limbo, ... not linked to the rest of psychical life" (*Life and Death in Psychoanalysis*, 41).

show that it is in the very nature of sexuality to have a traumatic effect and, inversely, that one cannot speak of trauma as the origin of neurosis except to the extent a sexual seduction has occurred." They add that, for Freud through 1895, "the notions of defense and trauma are closely articulated one to the other: the theory of seduction, by showing how only a sexual trauma has the power to activate a 'pathological defense' (repression)[,] is an attempt to do justice to a clinically established fact (*Studies in Hysteria*) that repression concerns specifically sexuality."[12] It is worth reminding ourselves that, within the seduction model, repression does not happen initially. Because of the peculiar temporality of human sexual development (the delay in sexual maturation), the initial event (for Emma, the sexual groping she endured) does not "activate a pathological defense"; it is only the second event, occurring in temporal proximity to the pubescent emergence of sexuality, that, by (re)activating the first event (transcribing it, as Freud might say), reconstitutes a memory-trace as something closer to an actual memory; it is this memory (or "reminiscence" as he and Breuer had described it) that then undergoes repression.[13] As Freud himself puts it, repression emerges as that form of "pathological defense ... directed only against memory traces from an earlier phase which have not yet been translated" (*Origins*, 175–76; Freud adds that "a failure of translation is what we know clinically as 'repression'"). The emergence of the pathological defense (repression) after a period of delay (latency) is thus, from Freud's point of view, the real beginning of a traumatic neurosis.

In theorizing the various psychical processes at work in the etiology of trauma, at this early point in his researches Freud is still focused on a real event as and at the point of origin: Emma really had been sexually assaulted by an adult even if, because of her prepubescent lack of sexual awareness, that real event was not experienced as traumatic while it was happening. The evolution of psychoanalysis from 1897 onward, however, leads to a series of major conceptual transformations. Two key developments appear in that year. First, in his now infamous abandonment of the seduction theory, Freud came to reject as implausible the likelihood that so many of his (hysterical female) patients had actually been sexually assaulted by male acquaintances and in particular by close relatives and more particularly by their fathers. Thus, to the extent hysteria could still be understood as involving, indeed as being grounded in, a sexual component, Freud hypothesized that what had been recounted as

12 "Fantasy and the Origins of Sexuality," 4.

13 "On the Psychical Mechanism of Hysterical Phenomena: Preliminary Communication" (1893), in *Studies in Hysteria*, *SE*, 2:1–17. Their most famous statement from this paper is that "hysterics suffer mainly from reminiscences" (7; original italics deleted).

episodes of abuse were actually sexual fantasies.[14] The shift here away from the acceptance of an original sexual assault and toward the theory of fantasy is then tied to a second transformation: what Freud understood as the discovery of infantile sexuality and more specifically of how unconscious sexual impulses, if in some fundamental way grounded in human biology, are necessarily at once expressed and experienced as psychical reality. The most famous formulation of these paired concepts will first appear in an 1897 letter to Fliess regarding the Oedipus complex (*Origins*, 223–24).

For our purposes here, what is most crucial is that this new conceptualization of fantasy, infantile sexuality, and the connection between them (the Oedipus complex being just one expression of this connection) also leads Freud to revise his understanding of the temporality of trauma, both its origin and the various phases through which it travels before developing into a neurotic condition. Even with the shift in his thinking, Freud is still committed to the "two-event" notion of traumatic etiology, a point to which we shall return shortly. But within the new schema the trauma itself is no longer understood as constituted by the *retrospective construction* of a relationship *between* the two events (for example, a fantasized scene and a subsequent dream, as in the case of the Wolfman). In Freud's initial formulation, the trauma is equivalent to the act of repressing the memory of the original event which now must be defended against precisely because, at some point later in time, it is recognized for what it was: a sexual act. By contrast, in the second formulation (again, the case of the Wolfman exemplifies Freud's changed view) the trauma emerges at the originary moment as fantasy that arises in the earliest phase of sexual development almost immediately prompts a pathological defense; it is a defense, however, not against an overt act of seduction or assault but against

14 In a September 1897 letter to Wilhelm Fliess, Freud observes in regard to the revelations of his patients that, because "there is 'no indication of reality' in the unconscious," it is effectively impossible "to distinguish between truth and emotionally-charged fiction" (*Origins*, 216). In "Femininity" (*New Introductory Lectures*, 1933), Freud will write that "hysterical symptoms are derived from phantasies and not from real occurrences" (22:120). That said, as Laplanche and Pontalis point out, from about 1896 forward, Freud approaches the question of fantasy

> "from two aspects at once, both as manifest data and latent content; and located thus at the crossroads, [fantasies] acquire in due course the consistency of an object, the specific object of psychoanalysis. Henceforward analysis will continue to treat fantasy as "psychical reality," whilst exploring its variants and above all analyzing its processes and structure. Between 1897 and 1906 appear all the great works which explore the mechanisms of the unconscious, that is to say, the transformations … of fantasy … [F]antasy is shown to be an autonomous, consistent and explorable field." ("Fantasy and the Origins of Sexuality," 7–8)

the infant / child's own auto-erotic impulses. As Freud remarks in 1906, "I have learned to explain a number of fantasies of seduction as *attempts at fending off memories of the subject's own sexual activity* (infantile masturbation)" ("On the part played by sexuality in the neuroses," *SE*, 7:274; my emphasis). And in the 1914 "History of the Psycho-analytic Movement," he writes:

> If hysterical subjects trace back their symptoms to traumas that are fictitious, then the new fact which emerges is precisely that they create such scenes in *phantasy*, and this psychical reality requires to be taken into account alongside practical reality. This reflection was soon followed by that discovery that *these phantasies were intended to cover up the auto-erotic activity of the first years of childhood* ... And now, from behind the phantasies, the whole range of a child's sexual life came to light. (*SE*, 14:17–18)

We might understand the full process as kind of double-defense. First, the infant / child creates a fantasy of being seduced and thereby creates a *passive* version of itself in relation to its own sexual urges; in other words, the infant / child effectively disavows its own auto-erotic impulses by projecting them onto the seducing other in the form of a myth of origin.[15] Then, through repression, the infant / child relocates what is already disguised in the form of the seduction myth into the Unconscious. (Part of what is remarkable here is that Freud comes see that the subject's own fantasies can be the origin of trauma even if completely unconnected to actual events.)

That said, if, as Laplanche and Pontalis note, the "quest for [trauma's] origins" has through this reformulation taken on "a new dimension," Freud maintains key elements of the initial formulation and in particular the temporal coordinates (the first and second events or the before-and-after sequence) by which he maps out the development of a traumatic neurosis.[16] Freud retains the two-event schema for two related reasons. First, whether the original event

15 Laplanche and Pontalis observe that, at this point in the evolution of Freud's thought, "the scene in which the subject describes ... seduction by an older companion is, in fact, a double disguise: pure fantasy is converted into real memory, and spontaneous sexuality activity into passivity" ("Fantasy and the Origins of Sexuality," 7).

16 As Laplanche and Pontalis observe, "the discovery of infantile sexuality has not invalidated in Freud's mind the fundamental schema underlying the seduction model: the same deferred action (*Nachträglichkeit*) is constantly invoked; we meet once more the two events (here the scene and the dream), separated in the temporal series, the first remaining un-understood and, as it were, excluded with the subject, to be taken up later in the elaboration of the second occasion." ("Fantasy and the Origins of Sexuality," 8).

really happened (the groping Emma experienced in the shop) or is merely a construction of the mind (a psychical reality), it is followed by a period of latency that essentially coincides with the period of sexual dormancy Freud believed to be unique to human evolutionary development.[17] Second, in both cases the emergence of a neurosis in some fundamental way depends upon the latency; that is, the neurosis would not develop without the period of sexual dormancy followed by the reawakening of sexual impulses with the onset of puberty.

But something then must happen at or near the onset of puberty to (re)activate the initial experience or, we might say, trigger a new response to it. In the first model, as noted above, the trauma and its attendant neurosis only truly exist at this moment, for it is the repression of the retrospective "reminiscence" of the original event that creates the neurosis in the form of unresolved pathological defense. In the second model, there is with the pubescent renewal of dormant sexuality a corresponding stirring of the repressed trauma, the infant / child's own early defense against the awareness and acceptance of its own sexual impulses. As repressed awareness (still couched in the form of, while being deflected by, the seduction myth) begins to rise to consciousness, it must be defended against even more vigorously because of the more powerful emotional surge characteristic of sexual maturation. In other words, in the second formulation it is precisely because the psyche must work that much harder to keep an endogenous sexuality hidden away that the neurosis emerges (the original repression did not generate a neurotic response).[18] The psyche cannot completely eliminate conscious awareness of these unwelcome matters, however, and so it must redirect the truth into dreams or other neurotic symptoms (either through repetition or inhibition). In this way, the true starting point of the neurosis is at once concealed and revealed albeit in the distorted form of the return of the repressed.[19] This understanding of the etiology of traumatic

17 For Freud's summary statement, see *Moses and Monotheism*, 94.

18 Freud offers a summary in *Moses and Monotheism*, 97.

19 In summarizing the "mechanisms that lead to a neurosis," Freud writes in *Moses and Monotheism* that

> "the decisive experiences in early childhood exert a lasting influence, yet in this case the stress falls not on the time, but on the process opposing that event, the reaction against it.... The Ego guards against this danger by repression. The excitation becomes inhibited in one way or another; the incitement, with the observations and perceptions belonging to it, is forgotten. This, however, does not bring the process to an end; either the instinct has kept its strength, or it will regain it, or it is reawakened by a new situation. It renews its claim, and—since the way to normal satisfaction is barred by what we might call the scar tissue of repression—it gains at some weak point new access to a so-called substitutive satisfaction, which now appears as a symptom, without the acquiescence

neurosis first fully emerges in Freud's account of the Wolf Man ("From the History of an Infantile Neurosis" [1918]) and is developed in some detail in his final metapsychological work (*Inhibitions, Symptoms and Anxiety* [1926]). As we shall see in the following section, it is also central to Freud's effort in *Moses and Monotheism* to locate the emergence of Judaic monotheism in a collective experience of trauma.

2

"Early trauma – defense – latency – outbreak of neurosis – partial return of the repressed material: this was the formula we drew up for the development of the neurosis. Now I will invite the reader to take a step forward and assume that in the history of the human species something happened similar to the events of the life of the individual" (*Moses and Monotheism*, 101). While the phrase "history of the human species" here points back to the events of human prehistory as Freud had described those in *Totem and Taboo*, it is also clear that, as he proceeds in what he calls the "application" (101) to mass psychology of an "analogy" (90) from individual psychology, his real intent is to deploy the concept of traumatic neurosis to understand the complex relationship between Jewish history (especially Jewish religious history) and Jewish cultural identity.[20] More precisely, as the particular sequence of the formula indicates, Freud aims to interpret this history through what I described in section 1 as the second schema for the etiology of traumatic neurosis, essentially the model he had formalized in the case of the Wolfman.

As we saw in Chapter 1, in the case of Jewish history Freud understands the "early trauma" not as fantasy but as an actual event, the murder of Moses. Then comes a collective "defense": while after the murder there was likely a continuing commitment to Moses—the "great man" (141), this magnificent figure" (76), the "eminent father substitute" (113)—and all he stood for, as Freud imagines it "there came a time when the people regretted the murder of Moses and tried to forget it"; and again, "the painful fact of his violent removal was … successfully denied" (58–59). Even his most devoted followers "had good reasons … for 'repressing' the memory of the fate that had befallen their leader and lawgiver" (85). Recognizing then that, despite the attempt by the postexilic priests

and also without the apprehension of the Ego. All phenomenon of symptom formation can be fairly described as "the return of the repressed." (163–64)

20 For Freud's clearest statement on this matter, see Moses and Monotheism, 71.

"to establish a continuity between their own times and the Mosaic period," "in the history of the Jewish religion there is a long period, after the breaking away from the Moses religion, during which no trace can be found of the monotheistic idea" (81, 84), Freud interprets this temporal gap as the historical time-frame for the working out of the final three terms of the formula: latency, outbreak of neurosis, partial return of the repressed material. That said, the analogy Freud aims to establish between individual and mass psychology lies on much shakier conceptual terrain than he is willing (or able) to admit.

We might start with some simple questions about the murder itself, the first event in the two-event sequence constituting the founding traumatic temporality of Jewish culture. If, as Freud claims, the Egyptian Moses was a tyrant to the people of the Exodus (forcing upon them the Aton religion they did not want), why was the murder traumatic at all? And in what sense would the people subsequently have denied or, even more mysteriously, have forgotten what they had just done? While we will have reason to revisit this claim in Chapter 2, for now we might note that, for Freud, the traumatic quality of the murder derives from the fact that it is not an isolated event and can be better understood as the *second* event in the two-event sequence. In other words, the murder was not the "early trauma" itself but was rather the reactivation after a period of latency of what had been previously repressed: the prehistoric slaying of the primal father. But within this framework it is not clear in what sense the murder of Moses can be understood as the "partial return of the repressed" especially if by "partial return" Freud wants to call attention to the fact that neurotic symptomology marks a recollection of an earlier (repressed) event in *distorted* form.

We might contrast Freud's conceptualization in this case to his understanding of the development of totemic religion, which he briefly summarizes as a condensed version of the thesis of *Totem and Taboo* (*Moses and Monotheism*, 101–05). Whether or not modern anthropologists or historians of religion would accept the theory (few would), in Freud's reconstruction a tribal group's acquisition of a totem animal and, more particularly, the development of the ritual of the totem feast can much more clearly be understood as a partial return of the repressed: the honored totem animal—effectively the tribe's spirit animal—stands in for even as it disguises the (slain) father (the tribe members do not consciously recognize the father in the animal) and the ritual killing and eating of the totem (it can only ever be killed and eaten under ritual conditions) recreates the original ambivalence toward the hated-and-revered father of the horde: the (repressed) memory of the murdered father is honored through the ritual even as the hostility that led to the killing is effectively re-expressed through symbolic reenactment. In short, the killing of the father partially returns in a ritual that, even as it repeats, simultaneously deflects any actual confrontation with or even memory of the killing. In that sense, while in Freud's interpretation totemism in general and the feast in particular point to a neurotic attachment to the past, they do so in a distorted form that preserves the recollection of the original deed in the Unconscious.

When we turn to the murder of Moses, however, it is much more difficult to conceptualize it as the return of the repressed slaying of the primal father. Even if, as Freud, argues, all human beings have retained a repressed memory of this prehistoric event (an issue we shall take up in later chapters), the only thing that links the two killings is that they both involve fathers—and in the case of Moses it is not even an actual father, only a "father imago" (140). (It is worth noting that Freud provides no evidence that the murderers actually viewed Moses in these terms.[21]) More to the point, unlike the symbolic reenactment we find in the totem feast, the murder of Moses is a singular event with no ritual status (hence, not the focus of symptomatic repetition) and, as a singular event, has its own unique motivation: the killing of the tyrant Moses was, by Freud's own estimation, a political act with none of the sexual overtones he had theorized as motivating the primal slaying.[22] Perhaps most tellingly, Freud cannot explain how the murder of Moses could be understood as preserving the primal slaying in its repressed state. While one can imagine that the ritual of the totem feast could disguise the very killing it commemorated, the same can hardly be said for the murder of Moses: how does the second murder of the "father" sustain the psychical coverup of the first? Freud bizarrely argues that, even as in the murder of Moses "the great deed and misdeed of primeval times was brought home to the Jews," their very "acting"—repeating the primal deed "on the person of Moses" (113)—inexplicably *blocked* the recollection of the repressed memory of the prehistoric killing.

---

21 Freud writes that "*without doubt*" (German: "*unzweifelhaft*" [16:217]) it must have been a tremendous father imago that stooped in the person of Moses to tell the poor Jewish laborers that they were his dear children" (140; my emphasis). But Freud cannot document that claim in any way. Moreover, he earlier casts plenty of doubt on it in remarking that these "poor Jewish laborers" were in fact "savage Semites [who] took destiny into their own hands and did away with their tyrant" (58).

22 Reflecting on the primeval events that set the stage for what he believes transpired during the Mosaic period, Freud writes that "mankind as a whole also passed through *conflicts of a sexual-aggressive nature which left permanent traces*, but which were for the most part warded off and forgotten, later after a long period of latency, *they came to life again and created phenomenon similar in structure and tendency* to neurotic symptoms" (101; my emphases).

If there are problems looking backward from the murder of Moses, there are also problems both with the time of the murder itself and with its aftermath. In terms of the murder, Freud is explicit in claiming that it was a "real repetition" (129) of the primal killing; thus, it is the second event in a two-event sequence. As noted above, however, Freud effectively argues that it generates its own pathological defense rather than creating a neurotic response to the already repressed memory of the primal slaying (the "early trauma" in Freud's schema). In other words, the murder of Moses becomes its own "early trauma" (the first event in a *new* traumatic sequence) against the memory of which a new defense must be erected. Thus, as we have seen, Freud argues that the very murderers quickly, and inexplicably, lost sight of what they had done: they tried to forget it, they denied it, they repressed it.[23] To apply the full formula for the etiology of a neurosis to this cultural situation, Freud must then establish the final three terms: 1) a period of latency during which the repressed memory is essentially dormant, 2) the emergence of a neurosis as that dormancy comes to an end (something triggers or reactivates the repressed memory), and 3) the return of the repressed as the memory breaks through into consciousness but only in a distorted form.

As regards the period of latency, Freud conceives it in terms of the temporal gap referred to above: so he writes that "the religion of Moses did not achieve it effects immediately, but in a strangely indirect manner.... It took a long time, many centuries, to do so" (159). At the end of this period, the very idea of a loving if severe father-god who chose the people of Israel as his own marks the return of the repressed "great father" (113), Moses: as Freud puts it, the recollection of Moses eventually morphed into "the conception of a unique, eternal, omnipotent God ... who thought [the people of Israel] worthy to make a bond

---

23 We might give special attention to Freud's statement that the people of the Exodus "repress[ed] the memory of the fate that had befallen their leader and lawgiver" (85). The phrasing is particularly odd because the passive construction ("...the fate that had befallen their leader and lawgiver"; *SE*: "... the fate with which their leader and lawgiver had met" [23:68]; the full German sentence reads: "*Sie hatten aber gute Motive, die Erinnerung an das Schicksal zu verdrängen, das ihrem Führer und Gesetzgeber bereitet worden war*" [16:172]) conveniently permits Freud to suggest that there is a question of agency here: who actually committed the murder if Moses' death was just *the fate that had befallen him*? In effect, it is Freud's own phrasing that creates the denial he then assigns to the murderers themselves. As a point of comparison, we might note that the totem feast is never similar denied, forgotten, or repressed; that is, while as the part of the second event in the traumatic sequence—the return of the repressed—it preserves the recollection of the first event (the primal slaying) in the Unconscious, the feast itself is always consciously retained as an event in itself: those who celebrate the feast know that they are doing so even if they don't know why.

with him ... if only they remained faithful to his worship" (140). Within the formula, the only thing left unaccounted for, then, is the triggering event that reactivates the repressed memory of the murder. Freud knows that identifying this event is absolutely crucial because, without the completed formula, he cannot explain Jewish faith as a mass-psychological phenomenon analogous to the development of a neurosis in an individual. In other words, Freud will not be able to solve the riddle of "why the monotheistic idea should make such a deep impression on just the Jewish people, and why they adhered to it so tenaciously" (113) unless he can adequately describe Jewish attachment to "the monotheistic idea" in terms of the *reactivation* of the repressed memory of the murder of Moses, a reactivation that then functions as the never-to-be-resolved compulsive conviction at the heart of Judaic faith and of Jewish cultural identity more broadly.

What was this triggering event? Though not for lack of trying, Freud clearly struggles both to define it conceptually and to locate it historically. The confusion is evident, for example, in what we have previously observed: at times he positions the murder of Moses as the second event in the two-event sequence (the "real repetition" of the primal slaying [129]), and at other times he positions it as the first event (the "early trauma") initiating a completely separate sequence. The lack of clear distinction seems almost a deliberate strategy on Freud's part: to confuse his readers into thinking he has already established the second event—the one completing the traumatic sequence set in motion by the murder of Moses—because the murder is itself a second event.

Elsewhere, he muddies the entire issue by acknowledging that the Mosaic tradition, once established by Moses himself and taking the form of Mosaic doctrine, never truly disappeared from Israelite religious discourse. But even this assertion isn't stated clearly or consistently. Freud cites Ernst Sellin's contention that that "the tradition of the murder of Moses was always present among the priests, until at last it was set down in writing."[24] While Freud

24 Freud is referring to Sellin's argument in *Mose und seine Bedeutung für die israelitisch-jüdishe Religionsgeschischte* (Leipzig: A. Deichert, 1922). Freud claims (42ff.) that it was not until he read Sellin's work that he thought he could come back to the "character study of Moses" that he had effectively abandoned after completing a draft of it in 1934. But since Freud wasn't satisfied with his own 1934 draft because it lacked a true historical ground—ground that he claimed in the published version of *Moses and Monotheism* to have borrowed from Sellin's book—it seems likely that Freud did not read it before he had finished the 1934 draft. Indeed, it may have been his reading of the book in 1935 or 1936 that spurred him to revise his "character study of Moses." (Parts I and II of *Moses and Monotheism* were first published in essay form in *Imago* in 1937.) This dating might lead us to rethink Ernest Jones' assertion that "it was Sellin's suggestion that made Freud

himself is more inclined to view the Hebrew prophets as the true preservers of the Mosaic tradition (see 42, 63–64, 80, and *passim*), he is willing at times to follow Sellin's lead at least in terms of the doctrinal elements of that tradition if not of the murder itself:

> The religion of Moses did not achieve its effects immediately, but in a strangely indirect manner.... It took a long time, many centuries to do so.... The Jewish people shook off the religion of Moses after a certain time ... The religion of Moses, however, had not perished. *A sort of memory of it had survived, obscured and distorted but perhaps supported by individual members of the priest caste through the ancient scripts.* It was this tradition of a great past that continued to exert its effect from the background; it slowly attained more and more power over the minds of the people, and at last succeeded in changing the God Jahve [Yahweh] into the God of Moses and in bringing again to life the abandoned religion Moses had instituted centuries before. (159–60; my emphasis)

---

decide to write his book" (*The Life and Work of Sigmund Freud*, 3 vols. [New York: Basic Books, 1953–57], 3:373). In any event, in the second prefatory note to Part III of *Moses and Monotheism*, Freud writes that without "Sellin's suggestion concerning Moses' end, the whole treatise would have ... remain[ed] unwritten" (71). Yerushalmi observes, as much as a question as a statement, that

"the correlations to *Moses and Monotheism* are so striking that we must wonder if Sellin's work merely confirmed Freud's prior intuitions or whether it was a reading of the book that triggered his own thinking. Beyond the slaying of Moses, Freud found in Sellin the historicity of Moses and the purity of his monotheism; a hidden link between Moses and the rise of Christianity through the expectation of his messianic return; the parallel between the murder of Moses and that of Jesus; above all, the survival of Moses' teaching and the memory of his murder as subterranean traditions." (26)

For Sellin's thesis provided the "secure foundation" in history without which, Freud fretted, his reconstruction of Moses would be "like an iron monument with feet of clay" (17). Even when he subsequently learned that Sellin had abandoned his claim about the murder, Freud is reported to have quipped, "He was right the first time." (qtd. in Yerushalmi, 83). Jones wrote that, when told by the scholar Abraham Shalom Yahuda in 1938 that Sellin had later "with[drawn] his suggestion and apologized for having made it ... Freud could only shrug his shoulders and say 'It might be true all the same'" (3:373). That said, it is not clear that Sellin did repudiate his argument. He actually cited more evidence in support of it in a study published in 1924 (and re-issued in 1935): *Geschichte des israelitische-jüdischen Volkes* (History of the Israelite-Jewish People). And in none of his other published writings does Sellin hint that he was not still fully on-board with his 1922 position; if anything, he appears to have felt that he had uncovered more confirmation of it. Still, as Jones comments, Sellin's argument was "immediately rejected by all Jewish scholars" (3:373).

Freud wants, even needs, to avoid the obvious implication of this claim: a tradition that had survived for centuries (even recorded at some stage in written form) could hardly be understood as existing only in the Unconscious. His way around this problem is the qualifying assertion that the tradition "could not have been known to many; it was not general knowledge." He immediately adds that, even to the extent some priests (or perhaps prophets) might have consciously preserved the tradition, it didn't pass into culture-wide acceptance simply through the transmission of a body of ideas: "And is this form of transmission enough to explain its effect? Can we credit such knowledge on the part of a few with the power to seize the imagination of the masses so lastingly when they learn of it? It rather looks as if there were something also in the ignorant masses akin to this knowledge on the part of the few, which comes forward to meet it as soon as it is uttered" (119–20). In other words, while the memory of Moses (possibly including his murder) was not repressed among all the people of Israel, for the bulk of the population (the "masses") the memory *was* repressed. Freud thus feels justified in describing the full (re)emergence of the religion of Moses—"bringing again to life the abandoned religion Moses had instituted centuries before"—as a neurotic reactivation of the repressed memory. As Freud had generalized slightly earlier,

> It is especially worthy of note that every memory returning from the forgotten past does so with great force, produces an incomparably strong influence ..., and puts forward an irresistible claim to be believed, against which all logical objections are powerless.... This strange characteristic can only be understood by comparison with ... delusions ... It has long been recognized that delusions contain a piece of forgotten truth, which had at its return to put up with being distorted and misunderstood, and that the compulsive conviction appertaining to the delusion emanates from this core of truth and spreads to the errors that enshroud it. (119–20)

If, as he adds "such a kernel of truth ... must also be conceded to the doctrines of the various religions," the purest example of this process—religion as a collective neurosis that takes the form of "distorted and misunderstood" delusions emanating from a forgotten past—is the return of the repressed "kernel of truth" that Freud, following Sellin, locates in the murder of Moses at the hands of the people of the Exodus. That return will, centuries later, take the distorted form of Yahwistic monotheism.

While there are obvious problems in trying to have it both ways (the murder was repressed for some but not for all), even among those who *consciously* retained the tradition (those who transmitted the knowledge orally or in writing), Freud appears to imagine that their preservation of the Mosaic tradition followed its own neurotic path. Our initial impression might be that he reserves this path for "the masses" who had no conscious recollection of the tradition. In suggesting that their memories returned "from the forgotten past" as delusions and thus in "distorted and misunderstood" form (they did not recognize the true origin of their own Yahwistic faith), Freud is simply following one of his key psychoanalytic principles: "All phenomenon of symptom-formation can be fairly described as 'the return of the repressed.' The distinctive character of them … lies in the extensive distortion the returning elements have undergone, compared with their original form" (164). But in a passage cited above, Freud seems to hold much the same view of how Mosaic tradition was preserved among those who wrote it down: "The religion of Moses … had not perished. A sort of memory of it had survived, obscured and distorted but perhaps supported by individual members of the priest caste through the ancient scripts." The phrase "a sort of memory … survived, obscured and distorted" (German: "*eine Art von Erinnerung an sie hatte sich erhalten, verdunkelt und entstellt*" [16:232]) suggests that the experience of "members of the priest caste" was not so different from that of the masses. Indeed, the fact that Freud views the priests holding onto Mosaic tradition in their own quasi-delusional way ("obscured and distorted") comes close to venturing that they had simply gone through the reactivation of the repressed memory before anyone else among the people of Israel and had already developed a neurotic response to it. To think of this another way, Freud may be unwittingly implying that the priestly "scripts" were just the earliest version on record of the return of the repressed (the "distortion" undergone by "the returning elements … compared to their original form"). In short, while Freud appears to want to argue that the priests (or prophets) were consciously aware that they were preserving a tradition that had fallen into neglect, he may be more strongly pushing the notion that Mosaic *tradition* was, from the start, a pathological defense against a memory that could not be consciously admitted.

But none of this truly answers the question that, by now, we might suspect Freud of studiously trying to avoid: what happened in Jewish history to reactivate the repressed Mosaic tradition? Even when he does make the effort to supply an answer, his very vagueness might make us wonder if, despite the importance he accords it as a way of bridging individual and mass psychology, he has any insight to offer into the matter. In theorizing how the return of the repressed functions at the level of the (neurotic) individual, at one point he describes the triggering event in very general terms: "new problems of life" and the "demands of the outer world" (97); and still later he says that what has been "forgotten" (repressed) can be "reawakened by a new situation" (163).[25] At the mass psychological level, he operates at the same level of generality: critical changes in culture might come about because of "the individual gifts of [a] people …, the direction their activities take and their general social condition" (118). Even in the specific instance where such cultural changes mark "the return of the repressed," after noting that such a return operates "under the influence of all the changes in the conditions of life that abound throughout the history of civilization," he concedes that he "can give … neither a survey of the conditions on which it depends nor any more than a scanty enumeration of the stages in which the return proceeds" (171). We are not surprised then that, with regard to the point at which Mosaic tradition "proved … strong enough decisively to influence the thought and activity of the [Jewish] people," Freud can only weakly gesture toward undefined "conditions … that made such development possible" (87). When he later describes how "the monotheistic idea … after a long latency period [took] hold of this people" (108), he has nothing to add to explain the transformation. In short, he doesn't even try to identify any second event—a condition, a problem, a demand, a situation—that could have reactivated the repressed memory of the murder of Moses.

Even on the single occasion when he tries to be more specific, whether intentionally or not, Freud misleads at least as much as he enlightens. Having noted that "how this process [the monotheistic idea taking hold of the Jews] was set in motion is not easy to say," he points to a kind of cultural malaise as a possible cause: "it seems that a growing feeling of guiltiness had seized the Jewish people—and perhaps the whole of civilization of that time—as a precursor of the return of the repressed" (109). While Freud doesn't try to define this guiltiness or say what prompted it or locate it within any particular time-frame, the primary link here between the return of the repressed and the Jewish people might lead us to assume that whatever social conditions had developed (we might think of this "feeling of guiltiness" as a neurotic response) were inseparable from the emergence of Yahwistic monotheism as a distorted return of the religion of Moses.[26] But Freud then makes no effort to

25 Freud notes elsewhere regarding traumatic etiology that "often we must be content to say that there is nothing else but an unusual reaction to experiences and demands that apply to all individuals; many people deal with them in another way which we may term normal" (91).

26 Although Freud returns to this hypothesis in the final section of *Moses and Monotheism*, he doesn't offer any new information to support it: "The consciousness of guilt in that epoch"—and what epoch is this exactly?—"was no longer restricted to the Jews; it had seized all Mediterranean peoples as a vague discomfort, a premonition of misfortune, the reason for which no one knew" (174).

describe how (or when or where) this new religious orientation took sufficient cultural hold to become the essence of Jewish identity. In fact, he immediately shifts away from Judaism itself to focus on the Christian tradition that would rise only centuries later: "This [feeling of guiltiness] went on until a member of the Jewish people, in the guise of a political-religious agitator, founded a doctrine which ... separated from the Jewish one. Paul, a Roman Jew from Tarsus, seized upon this feeling of guilt and correctly traced it back to its primeval source" (109). Shortly after, having noted that "the murder of Moses by his people" was the critical bridge "between the forgotten deed of primeval times and its subsequent reappearance in the form of the monotheistic religions," Freud once again disappoints: for not only does he fail (again) to explain how a transformative cultural guilt arose in the first place, but he also (again) jumps over any detailed consideration of Judaism to focus exclusively on the emergence of (Pauline) Christianity (114ff.). We might conclude, then, that, while Freud has a very clear sense of why Christianity might be described in terms of the return of the repressed—he equates the Christian Eucharistic meal with the totem feast (106, 111, 168–69)—despite his entire project being grounded in this hypothesis he really has no way of explaining the conditions under which the neurosis he knows as Judaism actually emerged. We might also conclude that, precisely because he has no explanation, Freud's description of the rise Christianity in the person of "a member of the Jewish people" aims to create the illusion of one: in other words, his account of how Paul traced the feeling of guilt "back to its primeval source" is presented as a follow-up example to what he (Freud) can only pretend to have already fully explicated in the context of Judaism. Of course, that full explication is precisely what he does not and perhaps cannot offer.

Can anything be salvaged from this conceptual morass? We might find one promising idea in Freud's linking of Judaism to Christianity through the pairing of Moses and Christ: "the guilt attached to the murder of Moses may have been the stimulus for the wish-phantasy of the Messiah, who was to return and give to his people salvation and the promised sovereignty over the world. If Moses was this first Messiah, Christ became his substitute and successor" (114). The suggestion that Moses should be understood as a messiah-figure might appear to come out of the blue, but Freud had alerted us to this association in Part II (once again his source is Sellin): "In 1922 Ernst Sellin made a discovery of decisive importance. He found in the book of the Prophet Hosea ... unmistakable traces of a tradition to the effect that the founder of their religion, *Moses, met a violent end* in a rebellion of his stubborn and refractory people.... This tradition was not limited to Hosea; it recurs in the writings of most of the later Prophets; indeed, according to Sellin, *it was the basis of all the later expectations of the Messiah.*" What immediately follows is just as crucial: "*Towards the end of the Babylonian exile* the hope arose among the Jewish people that *the man they had so callously murdered would return* from the realm of the dead and lead *his contrite people* ... into the land of eternal bliss" (42–43; my emphases). Without making any explicit effort to situate these events within a defined traumatic sequence, in this summary-account Freud links the murder of Moses to a specific subsequent development in Jewish religious history ("*later* expectations of the Messiah"; or even "the wish-phantasy of the Messiah") that itself has at least a loose association with both the *return* of the victim of the violence in a new or even a distorted form (the Messiah who, like Yahweh, has a particular regard for the Jewish people) and the people's *guilt*, marked by their contrition, for the callousness of their deed. (That Moses is able to return as the Messiah might be understood as a disavowal of the murder: the people's guilt for something that happened in the past is partially denied by being transformed into their hope for something better that will happen in the future as a result.) Freud even locates this progression of events—initial violence, collective guilt, latency, return-as-distortion—as reaching a critical stage of development at a specified moment in the people's history: in relationship to the Babylonian Exile (so sometime *after* the fall of Judah to Nebuchadnezzar's army in 586 BCE).

For the most part, Freud doesn't make these interconnections central to his argument. But neither does he completely ignore them. (It might be more accurate to say that he recognizes something important in the conceptual grouping without quite knowing what to do with it.) In Part III, for example, he once again hints that there might be some critical link between the return of Mosaic tradition after its strange dormancy (and now in the form of Yahwistic monotheism) and the time of the Exile (just before and just after): "... the *lost cause was once more regained.* In the constant endeavor of centuries, and last but not least through two great reforms—*the one before, the other after the Babylonian exile—there took place the change* of the popular God Jahve into the God whose worship Moses had forced on the Jews" (142; my emphases). At a very different point in his reconstruction of Jewish history (here focused on the evolution of the written tradition), he observes that the completed Pentateuch also emerged at roughly this time: "In the time after the [Babylonian] destruction of the Temple, in 586 [BCE], *during the Exile and after the return*, is placed the rewriting called the Priestly Code. The fifth century saw a definitive revision, and since then the work has not been materially altered" (51; my emphasis). Freud's accompanying footnote adds some key details:

> It is historically certain that the Jewish type was definitely fixed as a result of the reforms of Ezra and Nehemiah in the fifth century [BCE], therefore after the Exile, during the reign of the friendly Persians. According to our reckoning, approximately nine hundred years had then passed since the appearance of Moses. By these reforms the regulations aiming at the consecration of the chosen people were taken seriously: the separation from the other tribes was put into force by the forbidding mixed marriages; the Pentateuch, the real compilation of the law, was codified in its definitive form; the rewriting known as the Priestly Code was finished. (51n1)

I need to reiterate that Freud doesn't explicitly treat this watershed moment in Jewish history as especially important to the development of Judaism from an initial traumatic experience (the murder of Moses) into a collective neurosis. That said, he clearly intuits that something connected to the postexilic (and in particular the Persian) period merits our attention. Indeed, he appears to recognize that the true origin not just of Judaic (biblical / Yahwistic) monotheism but also of the very concept of people of Israel as "the chosen people"—"consecrated" because set apart from other peoples (and it is only at this historical moment that the concept can be "taken seriously")—is in some fundamental sense marked in the "return" of Moses after this "approximately nine hundred year" latency. While consciously located in the priest-driven restoration of the figure of Moses in a body of canonical writings focused chiefly on Mosaic doctrine (the Law), this return is, for Freud, inseparable from the emergence of a peculiarly Jewish personality "type" ("fixed as a result of the [priestly] reforms").

At the end of the footnote just cited, Freud writes that the postexilic reforms with their privileging of Mosaic teaching "did not adopt any new tendencies, but simply took over and consolidated former suggestions." I want to counter this claim, though in a way that still recognizes its insight: Freud is absolutely wrong here, but so absolutely wrong that he unwittingly points the way to an essential truth. If the postexilic priests "took over and consolidated former suggestions" regarding the Mosaic past, they did so precisely by adopting "new tendencies" that had not previously been associated with that past. Those new tendencies included a reconceptualization of the centrality of Mosaic law to Jewish cultural identity, a new cultural role assigned to the written text of Torah not just as a collection of legal stipulations but also, in the form of the Exodus narrative, as the centerpiece of the national foundation myth (especially important while the people were living under foreign domination), and a concept of chosenness that, while perhaps deriving in part from "former suggestions," came to exert a new kind of pressure or demand ("taken seriously") at both the individual and collective levels, the focus of the compulsive conviction that, as Freud was convinced, could explain "how the Jews have come to be what they are." All these tendencies emerged after and, more to the point, as a consequence of the people's experience of exile in Babylon. It is this postexilic constellation of conditions—precisely what Freud himself had identified without knowing he had—that, as I will try to demonstrate in chapters 2 and 3, constitute the true "traumatic experience" at the heart of Judaic monotheism. That said, and perhaps paradoxically, even acknowledging how much my own reconstruction owes to Freud's account, I will also attempt to show why understanding this foundational trauma does not require the hypothesis that Moses had been murdered.

CHAPTER 2

"How can we sing a song of the LORD?": the Compulsions of the Postexilic Unconscious

> In Judaism, man is always somehow a survivor, an inner something, whose exterior was seized by the current of the world and carried off while he himself, what is left of him, remains standing on the shore. Something within him is waiting.
>
> —FRANZ ROSENZWEIG, *The Star of Redemption*

∴

This chapter aims to revisit and reframe the question that Freud saw as the starting point of *Moses and Monotheism*, a question posed to Arnold Zweig in 1934: "how [have] the Jews ... come to be what they are[?]"[1] While diverging from Freud in many ways, what follows will venture a new answer in the context in which he sought his own: not just the enduring mystery of "the origin of monotheism among the Jews" (*Moses and Monotheism*, 81) but more particularly how that origin and the historical path emanating from it could only be grasped through the lens provided by psychoanalytically-informed inquiry.

As we saw in Chapter 1, in very broad terms Freud had first broached this subject within the context of primordial religion.[2] He would return to and clarify the conceptual problem in *Moses and Monotheism*: "A tradition based only on oral communication [of ideas] could not produce the *obsessive character which appertains to religious phenomena*" (130; my emphasis). From the perspective of psychoanalytic inquiry, Freud then sought to understand "in what exactly consists the ... nature of a tradition, and in what resides its peculiar power, ... [and] from what sources certain ideas, especially religious ones, derive the power to subjugate individuals and peoples." In is within that context that Freud takes up the "particular case of Jewish history," as case

1 *Letters of Sigmund Freud and Arnold Zweig*, ed. Ernst L. Freud, trans. Elaine Robson-Scott and William Robson-Scott (New York: Harcourt, Brace & World, 1970), 91.

2 See *Totem and Taboo*, *SE*, 13:158.

DOI:10.1163/9789004701663_005

that, as he adds, has its origin in "what may be properly termed a traumatic experience" (65).

If we were only concerned with the continuation of a traumatic experience itself, we wouldn't even need to have recourse to psychoanalysis. For the trauma at the heart of Jewish experience has not simply been passed down generation after generation but has also been repeated. What in his 1934 letter to Zweig Freud refers to as the "new persecutions"—while taking a more virulent form in the early 1930s—were in many ways the old persecutions: from the Jewish perspective, the Nazis of earlier times were known as Assyrians, Babylonians, Greeks, Romans, European Christians of Catholic, Protestant, and Eastern Rite varieties in England, Spain, France, Poland, Russia, Ukraine, and elsewhere. Even before the emergence of the Nazi threat, which finally prompted him to flee to England, Freud personally experienced the constant provocations and harassments of chronic anti-Semitism even in the Vienna under the rule of the slightly more enlightened Emperor Franz Joseph I.[3] But Freud's point is that Jews are bound to their religious-cultural identity even in the face of ceaseless cultural aggression: "they defy oppression, [so] that even the most cruel persecutions have not succeeded in exterminating them" (*Moses and Monotheism*, 116). It is this defiance in the face of "political misfortune" (147) and other "burden[s]" deriving from their adherence to "Mosaic religion" (142) that Freud wants to understand by turning upon Jewish history and the practices of Judaism the interpretive lens of his psychoanalytic method. As he writes in the study's final paragraph, while he has been particularly intrigued by "the question of how the Jewish people acquired the qualities that characterize it[,] ... the problem [of] how they could survive until today as an entity has not proved so easy to solve" (176). In broad terms, the answer as provided in *Moses and Monotheism* is to be found in how Judaism became a "tradition" and in that form took hold and, across countless generations, would continue to "take ... hold" of its Jewish adherents with an "irresistible claim to be believed, against which all logical objections become powerless" (107–08). In this context, as we noted in Chapter 1, Yosef Hayim Yerushalmi has argued that the "true axis" of *Moses and Monotheism* became the "problem of [Jewish] tradition" conceived first and foremost in terms of its "dynamics": how the experience of passing on Judaic monotheism was constituted less by the unfolding history of its core

3 As a telling instance of what he experienced throughout his life, in *The Interpretation of Dreams* Freud describes an incident in which his father's restrained response to an anti-Semitic taunt had led the young Freud to an awareness not just of the social consequences of Jewish identity generally but also of his own critical feelings towards the "unheroic conduct" of his father (*SE*, 4:197).

ideas and the corresponding cultural and religious practices than by the emergence of a largely unconscious attachment.[4] Freud's goal, in short, is to unearth the long-buried and ever-present "compulsive conviction" (108) that has its historical roots in an originary traumatic experience.

That said, while the central argument of this chapter is premised on reaffirming the notion that a cultural trauma stands at the origin of Jewish monotheism, I will now change directions and reject Freud's specific claim that the traumatic event was the murder of Moses. In other words, even as I will retain Freud's foundational position that Judaic-monotheistic faith must be understood not simply in terms of a body of doctrines and practices but more fundamentally in terms of powerful unconscious elements, I will explicitly shift away from the idea that made it conceptually possible for Freud to complete and publish *Moses and Monotheism*—Ernst Sellin's reconstruction of a biblical tradition that Moses had been murdered sometime during the period of the people's wandering in the desert after their exodus from Egypt. In so challenging the very premise of Freud's psychoanalytically-grounded argument about the origins of Jewish monotheism, I will also attempt to realign his concept of an originary cultural trauma with something other than his historically unsubstantiated reconstructions of the Mosaic-Exodus period. In short, this chapter aims to show that the originary trauma has a verifiable time and place in documented Jewish history. Just as important, this time and place (and their aftermath) are directly related to how monotheism has come to be understood in Judaism and beyond, a tradition that is inextricably linked to the final emergence of Torah sometime in the mid- to late-fifth century BCE.

1

In Chapter 1, I ventured that the burden of Jewish chosenness might be more precisely understood as the burden of always already *having been chosen*, or, borrowing a term from Jean Laplanche, the experience of Jewish afterwardsness.[5] I now want to offer a different take on what this burden entails (both what it involves and what it bequeaths as an inheritance) by drawing on Cathy

---

4 *Freud's Moses: Judaism Terminable and Interminable* (New Haven: Yale University Press, 1993), 29.

5 *Essays on Otherness*, ed. John Fletcher (New York: Routledge, 1999), 263; for a fuller accounting of this idea as an unacknowledged foundation of Freud's thought, see my *Coming Too Late: Reflections on Freud and Belatedness* (Albany: SUNY Press, 2017).

Caruth's effort to apply a retheorized understanding of Freud's concept of trauma to the psychohistory offered in *Moses and Monotheism.*

Building on Freud's own position that the Jewish "people passed through what may properly be termed a traumatic experience," Caruth reconsiders the idea of "latency" or delayed effect that Freud himself had associated with the time-gap between the murder of Moses and the subsequent (re)emergence of Mosaic tradition some eight or nine centuries later (*Moses and Monotheism,* 82–117). Although Caruth will come to explain the psychical process at work in such a situation differently from how Freud himself does, in her first attempt to treat the issue of latency in Jewish tradition she simply follows Freud in locating the originary traumatic moment in the murder of Moses: "it is this latency of the event that ... explains the peculiar, temporal structure, the belatedness of the Jews' historical experience: since the murder is not experienced as it occurs, it is fully evident only in connection with another place, and in another time."[6]

Before taking up the implications of that passive construction ("the murder is not experienced as it occurs"), we might observe that Caruth's formulation depends on applying in the context of Jewish history a model for the origin of trauma that Freud himself had put forward only to reject in favor of one he linked to the diagnosis of obsessional neurosis, a psychical condition in which latency (associated with *Nachträglichkeit* or deferred action) is typically grounded in the symptomatic and so distorted and unrecognizable return of repressed sexual desires. (Caruth will refer to this as "castration trauma."[7])

Freud introduces this topic at the point in *Moses and Monotheism* where he is trying to understand how "Mosaic doctrine, which at first found no hearing" among the people of Israel, "came into its own after a long space of time and finally prevailed." In that context, he asks "how is such a delayed effect to be explained and where do we meet with similar phenomena?" (82). After exploring other interpretive possibilities drawn from his own psychoanalytic researches, he concludes that "the only really satisfactory analogy to the remarkable process we have recognized in the history of Jewish religion is to be found in the domain apparently remote from our problem. It is very complete, however, approximating to identity" (even "in the nature of an axiom"). "This analogy is met with in psychopathology, in the genesis of human neurosis[,] ... always goes back to the very early impressions in childhood" (90–91). He later elaborates: "Early trauma—defense—latency—outbreak of the

6 *Unclaimed Experience: Trauma, Narrative, and History* (Baltimore: Johns Hopkins University Press, 1996), 17.

7 *Unclaimed Experience*, 135n18.

neurosis—partial return of the repressed material: this was the formula we drew up for the development of a neurosis." As we saw in Coda 1, Freud then applies the "formula" to the events of primeval history (essentially summarizing his account of the rise of totemic religions originally offered in *Totem and Taboo* [*Moses and Monotheism*, 101–08]) before employing it to describe the development of Jewish tradition as the reenactment and re-intensification of "the great deed and misdeed of primeval times": "the murder of the father ... was brought home to the Jews, for fate had decreed that they should repeat it on the person of Moses, an eminent father substitute" (113).

Among the other possibilities Freud considers before settling on obsessional neurosis as the "only really satisfactory analogy" is what Caruth refers to as "the model of ... accident trauma"[8]:

> It may happen that someone gets away apparently unharmed, from the spot where he has suffered a shocking accident, for instance a train collision. In the course of the following weeks, however, he develops a series of grave psychical and motor symptoms, which can be ascribed only to his shock or whatever else happened at the time of the accident. He has developed a "traumatic neurosis." ... [W]e observe that—in spite of the fundamental difference in the two cases, the problem of traumatic neurosis and that of Jewish monotheism—there is a correspondence in one point ... *latency*. There are the best grounds for thinking that in the history of the Jewish religion there is a long period, after the breaking away from the Moses religion, during which no trace is to be found of the monotheistic idea. (*Moses and Monotheism*, 84)

It is important to observe that Caruth for the most part ignores Freud's own reservation and thus sees no "fundamental difference in the two cases."[9] Or, more accurately, in attempting to answer Freud's question about the "delayed effect" of the full embrace of Mosaic doctrine, Caruth understands the "interruption of the symbolic system" as "linked, not to repression, unconsciousness, and symbolization" as Freud himself had (castration trauma) but rather to the dissociative effect of an original "temporal unlocatability" experienced in response to a "shocking accident."[10]

---

8 *Unclaimed Experience*, 135n18.

9 Caruth takes this position in part because, as she observes, "Freud generally placed his examples of the two kinds of trauma [castration trauma and accident trauma] side by side ... and admitted ... that he was not sure how to integrate the two" (*Unclaimed Experience*, 135n18).

10 *Unclaimed Experience*, 133n8, 135n18.

In broad terms, taking accident trauma as the archetype for traumatic etiology, Caruth also repurposes Freud's concept of *Nachträglichkeit* (deferred action) to describe not simply the temporal delay between the event and the onset of symptoms but also the mind's original relation to the event itself. Caruth thus comes to define trauma in terms of the mind's temporal dislocation relative to the traumatic event, a dislocation experienced as an inability to encounter the event in the mediated form of narrative memory.[11] Within that psychical setting, as a "breach in the mind's experience of time," the traumatic event "is experienced too soon, too unexpectedly, to be fully known and is therefore not available to consciousness until it imposes itself again, repeatedly, in the nightmares and repetitive actions of the survivor." Caruth thus concludes that "trauma is not locatable in the simple violent or original event in an individual's past, but rather in the way that its very unassimilated nature—the way it was precisely *not known* in the first instance—returns to haunt the survivor later on."[12]

If Freud's "formula ... for the development of a neurosis" is "early trauma—defense—latency—outbreak of the neurosis—partial return of the repressed material," Caruth's formula, by contrast, might be schematized as follows: *accident* (an unexpected violent event)—*dissociation* (the "inherent forgetting" in and through which the event "is first experienced" and can only be experienced)—*latency* (inseparable from and indeed simultaneous with dissociation: a sense of missing in relation to the event in which a kind of foundational incomprehensibility emerges from the psychical perception that the event was not actually experienced as it occurred)—*emergence of repetitive symptoms*

11 In discussing the impact of traumatic experience on the workings of memory and in particular how memories related to a trauma are stored in the mind, Bessel van der Kolk and Onno van der Hart argue against Freud's "use of the term 'repression'" because it "evokes the image of a subject actively pushing the unwanted traumatic memory away." Remarking that "contemporary research has shown that dissociation of a traumatic experience occurs as the trauma is occurring," they go on to observe that "there is little evidence for an active process of pushing away of the overwhelming experience; the uncoupling seems to have other mechanisms. Many trauma survivors report that they are automatically removed from the scene; they look at it from a distance or disappear altogether, *leaving other parts of the personality to* suffer and *store the overwhelming experience....* [W]hen a subject does not remember a trauma, *its "memory" is contained in an alternate stream of consciousness.* ("The Intrusive Past: The Flexibility of Memory and the Engraving of Trauma," in *Trauma: Explorations in Memory*, ed. Cathy Caruth [Baltimore: Johns Hopkins University Press, 1995], 168; my emphases). For related discussion, see Kay Young and Jeffrey L. Saver, "The Neurology of Narrative," *SubStance* 30 (2001): 72–84.

12 *Unclaimed Experience*, 3–4. The complex relation between memory and repetition treated in Freud's 1914 essay "Remembering, Repeating, and Working-Through" would be taken up again as a central concern of his 1920 *Beyond the Pleasure Principle*.

(not as Freud's return of the repressed but as the symptomatic expression of a psychically haunted consciousness that looks back, repetitively, longingly, futilely, compulsively on an event it experienced but never truly knew).[13] Applying the formula to Jewish history as Freud had reconstructed it in psychoanalytic terms (a history of trauma and the compulsiveness of traumatic return), Caruth concludes: "Thus we might say, on the basis of the understanding of traumatic repetition that Freud outlines in *Beyond the Pleasure Principle*, that the murder of Moses ... [is] suffered as the traumatic separation from the father"; and this separation psychically returns as "an endlessly incomprehensible violence" in the form of "traumatic repetition of the [original] violent separation."[14]

Taking up Caruth's notion that the temporal deferral within the experience of trauma "would thus seem to consist ... in *an inherent latency within the experience itself*," we might now return to the question lurking in her assertion that the murder of Moses was not experienced as it occurred.[15] We should note first that, explicitly following Freud's reconstruction of the immediate aftermath of the Jewish exodus from Egypt under the leadership of Moses, Caruth never wavers in her acceptance of Freud's two core claims: that Moses was murdered by his Jewish followers and that the murder initiated the trauma to which Jewish identity has ever-after been compulsively bound (even if the Mosaic tradition itself took centuries to fully develop).[16] But precisely because she employs the concept of accident trauma as the proper model for understanding Freud's account of "the traumatic history of the Jews," a history defined by "the murder of Moses and his return in the form of Jewish monotheism," Caruth is compelled by the logic of her own argument to suggest not only that the murder was akin to an accident (rather than the purposefully

13 The work of Jean Laplanche and Jean-Bertrand Pontalis in many ways anticipates Caruth's position in observing that a deferred response to a past experience acts on "whatever ... has been impossible in the first instance to incorporate fully into a meaningful context. The traumatic event is the epitome of such unassimilated experience" (*The Language of Psycho-analysis*, trans. Donald Nicholson-Smith [New York: Norton, 1974], 112).

14 *Unclaimed Experience*, 69.

15 *Unclaimed Experience*, 17; my emphasis. This claim is a specific instance of what Caruth considers a broader principle of trauma. As she writes elsewhere, "if repression, in trauma, is replaced by latency, this is significant in so far as its blankness—the space of unconsciousness—is paradoxically what precisely preserves the event ... For history to be a history of trauma means that it is referential precisely to the extent that *it is not fully perceived as it occurs*" (Introduction to *Trauma: Explorations in Memory*, 8; my emphasis).

16 While regularly designating Freud as the source of the idea, Caruth insists over and over again on the historical reality of the murder as the foundational event in Jewish history: see 14–20, 67, and 70.

aggressive act Freud himself describes: "the savage Semites took destiny into their own hands and did away with their tyrant" [58]) but also that, quite mysteriously, the murderers were psychically absent from the scene of the crime.[17] Caruth can thus bizarrely juxtapose the words "accident" and "murder" and ask us to imagine that Moses' murderers were "like the victim of a crash … never fully conscious" while committing the murder. While more implicit than explicit, this assertion then permits her to claim that "the murder [was] not experienced as it occur[red]" and could only become "fully evident only in connection with another place, and in another time," that is, in a "return … displaced by trauma." Of course, it is one thing to say, as Freud does, that guilt led the murderers subsequently *to repress their memories of the murder*, but it is another thing entirely to suggest that Moses' murderers—traumatized by the very murder they had committed—could only experience the murder in a dissociative state, what Caruth calls the "inherent forgetting" of an experience "that can hence never be fully known."[18]

So (re)conceptualized, the murder of Moses seems an unlikely candidate for the founding trauma of Jewish history. For only the most strained reading of the murder would suggest that the murderers themselves did not experience the murder as it occurred, that they were also victims (perhaps even the main victims) of the murder, that the murder "was *suffered* as a traumatic *separation*" from the one murdered, and that, consequentially, the very "monotheistic idea"—a religious orientation that "comes back after the latency of the Jewish people" (which is to say, returns as a compulsive conviction because of the very fact of their missing of the original "event of violent separation")—emerges as a response to what is "incomprehensible …, precisely of having violently separated from Moses *and survived*." Following Freud's own attempt to theorize how the repressed memories that were the aftereffects of the murder could be passed down to those who had not been present, Caruth will even go so far as to say that a murderous act experienced by the murderers themselves as a painful separation that could only be *survived* could then be passed on to subsequent generations in a similarly dissociative form: "The belated experience of trauma in Jewish monotheism suggests that history is not only the passing on of a crisis but also *the passing on of a survival* that can only be possessed

17 *Unclaimed Experience*, 70.

18 *Unclaimed Experience*, 17. We should note how the passive construction "the murder *is not experienced* as it occurs" has the odd effect of obfuscating the agency of the murder(ers) precisely by transforming murder from an intentional act into an *experience*. For a detailed critique of Caruth's position on this issue, see Ruth Leys, *Trauma: A Genealogy* (Chicago: University of Chicago Press, 2000), 293–97.

within a history larger than any single individual or any single generation."[19] By this point in her argument, any sense that what Freud calls a "crime" or "murderous deed" (*Moses and Monotheism*, 109) stood at the beginning of Jewish history has completely disappeared. And we are left with the almost impossible to understand assertion about Freud's effort to ground that history in "a traumatic experience" that "the very possibility" resides "in the nature of traumatic departure," a national (hi)story centered on "leaving … and returning, constituted by trauma."[20]

As an application of the accident model, in short, the murder of Moses is a particularly poor choice as a key element of the answer to one of Caruth's central questions regarding Jewish history: "what does it mean, precisely, for history to be the history of a trauma?"[21] Moreover, it is a surprising choice given that, within the theoretical parameters Caruth herself lays out, there is a much more obvious one. Indeed, there is an event from Jewish history that can be easily interpreted as traumatic for the Jewish people, an event in relation to which they can truly be understood as victims and not murderers who have magically forgotten their crime, an event that includes both suffering and (violent) separation—indeed marks suffering precisely as the result of (violent) separation—and necessitates the commitment to survival that will, in turn, sustain the cultural trauma through future generations, an event that will at once be repeated in history (many times over in fact) and become a chief motivation for Jewish culture to develop its own forms of repetitive behavior in response, an event whose central dynamic is shaped by the paired acts of leaving and returning even as that very pairing is, from the perspective of Jewish identity formed and thereafter haunted by its shadow, almost incomprehensible, an event that, to borrow from Caruth's own phrasing, was for the Jews "an arrival within a history no longer simply their own."[22] And beyond all that, not only does this event provide a specific answer, locatable in time and place, to "the question of the origin of monotheism among the Jews" that Freud himself sought through his very work on *Moses and Monotheism* (no mere "iron monument with feet of clay" [17] as he had fretted about his own argument) but it also, to draw on Caruth's phrasing again, "delineates the structure of Jewish historical experience" in a way that directly connects the origin of monotheism as we understand it today both to the completion of the Torah narrative (at the heart of which is the Moses-Exodus account) and to the historical starting

19 *Unclaimed Experience*, 71; my emphases.

20 *Unclaimed Experience*, 15.

21 *Unclaimed Experience*, 15.

22 *Unclaimed Experience*, 18.

point of a religious tradition defined by a culture-wide commitment to Torah in its root meaning, the compulsive (Freud might even say obsessional) adherence to Mosaic *law* among a people who only at this point in history could truly be called the Jews.[23] That event is what history knows as the Babylonian Exile.

2

The problem of applying either psychoanalytic model of trauma to the Babylonian Exile is that it was never forgotten; or, in psychoanalytic terms, the memory-traces that were the residue of the Exile were neither repressed (as in castration trauma) nor dissociated through what Caruth describes as an originary "missing" whereby it was "not experienced *in time*" (as in accident trauma).[24] In fact, it was just the opposite: the Exile was (all too) well remembered, at times in literal, quasi-objective terms (as a specific event or period in Jewish history) and at other times in figurative or affective terms.

In the former category we would certainly put the chronicle-history accounts in the final two chapters in 2 Kings (these deal primarily with the Babylonian destruction of Jerusalem and specifically of Solomon's Temple but also include the laconic statement "Thus Judah was exiled from its land" [25:21]) as well as in the final chapter of 2 Chronicles, which includes both a brief description of the fall of Jerusalem (including the statement "All the vessels of the House of God, large and small, and the treasures of the House of the LORD and the treasures of the king and his officers were all brought to Babylon" [36:18]) and a closing reminder (the final words of the Hebrew Bible) that, having defeated Babylon, Cyrus of Persia invited the exiles from Judah to return to their homeland and rebuild the Temple (36:22–23). We also find historical material elsewhere, for example, interwoven with poetic passages in the final section of Jeremiah (chapters 39–52), which ends during the Exile itself, and in Ezra, which effectively begins (1:1–4) where 2 Chronicles ends (with Cyrus' proclamation to the exiles in Babylon) and consistently looks back to recent history and a way of justifying Ezra's efforts to establish Torah as the governing law among the self-identifying Jewish population of the Persian province of Yehud Medinata.

Among the more figurative recollections of the Exile we would certainly list Ezekiel's prophetic depictions of God's judgment upon Judah (chapters 4–24, the centerpiece of which is the narration of the departure of divine glory from

23 *Unclaimed Experience*, 67.

24 *Unclaimed Experience*, 62.

the Temple in anticipation of the Babylonian invasion: 10:18–19) as well as his final imagining of the return from exile culminating in the vision of the paired restorations of the Temple (to which the divine glory would come back) and of the nation as a whole (chapters 36–48). We could also cite in this context Daniel's apocalyptic fever-dream that is not only set during the period of the Exile (Nebuchadnezzar is Daniel's king) but also presents Babylon as the first of the four world empires that would rule in succession prior to God's restoration of Israel (chapters 2 and 7). Finally, we might observe the way in which departure, often forced, or some analogous separation from one's homeland (usually from the Promised Land itself) is a recurring feature of the biblical narrative as though the condition of exile had become the narrative's central theme. The entire Hebrew Bible is framed by departure, beginning with the expulsion of Adam and Eve from the Garden of Eden (Genesis 3:23–24) and ending with the departure from Babylon (itself the result of the exile from Judah in the wake of Nebuchadnezzar's invasion) following the edict of King Cyrus. If we never expect that Adam and Eve will return to the Garden, Cyrus' edict is rather more typical in its balancing of exile (the people he invites to go back to Jerusalem haven't even started their journey as the Bible ends) with the hope, even the expectation, of successful return. Thus after their two initial journeys (from Ur to Haran and then from Haran to Canaan [Genesis 11:31, 12:1–5), we get Abram and Sarai's journey from Canaan to Egypt because of a famine (a journey that is effectively forced upon them despite the fact that God has just revealed Canaan as the future homeland of Abram and Sarai's descendants [Genesis 12:6–10]), a journey that then concludes with a return from Egypt to Canaan (Genesis 13:1); Jacob's flight to Haran following the threat to his life made by Esau (Genesis 27:41ff.), a flight that includes Jacob's vow to God regarding the period of his living outside the Promised Land and the anticipation of future return (Genesis 28:20–22); the several journeys of Jacob and his family from Canaan to Egypt in last section of Genesis (chapters 37–46), followed by the paired accounts of the deaths in Egypt first of Jacob and then of Joseph (chapters 49–50; the bodies of both will eventually be returned for burial in Canaan); Moses' flight from his Egyptian birthplace to Midian and his later return (Exodus 2, 4), the people's exodus from Egypt (where all of them had been born) with the goal of returning to the land of their ancestors (Exodus 12ff.); and finally the account of Moses' death which, while narratively set at the very end of the journey from Egypt to Canaan, occurs before the crossing of the Jordan River so that Moses effectively ends his life in exile from all the lands with which he is associated (Egypt, Midian, and Canaan): Deuteronomy 34:1–6.

Several of the psalms fit into the affective category in the sense that, whatever historical details they provide, their primary aim is to portray the emotional-psychological impact of the Exile either on those who experienced it first-hand or on those who viewed it with historical hindsight. Psalm 137, for example, famously offers a collective lament from the perspective of the lived reality of exile:

> [1] By the rivers of Babylon,
> there we sat,
> sat and wept,
> as we thought of Zion [Jerusalem]
> …
> [4] How can we sing a song of the LORD
> on alien soil? (Psalm 137:1, 4)

Psalm 22, most famous because of how the Gospel of Mark will borrow its opening line and verse 19 for the scene of Jesus' crucifixion, lacks Psalm 137's historical specificity, but it is typically understood as expressing the feeling of abandonment among the exiles in response to God's inexplicable absence from his role as national protector:

> [1] My God, my God,
> why have you abandoned me;
> why so far from delivering me …?
> …
> [5] In You our fathers trusted;
> they trusted, and You rescued them.
> [6] To You they cried out
> and they escaped …
> …
> [12] Do not be far from me,
> for trouble is near
> …
> [17] Dogs surround me;
> a pack of evil ones closes in on me …
> …
> [19] They divide my clothes among themselves,
> casting lots for my garments. (Psalm 22:1, 5–6, 12, 17, 19)

Psalm 89 is even more pointed in connecting God's absence to the national failure, in this case marked in the end of the House of David:

37 His [David's] line shall continue forever,
his throne, as the sun before Me [God],
38 as the moon, established forever,
an enduring witness in the sky.
39 Yet You have rejected, spurned,
and become enraged at Your anointed.
40 You have repudiated the covenant with Your servant;
You have dragged his dignity in the dust.
41 You have breached all his defenses,
shattered his strongholds.
...
45 You have brought his splendor to an end
and have hurled his throne to the ground.
...
50 O LORD where is Your steadfast love of old
which You swore to David in Your faithfulness? (Psalm 89:37–41, 45, 50)

The psalm is particularly noteworthy because the sudden shift in perspective following verse 38 (from triumph to despair) indicates that its second half (vv. 39–51) was added long after verses 1–38 were composed and no doubt because the experience of the Exile raised questions about the value of God's promises to his people, even what he "swore to David" and thus to the line of messianic kings he had established.

Taken together, these few examples amply show that, within the Bible at least, the Exile was never forgotten. But precisely because it was never forgotten, it is not immediately clear how, within the Freudian paradigm, it could have functioned as an instance of unassimilated (or, to use Caruth's word, "unclaimed") experience. For it is only in that form—as Freud puts it, "the state of being unconscious"—that "it could produce such mighty effects on its return," emerging finally as a "religious tradition" capable of "forc[ing] the masses under its spell" (*Moses and Monotheism*, 130). But in what sense can an event almost obsessively remembered and thus not repressed, dissociated, or otherwise psychically inaccessible have prompted within the cultural Unconscious of postexilic Judaea the sort of "compulsive conviction" (108) required to "force [the Jewish people] under its spell?" For Freud, this is vexing question in part because, as he puts in the final section of *Moses and Monotheism*, "the people met with hard times; the hopes based on the favor of God were slow in being fulfilled; it became not easy to adhere to the illusion, cherished above all else, that they were God's chosen people" (173). How, in short, could an event that was ever-present in the minds of the Jewish people and that initiated an historical trajectory, one that over and over again dispelled the illusion of chosenness, have attained, in some distorted or delusional form, an "obsessive quality" sufficient to compel continuing belief?

Before giving up on this approach as an interpretive dead-end, it is worth considering how the people's continued adherence to the illusion of their own chosenness in the face of an otherwise undeniable reality (the Exile, subsequent "hard times," covenantal promises never fulfilled, etc.) might be reconceptualized as the gravitational center of the originary cultural trauma. For Freud, of course, the idea (or more precisely the conviction) of chosennness is best understood as a reactive consolation for—and in that form a defense against—the murder of Moses, the return of the repressed guilt for the murder of the cultural father-figure in the guise an ever-cherished and ever-cherishing father-god. But moving passed this particular claim while yet retaining something of Freud's own interpretive procedure, we might think of the very question he poses (how did the Jews sustain the belief in their own chosenness against all odds?) as containing a key element of its own answer. It was not the fact of the Exile that was traumatic; rather, in the wake of the very incomprehensibility of their own survival as a people (a nation without a nation), what was traumatic for the Judaeans was the impossibility of answering the most basic question: what did it mean, or what did it *still* mean, to be the chosen people of God? While the rest of Chapter 2 will explore this question in more detail, as a way of concluding this section, we might briefly revisit Caruth's effort to reformulate Freud's theory regarding the emergence of monotheism as linked to and indeed inseparable from the traumatic origins of the Jewish people.

Despite her constant recourse to Freud's claim concerning the murder of Moses as the founding trauma of Jewish history, at other points Caruth relocates the trauma to a situation that would seem to predate the murder: "Thus, we might say, on the basis of [Freud's] understanding of traumatic repetition ..., that the murder of Moses, ... ultimately leads to a belated attempt to return to *the moment before the murder, to Moses' doctrine of chosenness*." Caruth is not especially clear as to why the experience of chosenness would be traumatic or how it is specifically connected to the murder of Moses. But this is not an isolated assertion on her part; indeed, she insists on its central importance:

> Arguing that monotheism is truly operative in Jewish history only as a "tradition," Freud suggests that the *sense of being chosen is precisely what cannot be grasped in the Jewish past,* the way in which the past itself has imposed itself upon it as a history that it survives but does not fully

> understand.... Monotheism, in shaping Jewish history ... thus becomes, in the history of the Jews, *the crucial and enigmatic query, What does it mean to be chosen?*[25]

There are several intriguing concepts here, most especially the notion that the chosenness associated with God's action in history with respect to the people of Israel is in some sense incomprehensible from the very start. While Freud associates this incomprehensibility with the repression of Moses' foundational role in establishing the Jews ("Moses ... created the Jews" [136]; "they were his 'chosen people'" [55]), drawing more directly on Caruth's account, we might go beyond Freud's limited frame of reference to infer that, even apart from the alleged murder, the sense of national chosenness fixed a crucial if hard to define aspect of Jewish experience in contrast to that of other ancient peoples: as Freud puts it, while in other religious traditions "the people and their god belong inseparably together[,] ... one from the beginning," Jewish tradition offers the unique "conception of a god suddenly 'choosing' a people, making it 'his' people and himself its own god" (55). Building on Caruth, we might then imagine that the very inexplicability of this act of choosing—as Freud observes this may be "the only case [of its type] in the history of human religions" (55)—has a role to play in the national trauma, its very uniqueness constituting a kind of inherent incomprehensibility (in Caruth's terms an "inherent latency" or "missing") at the very origin of the Jewish people. But in a way that Freud himself would understand latency (linked to *Nachträglichkeit* or "deferred action") as the time-lag between an original event and its retrospective traumatic reconstruction, we might then also conclude, *pace* Caruth, that it wasn't the murder of Moses that marked the temporal gap defining the origin of the national trauma; rather, it was the Exile that marked this gap, the point at which what was originally incomprehensible became traumatic. And it became traumatic not because (or not simply because) it happened (which was never denied) but because the Exile rendered even more unintelligible what never made sense to begin with: why a god (if not the one and only god), from out of the hidden recesses of his own inscrutability, stepped into history to choose this people—just this one people—as his own, one people for one god.[26] Most simply put, I want to venture that, after and in consequence of the Exile, the concept of chosenness that had previously circulated as an idea

---

25 *Unclaimed Experience*, 68–69; my emphases; original italics deleted. For related comments on the traumatic element of chosenness, see 67 and 71.

26 We shall consider in more detail in Coda 3 how God's very act of choosing the people of Israel might be understood as what Jean Laplanche calls the implantation of an

among the preexilic Israelites and Judahites acquired an unconscious dimension and, in the form of a compulsive conviction, would become what Freud might have called the "kernel" of the traumatic experience that would thereafter define Jewish history.

Building on the notion that one might be "confronted by an excess of validity over meaning," an excess that subsequently "drives ... a desperate search for a meaning," Eric Santner draws of the work of Jean Laplanche to suggest that this dynamic can work at the intersection of the individual and culture: "every induction into the domain of socio-symbolic relations is also, at least to some extent, a *seduction*; one's solidarity with the spirit of one's family / community / institution is always in part sustained by ... transgressive enjoyment sustained in fantasy.... [T]he psychic registration of validity in excess of meaning ... is *constitutive of the social bond itself*."[27] Fantasy so presented does not refer simply to something we desire but rather to the fantasmatic experience of attempting to reclaim what we never had to begin with (where the experience of loss paradoxically creates the very object of our desire). I would like to suggest that, for the people of Israel, the self-perception of being God's chosen people only acquired its unconscious dimension (and within that framework became structured by fantasy) during and after the Exile. (The concept of fantasy and its relation to the construction of the Jewish subject will be the chief concern of Coda 3.) That is, the notion of reclaiming what had never previously been crucial to Israelite / Judahite identity (in the preexilic period there was meaning but little validity) acquired validity in excess of meaning precisely in response to the Exile. In that scenario, the claim of chosenness functioned in part as a defense of the trauma of exile and its attendant foreign domination even as that very claim transformed the experience of exile (and foreign domination) into a trauma because the national failure thereby became incomprehensible. As a response to what Santner aptly calls the "enigma of election" in the wake of God's absence at the time of national need, the trauma was

"enigmatic message": see, for example, *New Foundations for Psychoanalysis*, trans. David Macey (Oxford: Basil Blackwell, 1989), 130.

27 *On the Psychotheology of Everyday Life: Reflections on Freud and Rosenzweig* (Chicago: University of Chicago Press, 2001), 102–03. Drawing on a letter written to Walter Benjamin in September, 1934 (the topic is Kafka), Santner credits Gershom Scholem with the idea that the validity of an experience might be encountered in excess of its meaning or significance (38–39, 44). Scholem's idea has been discussed in more detail in Giorgio Agamben, *Homo Sacer: Sovereign Power and Bare Life*, trans. Daniel Heller-Roazen (Stanford: Stanford University Press, 1998), 51 and *passim*.

structured by psychical disavowal, the attempt to reject (or at least to refashion as meaningful) what could not be denied.[28]

What we might say, then, was that what was "forgotten" or "latent" in the experience of the Exile was not its objective reality—it was too shocking, too real, too ever-present to ever be denied—but rather its meaning in relation to a cultural identity ("chosen people") mysteriously handed down from a distant past. To put this another way, as the validity of chosenness took precedence over its meaning, the very compulsion of fantasy drove the postexilic Judaeans into a "desperate search for a meaning."

Without saying this explicitly, drawing on Franz Rosenzweig's notion that, unique among the peoples of the world, Jewish identity "is neither simply *historical* nor simply *ahistorical*," Santner argues that something emerged in Jewish discourse to transform its notion of history into destiny, something "*meta-historical*, articulated with the remnants *immanent* to history." In his *Star of Redemption*, Rosenzweig writes, for example, that "in defiance of all secular history, Jewish history is the history of the remnant; the word of the prophet, that it 'will remain,' ever applies to it."[29] Santner comments that "Rosenzweig's argument in the *Star* allows us to understand Jewish 'stuckness' ... not, or at least not simply, as the unredeemed hauntedness pertaining to the violence of ethnogenetic foundations but rather as placeholder ... of a certain *rupture* with the time and space of ethnic and national histories." Santner's "at least not simply" is a crucial qualification, even an acknowledgement: whatever else it is, Jewish "stuckness" (neurotic compulsion) *includes* an "unredeemed hauntedness pertaining to the violence of ethnogenetic foundations." Indeed, Santner goes on to observe that it is in Jewish history that we first come to appreciate Freud's key idea that a "discontent ... haunts civilization" (he then adds that "Freud and Rosenzweig are ... in agreement that Judaism distinguishes itself by, as it were, *refusing to exorcise those ghosts*)."[30] Of course, Santner would be in a better position to recognize the full ramifications of his own insight if he, like Caruth, did not simply assume Freud's position in thinking of "violence of

28 *On the Psychotheology of Everyday Life*, 112. While overly invested as so many commentators on *Moses and Monotheism* are in Freud's theory that the murder of Moses was the true beginning of Judaic monotheism, Santner yet rightly perceives, without grasping why, that the experience of loss or what he calls "a series of traumatic cuts or separations" is "correlative to the advent of monotheism" (105). In Chapter 3 we shall also see how and why this transformation included and was inseparable from the completion of Torah and its full assimilation into Judaean culture.

29 *The Star of Redemption*, trans. William W. Hallo (New York: Holt, Rinehart and Winston, 1970), 404.

30 *On the Psychotheology of Everyday Life*, 113–15.

ethnogenetic foundations" in terms of the alleged murder of Moses. That is, if he more properly understood his choice of "violence," "rupture," and "ethnogenetic foundations" in connection to the postexilic experience of Judaeans who, with the memory of the Exile fresh in their collective minds, lived under Persian colonial rule, he would see that "hauntedness" defined the rupture at the heart an emergent ethnic and national history. In this context, Jewish "stuckness" can be understood as a particularly telling *cultural* instance of what Freud means by the phrase "fixated to the trauma" (*Beyond the Pleasure Principle*, *SE*, 18:13).

Within this historical framework, we might also say, then, that what was lost in the Exile was not just the land, the monarchy, the nation itself, and the cultural self-determination belonging to the nation but the very past in which land, monarchy, nation, and self-determination could have been taken as signs of the fulfillment of the divine promises first made to Abraham and later affirmed in covenants made through Moses and David. And necessarily included in this loss was the sense that God's choosing of the people could ever have been meaningful if everything that choosing included could all fall apart while God simply disappeared. In short, it was not the death of Moses that, as the origin of a cultural trauma, the people had to survive; rather, it was the death of God.

3

As noted, the fact of the Exile was never denied, nor for large portions of the biblical narrative was it ever deemed as lacking meaning or as otherwise incomprehensible. We might put this second point in slightly different terms: if the fact of the Exile itself was never denied, what was denied—often actively denied—was precisely that it had no meaning or was otherwise incomprehensible. Biblically speaking, denying the incomprehensibility of the Exile was the explicit goal of what has traditionally been known as the Deuteronomistic History.

While the Deuteronomistic History is sufficiently established in modern scholarship to make a lengthy summary here unnecessary, some keys elements are worth keeping in mind as we proceed. Firmly associated in its earliest phase with the reform movement set in motion by the late seventh-century king Josiah and the prophet Jeremiah, the Deuteronomistic History reworked what historical narrative was already established in Israelite and Judahite culture to place a new nationalistic emphasis on the centrality of Mosaic law and the cult of Yahweh as practiced (from the perspective of the reformers, hereafter to be exclusively practiced) at the Temple in Jerusalem. These reforms included the discovery (aka the writing) of a new book, Deuteronomy, that would eventually be included in Torah (see 2 Kings 22:8–13 and 23:1–3; the largely postexilic priestly-oriented Leviticus is also the product of this movement) as well as a series of additions to or other revisions of earlier writings. More an interpretation of history than a free-standing historical account (often merely overlaying an earlier historical narrative), the Deuteronomistic History is best understood as an effort to redefine the notion of the people's covenant with Yahweh as conditional in a way that neither the Abrahamic covenant nor the Davidic covenant had been. In simplest terms, the Deuteronomistic History states that the nation will succeed when the kings and the people fully commit themselves to observance of Mosaic law (see 2 Kings 23:21–25) and it will fail (it will be punished) when it does not observe Mosaic law.[31]

It was one thing, however, to formulate such a theory of national history from the perspective of the first phase of reforms, a period during which Josiah-ruled Judah pursued a policy of national revival, including an initially successful effort of territorial expansion to reclaim portions of the land lost when Assyria conquered the northern kingdom of Israel in the late-eighth century (e.g. 2 Kings 23:19). But it was harder to maintain the theory in the wake of Josiah's sudden defeat at the hands of the Egyptian army under Pharaoh Necho II. Josiah's fall (usually dated 609 BCE) predated the Babylonian conquest of Judah by just over twenty years, and the exilic and postexilic writers and redactors were then in the awkward position of having to revise the core claim of the Deuteronomistic History while retaining its primary purpose. For how could a Davidic king who "with all his heart and soul and might, [lived] in full accord with the Teaching [Law] of Moses" (2 Kings 23:25) have failed so immediately after his (re)commitment to Mosaic law and at the hands of

31 Though somewhat vague about when this happened historically and what precisely prompted it, Freud gets at the basic issue in observing that

"the priests in their rewriting of the Biblical text as we have it [this would be mostly exilic and / or postexilic revision] ascribe too much to Moses. Institutions as well as ritualistic rules undoubtedly belonging to later times are declared to be Mosaic laws, with the clear intention of enhancing their authority.... The priests, in the accounts they present, desired to establish a continuity between their own times and the Mosaic period. They attempted to deny just what we have recognized to be the most striking feature of Jewish religious history: namely, that there was a gap between the Mosaic law-giving and the later Jewish tradition.... Their presentation denies this sequence of events with all the means in its power." (*Moses and Monotheism*, 81)

For broader discussion of the postexilic period of priestly rule and more specific discussion of the development of the Mosaic legal codes, see Michael Walzer, *In God's Shadow: Politics in the Hebrew Bible* (New Haven: Yale University Press, 2012), chs. 2 and 8.

the very people (the Egyptians) from whom God had liberated the enslaved Hebrews just prior to the institution of the Mosaic covenant? And how could God shortly thereafter have departed from his own Temple and, in so doing, have completely abandoned his nation and his people to the Babylonian invaders?

Luckily, the Deuteronomistic History already contained the answer to that question: the nation failed when the kings and / or the people failed to obey the covenantal law. Thus, while 2 Kings' single-verse account of Josiah's ill-fated encounter with Necho II (2 Kings 23:29) provides no interpretive context, the postexilic revision in 2 Chronicles 35:20–22 offers a theologically-inflected portrayal of the events, a portrayal that explicitly condemns Josiah for acting against God's will.[32]

The idea that even the greatest of the kings might fail (or might act in such a way as to effectively guarantee some later divine rebuke: even Moses falls into this pattern) is so stamped over the historical narrative that it hardly needs extra documentation. But two examples narratively set before the period of Josiah quite clearly establish the general point even as they show the revisionary process at work in biblical composition. When we look at the account of the splendor of Solomon's reign in 1 Kings 4–5 and 1 Kings 10, it is easy to imagine that, during the time of the third and final king of the United Monarchy, all the promises God had made to Abraham at their first encounter were understood as having reached fulfillment in the greatness that was monarchical Israel.[33] But contradicting this depiction both in

32 Significantly in the account in 2 Chronicles it is the Egyptian Necho II who is acting in accordance with Yahweh's designs: Josiah went into battle "heedless of *Necho's words from the mouth of God*; and he came to fight in the plain of Megiddo" (35:22; my emphasis).

33 We might compare the accounts in 1 Kings 4–5 and 1 Kings 10 to the covenantal promises in Genesis 12, 15, Genesis 17:

"[4:20] Judah and Israel were as numerous as the sands of the sea; they ate and drank and were content. [5:1] *Solomon's rule extended over all the kingdoms from the Euphrates to the land of the Philistines and the boundary of Egypt*. They brought Solomon tribute and were subject to him all his life." (1 Kings 4:20, 5:1; my emphasis)

"[14] The weight of gold which Solomon received every year was 666 talents of gold, [15] besides what came from the tradesmen, from the traffic of the merchants, and from all the kings of Arabia and the governors of the regions.... [23] *King Solomon excelled all the kings on earth in wealth and in wisdom.* [24] *All the world came to pay homage to Solomon and to listen to the wisdom with which God had endowed him.*" (1 Kings 10:14–15, 23–24; my emphasis)

tone and content, the very next chapter suggests that Solomon's and thus Israel's greatness were more appearance than reality (at least from God's perspective):

> [1] King Solomon loved many foreign women ... [2] from the nations of which the LORD had said to the Israelites, "None of you shall join them and none of them shall join you, lest they turn your heart away to follow their gods." Such Solomon clung to and loved. [3] He had seven hundred royal wives and three hundred concubines; and his wives turned his heart away. [4] In his old age, his wives turned away Solomon's heart after other gods, and he was not wholeheartedly devoted to the LORD his God as his father David had been.... [9] The LORD was angry with Solomon, because his heart turned away from the LORD, the God of Israel, who had appeared to him twice [10] and had commanded him about this matter, not to follow other gods; *he did not obey what the LORD had commanded.* [11] And the LORD said to Solomon, "Because you are guilty of this—*you have not kept My covenant and the laws which I enjoined upon you—I will tear the kingdom away from you.* (1 Kings 11:1–4, 9–11; my emphases)

Though portrayed as a divine warning regarding the future, that concluding "I will tear the kingdom away from you" is no doubt a reflection backward in time from the perspective of a later point in history when the kingdom had already been torn away from the heirs of David (see 2 Kings 25:1–7).

"[1] The Lord said to Abram, 'Go forth from your native land and from your father's house to the land that I will show you." // [2] *I will make of you a great nation, // And I will bless you; // I will make your name great,* // And you shall be a blessing. // [3] I will bless those who bless you // And curse him that curses you; // And *all the families of the earth // Shall bless themselves by you.*" (Genesis 12:1–3; my emphases)

"[18] On that day the Lord made a covenant with Abram, saying, "To your offspring I assign this land, from the river of Egypt to the great river, the river Euphrates." (Genesis 15:18)

"[1] When Abram was ninety-nine years old, the Lord appeared to Abram and said to him, "I am El Shaddai. Walk in My ways and be blameless. [2] I will establish My covenant between Me and you, and I will make you exceedingly numerous.... [6] *I will make you exceedingly fruitful, and make nations of you; and kings shall come forth from you.*" (Genesis 17:1–2, 6; my emphasis)

Much the same could be said of the second example, a passage from Moses' final sermon to the people near the end of Deuteronomy:

> 15 See, I set before you this day life and prosperity, death and adversity. 16 For I command you this day, to love the LORD your God, to walk in His ways, and to keep His commandments, His laws, and His rules, that you may thrive and increase, and that the LORD your God may bless you in the land that you are about to enter and possess. 17 But *if your heart turns away and you give no heed*, and are lured into the worship and service of other gods, 18 I declare to you this day that … *you shall not long endure on the soil that you are crossing the Jordan to enter and possess.* (Deuteronomy 30:15–18; my emphases)

Directed at a people who had never even set foot in the Promised Land, Moses' listing of exile as among the punishments for failing to "keep His the commandments" makes much more sense as a fictionalized foreshadowing of what had already occurred (known history told in the future tense); in fact, these four verses were most likely either a postexilic addition to or a postexilic revision of the preexilic text of Deuteronomy written during the reign of Josiah.[34]

In sum, both examples suggest how invested the biblical narrative is in retrospectively depicting the people's violation of the Law as either a constant threat or, worse, already at work and so establishing the grounds on which at some point in the future God would effectively be forced to exact the cost for disobedience: foreign destruction of the nation followed by exile. In other words, the people's real or potential failure lurked even in moments that on the surface would appear to have testified not just to national greatness but also to God's fulfillment of his side of the covenantal bargain. Casting its shadow over future Israelite and Judahite / Judaean history, disobedience was, we might say, present from the beginning; hence, when the Exile actually happened, God's apparent breaking of his promises and indeed his very abandonment of the people to whom he had sworn his *hesed* (commitment, loyalty, devotion, steadfast love) had already been explained because always anticipated. In that context, the Exile ceased to defy understanding; it was, rather, the to-be-expected consequence of the people's sin. And where responsibility was so clearly delineated, the Exile's very incomprehensibility could be rendered intelligible—a simple relation of cause and effect—and so denied. As Freud

34 The reality of the Exile represented as a prophetic statement made by Moses is even more obvious in Deuteronomy 29:24–27.

might have put it by drawing on the distinction between fright and anxiety he had made in *Beyond the Pleasure Principle*, one of the main effects of the Deuteronomistic History (especially its final postexilic revisions) was to impose a sort of proleptic anxiety on the preexilic narrative.[35] The postexilic Jewish Unconscious aimed, in short, to master the trauma of the Exile by retroactively foreseeing it and thus, by means of an anxiety-induced and -inducing anticipation, preparing retroactively for what could not have been avoided. If the Judaean survivors could not thereby deny the Exile itself, they could refuse or at least dilute its full traumatic impact.

Though operating within the broad interpretive parameters of the Deuteronomistic History's explanation for the Exile, this refusal took a variety of specific forms in postexilic Jewish writing and culture. In their different ways, these should be understood as accepting the historical reality of the Exile while rejecting—disavowing, deflecting, or otherwise denying—its incomprehensibility in relation to preexilic history and in particular to the idea of chosenness that had taken root in Israelite and Judahite consciousness. Three examples will have to suffice, all among the most important developments in postexilic Jewish religion and culture.

The first of these is the evolution of the very idea of monotheism, the transformation of what Jan Assmann has called the preexilic "monotheism of loyalty"—one god for one people, a relationship based on mutual loyalty and exclusivity—to the postexilic universal monotheism—there is only one god in the universe, the god of all peoples and all nations.[36] The postexilic development wasn't completely new since it brought to completion an idea that had been occasionally treated in preexilic writings, the idea of Yahweh's future engagement with other nations as part of the fulfillment of his plan for Israel. The eighth-century Proto-Isaiah, for example, offers a vision of "days to come" at which time

---

35 For Freud's distinction between fright and anxiety, see *Beyond the Pleasure Principle*, SE, 18:12, 32.

36 Assmann, *The Invention of Religion: Faith and Covenant in the Book of Exodus*, trans. Robert Savage (Princeton: Princeton University Press, 2018), 79–90. Assmann here distinguishes "monotheism of loyalty" (one god for one people) from what he calls "monotheism of truth," an evolution in the earlier concept he associates with exilic and postexilic prophets and showing "the influence" in the Persian period "of Achaemenid Zoroastrianism. This monotheism," Assmann notes, "concerns not the God who freed his people from Egyptian bondage but the creator of heaven and earth, beside whom there are no other gods" (84).

[2] The Mount of the LORD's House
Shall stand firm above the mountains
And tower above the hills;
And all the nations
Shall gaze on it with joy.
[3] And the many peoples shall go and say:
"Come,
Let us go up to the Mount of the LORD,
To the House of the God of Jacob;
That he may instruct us in His ways,
...
For instruction shall come forth from Zion,
The word of the LORD from Jerusalem.
[4] Thus He shall judge among the nations,
And arbitrate for the many peoples. ([Proto-]Isaiah 2:2–4)

This vision of a world unified under Yahweh is affirmed and even expanded in a series of passages normally ascribed to the exilic Deutero-Isaiah and / or the postexilic Trito-Isaiah:

[5] And now the LORD has resolved,
...
[6] "It is too little that you should be My servant
In that I raise up the tribes of Jacob
And restore the survivors of Israel:
I will also make you a light of nations,
That My salvation may reach the ends of the earth. ([Deutero-]Isaiah 49:5–6)
...
[7] How welcome on the mountain
Are the footsteps of the herald
...
Announcing victory,
Telling Zion, "Your God is King!"
...
[8] For every eye shall behold
The LORD's return to Zion.
...
[10] The LORD will bare His holy arm
In the sight of all the nations,

And the very ends of the earth shall see
The victory of our God. ([Deutero-]Isaiah 52:7, 10)
…
5 So you shall summon a nation you did not know,
And a nation you did not know
Shall come running to you. ([Deutero-]Isaiah 55:5)
…
1 Thus said the LORD:
Observe what is right and do what is just;
For soon My salvation shall come,
And My deliverance be revealed.
…
6 As for the foreigners
Who attach themselves to the LORD,
To minister to Him,
And to love the name of the LORD,
To be His servants,
…
7 I will bring them to My sacred mount,
…
Their burnt offerings and sacrifices
Shall be welcome on My altar;
For My House shall be called
A house of prayer for all peoples. ([Trito-]Isaiah 56:1, 6–7)

What is particularly noticeable in this prophetic discourse is that, even as Yahweh becomes the one god in the universe, he maintains his unique bond with Israel: that is, the earlier, much narrower monotheism of loyalty still inhabits the emergent universal monotheism. Thus it is that, even in their defeated, colonized condition, the Judaeans can still identify themselves as the chosen people and, consequently, even within the more expansive view of God's reach, the focal point of world history.[37]

---

37 Freud finds this particular development in Jewish history almost inexplicable given its limited political success on the world stage; he contrasts the Jewish situation to that of Egypt where the concept of universal monotheism had emerged during the reigns of Amenhotep III and IV: "In Egypt monotheism had grown … as an ancillary effect of imperialism; God was the reflection of a Pharaoh autocratically governing a great world Empire. With the Jews the political conditions were most unfavorable for a development away from the idea of an exclusive national God towards that of a universal ruler of the

In this context, even as foreign agents, either as scourges or defenders and often acting outside of Israel's own borders, could play a role (whether knowingly or not) in God's larger plan for history, that role was never independent of God's unique relationship with the covenantal people. As the Babylonian invasion approaches, Jeremiah, for example, first warns the inhabitants of Jerusalem that God is planning a disaster for the nation (18:1–12); subsequently, he tells the Judaeans living in Babylon that the period of the Exile, having already been determined ("… When Babylon's seventy years are over…" [29:10]), will serve God's redemptive purposes (29:1–23). Later still, Jeremiah will lay out God's specific judgments upon the nations and will even go so far as to predict God's deployment of Babylon to punish Egypt (chapters 46–51).[38] Ezekiel will draw on both these elements from Jeremiah: he will similarly describe Babylon's destruction of Judah as a sort of purifying chastisement of the people prior to their restoration to the Promised Land and the return to the path of destined national greatness (Ezekiel 21:1–27 and *passim*); and he will go on to describe God's condemnation of the other nations, including those that, like Babylon, unknowingly work on his behalf (chapters 25–32). And in the last book of the Hebrew Bible in terms of its date of composition, the author of Daniel will represent God's oversight of a line of empires that, starting with Babylon and ending with the Seleucid Greek empire, would dominate the region (chapters 2, 7) until at the "time of the end" (12:9) God would intervene in history by sending Michael, prince and protector, to deliver the people (12:1).[39] Finally, in a passage we previously considered, in the last book of the Hebrew Bible in terms of the final ordering of texts, the author of 2 Chronicles portrays Cyrus of Persia "in fulfillment of the word of the LORD spoken by Jeremiah" first, in defeating Babylon (and so freeing the Judaean captives) and then, in delivering an edict whereby those captives are invited to return to their homeland to rebuild the Temple (36:21–23). In this particular instance, the foreign ruler actually knows that he governs under the authority of the god

world. When, then, did this tiny and impotent nation derive the audacity to pass themselves off as the favorite child of the Sovereign Lord?" (80).

38 These chapters conclude with the prophecy of the destruction of Babylon itself: "… the Lord's purpose is fulfilled against Babylon, // To make the land of Babylon // A waste without inhabitant" (51:29).

39 In chapter 12, deliverance appears to mean the resurrection of the dead in concert with a final judgment, some awakening "to eternal life, others to reproaches, everlasting abhorrence" (Daniel 12:2). But the earlier vision of the Son of Man (or simply "a human being") coming "with the clouds of heaven" and claiming "an everlasting dominion" (7:13–14) is more suggestive of an end time defined by the final triumph of Israel as God's once and future kingdom.

of the Judaeans. Yahweh is, in Cyrus's own words, "the LORD God of heaven" who rules everyone and everywhere and from that position has delegated to a non-Judaean the right and responsibility to rule "all the kingdoms of the earth" (36:23). Whether the foreign rulers are wicked or righteous, in all these cases, a reimagined Yahweh becomes the master of human history and sovereign of the cosmos whose permitting of the destruction of Israel and then of Judah with the subsequent domination of Judaean culture by various Near Eastern empires could be seen as part of his larger purposes. So understood, the period of the Exile was anything but meaningless because it served a necessary if counterintuitive function in the fulfillment of the ancient promises made to God's still chosen people.

The second and third examples both center on the completion of Torah and its subsequent importation into Persian-ruled Judah by the priest-governor Ezra sometime in the mid- to late-fifth century. The second example considers Torah specifically as a narrative of the people's history prior to the founding of the nation: Ezra's completed Torah primarily told the story of the exodus from Egypt under Moses' leadership along with the establishment of the Law that would, as the narrative consistently emphasizes, make the nation distinct from all other nations (Exodus 8:19, 33:16, and *passim*). While the core Moses-Exodus story was likely given something close to its final form in the late-seventh century as part of the reforms instituted by King Josiah, it would have taken on new meaning in the aftermath of the Exile and during a time when the Judaeans had once again been reduced to a subject people under foreign domination (even if Persian imperial policy granted them a fair bit of local control).[40] Although the Exodus was a story of the people's past, in the context of fifth-century Persian hegemony it could also be understood as foreshadowing what lay ahead: rather than serving as the nation's foundation myth as it had during Josiah's reign, under the priestly theocracy of the Persian (and later Greek) period the Exodus account projected a future time when God would once again intervene in history to liberate his people from foreign servitude.[41] And if the full restoration of Israel after its second exodus was yet

40 For a persuasive account of how and why the basic narrative of Torah was established in the late-seventh century (prior to the final revisions of the exilic / postexilic period), see Israel Finkelstein and Neil Asher Silberman, *The Bible Unearthed: Archaeology's New Vision of Ancient Israel and the Origin of Its Sacred Texts* (New York: The Free Press, 2001), especially Part III. For related discussion, see Donald B. Redford, *Egypt, Canaan, and Israel in Ancient Times* (Princeton: Princeton University Press, 1992), chs. 14–15.

41 Following Sellin's account, Freud himself links this future orientation to messianic expectations explicitly associated with the return of the slain Moses: *Moses and Monotheism*, 42–43.

to come (perhaps even to include the return of the northern tribes into a fully reintegrated united monarchy), then the Exile could be reimagined less as a national catastrophe than as a delay (even a necessary correction) on the path to the promised national greatness.

The third example relates to Torah in a different sense. While the expected restoration of the nation might require that God send a new Moses (whether prophet, priest, king, messiah, or some combination thereof), it also demanded national revival in the form of recommitment to the Mosaic legacy (Torah) in its more fundamental meaning of instruction: the Law that God had revealed to his people through Moses. If according to the Book of Nehemiah, Ezra had the entirety of Torah read aloud to the people gathered in a square in Jerusalem (Nehemiah 8:1–8), the specific focus of that reading were the legal requirements that God had imposed at Sinai as a condition of the covenant.[42] The need to remind the people of their covenantal obligations would, of course, have been directly related to the Deuteronomistic perspective in the sense that national failure generally and the Exile in particular were explicitly understood as the punishments inflicted by Yahweh in consequence of the people's neglect of those obligations. But the recommitment to the Law could also be understood as an act of hope that the loss of national sovereignty was temporary: if the people had been justly punished for the sins for which they were responsible, then as free historical agents they could reverse their fortunes—and reclaim God's favor—by dedicating themselves anew to proper legal observance.

From Freud's point of view, the notion that the people "deserved nothing better than to be punished … because they did not observe the laws" (that is why God had sent them into exile) led the Jews—and, though Freud himself does not say this, these are best understood as the Jews *after* Ezra's arrival in Jerusalem with the completed Torah—to "render their religious precepts ever and ever more strict, more exacting, but also more petty" (*Moses and Monotheism*, 173). But strictness to the point of pettiness was precisely the point. The edict of Ezra 10:3–5 that Judaean men must divorce their non-Jewish wives and disown any children of those unions serves as an apt synecdoche of one of the key aims of the reclamation of Torah in the postexilic period: to redefine the concept of ethno-national distinctiveness in terms of the holiness that derived from remaining apart from other peoples (see, for example,

42 Ezra is referred to here as "a scribe" who reads from "the Teaching of Moses" or from "the scroll of the Teaching." And the point of the reading is to "explain the Teaching to the people, … translating it and giving the sense; so they understood the reading" (Nehemiah 8:1, 3, 7–8). In other words, Ezra reads Torah not to teach the people the story of their past but to make known their present obligations under the Law.

Exodus 19:3–6, Leviticus 20:26, and Deuteronomy 7:1–6). And that cultural separation would, in turn, reinvigorate the concept of chosenness that the Exile had called into question by transforming the Judaeans' status as a subjugated people into an opportunity to assert their very difference from their colonial overlords (Persian, then Greek, then Roman) and the non-Jewish populations among whom they increasingly lived. The very weakness of the claim of chosenness (how could God have permitted the nation of his chosen people to be destroyed?) could thus become the source of its strength: we are chosen (still) because, even in our current debased state, we are holy because we are separate because we are committed to the laws our God has commanded no matter how strict, exacting, or petty (indeed, our very willingness to accept such laws is what sets us apart as a holy nation). And with a complete Torah available for the first time, it was now possible for the entire nation to "turn ... to the LORD ... with all [its] heart and soul and might, in full accord with the Teaching of Moses" (2 Kings 23:25).

In that context, what Freud viewed as the mere pettiness of rules in the form of religious precepts points beyond the strictness of the rules themselves to the obsessional state necessary to adhere to them. Although Freud himself would interpret that obsession—the insistence on self-imposed legal restrictions (more don'ts than do's)—as evidence of Jewish culture's insatiable need to express its guilt for the murder of the cultural father, Moses, in the historical setting of the postexilic period it makes more sense to view the strictness and commitment (the pettiness) as constituting a psychologically compelling way of acknowledging the fact of the Exile while denying the trauma that derived from it. In short, the obsessional observance of ever stricter and pettier precepts erected a psychical defense in the form of a rationalization. For if all could be salvaged by a (re)commitment to Torah, the horrors of the Babylonian destruction of Jerusalem and its aftermath could be reimagined as a merely a setback, and the promises of the covenant could become fully intelligible once again because still fully in effect: the Judaeans were still God's chosen people and a glorious future still beckoned. Indeed, God had given his people a second chance precisely to the extent they took upon themselves the responsibility for the Exile ("because they did not observe the laws"). By devoting themselves to the Law in an even more rigorous version, they would by their very holiness (the separateness that proved their continuing chosenness) not only prevent the repetition of catastrophe but also guarantee that God would at some point in the future make good on his covenantal promises.[43]

---

43 Ezra effectively blames the people for the Exile despite the fact that their sin in not observing Torah was not a possibility until after the Exile. In this context, Ezra might

To put this another way, by doubling down on the Law, the Judaeans could sidestep the inconvenient fact that Josiah's commitment hadn't saved him from death at the hands of Israel's great enemy or that, shortly thereafter, the Babylonians had burned God's own temple to the ground and taken the chosen people into captivity.[44] (Re)commitment to Torah thus became a way for Judaeans living under Persian colonial rule to disavow that God had already failed to keep his word. As a cultural reaction formation, the inverse of this recognition—that the responsibility for the catastrophe fell on the people themselves—served, in short, to deny God's own responsibility. That denial was necessary because to admit that the god who had promised his steadfast love had simply abandoned his people in their time of distress would undermine the essence of the people's identity, everything the people understood of themselves from the past they had inherited. Chosenness was the site of the postexilic trauma because the very divine choosing that had brought the people of Israel into existence and that had given the nation its distinctive identity (a holy nation) would be meaningless if God were recognized as incapable of fulfilling his promises. Paradoxically, the completion of Torah and its institutionalization among the Judaeans was first and foremost an act of refusal, the refusal to admit the possibility that there was no god of Israel or at least no god the people of Israel could trust.

Of course, other parts of the biblical narrative would refuse the refusal itself, would refuse, that is, to accept either the explanation (the people were themselves to blame) or the past-refuting hope of a future restoration. We have already seen examples of the acknowledgement of the Exile without the excuses or the consolations: Psalm 22's anguish at God's inexplicable absence; Psalm 137's sense of despair at life in exile from the Promised Land; and Psalm 89's sudden shift from a sense of triumph under the rule of God's anointed king whose "line shall continue forever" to lamentation in the face of God's

---

be understood as the inventor of the cultic function of Torah as a response to the loss of national self-determination.

44 That said, the notion that the Judaeans had never properly observed the Law because they had never truly known it was part of the preexilic narrative as well; thus, 2 Kings 22 observes that after Josiah "heard the words of the scroll of the Teaching" (Deuteronomy) for the first time, "he rent his clothes" out of anguish (2 Kings 22:11). In the following chapter, anticipating Ezra's own reading of the Torah to "the entire people" in Jerusalem as recounted in Nehemiah 8:1, Josiah goes to the Temple and to "all the people, young and old ... read[s] to them the entire text of the covenant scroll" (2 Kings 23:2).

inexplicable betrayal ending with the most pressing of questions: "O LORD, where is Your steadfast love of old …?" (Psalm 89:37, 50).

And then there is the Book of Job.

4

Slavoj Žižek makes the intriguing suggestion that, as it moves from the test of Job laid out in its opening chapters to the test of God himself in its final chapters, the book deliberately exposes in the "farcical spectacle" of God's "empty boasting" (chapters 38–41) not the incomprehensibility of the divine (to the human mind at least) but, quite the opposite, God's "impotence—or, at the very least, weakness." For, in Žižek's reading, God is actually unable to answer Job's simple question: why was he made to suffer?[45] Žižek gets a bit off the mark in arguing that Job's "properly ethical dignity lies in the way he persistently rejects the notion that his suffering can have any meaning."[46] It would be more accurate to say that Job assumes there is meaning to his suffering, but he rejects the claim consistently made by the three friends (Eliphaz, Bildad, and Zophar) that, because God is just, Job must have sinned in some way and that, therefore, his current suffering must be his due punishment (chapters 4, 8, and 11 and *passim*). While Job does regularly assert his innocence ("You know that I am not guilty") and refers to himself as "Blamelessly innocent," one who "saved the poor man who cried out, // The orphan who had none to help him. // … gladdened the heart of the widow. // … was a father to the needy, // … looked into the case of the stranger" (10:7, 12:4, 29:12–16), he doesn't completely reject the possibility that he has unknowingly sinned. But even or especially if that is the case, he wants to know how exactly: "How many are my iniquities and sins? / Advise me of my transgression and sin" (13:23; see also 6:24–30). More broadly, he wants God to appear in person to explain the reason for the suffering since, on the surface, it cannot properly be described as a punishment in any normal sense (of course, the reader, but not Job himself, already knows that because we earlier read chapters 1 and 2).[47] While God as the voice from

45 *The Puppet and the Dwarf: The Perverse Core of Christianity* (Cambridge, MA: MIT Press, 2003), 124–25.

46 *Puppet and the Dwarf*, 125.

47 So Job says to the three friends:

[3] "I would speak to the Almighty; // I insist on arguing with God. // … // [13] Keep quiet; I will have my say, // Come what may upon me. // … // [15] He may well slay me; I may have no hope; // Yet I will argue my case before Him. // … // [18] See now, I have prepared a case; //

the whirlwind does finally appear (38:1ff.), he (in)famously doesn't answer Job's question or, in Žižek's view, he cannot answer (his impotence is marked by that very incapacity). While never saying this explicitly, Job is thus left to infer that the question about his suffering has no answer.

Žižek's anachronistic decision to label Job's three friends as "theologians," while not entirely inapt given the doctrinal position they collectively espouse, makes most sense if we imagine them as theologians of the Deuteronomistic school. Job (both book and character) makes a mockery of this school or, we might say, makes a full frontal assault on the Deuteronomistic History's core claims. For, as Job notes, life shows us that the good often suffer while the wicked often prosper, and there is no life beyond the grave to compensate for that fundamental unfairness (chapters 21 ,14 and *passim*). Tellingly, as Žižek is right to observe, "God takes [Job's] side at the end, claiming that every word Job spoke was true, while every word the three theologians spoke was false."[48] God even threatens to punish the "theologians" (the friends) because they have not spoken the truth as Job has (Job 42:7–8): their claim that God is just and that, therefore, the innocent do not suffer is completely belied by the fact that God in every meaningful sense causes Job's suffering precisely *because* Job is "blameless and upright" (1:1), the very fact with which the book opens. More generally, suffering and prosperity are equally meaningless because they have no causal relation to moral conduct, and God is unwilling or unable to change the world that is foundationally incomprehensible at least from the perspective of the human mind that might reasonably expect the omnipotent designer of the universe to promote moral goodness and to reward it at every opportunity. The likelihood that Job was written in close temporal proximity to Ezra's arrival in Jerusalem, perhaps even as a response to Ezra's championing of Mosaic law as the path to national revival, points to the Deuteronomistic theory of history (and in particular its simple cause-effect understanding of the Exile) as the writer's prime target.

That said, the very fact that God causes Job's suffering—he is no helpless, passive observer here—suggests that God is not in fact impotent in the way Žižek asks us to imagine. Indeed, thinking of Job's God as *merely* impotent

I know that I will win it. // [19] For who is it that would challenge me? // I should then keep silent and expire." (13:3, 13, 15, 18–19)

Job's "properly ethical dignity," in short, lies not in what Žižek calls his insistence "on the utter meaningless of his suffering" (125) but rather in his refusal to accept the accusation that he has done something wrong. What he wants is not that his suffering end (his children, wealth, bodily integrity restored) but only that God explain himself, that is, justify Job's suffering.

48 *Puppet and the Dwarf*, 125.

misses the point; or, more precisely, such a perspective understates the very radicality of the book especially if we understand it as a response to the dominant postexilic (re)conceptualization of Jewish theology and religious history as laid out in the biblical narrative (in short, the Deuteronomistic History). Job's God is not impotent; rather, he is powerful (absolutely so: omnipotent) but in a way that is irrelevant to Job's chief concern (why did he have to suffer?) and thus also to the chief concern of the postexilic Judaeans inspired by Ezra's gift of Torah to (re)commit themselves to Mosaic law as the centerpiece of a national reward-punishment system.

The God of the final chapters of Job (38:1–42:9) is in every meaningful sense a creator-god and, as presented, not so remarkably different from the god-figure portrayed in Genesis 1. In fact, the book constantly echoes passages from Genesis 1.[49] But this creator-god is decidedly not, as the core historical narrative of the Bible would have it, the god of history and, even more noticeably, not the god of Jewish history, which, except by way of a sort of negative allegory, is not present in the book at all: there is no concept of a people or the covenant or Mosaic law or freedom from liberation in Egypt (the very foundation of the covenantal relation understood as Yahweh's direct intervention in time) or of any of the phases of Israelite or Judahite national history (Job is not even identified as an Israelite).[50] What those final chapters of Job put on display, mostly in the form of what Žižek calls "empty boasting," is simply the raw power of creation, and in particular its ceaseless cycle of life and death (what we might call a primal energy), in which this God

49 These echoes are particularly pronounced in chapters 38–39, but they show up elsewhere including in several of the speeches of the three friends. For broad discussion of this adaptive pattern, see Robert Alter, *The Art of Biblical Poetry* (New York: Basic Books, 1985), ch. 4.

50 Alter quite correctly observes that, biblically speaking, the "God of Israel ... is above all the God of history" (*The Art of Biblical Narrative* [New York: Basic Books, 1981], 32). Yerushalmi remarks in a related context that the "novel perception" regarding human history as the site of divine revelation and activity "was not the result of philosophical speculation, but of the peculiar nature of Israelite faith. It emerged out of an intuitive and revolutionary understanding of God, and was refined through profoundly felt historical experiences.... Suddenly, as it were, the crucial encounter between man and the divine shifted away from the realm of nature and the cosmos to the plane of history, conceived now in terms of divine challenge and human response" (*Zakhor: Jewish History and Jewish Memory* [Seattle: University of Washington Press, 1982], 8). The Book of Job, however, offers no sense of "history" as the primary locus of divine revelation.

takes obvious pride.[51] What is most radical in the Book of Job, in short, or what is most threatening to postexilic Jewish consciousness bound to the core concepts of covenantal election and the rigors of legal observance is not that the God of Israel is impotent, though that would be challenge enough and a real fear in the wake of the Exile where God could not defend his people from the Babylonian invaders.[52] Rather, what is most radical and most threatening is that the God of Israel, newly (re)imagined in the postexilic world as the one and only god of the cosmos, the creator of all things and master of existence, is no different from the life-cycle god of the pagans—merely the Hebraic version of the Greek "artist-god" of Nietzsche's *Birth of Tragedy*.[53] The Book of

---

51 Here is just one of the many examples of how Job's God (the Voice from the Whirlwind) glories in his own creation even or especially when it involves the intermingling (we might think of it as the constant oscillation) of life and death:

"[27] Does the eagle soar at your command, // Building his nest high, // [28] Dwelling in the rock, // Lodging upon the fastness of a jutting rock? // [29] From there he spies out his food; // From afar his eyes see it. // [30] His young gulp blood; // Where the slain are, there is he." (39:27–30)

52 Translated into Jewish historical terms, Job asks why those who faithfully adhere to the terms of the covenant will not receive any particular rewards for their fidelity and why they should follow the covenant at all if there is no guarantee that Yahweh will fulfill (or will be able to fulfill) his promises. And there would be a series of related, unanswerable questions. What does it mean to be the chosen people if God's special favorites suffer just like everyone else? What good is the covenant, its promises, God himself, and who for that matter is this God who chose the people of Israel? What does God's choosing even mean, and does it mean anything at all if it can so easily come to nothing? In Žižek's terms, the Jews living under Persian imperial rule would then have had to admit that they were truly and irreversibly "abandoned by God" (131) or even worse, that God had never been there to begin with (so less an impotent god than a fictional one).

53 So Nietzsche writes in his opening "Attempt at a Self-Criticism":

"In fact, the entire book knows only one overt and implied artistic meaning behind all events—a "god," if you will, but certainly only an entirely thoughtless and amoral artist-god, who in both creating and destroying, in doing both good and ill, wishes to experience that same joy and glory; who, creating worlds, rids himself of the affliction of abundance and super-abundance, of the suffering of his internal contradictions. The world: at every moment the successful redemption of God, the ever-changing, ever-new vision of the most afflicted, contrary, contradictory being." (*The Birth of Tragedy: Out of the Spirit of Music*, ed. Michael Tanner, trans, Shaun Whiteside [London: Penguin Books, 1993], 8; original italics deleted)

The Hebraic artist-god of the Book of Job is rather more interesting in that he takes perpetual delight in what he has created. In that context, we might understand God's boasting of Job to the Satan in the book's opening chapter as quite genuine. God has designed humankind to have both the practical capacity for moral goodness and the imaginative capacity to articulate the concept of justice in an abstract sense, to believe

Job thus goes much further than Žižek suggests in its challenging the very notion of God that most of the Hebrew Bible portrays or at least imagines itself portraying. To put this another way, the book exposes what had been visible in the biblical narrative all along though quite thoroughly repressed: that, as Harold Bloom once so aptly put it as a description of the god-figure on display in the so-called Book of J, "Yahweh is ... just the name for reality."[54] And reality (though worthy of being proclaimed the one true god) does not make covenants or promises or recognize right and wrong or institutionalize law or choose a people as its own.

Following Žižek, we might say that what the Book of Job does more than any other book in the Hebrew Bible is reveal the "split" in the narrative "between the official / public text and its obscene initiatory supplement," the gap between what it wants to reveal and what it can't help revealing even in the very effort to conceal.[55] That said, while Žižek associates the "obscene supplement" with the operations of the Unconscious (manifested particularly in the superego's effort to "mask ... the big Other"), at times the biblical text quite explicitly puts the gap on display. For example, the Book of Job's closing image of Job receiving from God a series of rewards for his uprightness even in the face of suffering—"The LORD restored Job's fortunes ..., and the LORD gave Job twice what he had before.... Thus the LORD blessed the latter years of Job's life more than the former" (42:10, 12)—appears to be the final mockery (the obscene supplement) of the (official) Deuteronomistic perspective. The fairytale ending in which God bestows health, prosperity, long-life, and, most shockingly, ten replacement children on the morally deserving Job so blatantly disregards everything we have encountered from the opening verse to 42:9 that we can only imagine the author as taking deliberate aim at the vision of life promoted in the Ezra-tradition. Precisely by presenting that tradition in such hyperbolic terms (now the "blameless" Job receives *extra* rewards for his proper conduct), the book's final eight verses force us to see just how false the basic concept is. (The replacement "sevens sons and three daughters" [42:13] is undoubtedly the most obscene part of the final rewards.) The morally deserving (whether individuals like Job or the Judaeans as a whole) do not typically experience

that justice *should* exist even to the point of questioning why it appears to be all too often absent from life. In short, God creates humankind in such a way that it is able to discern the discrepancy between what is and what ought to be. Job's God loves this part of humankind—takes pride in it—just as he loves and takes pride in the eagle that kills its prey without remorse.

54 *The Book of J*, trans. David Rosenberg (New York: Vintage Books, 1990), 286.

55 *Puppet and the Dwarf*, 127.

their lives in that way; indeed, as Job himself observes, they are just as likely to suffer as to prosper. Just as important, the Book of Job ventures that God is less a bystander of that suffering than its cause and so not a being to be trusted to fulfill his promises. In terms of the history on display in the biblical narrative more broadly, the postexilic writings particularly show the split between official and supplemental caused by the Exile (what can be admitted vs. what cannot) even as they typically (but not always) deny the split by claiming that the Exile was part of God's plan all along and, in that form, was inseparable from the fulfillment of the covenant rather than a repudiation. As Freud muses towards the beginning of Part III, "it might not have been easy for [the] people to reconcile their belief in their being preferred before all others by an all-powerful God with the dire experiences of their sad fate. But they did not let doubts assail them"—the Book of Job might refute this particular claim—"and perhaps in the end they referred to 'God's unfathomable will,' as religious people do to this day" (*Moses and Monotheism*, 79).

Returning to Freud's own account, we might note Žižek's approving comment that *Moses and Monotheism* aims finally to reconstruct the "spectral history that haunts the space of Jewish religious tradition," a haunting we have explored in terms of Freud's attempt via the lens of psychoanalysis to unearth that tradition's sustaining, if unconsciously held, "compulsive conviction." Žižek adds that what Freud especially succeeded in demonstrating is that "one becomes a full member of a community not simply by identifying with its explicit symbolic tradition, but only when one also assumes … the secret history of traumatic fantasies transmitted 'between the lines,' through the lacks and distortions of the explicit symbolic tradition." Drawing on this theoretical perspective as the general framework for understanding Freud's final verdict on Jewish history, Žižek concludes that

> Judaism's stubborn attachment to the unacknowledged violent founding gesture that haunts the public legal order as its spectral supplement enabled the Jews to persist and survive for thousands of years without land or a common institutional tradition: they refused to give up their ghost, to cut off the link to their secret disavowed tradition. The paradox of Judaism is that it maintains fidelity to the founding violent Event precisely by not confessing, symbolizing it: this "repressed" status of the Event is what gives Judaism its unprecedented vitality.[56]

56 *Puppet and the Dwarf*, 128.

While implicit in this statement is a different way of understanding how a tradition once created is passed down from one generation to the next, in its fundamentals Žižek is here in accord with Freud's answer to "the question of the origin of monotheism among the Jews" and, more particularly, to how that origin is inseparable from the solution to "the problem [of] how [the Jewish people] could survive until today" (*Moses and Monotheism*, 80–81, 176).

Yet Žižek's full interpretive context should give us pause. For even as his phrase "secret history of traumatic fantasies" recalls Freud's own claim in *Moses and Monotheism* that, at the beginning of Jewish history, "the people passed through what may be properly termed a traumatic experience" (64–65), other phrases in the passage just quoted suggest that he is following Freud's account in another, more problematic way. Indeed, the phrases "the unacknowledged violent founding gesture," "their secret disavowed tradition," and "the founding violent Event" that could not be directly confessed because unconsciously "repressed" all point to the originary traumatic event as Freud himself had hypothesized it, an event that Žižek so reflexively replicates from Freud's account that he cannot even be bothered to put it in its own sentence. And so Žižek begins his summary of Freud's conclusions in *Moses and Monotheism* as follows: "What Freud endeavors to reconstitute in *Moses and Monotheism* (the story of the murder of Moses, etc.) …" The parenthetical addition with the closing "etc." says it all: Freud's hypothesis, itself borrowed from Sellin, regarding the murder of Moses as "the founding violent event" and thus as the very (traumatic) origin both of Jewish monotheism and of Jewish culture as a whole requires no theoretical elaboration or even the effort to acknowledge just how historically suspect Freud's claim actually is. It is as though the murder and the ensuing trauma were simply established facts and recognized as such.[57]

As I have argued first against Caruth and now against Žižek (though many others could be included in this list), the Babylonian Exile has a much better claim on the phrase "founding violent Event." Part of the conceptual resistance to focusing on this much more obvious choice—beyond question an "event" and one fully attested in both history and the biblical narrative, a "founding" in the sense that it clearly established something new in Jewish history, and indisputably violent (this needs no explanation except to say that the founding and the violence go together)—is that the Exile is all too openly acknowledged and so not repressed in the way Freud saw as a necessary aspect of Judaism's

57 In much the same vein Žižek subsequently and all too casually suggests that the early Jewish community was mysteriously "formed and held together through the mechanism described by Freud in … *Moses and Monotheism*[,] … *the shared guilt of parricide*" (130; my emphasis).

capacity to compel belief against all reason. But, as I have also argued, the Exile was acknowledged and denied simultaneously; or, more accurately, while the facts of the Exile and its aftermath (including ongoing colonial occupation in the Jewish homeland) were never denied, their meaning was in various ways psychically deflected or disavowed, unassimilated, unclaimed, unacknowledged precisely because, for all the reasons we have considered, their terrifying implications were the very site of a cultural trauma.

Nevertheless, following Freud's own argument Žižek is still correct in calling attention to the "paradox" inhabiting this disavowed, if never truly secret, tradition, a paradox through which, by "maintain[ing] fidelity to the founding violent Event," Judaism and Jewish culture more broadly have been able to sustain their "unprecedented vitality." As a way of demonstrating this point especially in relation to the emergence and development of Jewish *tradition* as Freud understood that term, we might by way of concluding this chapter consider a single post-biblical example from among an endless number of choices, part of the lament from the liturgy for Tisha B'Av (the ninth of Ab), a day of fasting in commemoration primarily of the destruction of the First and Second Temples:

> A fire kindles within me as I recall—*when I left Egypt*,
> But I raise laments as I remember—*when I left Jerusalem*.
>
> Moses sang a song that would not be forgotten—*when I left Egypt*,
> Jeremiah mourned and cried out in grief—*when I left Jerusalem*.
>
> The sea-waves pounded but stood up like a wall—*when I left Egypt*,
> The waters overflowed and ran over my head—*when I left Jerusalem*.
>
> Moses led me and Aaron guided me—*when I left Egypt*,
> Nebuchadnezzar and the Emperor Hadrian—*when I left Jerusalem*.[58]

Yerushalmi's comment on the passage is particularly instructive as a way of understanding the workings of Jewish collective memory especially as regards the Babylonian Exile (marked here both in the reference to Nebuchadnezzar and in the repeated "*when I left Jerusalem*," though that leaving of Jerusalem is also connected to the Roman Hadrian's expulsion of the Jewish population from the national homeland following the Bar Kochba revolt):

---

58 Qtd. in Yerushalmi, *Zakhor*, 43. Yerushalmi notes that the author of the lament … is not known," though "the poem appears in many liturgies" (118n27).

> It is the antiphony of the hammering refrain that first catches our attention. The "memory" of being exiled from Jerusalem is established and heightened by a repeatedly inverted comparison with the exodus from Egypt, the archetypal locus of Jewish historical references.... [T]he lament is almost devoid of any historical details. That which is remembered here transcends the recollection of any particular episode in an ancient catastrophe. It is rather the realization of the structural contrast in Jewish historical experience, built around the dramatic polarity of two great historical "departures" (Egypt / Jerusalem—Exodus / Exile), each with its obvious though unstated clusters of meanings and implications. Most striking of all is the continual speech in the first person singular ("I left Egypt"; "I left Jerusalem") in lieu of the ancestral "they" or even a collective "we." We should be quite mistaken, I think, were we to attribute this usage merely to the liberties of poetic diction. The deliberate uses of the "I" is more serious than that, and it points to a larger phenomenon.[59]

Minimally, that "larger phenomenon" is the communal ritualization of the past in Jewish consciousness whereby an event as ancient, and so disconnected, from the speakers' present as the Exile is (re)imagined as having happened to the speakers themselves. What they never directly experienced, in short, is represented as though it were part of their own memory, the distant past not distant at all but an ongoing reality for those who had never lived through it.

To draw once again on Caruth's effort to apply Freud's "accident trauma" to Jewish history, traumatic neurosis is not simply "the reaction to any horrible event, but rather, [to] the peculiar and perplexing experience of survival. If the dreams and flashbacks of the traumatized"—that is, the compulsions to return to the site of the trauma—"engage Freud's interest, it is because they bear witness to a survival that exceeds the very claims and consciousness of the one who endures it." In short, "the repetition at the heart of catastrophe ... emerges as the unwitting reenactment of an event that one simply cannot leave behind."[60] Read in conjunction with Yerushalmi's "larger phenomenon," what Caruth understands as traumatic excess does not involve the forgetting (the dissociative missing) of the original event—in this case the forced leaving of Jerusalem and exile from the homeland more broadly, which were never forgotten. Rather, the excess lay in the incomprehensibility of the *survival* of the

59 *Zakhor*, 43–44.
60 *Unclaimed Experience*, 61, 2.

Exile ("I left Jerusalem"), an event that, as measured by the incessant, indeed relentless need to return to it, could never simply be left behind.

Yerushalmi's point permits us to see how and why traumatic neurosis functions at a cultural level. For, as regards the self-fashioning at the heart of Jewish identity, Caruth's traumatized "one" is always simultaneously individual and collective, even as past and present are fused within the dual figure. The "I" in "I left Jerusalem," that is, marks how the Jewish individual belongs to a greater whole (the chosen people) and is always participating in a past that is ever-alive in the present. But the very need to return—both return to the past and rhetorically return in the form of the liturgy's "hammering refrain"—is obsessive precisely because the trauma, originating not in Moses' murder but in the Exile, has never truly been resolved.

Freud himself understood that "the doctrine that the Jews were [God's] chosen people" as central to their survival "until today as an entity," a mindset that "kept the scattered people together," their almost miraculous way of "defy[ing] oppression" so "that even the most cruel persecutions have not succeeded in exterminating them" (*Moses and Monotheism*, 79, 176, 147, 116). Caruth is thus absolutely correct in remarking that "Jewish monotheism, as the sense of chosenness, thus defines Jewish history around the link between survival and a traumatic history that exceeds their grasp."[61] And she is right again to say that what exceeds their grasp is "the sense of being incomprehensibly chosen by God to survive," an incomprehensibility clearly expressed through the pairing of "I left Egypt" / "I left Jerusalem." But she is wide of the mark in her insistence that the incomprehensibility of chosenness and survival emerges "after" (and she might have added in response to or in consequence of) "the return of the repressed murder of Moses."[62] Caruth actually speaks more wisely than she knows in observing how in response to a traumatic event the mind "can do nothing but repeat *the destructive event* over and over again." For, as she concludes, "the history of the traumatized individual"—or in the case of Jewish identity, the history of the traumatized culture—"is nothing other than the determined repetition of *the event of destruction*."[63] But the "determined repetition" of "I left Egypt" / "I left Jerusalem" points not to the murder but to the Exile as the "event of destruction"—what Žižek should have recognized in his apt phrase "founding violent Event"—that would ever-after, as what Freud himself called "an unlaid ghost" (132), exceed the claims of collective Jewish (un)consciousness. More accurately, the "traumatic experience" that

61 *Unclaimed Experience*, 67.
62 *Unclaimed Experience*, 68.
63 *Unclaimed Experience*, 63; my emphases.

truly founded the Jewish people was less the Exile than what followed in its wake, the paired incomprehensibility of chosenness and survival. To draw on Caruth one last time, the origin of the trauma coincident with the origin of monotheism among the Jews was "not simply a fact of the past but the experience of [the people's] being shot into a future ... not entirely [their] own."[64] As Freud amply documented in *Moses and Monotheism*, the paradox is that this experience of dispossession has been, from the standpoint of Jewish culture, disabling and enabling simultaneously.

At the close of a subtle and at times moving reflection on the impact on Jewish, Christian, and Muslim sensibilities of modern Israel's annexation of East Jerusalem in the wake of its victory in the Six-Day War, Lawrence Wright comments that "the religious carnage that has marked every era of this maddened city will continue, because whoever controls Jerusalem controls access to the sacred places. It is a way of owning God."[65] Wright's phrase "maddened city" might remind us of the anti-Zionist Freud's own musing in his May, 1932 letter to Zweig on the "heritage from this land [Israel] we have taken over into our blood and nerves," a heritage Freud thought well in excess of the land's actual historical importance.[66] Wright's remark that the annexation effectively meant that Jerusalem and all it contained and symbolized "would be back in Jewish hands for the first time in nearly two thousand years" might also remind us of the end of the Hebrew Bible with its hope, expressed through the edict of King Cyrus, that the reclamation of Jerusalem from the Babylonian invaders marked the restoration of the people of Israel to God's favor, a restoration that would be especially enacted in the rebuilding of the Temple.[67] For the Jews of Ezra's time and indeed for modern Jews, we might imagine that, to the extent controlling Jerusalem and its sacred places (the Temple in particular) was and is "a way of owning God," such ownership was and is *consciously* understood in just the opposite way: living in the land God first promised in the covenant made with Abraham meant and means that God has fulfilled his side of the bargain, a fulfillment demonstrating without the nagging doubt brought on by exile that Abraham's descendants were—and still are—God's chosen people.

---

64 *Unclaimed Experience*, 71.

65 "Letter from Jerusalem: Forcing the End," *The New Yorker*, July 20, 1998, 53.

66 *Letters of Sigmund Freud and Arnold Zweig*, 40.

67 For a rich discussion of the biblical narrative's complex understanding of the land of Israel, see Regina M. Schwartz, *The Curse of Cain: The Violent Legacy of Monotheism* (Chicago: University of Chicago Press, 1997), ch. 2 ("Owning Identity: Land").

CODA 2

The Christian Unconscious: Pauline Disavowal

> The future is no future without this anticipation and the inner compulsion for it, without this "wish to bring about the Messiah before his time" and the temptation to "coerce the kingdom of God into being"; without these, it is only a past distended endlessly and projected forward. For without such anticipation, the moment is not eternal; it is something that drags itself everlastingly along the long, long trail of time.
>
> —FRANZ ROSENZWEIG, *The Star of Redemption*

∵

In section 3 of the preceding chapter, I offered three examples of the way the cultural trauma of the Babylonian Captivity was disavowed in the postexilic biblical tradition. (We might even say the trauma was sustained, in part at least, in the very act of disavowing it.) I would now like to add a fourth example, which, though it has an obvious share in that tradition and in fact derives directly from it, would have been out of place in the chapter proper because it comes not from the Hebrew Bible but from the New Testament. While this example might be said to be coincident with Christianity as a whole—in a very real sense Christianity might be understood as an elaborate disavowal of everything the Exile represented in postexilic Jewish culture—after laying out some of the basic history, my primary focus here will be the particular formulation of the disavowal on display in the writings of Saint Paul.

Before taking up that Pauline formulation, I want to provide contextualization in the form of two crisis-points of first-century Christianity (at this stage in history more properly termed Jewish-Christianity or messianic Judaism). I aim to demonstrate by these examples how an event from the distant past (the Exile of the sixth century BCE) could be reactivated in the new cultural setting. The trauma was reactivated, moreover, and so needed to be disavowed yet again, precisely because the circumstances giving rise to it had never truly been resolved; to borrow from Freud's famous phrasing, postexilic Jewish culture remained in a very real sense "fixated to the trauma" (*Beyond the Pleasure Principle*, SE, 18:13). Over many centuries the Judaeans' experience of

 DOI:10.1163/9789004701663_006

the trauma oscillated between a kind of dormancy and more open expression depending on the particular situation in which they found themselves.

For example, while there were undoubtedly long stretches under Persian and then Greek rule during which the population of Judaea effectively settled into its colonized condition and even thrived under it, the Hellenization project that came to a head under the Seleucid Greek ruler Antiochus IV didn't just provoke political rebellion (the Maccabean uprising that led to the brief period of national independence under the Hasmoneans) but, prior to the end of the rebellion, also prompted the writing of the apocalyptic Book of Daniel. To the extent Antiochus's efforts repeated key elements of the Babylonian invasion (while there was no equivalent to the Exile, the Seleucids took Jerusalem after a siege, slaughtered thousands, and desecrated if they did not destroy the Temple—according to Josephus' *War of the Jews*, the Greeks forced the priests to sacrifice pigs upon the Temple altar), the Book of Daniel can be understood, in broad terms at least, as responding to the Antiochene crisis in much the same way earlier writers had responded to similar situations: by at once acknowledging the traumatic moment and denying or otherwise deflecting it. Thus, while Daniel portrays the violation of the Temple (9:27, 11:31, 12:11) as an abomination, it is an abomination worthy of divine intervention in history through the power of the Son of Man (chapter 7) and, later, of the prince and protector, Michael (chapter 12). The horror of the threat of complete cultural assimilation is, in effect, turned around in Daniel's end-time vision precisely to the extent the threat pushes God to act to restore his people to the promises of the covenant (the Son of Man figure is less a Davidic messiah than an allegorical representation of Israel itself as a beloved human being in opposition to the beastliness of the non-Jewish empires whose historical line will end with the hoped-for Judaean triumph over the Seleucids). As Daniel portrays it, if the crisis is very real, so too will be the resolution, one that famously includes the sole reference in the Hebrew Bible to bodily resurrection (Daniel 12:2) as the fullest manifestation of divine justice and a fitting marker of what the close of Daniel simply calls "the time of the end" (12:9) and then "the end of the days" (12:12).

The brief period of Hasmonean rule would, of course, abruptly end with the arrival of yet another beast, this time in the form of Pompey the Great's Roman legions (ca. 63 BCE). As Roman imperial domination led, after another failed rebellion, to yet another siege of Jerusalem and later, after the Bar Kochba revolt, to yet another exile, the national trauma would come back with a vengeance.[1] After the failure of the first revolt with its terrible reminder of the

1 In one of the verses from the liturgy for Tisha B'Av (a day of fasting in commemoration primarily of the destruction of the First and Second Temples) I quoted in Chapter 2, there is a

Babylonian invasion—both Jerusalem and the Temple were destroyed by the Romans in 70 CE—Jewish culture faced a crisis of self-definition: what is the source of Judaic faith, without the priesthood, what is the structure of Judaic authority, what is it that God wants? Venturing a conceptual parallel between situation faced by Job and that of the dying Jesus of Mark's gospel who, borrowing from Psalm 22, despondently asks, "My god, my god, why have you forsaken me?" (Mark 15:34), Slavoj Žižek remarks that this is "not a complaint to the *omnipotent* capricious God-Father whose ways are indecipherable to us, mortal humans, but a complaint that hints at an *impotent* God: it is rather like a child who, having believed in his father's powerfulness, discovers with horror that his father cannot help him."[2] It is worth noting, because Žižek himself does not, that the feeling of abandonment Mark's expresses through the forsaken Jesus derives primarily from the fact that the Second Temple had just been destroyed and, once again, God had done nothing to save it or his people. The image of an absent Jesus with which Mark ends his Gospel ("he has been raised; *he is not here*" [16:6; my emphasis]) makes the resurrected Jesus complicit: even as the enemy of the chosen people destroyed the House of God, the Messiah too had been inexplicably elsewhere. The gospel-tradition as we now have that in the New Testament begins as a response to this catastrophe: the author of Mark (the first of the gospels) aims not to tell the story of the life of Jesus so much as to use that story to explain a cultural crisis that is also a crisis of religious faith. From Mark's point of view, the destruction of the Temple was not some terrible mistake or some incomprehensible moment; rather, God permitted the destruction of the Temple (his own house)—in this, Mark's God is very much like Ezekiel's God whose glory or *kavod* departs from the Temple in advance of the Babylonian takeover of Jerusalem (Ezekiel 10)—because Jesus himself (God's anointed) stood against the Temple or at least

direct link made across the more than seven-century gap between the Babylonians and the Romans as enemies of Israel:

"Moses led me and Aaron guided me—*when I left Egypt,* // Nebuchadnezzar and the Emperor Hadrian—*when I left Jerusalem.*"

The association here between Nebuchadnezzar and Hadrian has less to do with the destruction of the two temples than with exile from the homeland ("when I left Jerusalem"). Jerusalem itself and the Temple had been destroyed by the Romans during the reign of Vespasian (70 CE) whereas Hadrian, whose reconstruction of Jerusalem as a Roman city and his plan to build a temple dedicated to Jupiter on the Temple Mount had prompted the Bar Kochba revolt, was responsible for the retaliatory banishment of Jews from Jerusalem and the large-scale depopulation of other Judaean communities.

2 *The Puppet and the Dwarf: The Perverse Core of Christianity* (Cambridge, MA: MIT Press, 2003), 126.

against the Temple priesthood who had in their own way, as Mark depicts it, already desecrated it.[3]

If for Mark's community the focus of the trauma was the loss of the Temple and the the risen Christ's inexplicable absence, even before the First Roman War followers of Jesus faced a different though related crisis: how to explain Jesus' death or, more abstractly, to explain the meaning of the death of God's anointed. In short, if Jesus really was the messiah, why did he have to die? While the retrospective reconstruction of the expectation, even the necessity, of Jesus' suffering and death clearly drew on (Deutero-)Isaiah's portrait of the suffering servant (Isaiah 52:13–53:12), that portrait didn't connect the servant-figure to the messiah and in fact appears to have understood the servant-figure as an allegory for the nation of Israel itself in its condition of exile. The difference suggests that, as the tradition of Jesus-as-messiah developed among Jewish-Christians after the crucifixion, writers within the tradition intentionally searched the Hebrew scriptures for some anticipatory moment (an explanation that could be read as prophecy) that they could then align with the idea of the messiah, a role for which Jesus' very death at the hands of the Romans would, by definition, otherwise have disqualified him. In other words, though crucified by the enemies of God's people, Jesus could still be the messiah if God had intended the messiah's suffering and death all along, Jesus knew about his own suffering and death in advance (see Mark 8:31–33, 9:30–32, and 10:32–34), and suffering and death were not incidental to but in fact central aspects of a radically new understanding of messiahship. In the wake of the crucifixion, the task of the messiah was and indeed had to be redefined: now, the messiah was not sent to liberate the nation from foreign domination (Jesus had not even pursued this task, and those who had among the people had failed miserably over and over again) but to usher in something that, while conceptually drawing on a body of political ideas associated with the covenant, could not simply be equated with previous covenantal expectations: that something was the kingdom or reign of God. In short, the disturbing question—why did Jesus

3 The so-called "cleansing of the Temple" scene of Mark 11:15–18 (repeated in Matthew 21:12–16 and Luke 19:45–47) has a non-Markan version in John's gospel (2:13–22). The two versions suggest that the incident goes back to an even earlier tradition, possibly to something the living Jesus actually did in Jerusalem (a challenge to the Temple priests that led to his arrest and execution): for discussion, see John Dominic Crossan, *Jesus: A Revolutionary Biography* (San Francisco: HarperSanFrancisco, 1989), 127–33. We might note that Mark's vision of the "desolating sacrilege" (13:14; part of the mini-apocalypse of chapter 13) not only portrays Jesus predicting the destruction of the Temple, which from Mark's point of view had already taken place, but specifically draws much of its language from the account in the Book of Daniel, which, as noted, was a response to the desecration of the Temple by Antiochus IV.

have to die?—would cease to be disturbing if it had an answer (the messiah *had to* die, was destined to die) that itself restored confidence that God had not abandoned or simply forgotten his people and that, therefore, his promises would one day be and in fact were even now in the process of being fulfilled.

But what specific function did Jesus' crucifixion serve in that fulfillment? While Mark's Jesus foretells his death on three different occasions and specifically links that death to the greatest of all Christian mysteries, the resurrection (in each case Jesus tells his disciples that he will rise "three days" after the crucifixion), there is little in either Mark's gospel or in the other canonical gospels that lays out a doctrinal position on the matter: that is, while death logically precedes resurrection, the four gospels never explain why the glorification that comes with resurrection requires death at all. In the final chapter of his First Letter to the Corinthians, Paul strongly implies that death is not a requirement for others to experience such glorification ("Listen! I will tell you a mystery. We will not all die [literally: fall asleep], but we will all be changed, in a moment, in the twinkling of an eye, at the last trumpet ... the trumpet will sound, ... and we will be changed ... this mortal body must put on immortality" [1 Corinthians 15:51–53]). Nevertheless, he also asserts that the passage through death is not just what precedes glorification but also what makes it possible: "what you sow does not come to life *unless it dies*" (15:36; my emphasis; it should be noted that Paul at times appears to understand death in figural rather than literal terms). In that sense, Jesus' death was necessary (though perhaps not in the cruel form of crucifixion) because it was only through death that Jesus could emerge triumphantly as the risen Christ. Moreover, Jesus' path from death to life could be conceived as a model, even the gateway, for the process of glorification that others would subsequently follow (the "first fruits of those who have died" [15:20]). For Paul, we have a share in the promise of the resurrection only to the extent we also have a share in the death of Jesus that precedes the resurrection and is in some mysterious way its prerequisite.[4]

While he rather vaguely makes this point in 1 Corinthians 15 (e.g. 15:29), Paul is much more explicit about it in this Letter to the Romans:

4 While Paul himself appears to have interpreted the notion of sharing in Jesus' death as a fundamentally positive experience (see, for example, Philippians 2:3–4), others (the author of Mark comes to mind) depict sharing in Jesus' death as meaning or even requiring a literal dying as Jesus had: mocked, in agony, and feeling abandoned by God. The late-first century or early-second century *Epistle of Barnabas* portrays Jesus saying to his followers, "those who wish to see me and touch my kingdom *must take hold of me through pain and suffering*" (*The Apostolic Fathers*, ed. and trans. Bart D. Ehrman, 2 vols. [Cambridge, MA: Harvard University Press, 2003]. 2:41; my emphasis).

> [3] All of us who have been baptized into Christ Jesus were baptized into his death ... [4] Therefore we have been buried with him by baptism into death, so that, just as Christ was raised from the dead by the glory of the Father, so too we might walk in newness of life. [5] For if we have been united with him in a death like his, we will certainly be united with him in a resurrection like his. [6] We know that our old self was crucified with him so that the sinful body might be destroyed, and we might no longer be enslaved to sin. [7] For whoever has died is free from sin. [8] But if we have died with Christ, we believe that we will also live with him. [9] We know that Christ, being raised from the dead, will never die again. [10] The death he died, he died to sin, once for all; but the life he lives, he lives to God. [11] So you must also consider yourselves dead to sin and alive to God in Christ Jesus. (6:3–11)

What is clear from this passage is that, for Paul, the death of Jesus is required not so much for himself but for everyone else: the death that is now part of the job-description of the messiah in a way it had never been previously in Jewish thought is what is required so that we too (at least the true believers among us) can experience resurrection after our own deaths. And we benefit from Jesus' death precisely to the extent that, because death is, since the time of Adam's transgression, inseparable from the sin that is its cause, we are freed from sin by Jesus' death: by dying with Jesus or, as Paul sees it, being baptized into his death and so sharing in the resurrection that is its reward. So understood, Jesus' death was necessary as what Romans 3:25 famously calls Christ's ἱλαστήριον, variously translated as atonement, reconciliation, propitiation, expiation, or even the archaic seat of mercy.[5] As Freud would put it in *Moses and Monotheism*, in Paul's "phantasy of expiation" the innocent Christ "had thereby taken over the guilt of the world" (110). In Romans 5:18, Paul would write that "a single act of righteousness [Christ's atoning sacrifice] leads to acquittal and life for

5 The New Revised Standard Version translates the Greek ἱλαστήριον as "sacrifice of atonement"; the fuller passage reads: "[23] ... since all [people] have sinned and fall short of the glory of God ... [24] they are now justified by his grace as a gift, through the redemption that is in Christ Jesus, [25] whom God put forward as a *sacrifice of atonement by his blood*" (Romans 3:23–25; my emphasis). The KJV translates ἱλαστήριον as "propitiation," the New American Bible as "expiation," the New Jerusalem Bible as "sacrifice of reconciliation." On the NRSV's particular phrasing, although its etymological origin is unclear, the word "atonement"—"a setting or being at one"—appears to be an English neologism. William Tyndale seems to have first applied it to matters of Christian theology in 1526 as a way of translating 2 Corinthians 5:18's καταλλαγής (*OED*, Atonement 1–3); but he translated Romans 3:25's ἱλαστήριον as "seate of mercy."

all men." Or, as he had written earlier in 1 Corinthians 15:22, "as in Adam all die, so also in Christ all shall be made alive." This doctrine of the substitutive value of Christ's death (much like the redemptive quality of the Day of Atonement ritual described in Leviticus 16: Christ dies on our behalf; his innocence redeems our sin) was widely enough held among early Jewish-Christians that, while never put forward in such formal terms in the gospels, it appears as a foundational doctrinal claim elsewhere in the New Testament (see, for example, the Letter to the Hebrews 9:11–28). The larger point is that, once again, we see a crisis turned around to the point of denial: what could have easily led to doubts about God's commitment to the promises of the covenant becomes instead a reason to renew one's faith. Rather than being meaningless—the site of incomprehensibility that defines a trauma—the death of Jesus as the Christ is completely meaningful because, counterintuitive as it might appear, it was central to God's plan for human redemption.

It is within this very broad context that we might return to Paul's efforts to challenge the idea that observance of Mosaic law could lead to the fulfillment of the covenantal promises, an issue we took up in Chapter 1. As we saw there, championing the Abrahamic covenant over the Mosaic covenant and observing that the promise made to Abraham in Genesis 12:3—"all the families of the earth // Shall bless themselves by you"—could yet be fulfilled through faith in Christ rather than through the works of the law, Paul accepts the general principle underlying the Deuteronomistic History (we are sinners / we are to blame for our own suffering) even as he rejects the notion that, through our own actions (works or a rigorous recommittal to the Law), we might be restored to divine favor. Paul shares with Ezra and most of the postexilic writings the hope of future redemption (in the spirit of Isaiah 2 and 56 now extended to Gentile believers as well), but this redemption is imminent for Paul precisely because, with Christ's resurrection, the apocalyptic clock has starting ticking; hence, in sharp contrast to the patience of the Ezra-tradition (a tradition in which he locates himself as one zealous for the Law [Galatians 1:14, Philippians 3:6]), Paul is impatient: a fundamental sense of urgency governs his mission to the Gentiles, and his goal of reaching Spain appears to have represented in his mind the completion of human history itself. That very urgency suggests at once genuine expectation and a kind of desperation as though time were running out in both senses: the kingdom of God is at hand and, if this is not the promised end, then everything we have ever believed is meaningless. Paul's own frenetic energy in support of the former position (the time of the end is upon us: 1 Thessalonians 4–5 and elsewhere) might be understood then as commitment and terror simultaneously: Paul acts (he *needs* to act) in part to deny what he most fears—if the revelation made manifest in the risen Christ isn't real, then, as he laments in 1 Corinthians 15, "our preaching is useless and so is your faith ... and we are of all people the most to be pitied" (15:14, 19). And by "faith" Paul doesn't just mean faith in the messianic Jesus but Judaism—the covenantal religion—more broadly. Paul's fervent, oft-expressed conviction of an imminent end time thus aims to forget that God's promises are easily broken precisely by acting in a way (we might call it a desperate attempt) to fulfill those promises, to force the end by his very mission among the uncircumcised: when he gets to Spain, the general resurrection will begin.[6] It is in this context that Paul can imagine himself not just as God's servant but effectively as his coworker (1 Corinthians 3:9). And as a coworker (not just one who proclaims the revelation but also enacts its meaning) he can disavow the vexing question lurking in postexilic Jewish history: if we cannot trust God to keep his promises, how can we believe that we were ever chosen?

Although different from the Torah-committed Ezra in so many ways (for Paul, for example, circumcision, the very sign of the covenant, "is nothing," though the opposite is also true: "uncircumcision is nothing" [1 Corinthians 7:19], Paul is akin to Ezra in his determination to make the very weak point of faith (doubt about God's own fidelity to his own people) into the very driving force of (re)commitment. Just as Ezra recommitted to his faith through the act of reinterpreting its texts and traditions and then applying the newly

6 Capturing the special inflections of Paul's understanding, Žižek argues that

> "the shift from Judaism to Christianity with regard to the Event is best encapsulated in terms of the status of the Messiah: in contrast to Jewish messianic expectation, the basic Christian stance is that the expected Messiah has arrived, that is, we are already redeemed: the time of nervous expectation, of rushing precipitously toward the expected Arrival, is over; we live in the aftermath of the Event: everything—the Big Thing—has already happened. Paradoxically, ... the result of this Event is not atavism ("It has already happened, we are redeemed, so let us just rest and wait ..."), but, on the contrary, an extreme urge to act: it has happened, so now we have to bear the almost unbearable burden of living up to it, of drawing the consequences of the Act.... [T]hrough the Event (of Christ) we are formally redeemed, subsumed under Redemption, and we have to engage in the difficult work of actualizing it.... What this means, in theological terms, is that it is not we humans who can rely on the help of God—on the contrary, we must help God."

What Žižek refers to as Paul's "extreme urge to act" has a neurotic dimension that is especially marked in the strangely vexed temporality in many of Paul's descriptions of the task at hand: an "already but not just yet" or a "both now and soon" or a "it is done but the time is still short" or a "the work is completed but there is much work left to do." For if Paul feels the "almost unbearable burden" of acting in response to a redemption that has already happened, this is partly because only by acting can he sustain the belief that it actually has happened. Žižek effectively gets at the core of the Pauline complex in remarking that "the Event [of the resurrection] is a pure empty-sign, and we have to work to generate its meaning. 'The Messiah is here'—this summarizes the terrible risk of revelation" (135–37; original italics deleted).

reinterpreted terms to contemporary circumstances (recall, for example, his ruling based on his reading of Torah that Judaean men must divorce their non-Jewish wives [Ezra 9–10]), so Paul too came to a new understanding of what the covenant meant through acts of reinterpretation that aimed to reveal its true meaning: what it has always meant if never truly understood until the advent of the messianic age.[7]

As a way of exploring the centrality of (re)interpretation to the construction of Pauline doctrine (and Pauline doctrine itself as yet another instance of the disavowal of postexilic trauma), we might note, first, that Paul's letters have no first-hand account of the conversion experience (the Road to Damascus story) that the author of the Acts of the Apostles narrates on three separate occasions: 9:1–22, 22:1–21, 26:2–23. While Paul alludes to a conversion experience (see Galatians 1:11–24), he provides almost no specifics of his own; rather, the impetus to his conversion is what in Galatians 1:12 he simply calls a revelation (Greek: ἀποκαλύψεως), a word he uses on several occasions in his letters.[8] And what in 1 Corinthians 15 has normally been taken to refer to apparitions of the resurrected Jesus—

> [5] … he [Jesus] appeared [Greek: ὤφθη] to Cephas, then to the twelve. [6] Then he appeared [ὤφθη] to more than five hundred brothers and sisters at one time, … [7] Then he appeared [ὤφθη] to James, then to all the apostles. [8] Last of all, … he appeared [ὤφθη] also to me (1 Corinthians 15:5–8)—

would be better understood as referring to epiphanies or acts of comprehension of some kind: a more literal and indeed a better translation of the Greek ὤφθη would be "was revealed to," which does not suggest an actual visitation of

---

7 It is in this context that the following comment by Žižek is properly understood:

"[O]ne should read Paul from within the Jewish tradition—since precisely such a reading brings home the true radicality of his break, the way he undermined Jewish tradition from within.… [R]eading Saint Paul from within the Jewish tradition … allows us to grasp "Christianity-in-becoming": not yet the established positive dogma, but the violent gesture of positing it, the "vanishing mediator" between Judaism and Christianity … Paul did not simply pass from the Jewish position to another position; he did something with, within, and to the Jewish position." (10)

8 Paul at times uses the word (apocalypse) in a very generic sense as making something known: 1 Corinthians 1:7 and 14:26, for example. But at other times he uses it to refer to a direct communication from God of some type, though often not always intended for Paul personally: see 1 Corinthians 14:6; 2 Corinthians 12:1, 7; Romans 2:5 and 16:25; Galatians 1:12 and 2:2.

the risen Christ. In other words, Paul never says that he or anyone else actually "saw" the resurrected Jesus in the way we normally imagine.[9]

Just as important, what the preceding two verses of 1 Corinthians 15 tell us about Paul's own particular "revelation" is that it was something he received in the form of an idea from others and most likely one that derived from the reinterpretation of Hebrew scriptures as that could be applied to new beliefs about the life, death, and afterlife of Jesus of Nazareth: "[3] For *I handed on to you as of first importance what I in turn had received*: that Christ died for our sins *in accordance with the scriptures*, [4] and that he was buried, and that he was raised on the third day *in accordance with the scriptures*" (1 Corinthians 15:3–4; my emphases). While it is not immediately clear what Paul means by alluding to the scriptural basis of his "on the third day" phrasing, the most likely source is Hosea 6:1–2:

> [1] Come, let us turn back to the LORD:
> He attacked, and He can heal us;
> He wounded, and He can bind us up.
> [2] In two days He will make us whole again;
> *On the third day He will raise us up*,
> And we shall be whole by His favor. (my emphasis)

Within the patterns of prophetic discourse, Hosea's image of God raising up his people "on the third" day is probably meant only to signify *sooner rather than later*: maybe not immediately—the first day—or even very soon—the second day; God will act when he will act, but he will not make us wait forever (be prepared: the third day is coming). "On the third day" is still figural rather than literal for Paul; we should associate it with his equally famous phrasing for the unexpectedness of the "day of the Lord," which "will come like a thief in the night" (1 Thessalonians 5:2). (It is Mark who will create the actual narrative concept of three days between the crucifixion and the resurrection [16:2], a time-gap he aligns with Jesus' thrice-given prophecy that three days after his

9 No doubt Paul has been understood as referring to an actual visitation because of the post-resurrection accounts we find in Matthew 28, Luke 24, and John 20–21, though these too could easily be interpreted in figural terms: not statements of Jesus' literal appearance but symbolic representations of his abiding presence in the different communities represented in those three gospels. The Road to Emmaus story in Luke 24, for example, clearly aims to suggest that Jesus is still present to the community in the paired forms of scriptural interpretation and the ritual practice of the Eucharistic meal; when these are performed, the eyes of the two disciples are "opened, and they recognize" Jesus, who then "vanishe[s] from their sight" (24:31).

death he will rise again.[10]) But Hosea's description of God's "rais[ing] us up" will become decidedly literal for Paul in a way it might not have been for other early Christians.

To get a sense of the full implications of what Paul intends by saying that Jesus "was raised on the third day in accordance with the scriptures," we might consider a brief passage in Philippians 2. Verses 6–11 are generally understood to be an already existing unit that Paul simply quotes, a pre-Pauline prayer or hymn that he likely learned from a community he had visited during his missionary work. We might even go so far as to speculate that what actually converted Paul to the "the Way" (the very movement he had previously been persecuting) was his encounter with a proclamation concerning the post-crucifixion "living Jesus" that likely took liturgical form (that is, as a prayer or hymn). Whatever such a proclamation originally asserted (and it's worth noting that Philippians 2:6–11 do not refer specifically to Jesus' resurrection but only to his glorification as "Lord") was (re)interpreted by Paul as meaning that the living Jesus (or the once-dead-but-now-living Jesus) had been raised from the dead. That would be a concept a Pharisee (if that is what Paul was) might have been ready to accept as a prophetic fulfillment of Hosea 6:2 if he had first been convinced of its factual reality, if, in short, that had been his "revelation."[11]

---

10 Mark no doubt had inherited from an early-Christian tradition he shared with Paul the resurrection "on the third day" concept. He then takes what in Paul is formulated as a kind of pre-doctrinal assertion created "in accordance with the scriptures" (probably at this early stage serving more a liturgical than an explicitly theological function) and transforms this assertion into a prophecy that, as noted above, Jesus then makes about himself on three occasions. Mark then invents the scene at the empty tomb (chapter 16) to provide a narrative representation of an actual three days.

11 It is entirely possible that the impetus to Paul's conversion was his sudden apprehension that what members of the Way (people he met in his attempts to persecute the movement) actually meant when they talked about the living Jesus or the abiding presence of Jesus or about "seeing" Jesus or having visions of Jesus or about the imminent return of Jesus (which they may have described by drawing on "the third day" language of Hosea 6:2) was that a man who had been crucified was actually alive. Paul's "apocalypse," in short, was that this Jesus, whom Paul had never met, could only be alive if God had raised him from the dead. As Alain Badiou aptly observes, "in Paul's eyes, without the motif of the Resurrection, Christ's existence would have been of little more importance that that of any other Oriental mystic, however talented." As Badiou subsequently notes, for Paul "Jesus is resurrected; nothing else matters" (*Saint Paul: The Foundation of Universalism*, trans. Ray Brassier [Stanford: Stanford University Press, 2003], 61, 63).

As Paul then extrapolates the notion in 1 Corinthians 15:12–20, if Jesus has been raised, then the general resurrection has been set in motion and thus the time of the end is imminent. And if the death-and-resurrection of the messiah is understood as the beginning of the end time—if it is precisely the messiah's task to initiate the end time by means of his resurrection (God's act of raising him up as a reward for his obedience or what Philippians 2:7 mysteriously refers to as his act of "self-emptying" [*kenosis*])—then the true task of the messiah (Christ Jesus) is to defeat death itself:

> [20] But in fact Christ has been raised from the dead, the first fruits of those who have fallen asleep. [21] For as by a man came death, by a man has come also the resurrection of the dead. [22] For as in Adam all die, so also in Christ shall all be made alive. [23] But each in his own order: Christ the first fruits, then at his coming those who belong to Christ. [24] *Then comes the end, when he delivers the kingdom to God the Father after destroying every rule and every authority and power.* [25] *For he must reign until he has put all his enemies under his feet.* [26] *The last enemy to be destroyed is death.* (1 Corinthians 15:20–26; my emphasis)

Drawing out the logic of the original covenantal proclamation made to Abraham (Genesis 12:3), Paul concludes that the divine blessing intended for "all the families of the earth"—Paul will rephrase as "all the Gentiles shall be blessed in you" (Galatians 3:8)—is precisely what had been denied to humankind because of the Fall:

> [22] And the LORD God said, "Now that the man has become like one of us, knowing good and bad, what if he should *stretch out his hand and take also from the tree of life and eat, and live forever*!" [23] So the LORD God banished him from the garden of Eden, to till the soil from which he was taken. [24] He drove the man out, and stationed east of the garden of Eden the cherubim and the fiery ever-turning sword, to guard the way to the tree of life. (Genesis 3:22–24; my emphasis)

If the blessing of immortality is for everyone (children of the common ancestor, Adam, all living in exile from the paradise God had created as their natural homeland), then it is not the task of the messiah to liberate the people of Israel from Roman oppression. For the "apocalyptic" Paul, the imminent kingdom of God is not merely the restored kingdom of Israel, and the conquest to come does not aim to reestablish God's reign in the Promised Land under the rule of the Davidic messiah-king.[12] Rather, as Paul puts it, the messiah is just the means to the glorious culmination of history and indeed of creation itself:

> [27] "God has put all things in subjection under his feet." But when it says, "all things are put in subjection," it is plain that he is excepted who put all things in subjection under him.[28] When all things are subjected to him, then the Son himself will also be subjected to him who put all things in subjection under him, *that God may be all in all.* (1 Corinthians 15:27–28; my emphasis)

That is the ultimate promise of the covenant even if no one could truly understand it until the Christ "emptied himself" (Greek: ἐκένωσεν);

> and being found in human form,
> he humbled himself
> and became obedient to the point of death—
> even death on a cross. (Philippians 2:7–8)

So reconceptualized, the horror of Jesus' crucifixion, which to one more reasonably minded might have been taken as a powerful demonstration that God had abandoned his anointed one and so also the very people the messiah would be expected to protect, becomes, paradoxically, the beginning of the fulfillment of God's greatest, if until the coming of Jesus unrecognized, promise: the deification of humankind in the form of the imperishable body of the resurrection (see 1 Corinthians 15:35–57).

Paul's claim that the messiah's chief task is to defeat death (not just for himself but for humankind as a whole) at once acknowledges and refuses to fully acknowledge that, at the beginning of human history as the biblical narrative lays it out, we were effectively abandoned by the God who had created us: forced to live in exile from the land (Paradise) he had given as our home and doomed to a death that, as the close of Genesis 3 all but declares, marked an unbridgeable separation from our divine origin. In the very moment of recognizing this truth, Paul envisions the messianic triumph over death—a triumph the consequence of which will be our restoration to a fundamental

12 That is why Paul can say "[26] for in Christ Jesus you are all children of God through faith.... [28] There is no longer Jew or Greek, there is no longer slave or free, there is no longer male and female; for all of you are one in Christ Jesus. [29] And if you belong to Christ, then you are Abraham's offspring, heirs according to the promise" (Galatians 3:26, 28–29).

inseparability from God ("God will be all in all")—as a reversal of history itself: God had never truly abandoned his creation but had planned all along to establish the conditions of our final (comm)union.

At the heart of Paul's theology, then, is a conviction that attempts to deny the all but undeniable reality revealed by the painful lesson of the Exile: God doesn't care about his chosen people. By reinterpreting the scriptures, Paul now sees it differently: God's care is truly manifested in the gift always intended for *all* people. And when at the close of the messianic age God is truly "all in all," the experience of exile—whether that exile is the banishment from Eden or the captivity in Babylon—will mean no more than the ritual of circumcision or adherence to Mosaic law more broadly: which is to say, nothing at all. In a powerful act of disavowal of everything the Jewish past should have taught him, the more Paul believes, the more committed he is, the more real it all becomes.

CHAPTER 3

Torah and / as Tradition

> The life of an individual is measured in years and decades; the life of a culture in centuries and even millennia. A culture maintains its identity by passing on the sum of its values and experiences from one generation to the next. Its memory must be organic and trans-temporal, or else the culture dies or survives only as a hollow shell.
>
> —STEPHEN BERTMAN, *Cultural Amnesia*

•••

> In what exactly consists the intrinsic nature of a tradition, and in what resides its peculiar power, … from what sources certain ideas, especially religious ones, derive their power with which they subjugate individuals and peoples—to study all this in the particular case of Jewish history would be an alluring task.
>
> —FREUD, *Moses and Monotheism*

∵

1

In a moment of wistful reflection near the end of his life, Freud wrote to his son Ernst that "it is typically Jewish not to renounce anything and to replace what has been lost."[1] Although his departure was still more than four months away, Freud may have been anticipating his flight to England from German-occupied Austria (he left Vienna on June 4th). That said, Freud may also have been thinking about Jewish experience more broadly. To the extent his musings on what was "typically Jewish" included the promises of the covenant—land, nationhood and national greatness, divine presence and solicitude (love even), and a special place in human history—Freud was no doubt right at some basic

1 Letter to Ernst Freud (January 17, 1938), *Letters of Sigmund Freud*, ed. Ernst L. Freud, trans. Tania Stern and James Stern (New York: Basic Books, 1960), 440.

 | DOI:10.1163/9789004701663_007

level: devout Jews and even some not so devout tenaciously held onto those promises even in the face of the hard facts of their shared past and present.

Yet at a different level, Freud was clearly wrong. Especially in the transition from preexilic Judah to postexilic Judaea (from the self-ruled national homeland to a minor province in the Persian, Greek, and then Roman empires), Jewish culture, while never renouncing the covenantal promises, did "replace what had been lost." For, as Michel de Certeau rightly observes, "the loss of the ancestral land" was "the precondition of the appearance of the 'Bible,'" and in a different sense the biblical narrative "takes the place of lost prophetic speech."[2] Freud is not even following the terms of his own argument in *Moses and Monotheism*. For one of his main contentions there is that a Mosaic tradition was created precisely as a replacement for (the murdered) Moses himself. Reviewing what he calls the "historical truth" on display in the Moses-Exodus story, Freud explains that his various "psychological digressions" aim "to make it more credible that the religion of Moses exercised influence on the Jewish people only when it had become a tradition" (164). Of course, it is crucial that we then remind ourselves of one of Freud's other contentions: for Judaic monotheism to have become a tradition, it "must first have suffered the fate of repression, that state of being unconscious, before it could produce such mighty effects on its return, and force the masses under its spell" (130). In short, it is only as a consequence of repression and the subsequent return of the repressed in distorted form that Moses' own (Egyptian-Aton) religion could be replaced with "the religion of Moses" or Judaic monotheism. In other words, in the form of a distorted "memory from a forgotten past," a "compulsive conviction" was produced among the Jewish people regarding the truth of Mosaic tradition. And while it took conscious form as a body of laws, ritual practices, a shared history, and theological doctrines, among other things, this tradition

2 *The Writing of History*, trans. Tom Conley (New York: Columbia University Press, 1988), 319. De Certeau adds that, if the Exodus account "narrates the Jewish people's acquisition of their own land through the gesture of breaking away from the Egyptian," the act of writing itself "cannot forget the misfortune from which its necessity springs." Later in history, "*the* Book (the 'Bible' in the singular) is formed, but in Egyptian Greek (the so-called Septuagint Bible), from Hebrew books or scrolls (in the plural) translated by Jews *into* the language of the enemy country in which they find themselves living without any hope of return to Israel." In a related context, Eric Santner observes that, in Freud's view at least, loss is "correlative to the advent of monotheism"; moreover, "Freud understood the contingent and historical condition of *diaspora* as simply the next link in this logical sequence: the separation of a people from territory imagined to be proper to them" (*On the Psychotheology of Everyday Life: Reflections on Freud and Rosenzweig* [Chicago: University of Chicago Press, 2001], 105–06).

functioned *unconsciously* as "an irresistible claim to be believed, against which all logical objections remain[ed] powerless" (107–08).

Nevertheless, even as he thereby came to theorize the initial formulation of Mosaic tradition (including its content: among its other distortions, the god-father Yahweh now stood in the place of the founding-father Moses), Freud grappled with how to describe "tradition" in its other basic sense: the passing on of a heritage generation after generation. Following up his initial formulation of the problem in *Totem and Taboo* (1913)—"what are the ways and means employed by one generation in order to hand on its mental states to the next one?" (*SE*, 13:158)—in *Moses and Monotheism* he would observe, as noted previously, that "a tradition based only on ... communication [of ideas] could not produce the *obsessive character which appertains to religious phenomena.* It would be listened to, weighed, and perhaps rejected, just like any other news from outside; it would never achieve the privilege of being freed from the coercion of logical thinking" (130; my emphasis). Thus, the "true axis" of *Moses and Monotheism* became, as Yosef Hayim Yerushalmi puts it, the "problem of [Jewish] tradition" conceived first and foremost in terms of its "dynamics": how the experience of passing on Mosaic monotheism from one generation to the next was constituted less by the unfolding history of its core ideas and the corresponding cultural and religious practices than by the emergence of collective neurosis that could be transmitted over time.[3]

On one level, as Freud writes, "there is no problem here." For "such a tradition" could be "maintained by conscious memory of oral communications which had been passed on from forebearers of only two or three generations before." But he then asks:

> Can we believe the same ... for the later centuries—namely, that the tradition was always based on a knowledge, communicated in the normal way, which had been transmitted from forebearer to descendant? Who the persons were that stored such knowledge and passed it on from mouth to mouth we no longer know ... According to [Ernst] Sellin, the tradition of the murder of Moses was always present among the priests, until at last it was set down in writing ... Yet it could not have been known to many; it was not general knowledge. And is this form of transmission enough to explain its effect? Can we credit the knowledge on the part of a few with the power to seize the imagination of the masses so lastingly when they learn of it? It rather looks as if there were something also in

3 Yerushalmi, *Freud's Moses: Judaism Terminable and Interminable* (New Haven: Yale University Press, 1993), 29.

> the ignorant mass of the people akin to this knowledge on the part of the few, which comes forward to meet it as soon as it is uttered. (119–20)

This "something also in the ignorant mass of the people" was not *knowledge* of the murder of Moses but "memory traces of the past in the unconscious" (119) that could "come forward" via the return of the repressed in the distorted form of Mosaic tradition. But then Freud did face a conceptual problem: his explanation for such a cultural scenario (a collective neurosis) required him to make a leap of psychoanalytic faith to the idea that repressed memories could be transmitted across generations.

As Freud sees it, there is a definite upside to this position. For, he reasons, "if we accept the continued existence of such memory traces in our archaic inheritance, then we have bridged the gap between individual and mass psychology and can treat peoples as we do the individual neurotic." But he also recognizes that such a scientifically ungrounded theory had already been widely discredited "by the present attitude of biological science" (128). On one level what he calls a "bold step" is "inevitable" (the translation in the *Standard Edition* perhaps gets the idea more clearly: "the audacity cannot be avoided" [23:100]) simply because his theory of Jewish tradition-as-neurotic-compulsion requires it. That is, he simply cannot understand how tradition could have "force[d] the masses under its spell" without the concept of the return of the repressed functioning on a cultural level.[4] But on a different level his sense that Jewish tradition held the people's collective imagination centuries upon centuries after the religion's founding and in a form still "inaccessible to consciousness" (121) suggests that Freud accedes to the unscientific theory on other grounds.

Although he never mentions him by name, Freud is here rather notoriously applying to human psychology the pre-Darwinian theory of evolution most associated with the French biologist Jean-Baptiste Lamarck (1744–1829), who had argued that an organism can pass on acquired characteristics to its offspring (a theory sometimes referred to as "soft inheritance"). Darwin rejected this theory, and early twentieth-century genetic science eventually disproved it, facts that Freud no doubt knew by the time he wrote *Moses and Monotheism*.[5] Freud's earlier interest in Lamarckism had largely been confined to

4 Freud acknowledges that he "argue[s] as if there were no question that there exists an inheritance of memory—traces of what our forefathers experienced, quite independently of direct communication and of the influence of education." But he then "admit[s] ... that [he] cannot picture biological development proceeding without taking this factor [acquired qualities being transmitted to descendants] into account" (127–28).

5 For Freud's earlier reliance on Lamarckism, see "Overview of the Transference Neuroses" (1915), published in *A Phylogenetic Fantasy: Overview of the Transference Neuroses*, ed. Ilse

inheritance among prehistoric humans of the kind he had theorized in *Totem and Taboo*.[6] In *Moses and Monotheism*, by contrast, he attempts to apply psychological-Lamarckism in the context of historically specific events from the relatively recent past and developed over a short historical span (roughly eight to nine centuries), a shift in context that made an already discredited theory even more untenable.

In what remains of this chapter, I want to draw on de Certeau's observation—the Bible (and especially Torah) emerged as a response to and even a replacement for what had been lost (the ancestral land / the direct presence of God in the form of prophetic speech)—to offer an alternative to Freud's Lamarckism. In short, I want to suggest that, while there is no such thing as "soft inheritance" as regards the passing on of repressed memories, we can yet understand how the compulsive conviction that Freud makes central to Mosaic tradition (something akin to, even to the point of repeating, the original traumatic experience) could be transmitted across generations. But I will alter Freud's theory in two essential ways. First, as argued in Chapter 2, the trauma that was passed down through countless generations in and through the Jewish Unconscious was not the murder of Moses but the Babylonian Exile and the attending loss of the national homeland; second, precisely in the setting of the postexilic period (a setting that saw the emergence of Judaic monotheism as we now understand that concept), the container of the trauma and the vehicle of its transmission over time were not repressed memories but something highly visible and consciously, indeed obsessively, remembered, shared both within and between generations and so quite purposefully retained and passed down as among Jewish culture's most treasured possessions: Torah itself.

Grubitch-Simitis, trans. Axel Hoffer and Peter T. Hoffer (Cambridge, MA: Harvard University Press , 1987), 5–20; and *Outline of Psycho-Analysis*, *SE*, 23:167, 190n1, 200–02, 207. For discussion, see Frank J. Sulloway, *Freud, Biologist of the Mind: Beyond the Psychoanalytic Legend* (New York: Basic Books, 1979); Ilse Grubitch-Simitis, "Metapsychology and Metabiology: On Sigmund Freud's Draft Overview of the Transference Neuroses," in *A Phylogenetic Fantasy*, 75–107; and Henry Edelheit, "On the Biology of Language: Darwinian / Lamarckian Homology in Human Inheritance (with some thoughts about the Lamarckism of Freud)," in *Psychoanalysis and Language* (Psychiatry and the Humanities, v. 3) (New Haven, CT: Yale University Press, 1978), 45–74. Freud makes many direct references to Lamarck, for example in letters to Sándor Ferenczi on January 6, and December, 22, 1916, and January 28, March 2, May 29, and December 27, 1917. Ferenczi himself is still referring to the joint work on Lamarck as late at May 18, 1918.

6 In "Overview of the Transference Neuroses," for example, Freud writes that "one can justifiably claim that the inherited dispositions [of the human psyche] are residues of the acquisition of our ancestors," in other words a "phylogenetic disposition." "In this sense," Freud concludes, "neurosis is … a cultural acquisition" (*Phylogenentic Fantasy*, 10, 19).

2

To get at the full implications of this claim, I want to draw on Robert Paul's notion that, as a "source of *semiotic* replication," Torah is capable of producing copies of itself, as well as men, who are themselves 'copies' of it, its metaphorical 'sons' [ritually created through, among things, the aptly termed *bar mitzvah*], insofar as they are informed by and exemplify in their being and actions the instructions imparted to them by the Torah." Paul himself draws on the work of the evolutionary biologist, Richard Dawkins, who, as Paul notes, "asserts that genes are members of a wider class of 'replicators,' whose members include 'anything in the universe of which copies are made.' … [Dawkins] recognizes the independent existence of a cultural or semiotic replicator, which he calls a 'meme.'" Building on Dawkins's concept, Paul then describes how "a 'memic' or cultural replicator accomplishes its work by channeling the motivations and capacities of human actors into activities that result in the reproduction of copies of the meme …. [The meme] produces a population of humans who are 'like' it, in the sense that they actualize its instructions. And through the instructions it gives these people, it also motivates and directs them to produce more copies, so that the instructions can be disseminated and transmitted over generations." Paul concludes by arguing that, in its capacity as a recognized and widely disseminated text, "Torah has characteristics that suit it to … replication at the memic level":

> It is a symbol whose meaning, and ability to instruct authoritatively, comes from its own status as a … self-referential symbol, or meme, and thus as a fixed point in relation to which all other symbols derive meaning, that derives its own meaning from nothing but itself. The Torah, being a set of instructions, is clearly a replicator, insofar as it produces a community of individuals "similar" to it and to each other, in the sense that they all, as individuals, embody the Torah by enacting the instructions within it. In addition, the Torah not only enjoins those under its influence to practice the laws it gives but also insists repeatedly that it be transmitted across generations and that it itself be copied.[7]

Drawing one of Paul's earlier comments, we might view Torah and especially the Moses-Exodus story at its heart as a prime example of a culturally "shared and valorized myth … [that] is able to arouse, address, and organize

---

7 *Moses and Civilization: The Meaning Behind Freud's Myth* (New Haven: Yale University Press, 1996), 185–87.

in a culture- and ego-syntonic way the individual's own powerful but inchoate fantasies, molding them into a personality suited to abide by the rules and conventions governing the social system."[8] In short, (re)conceptualized as a meme, Torah can be understood as the chief cultural replicator of the Jewish past: not just the culture's foundation myth but the centerpiece of a coercively authoritative structure that in the form of what Freud calls a "tradition" disseminated across countless generations would "take … hold" of its Jewish adherents with an "irresistible claim to be believed, against which all logical objections become powerless." In short, "a compulsive conviction" (*Moses and Monotheism*, 107–08).

That said, Paul's very interest in the mythic patterns underlying Jewish (and Judeo-Christian) culture at the expense of historical reconstruction leads him to view Torah as strangely free-floating, outside the framework of any particular historical-cultural setting in which it might have achieved its memic status. Commenting, for example, on the specific "question of whether Moses was *really* an Egyptian or an Israelite, which so exercised Freud," Paul reflects that this question "does not concern me, since my analysis remains within the confines of the myth and makes no assumptions about who or what Moses might have been in historical terms." He later offers this generalization: "the history in the Bible, even when it is relatively realistic, is always to be seen in the larger mythic context in which it is embedded and from which it takes its present significance." And he adds for good measure, "in this regard [the history in the Bible] does not differ from any sort of history, which is always told from a certain point of view and from within a certain narrative construct."[9] That

8 *Moses and Civilization*, 171.

9 *Moses and Civilization*, 78, 234n8. For discussion of the cultural mnemotechnics at work in Torah (especially in evidence in Exodus and Deuteronomy), see Jan Assmann, *From Akhenaten to Moses: Ancient Egypt and Religious Change* (New York: The American University in Cairo Press 2014), 32–36; and *The Invention of Religion: Faith and Covenant in the Book of Exodus*, trans. Robert Savage (Princeton: Princeton University Press, 2018), 191–96. Elaborating on how in practice collective memory first forms and then continues to function within a particular cultural moment, Assmann argues that the mnemohistorical notion of "'reception' is not to be understood … merely in the narrow sense of transmitting and receiving. The past is not simply 'received' by the present. The present [rather] is 'haunted' by the past," and the way the present "invent[s], reinvent[s], and reconstruct[s]" its past may under certain conditions be marked by collective uneasiness, even anxiety, concerning an experience that is not truly past: *Moses the Egyptian: The Memory of Egypt in Western Monotheism* (Cambridge, MA: Harvard University Press, 1997), 89. Particularly in the form of what Assmann calls "counter-memory"—a mode of recollection that "strives at keeping present in the world of today an image of yesterday that contradicts it"—a present that resides in the shadow of a past that simply will not give up the ghost might distort what has come down from the past precisely to remember and to forget it simultaneously: *Moses the Egyptian*,

last assertion, justified as it may be as an appropriate caution about historical interpretation generally, is telling because thinking of Torah as being "told from a certain point of view"—and, we might add, from a historically specific and so limited point of view—"and from within a certain narrative construct" is precisely what Paul does not do.

Ironically, at one point Paul suggests that he is intentionally distancing himself from the notion that the Bible could or even should be studied as a completed whole as though it simply "existed" in the way that much of rabbinical tradition would have simply taken for granted: "The rabbis regularly depicted Moses and the patriarchs as engaged in scholarly disputation about passages in Torah, just as they themselves were. They considered such disputations a central focus of life, and it must have seemed natural to them to depict earlier generations of 'Jews' doing the same—*without regard for the fact that the Torah had not even come into existence in the time of the patriarchs*."[10] But while Paul's own work is grounded in the sense that Torah came into existence at some defined point in the past (and definitely later than the time of the patriarchs), he is consistently vague about when that point was. While he clearly rejects the old-fashioned idea that Moses wrote Torah, he implies without ever saying that it was likely written sometime in close temporal proximity to the Exodus conceived as an actual historical event. But the idea that Torah's very composition might (even must) be located in historical terms (as though those terms would then provide an important access point for interpretation) turns out to be irrelevant to Paul's primary focus on Torah's mythic importance to the shaping of Israelite-Jewish culture:

> Let us consider the question of where Torah came from. The answer, of course, is that it was revealed to Moses on Mount Sinai. But ... the whole Torah, as a narrative, is nothing other than the story of the revelation at Mount Sinai: what led up to it, what happened during the life of the prophet Moses who received the Law, and, of course, the Law itself. Thus we may say that the Torah was "created" ... at Sinai. But at the same time, the creation of the Torah is a story contained within the Torah narrative ... The book is at once container and contained .... [In that form] it is recited, copied, taught, studied, and otherwise infinitely replicated and disseminated. This capacity to replicate and disseminate itself as a

220n13; for theoretical elaboration, see Assmann, *Cultural Memory and Early Civilization: Writing, Remembrance, and Political Imagination* (Cambridge: Cambridge University Press, 2011.

10 *Moses and Civilization*, 57; my emphasis.

> memotype is underscored by its self-referential qualities ... Thus does the Torah stand as an uncreated but creative point of reference in relation to which all other signs [within Jewish culture] acquire significance.[11]

Paul here both answers and does not answer his own prompting "question of where Torah came from." Or, rather, his never strays beyond a kind of hermeneutical closed system. While it must have come from some place and time (definitely after the time of the patriarchs), all that matters finally is the memic / mythic function (self-referential and so effectively timeless) it eventually came to serve. For, as he has remarked earlier, "the power of myth does not depend on whether it tells a true story about ancient history but rather upon whether it is capable of providing an authoritative foundation for the continual construction, maintenance, and reproduction of an ongoing social order."[12]

In simplest terms, then, Paul's very ahistorical approach to the content of the biblical narrative extends to the history of the Bible's composition, and this despite his acknowledgement that historical claims of any kind must take into account the point of view from which they are presented. With reference to the composition of Torah in particular, Paul makes not a single reference to Ezra or to the Babylonian Exile in his entire study. Indeed, despite knowing this not to be the case, he writes as though Torah simply appeared whole cloth out of nowhere.[13] And so his lack of interest in the "true [hi]story" by which Torah came to serve as "an authoritative foundation for the continual construction, maintenance, and reproduction" of the "ongoing [Jewish] social order" begs the question or really two questions: 1) without any particular cultural setting, how is it that Torah came to be written in the first place? and 2) how (or why) did it became authoritative? We might reframe the second question as follows: how could Torah have become authoritative in Jewish culture unless members of that culture perceived it to be a response to some event or broader situation resonating deeply with their own experience?

Paul actually has an answer to the second question, an answer that is at once ahistorical and surprisingly predictable in the context of Freud's own appraisal

---

11 *Moses and Civilization*, 188–89.

12 *Moses and Civilization*, 10. Paul adds that the cultural authority of myth "does not appear to derive from anywhere in the present world. On the contrary, this world is made possible only by the myth itself."

13 Throughout the study, Paul behaves as a reader in much the same fashion as the rabbis he disparages, even to the point of acknowledging that he will avoid the question of when (or where or why) different parts of the Bible were composed—he writes that he will "not address the question of the origins and developments of the written works" (177)—and will treat it instead as a unified whole.

of the Exodus story and its aftermath. Drawing on Freud in suggesting that "the Torah text exemplifies an obsessional style of thought," Paul remarks that "the guilt that drives the obsessional or conscientious personality organization" is culturally reproducible not because of the inheritance of repressed memories but rather because of the unconscious reaction individuals have ("the unconscious guilt" they "feel"), "*regardless of cultural setting*, for fantasies of a broadly oedipal nature: fantasies involving some interplay of feelings of passionate attachment, jealous, sexual excitement, murderous rage, and dread of punishment."[14] Thus, even as Paul provides a real service in showing why Freud's psychoanalytic interest in what in *Totem and Taboo* he had called "the ways and means employed by one generation in order to hand on its mental states to the next one" did not need to rely on a scientifically discredited Lamarckism, in the end Paul arrives at the same place Freud himself did: the traumatic experience that stood at the origin of Jewish monotheism and Jewish history more broadly was an "oedipal murder."[15]

Because the attempt to refute that very claim was the central burden of Chapter 2, I will not here rehearse why I do not think it is supportable on either theoretical or historical grounds. That said, I do also want to affirm Paul's key concept of the memic function that Torah once played, and continues to play, in Jewish culture. Indeed, by his own terms, in its very multifaceted design and purpose Torah is not just ideally suited to serve this function, but it also came to into being in precisely the circumstances where it could serve the culture's demand for a new "authoritative foundation": the historical moment when, to draw on Eric Santner's work, Jewish culture—more precisely, postexilic Judaean culture—was "confronted by an excess of validity over meaning."[16]

Simply by acknowledging that Torah as a completed text entered into Jewish culture at a very particular crisis point in history, we might readily accept that it quickly assumed the function of a memic replicator. The biblical narrative itself makes this claim: the whole point of Ezra's reading Torah aloud in Jerusalem (Nehemiah 8:1–8) was to establish it as the dominant discourse of the postexilic period. (Even if we consider apocryphal Nehemiah's claim that Ezra was able to gather for the reading "the entire people … as one man in the square before the Water Gate" [8:1], we might accept the hyperbole as

14 *Moses and Civilization*, 171; my emphasis. By "obsessional," Paul means "a constellation of character traits composed of defenses against unconscious guilt associated with an unconscious fantasy of having committed a violent *and erotically motivated crime* for which the punishment would be death or castration" (my emphasis).

15 *Moses and Civilization*, 171.

16 *On the Psychotheology of Everyday Life*, 102.

yet representing an important truth: the theocratic governing structure of the Persian period provided the social setting in which the wide dissemination of Torah became possible for the first time, that very dissemination serving as a key part of the new cultural authority.[17]) Both its stories and its laws would thereafter define a new Jewish identity that could then be passed down from one generation to the next.

Among the numerous examples of the Torah's replicating effect, we might give special attention to these five verses in Deuteronomy 6:

> [4] Hear, O Israel! The LORD is our God, the LORD alone. [5] You shall love the LORD your God with all your heart and with all your soul and with all your might. [6] Take to heart these instructions with which I charge you this day. [7] Impress them upon your children. Recite them when you stay at home and when you are away, when you lie down and when you get up. [8] Bind them as a sign on your hand and let them serve as a symbol on your forehead; [9] inscribe them on the doorposts of your house and on your gates. (6:4–9)

There is a purposeful ambiguity here in the referent of the phrase "these words that I am commanding your today." "At one level," as Paul notes,

> *these words* (or *these instructions*) may be understood to refer to the Ten Commandments, which have just been revealed in the previous chapter ... But we may also understand by [the phrase] the whole of Torah itself ... On the other hand, 'these instructions' can also refer, in a literal way, to ... themselves. Judaic practice has taken the passage in just this way. Thus the prayer 'Hear O Israel ...' is, in fact, repeated every day by the observant Jew. Further, 'these instructions,' that is, this passage, together with a few other verses, is inscribed on parchment and inserted in *tefillin*, or phylacteries, as the passage instructs, as well as in *mezuzot*, small casings attached to the doorframes of houses, also according to a (literal) reading of the instructions.

---

17 So Freud reflects in one of his own notes:
"It is historically certain that the Jewish type was definitely fixed as a result of the reforms of Ezra and Nehemiah in the fifth century B.C., therefore after the Exile ... By these reforms the regulations aiming at the consecration of the chosen people were taken seriously: the separation from the other tribes was put into force by forbidding mixed marriages; the Pentateuch, the real compilation of the law, was codified in its definitive form; the rewriting known as the Priestly Code was finished." (51n1)

And, “on a more general level, the command to recite, take to heart, and teach one’s children … is the basis for the entire practice of the reading, study, and teaching of the Torah itself”; that is, faithful members of the covenantal people are explicitly commanded to repeat or replicate the Torah by reciting the words constantly and by teaching them to their children who will then also recite them constantly. Even the physical status of the words acquires an aura of the sacred because Torah is effectively “the material representation of the ultimate authority of God.” In short, culturally speaking, “the authority of Torah is supreme.”[18]

That said, Paul’s otherwise convincing description of Torah’s authoritative function leans all too heavily on the ahistorical (even anti-historical) claim of Freud’s oedipal economy as an explanation of its capacity to produce and perpetuate collective commitment; as noted, Paul argues that “fantasies of a broadly oedipal nature”—precisely the types of fantasy he believes sustained in Jewish culture an “unconscious guilt” for an ancient patricide—can have a broad social impact “*regardless of cultural setting*.”[19] This reliance on the Oedipus complex as the psychical force driving the culturally unconscious attachment to Torah clearly aims to conceptualize Torah’s memic status as possessing precisely the kind of “obsessive character” (*Moses and Monotheism*, 71, 130) Freud thought necessary to explain the tenacity of Jewish devotion in the face of constant hardship. Once again we find a scholar unable to separate his argument from Freud’s and so all too willing to theoretically endorse what was unpersuasive from the start. But if we move away from Freud’s foundational claim that the murder of the cultural father-figure was the originary traumatic event in Jewish history we can also move away from the oedipal-based castration model as the framework in which we must understand that history’s traumatic fixation. To put this another way, by placing the cultural emergence of Torah in its proper historical context, we can dispense with two paired notions, both adapted from Freud, on display in Paul’s work: the first, that the murder of the cultural father-figure subsequently fueled an unconscious guilt among the murderers; and second, that this very guilt, transmitted now not through the inheritance of repressed memories (Freud’s Lamarckism) but through Torah’s

18 *Moses and Civilization*, 187–88, 185.

19 In an astonishing admission, Paul later writes: “I am inclined to believe that major generic dimensions of certain *unconscious fantasies, especially oedipal ones, have innate genetic foundations* …: such fantasies as those associated with castration fears, the primal scene, and seduction scenes … [I]t does seem likely that *humans have, as part of their innate mental endowment*, fantasies and associated affects, mental representations, and structures that are the residues of our evolution from primates living in bands with male hierarchies that may have been related to mating strategies in the group” (243n1; my emphases).

status as an authorizing discourse, then enabled the collective and ultimately transgenerational replication of the distorted memory of the murder precisely to the extent the repressed figure of the murder-victim had "returned" in the simultaneously loving and law-giving, nurturing and punitive father-god Yahweh.

In short, by separating the concept of the culturally binding force of Torah-as-meme from the primal oedipal economy that Freud believed had been reactivated with the murder of Moses, we can set aside the notion that Judaic monotheism is, as Santner notes, "the ultimate religion of the superego."[20] By moving past the Oedipus complex as central to Jewish culture we can also give proper attention to Cathy Caruth's important but poorly framed argument, itself over-reliant, as we have seen, on Freud's claim about the murder of Moses: at the origin of Jewish history (an origin we should date in the postexilic period), we find "the experience of trauma" that "consist[s], not in the forgetting of a reality that can hence never be fully known, but in an inherent latency within the experience itself."[21] Central to the memic Torah's capacity to generate unconscious attachment is that, in its very revelation (at Sinai, through Ezra), something is yet concealed, missing, or even lost. As Franz Rosenzweig would put it so poetically and so mysteriously in his *Star of Redemption*, "in Judaism, man is always somehow a survivor, an inner something, whose exterior was seized by the current of the world and carried off while he himself, what is left of him, remains standing on the shore. Something within him is waiting."[22] In what follows, I want to offer a series of suggestions for how we might understand what precisely prompts this "waiting" and how it is experienced in the postexilic Jewish Unconscious. I would also venture that, as we shall take up in Chapter 4 and its accompanying Coda, Freud himself unwittingly went in search of just this understanding in his work on *Moses and Monotheism*: a sense of expectancy, even a longing, for "an inner something"

20 *On the Psychotheology of Everyday Life*, 104. Santner's point is that Freud himself viewed Judaism this way. That said, one of the main points of Santner's study is that Franz Rosenzweig's understanding of Judaism and Jewish culture more broadly provides a corrective to Freud that also enables us to see in Freud's own writings a counter-narrative in which something other than the superego emerges as central to Judaic faith's unconscious dimension: self-estrangement that makes possible the ethical encounter with the Other conceived as one's neighbor.

21 *Unclaimed Experience: Trauma, Narrative, and History* (Baltimore: Johns Hopkins University Press, 1996), 17.

22 *The Star of Redemption*, trans. William W. Hallo (New York: Holt, Rinehart and Winston, 1970), 404–05.

that, while absent, promises to return and by that very (unfulfilled) promise keeps the Jewish "survivor" compulsively attached to that very absence.

3

We might start by returning to Freud's notion that Jewish culture's traumatic fixation underlies and effectively creates Judaic *tradition*. Exploring that relation in more detail, we might consider Leon Wieseltier's contention that, "for the Jew, the idea of tradition holds a consolation for the loss of immediacy, or at least the immediacy of the founding illumination."[23] There is in this sense of tradition, we note, a simultaneous acknowledgement of loss and a consolation for it, with tradition taking on both psychosocial functions simultaneously.[24]

As a mode of compensation, Wieseltier suggests that Jewish ritual practice in particular aims to counter the lost immediacy of revelation precisely through the "ritual abolition of time[,] ... planned disruption[s] within a highly organized commitment to temporality." The extended example he offers is the climactic moment of the priestly anointing in Leviticus 8–9, where Moses and Aaron's (and Aaron's sons') meticulous adherence to the prescribed rules for the burnt offering culminates in the immediacy of God's self-revelation in the consuming fire (9:22–24). But his example *par excellence* for what he calls the "re-creation of contemporaneity" is "that theater of the recovery of experience ... known as the Passover seder."[25] Wieseltier consistently suggests that, in opposition to later rabbinical commentary which can at best offer a sort of record of a now lost simultaneity of God and his people, scripture itself enacts something akin to a full revelatory immediacy. In that context, however, it is especially noteworthy that Wieseltier refers here to the *ritual* of the seder and not to the account of Passover provided in Exodus. For what we cannot help

---

23 "Leviticus," in *Congregation: Contemporary Writers Read the Jewish Bible*, ed. David Rosenberg (New York: Harcourt Brace Jovanovich, 1987), 28.

24 Observing that Judaism "is based on a revelation that is over," Wieseltier goes on to describe how the loss of immediacy must confront what we might call the "pastness" of the past: "[T]he faith of the Jew is premised upon the denial of contemporaneity with revelation.... Coming too late, the Jew detests time. He attempts to abolish it. Naturally, it is not abolished.... Coming too late, he has nothing but time. History is oxygen for Jews. It is the essential environment for a faith that calls itself a transmission." In short, the loss of immediacy at the foundation of Judaism (Wieseltier calls the postexilic Leviticus "the origin" of Judaism) is inseparable from the experience of belatedness—a *coming too late*—it can never escape ("Leviticus," 27–28, 38).

25 "Leviticus," 27–28.

but notice in the text of Exodus 12 is just how much Jewish tradition carries the burden of its own afterwardsness even in what may be its most powerful attempt to reclaim its origin. For as presented, the actual story of the Passover is inseparable from the recounting of the construction of the very ritual that will later commemorate it. To put this another way, the account in Exodus 12 doesn't just describe an event from the past but engages that very pastness by effectively describing how immediacy is then repeated as ritual reenactment.

In this sense, Wieseltier's phrases, the "*re-creation* of contemporaneity" and the "theater of *the recovery* of experience," are particularly apt. That said, to the extent ritual and liturgical practices associated with the legal requirements of Torah aim to alter the culture's experience of time, the very linking of the Law to the Mosaic revelation at Sinai imaginatively resituates those who observe it (for Ezra, for example, the people who have heard Torah proclaimed in Persian-ruled Jerusalem) in a period before the nation was even founded and so necessarily prior to when it was destroyed. Loss in the form of national failure and the inexplicable absence of God in the time of need could thus be deflected if not completely denied. Subjugation to a foreign power merely put the de-nationalized Judaeans back in the time of pre-Israel Moses and the people of the Exodus, a collective ready for liberation, prepared to take on the burden of the covenant's legal requirements, and, through their very (renewed) commitment, living in expectation that God's promises would be fulfilled. To return to the biblical representation of the Passover, we might note that the very point of Exodus 12's narration on how the (future) Seder would ritualistically reenact the original event is effectively a declaration of cultural survival, the continuation of a people bound together by the terms of the Exodus: liberation from servitude, the establishment of the Law and related terms of the covenant, the acquisition of the Promised Land. If the ritual imaginatively relocates those observing the Law to Egypt during the time of God's saving action and, later, at Sinai for the revelation of the Law the observance of which is the condition for the fulfillment of God's covenantal promises, then the Passover conceived as ritual reenactment situates those participating in its "sacred time" as living before the Promised Land has been either gained or lost.[26] In his most optimistic mood, then, Wieseltier imagines that tradition so

26 In her anthropological analysis of Passover, Ruth Gruber Fredman remarks in a related context that "the sequence of the Haggadah, as its shifts its focus from past to present to future, mirrors the historical progression, but the symbolic identifications turn history into myth at each stage. The result is that those at the seder sit in … a moment in history *whose meaning has been predefined by the Exodus*" (*The Passover Seder: Afikoman in Exile* [Philadelphia: University of Pennsylvania Press, 1981], 113; my emphasis).

understood might point the way beyond loss, for "it ensures," he argues, "that those who come after are also those who come before, that the inheritors are also the bequeathers." To the extent tradition, paradoxically, can look more to the future than to the past ("the future," Wieseltier observes, "not the past, is the term of Jewish desire") it also has the "ironic consequence of restoring the Jew to a position of priority, of coming before."[27]

More pessimistically, however, Wieseltier also sees Torah as seeking to overcome the very loss it cannot help but acknowledge. As an instance of what he generally terms Jewish "fatalism" ("a willingness to settle for something less than experience in a relationship with God"), Wieseltier remarks with some sense of pathos that "the impatient Jew ... suffers his days in the deprivation of [divine] acknowledgement, or worse, in its commemoration."[28] It is worth noting in this context that the Jewish liturgical calendar ends with the death of Moses (Deuteronomy 34), which is then followed by a return to the creation story (Genesis 1). Liturgically speaking, the arrival in the Promised Land is indefinitely postponed. To put this in different terms, while the Exodus has already happened, its promise is yet to be fulfilled, an orientation that acknowledges while trying to deny the failure of the past: the meaning of the Exodus was never truly realized and could only then be projected into the future precisely as a way to deny the failure. In short, the fulfillment of God's covenantal promises are always "to come," which is another way of saying that they may never be fulfilled. But the future "to come" must be believed in with complete sincerity and conviction to refuse what history has already revealed.[29]

From this perspective, the very temporal reorientation Wieseltier describes—the past is effectively abolished by being reimagined as the present while the present becomes the gateway to an unfinished future defined as a repetition of the past—creates a cultural fantasy-structure: commitment to the future guaranteed by adherence to Torah enables the illusion that the Exile didn't really happen, for the triumph of the Exodus becomes in repeated form what awaits the Judaeans living under foreign rule. Nevertheless, if tradition so conceived emerges as a way of giving voice to nostalgia as the pained recognition of the elusiveness of what Wieseltier calls "the past without end," it

27 "Leviticus," 28.

28 "Leviticus," 27, 38.

29 Slavoj Žižek has argued that the very concept of covenantal deferral is central to Judaism, especially in contrast to Christianity: "Judaism reduces the promise of Another Life to a pure Otherness, a messianic promise which will never become fully present and actualized (the Messiah is always 'to come')" (*The Puppet and the Dwarf: The Perverse Core of Christianity* [Cambridge, MA: MIT Press, 2003], 140–41).

also serves a compensatory function.[30] For one way of taming the trauma of a terrible past that created an uncertain future would be to fix the "meaning" of the past under a dominant cultural symbol (Torah, itself the focal point of linked prophetic, ritual, liturgical, and national-historical discourses) in such a way that the future would become knowable precisely as a repetition of a triumphant past. And so Torah, and more particularly the Exodus story, came to function as what we might call the central ritual of Jewish consciousness. The past was transformed thereby from the site of failure into the site of expectation: in becoming one with the people of the Exodus (through the observance of Passover, for example) one Jewish person as part of the entire chosen people could (re)experience divine liberation from servitude in advance of the rise to national greatness in the Promised Land. In short, just as the chosen people (a nation before a nation) could look forward in response to Moses' leadership and, especially, to his demand for devotion to the Law, so postexilic Judaeans could live in anticipation that, by means of their own devotion, the nation of Israel would rise (again).

To the extent none of this can be properly understood as invisible to the Judaeans themselves, we might return one last time to Freud's assertion in *Moses and Monotheism* that "a tradition based only on ... communication [of ideas] could not produce the *obsessive character which appertains to religious phenomena.*" That is, the compulsiveness of religious faith required something more than traditional forms of teaching. For, as Freud thought, religious faith could only "achieve the privilege of being freed from the coercion of logical thinking" if it had "first ... suffered the fate of repression, the state of being unconscious, before it could ... force the masses under its spell" (130). But while unconscious at some level, the foundational truth did not need to be repressed as Freud imagined. For, as far as Judaism is concerned, the "something more" could be the inculcation of an obsessional identity deriving precisely through memic replication of Torah. For the Jewish psyche of the postexilic period, in short, it was the very replication of Torah and the impact of that replication on the mental structures of those operating within its culturally discursive dominance that operated unconsciously even as the instruction (as both content and practice) was highly public.

30 "Leviticus," 38. Although he gives this concept a generally positive spin, Wieseltier refers to the "apotheosis of alterity," or the separation from God, as the very "the condition of [Jewish] meaning." With special focus on Leviticus as the Book of the Law, he also notes that recognizing this separation becomes the "deeper objective of the law" and, more broadly, of the tradition expressed through the law (36).

We might think of Torah's memic capacity both to replicate and to compel (unconscious) repetition in terms of what Santner has called "ibidity." Reworking Freud's foundational ego / id distinction, Santner observes that "the *libidinal* component of one's attachments to … symbolic identity must also be thought of as 'ibidinal'" in that it "calls forth a largely unconscious 'citation' of authority": prompted, invited, summoned, provoked by a "primordial *ex-citation*," the subject is "called out to engage in a repetitive and interminable citational praxis in relation to a source of authorization that is at some level grounded in itself."[31] Santner's ibidity is particularly relevant to Paul's understanding of Torah as the prime Judaic meme in the sense that the idea of an "ex-citing" source of authority, "grounded in itself" (or what Santner earlier refers to as "magical" authority, "unsubstantiated, without ultimate foundation in a final ground qua substantive reason," but "grounded … [only] in its own meta-juridical act of self-positing") is conceptually akin to a key element in Paul's description of Torah: "a symbol whose meaning, and ability to instruct authoritatively, comes from *its own status as a self-created, self-referential symbol …* and thus as a fixed point in relation to which all other symbols derive meaning, that *derives its own meaning from nothing except itself*."[32] Torah might also be considered "ibidinal" in the way it "calls forth" from anyone imbued with its presence "a largely unconscious 'citation' of authority," where such *ex-citation* produces what Santner has earlier referred to as "a summons" and from that very summons prompts the one called "to engage in a repetitive and interminable citational praxis." The postexilic Jewish subject's engagement with Torah is all that: a response of one who, ex-cited by authority, cites that very authority in turn—repetitively, obsessively, interminably—in the fashioning of its own symbolic identity, an identity that, as Santner adds, "is never settled once and for all."[33]

Paul offers as what we might consider an exemplary instance of the ibidinal process the invitation offered through the Passover seder for Jewish sons "to form a fantasy identification with Moses" as savior of the people. That identification (Moses-as-cultural-hero) is paired with the "fear of the wrath" of God, which includes the warning derived from Moses' own final punishment: dying outside the Promised Land. The pairing together "underwrites the [Jewish / male] social contract." Paul concludes more broadly that "the here and now of the seder festival" is thereby "given culturally valorized form as the ceremony

---

31 *On the Psychotheology of Everyday Life*, 50.

32 Santner, 50; Paul, 187; my emphases.

33 *On the Psychotheology of Everyday Life*, 31, 50.

unfolds anew each year."[34] Beyond Passover itself, Torah as a whole is central to the ritualization of the time through the annual liturgical calendar of Sabbath observance as that centers on the reading aloud of the entire Torah within the synagogue. As Paul comments, "performed from beginning to end every year," Torah acquires in this setting the "central status" in Jewish culture: in particular, "the Laws contained in the Torah form the foundation of social life, and the narrative in which they are embedded constitutes an enacted, living myth constantly and repetitively experienced publicly in the present moment."[35] We might think of the liturgical cycle as modeled on Ezra's reading of newly completed Torah to the inhabitants of Jerusalem. And, of course, Ezra's reading of Torah was intended at some level to replicate Moses' original giving of the Law at Sinai. In that sense, the repetition organized annually in the liturgical calendar (its cycle of readings) is itself a repetition of (and a repetition of repetition of), and thereby a participation in, two founding events, both centrally concerned with fixing Torah (as Law and narrative) at the heart of Jewish culture. In short, what Paul says of the ritualization of the Passover event in the Seder and more broadly with the "Passover season" could be said of the memic authority of Torah as a whole: "the ritual techniques that set off the Passover season … demarcate and protect this period as *a reconnection with the mythic era*."[36] This reconnection, effected via ritualized reenactment, shapes symbolic identity as unconscious repetition. Restored to a time at the beginning of the cultural history, those "ex-cited" by Torah can look forward to the founding of the nation of Israel even in the aftermath of the Exile.

4

Reflecting on the "psychical dispositions" at work in creating and sustaining religious faith, Freud had written in *Totem and Taboo* that an "unconscious" capacity to "interpret" or even "undo the distortions which other people have imposed on the expression of their feelings" might help explain how "*all the customs, ceremonies and dogmas left behind*" in a particular religious tradition might survive as a "heritage of emotion" that "later generations" might "take over" into themselves (*SE*, 13:158–59; my emphasis). Paul concludes from this statement that a memory of a past event or action and even the "defenses associated with it" can be passed on to

---

34 *Moses and Civilization*, 180.

35 *Moses and Civilization*, 177.

36 *Moses and Civilization*, 178; my emphasis.

> each generation of individuals by means of religious myths, rituals, and practices. The customs, ceremonies, and dogmas that are a distorted re-representation of the original memory or fantasy, defensively transformed and translated into primary-process symbolic imagery, can be unconsciously deciphered by new generations of participants in their parents' practices and thus acquired by them as well without the intervention of an conscious critical judgment. What this theory tells us is that the supposed "memory" can be thought of as being actually produced *in individuals* by participation in the ceremonies and customs that express the dogmas of the mythic system .... All that is required ... in understanding how religious traditions are reproduced in undiluted force in succeeding generations of cultural actors, is that the new generation possess the unconscious "apparatus" ... that allows its members to decode the customs, ceremonials, and dogmas to which they are exposed and in which they participate during the formative years of their enculturation.[37]

So understood, the unconscious dimension compelling Judaic faith as a tradition (a collectively-held "compulsive conviction") is neither the memory of the (never-forgotten) Exile nor the very public commitment to Torah as a memic replicator in postexilic culture. What is unconscious, rather, and in that form able to generate unswerving loyalty in the face of constant contradiction, is what Freud calls the "unconscious understanding" of what lies underneath "all the customs, ceremonies, and dogmas left behind": in short, the perception (perhaps better termed an intuition) among members of one generation of the unconscious attachment both possessed by and bequeathed from members of the previous generation. This perception (or intuition) itself derives from the later generation's unconscious capacity "to undo the distortions" surrounding those emotions or, more broadly, the emotive, ethical, and psychosocial investments of the earlier generation in the tradition it had itself previously received from an even earlier generation. And so a tradition is culturally (re)produced.

It must be stated again: while Freud considers human beings as possessing an innate capacity "to undo the distortions which other people have imposed on the expression of their feelings," this undoing is itself precisely an "*unconscious* understanding." The undoing of another person's emotive distortions (distortions, often times defensive in nature, that are themselves the expression of unconscious attachments) should not then be understood as a decoding (Paul's terms) so much as a reception followed by unconscious replication.

37 *Moses and Civilization*, 173.

As Paul suggests, the one undoing the distortions of another is drawing on an innate disposition that pursues "a 'fit' [with] one's personal unconscious experience and fantasy." The receiver, as Freud puts it, thereby "take[s] over [a] heritage of emotion" without being aware either of the acquisition or of the previously existing unconscious framework that enables the acquisition. Freud, moreover, appears to believe that the acquisitive undoing can and does occur not just at the individual level but also between generations within a culture. In the latter case, what Paul calls the personal "fit" is not just with another individual but with a larger "public 'memory,' or fantasy / myth / story" even where, as in a typical case, that public memory comes in the form of "core mythic ideas to which [a] child is exposed through his or her parents, by way of the customs, ceremonies, and dogmas in which the parents themselves are actively and meaningfully involved."[38] As regards the acquisition / replication of a culture's prevailing religious ideas, Freud's contemporary Émile Durkheim referred to finding this fit as the act of "plac[ing] ourselves within their sphere of action," an act we then unconsciously repeat "every time we feel the need for renewing their effects"; for Durkheim such repetition effectively required that the individual function as a member of the cult understood "not simply as a system of signs by which faith is outwardly translated" but also as "a collection of the means by which this is created and recreated periodically."[39] Although he is thinking in terms of the individual rather than the collective, in this context we might borrow Santner's description of the subject's "traumatic encounter with the dense, enigmatic presence of the Other's desire as constitutive of the inner strangeness we call the unconscious."[40] Translated into cultural terms, we should understand the collective Unconscious of one generation as being answerable to without fully understanding that what it is answering in the form of narrative, ritual, liturgy, and legal observance is the collective Unconscious of the generation that has come before. Moreover, from the position of its own priority from which its enculturates the next generation (its own offspring), the earlier generation never fully understands that it is passing on the enigmatic messages of its own unconscious attachments.[41]

38 *Moses and Civilization*, 173–74.

39 *The Elementary Forms of Religious Life*, trans. Joseph Ward Swain (London: George Allen & Unwin, 1915), 417. For related discussion on religion as a cultural system with special attention to the central role played by ritual practices in generating lines of authority, see Clifford Geertz, *The Interpretation of Cultures: Selected Essays* (New York: Basic Books, 1973), 87–125.

40 *On the Psychotheology of Everyday Life*, 33–34.

41 For the notion of "enigmatic messages" from the Other that are retained as "unconscious residues" in the one receiving them, see Jean Laplanche, *New Foundations for Psychoanalysis*, trans. David Macey (Oxford: Basil Blackwell, 1989), 130.

If such unconscious transmission is the process by which a tradition is passed on, we must remind ourselves that, from the perspective of Freud's goal of understanding the compelling force of religious faith, what is crucial about tradition is how or why it generates the conviction of truth, what "simply must be believed" (*Moses and Monotheism*, 167). If, for the cultural heritage we now know as Judaic faith, a traumatic experience eventually leads to Torah as memic replicator and, through that replicator, produces repetition compulsion in the Freudian sense, the "customs, ceremonies and dogmas *left behind*" in the emergence of postexilic Judaism are not simply what is bequeathed from one generation to the next as the content of tradition. For more precisely and more crucially the unconscious residue is compulsive repetition itself, what Caruth calls "the unwitting reenactment of an event that one simply *cannot leave behind*."[42]

5

Accepting the need to think along with Freud's perspective without necessarily agreeing with his conclusions, Yerushalmi comments that "the force and longevity of religious tradition cannot be apprehended if tradition is presented essentially in terms of the history of ideas, or the history of education, or even as a system of symbols whose mythical, material, and social referents can be decoded, while its psychological dimensions are ignored. It is precisely here that psychoanalysis may be of help. The question is how to apply it."[43] As noted in section 1, Yerushalmi rightly observes that the "true axis" of *Moses and Monotheism* is the "problem of [Jewish] tradition"; as Freud himself would put it at the end of Part II: "Only then would the interest of our purely historical study be fully warranted. In what exactly consists the intrinsic nature of a tradition, and in what resides its peculiar power" (65). For Freud, tradition's "intrinsic nature" and "peculiar power" were inseparable because effectively indistinguishable: tradition was what was passed down over time as the compelling force of belief itself. And as part of any religious system (Judaism or otherwise), the psychoanalyst Freud thought that belief was best understood on the model of obsessional neurosis, one collectively held and capable of being transmitted across generations.

In taking this position generally and in then borrowing Lamarck's theory of soft inheritance as a way of explaining how the repressed memories at the heart of obsessional neurosis could be passed on from parents to children on

42 *Unclaimed Experience*, 2; my emphasis.

43 *Freud's Moses*, 87.

the model of genetic codes, Freud hoped to found a theory of cultural development on one of his key concepts for the development of individual personality: "If we accept the continued existence of … memory traces in our archaic inheritance, then we have bridged the gap between individual and mass psychology and *can treat peoples as we do the individual neurotic*" (128; my emphasis). Even in recognizing that such a scientifically ungrounded theory had already been effectively disproven, he was not deterred.

While Caruth, like so many others, gets off-track in too easily accepting that what Freud calls "the origin of monotheism among the Jews" had its beginning in the murder of Moses (for Freud himself an act that fit within the broad parameters of oedipal economy whose own origin he traced to prehistoric times), her attempt to explain the obsessive quality of Jewish faith, including how something essentially unconscious could subsequently be transmitted from person to person and, collectively, from one generation to the next, avoids Freud's oedipal terminology (the castration model of trauma). As we saw in Chapter 2, Caruth (re)theorizes both the original traumatic situation and the governing psychical process: the "accident model" whose traumatic force is driven by dissociation rather than by repression. A full discussion of how Caruth's ideas are more in line with contemporary applications of psychoanalysis to cultural formations is beyond the scope of my discussion here. But it is worth noting that trauma-theory and related concepts deriving from psychoanalysis have frequently been employed as a way of exploring the traumatic experience of entire peoples especially in colonial situations, situations not completely dissimilar from that faced by postexilic Judaeans living under Persian, Greek, or Roman rule.[44] These applications often attempt to address Yerushalmi's "problem of tradition, not merely its origins, but above all its dynamics," that is, how a historical situation that gives rise to a collective trauma (for example, a violent invasion and takeover by a foreign people of an

44 Among the many important works devoted at least in part to exploring the intersections of psychoanalytic theory and cultural trauma are the following: Homi K. Bhabha, *The Location of Culture* (New York: Routledge, 1994); Sam Durrant, *Postcolonial Narrative and the Work of Mourning* (Albany: State University of New York Press, 2004); Marianne Hirsch, *The Generation of Postmemory: Writing and Visual Culture After the Holocaust* (New York: Columbia University Press, 2012); Kali Tal, *Worlds of Hurt: Reading the Literatures of Trauma* (Cambridge: Cambridge University Press, 1996); Ranjana Khanna, *Dark Continents: Psychoanalysis and Colonialism* (Durham, NC: Duke University Press, 2003); Kai Erikson, "Notes on Trauma and Community," in *Trauma: Explorations in Memory*," 183–99; and several studies by Dominick LaCapra, including *Representing the Holocaust: History, Theory, Trauma* (Ithaca: Cornell University Press, 1994), and *Writing History, Writing Trauma* (Baltimore: Johns Hopkins University Press, 2001).

indigenous people) might, in its unresolved state, become a cultural fixation and in that form passed down over many generations. The colonized Unconscious, we might say, can neither truly forget nor truly remember the original violence, and in that setting the past is kept alive in the present (and as the present) through constant reenactment. To draw on Caruth again, "for history to be a history of trauma means that it is referential precisely to the extent that it is not fully perceived as it occurs; or to put it somewhat differently, that a history can be grasped only in the very inaccessibility of its occurrence." In this context, the original cultural wound is "not available to consciousness until it imposes itself again ... in the ... repetitive actions of the survivor[s]."[45] Precisely how the traumatic force of the original wound is *acquired* by subsequent generations—people who were not even present at the start—is not particularly clear in Caruth's account, but she imagines that the trauma can be passed down in the form of the communication of what was missed (the inherent latency) of the original event.[46]

Part of my effort of a corrective revision of Caruth's promising but flawed perspective is to draw on Paul's concept of memic replication as a way of linking together two of her key (fundamentally Freudian) ideas: that unresolved trauma returns in repetitive actions (symptoms) and that trauma can be transmitted in the form of *mis*communications, where what is passed on, from one person to another or even across generations, is at once intelligible and unintelligible. In the context of Jewish culture, we might think especially in terms of what Freud understands as the "insatiable" need among members of that culture—and, as I have been at pains to argue, this should be understood precisely as a postexilic phenomenon—"to render their religious precepts ever and ever more strict, more exacting, but also more petty" (*Moses and*

45 *Unclaimed Experience*, 18, 4.

46 Caruth herself theorizes the process of transmission as akin to the experience of witnessing the anguished testimonies of Holocaust survivors:

"How does one listen to what is impossible? Certainly one challenge of this listening is that it may no longer be simply a choice: to be able to listen to the impossible, that is, is to have been *chosen* by it, *before* the possibility of mastering it without knowledge. This is its danger—the danger ... of trauma's "contagion," of the traumatization of the ones who listen ... To listen to the crisis of a trauma, that is, is not only to listen for the event, but to hear in the testimony the survivor's departure from it; the challenge of the therapeutic listener, in other words, is *how to listen to departure*." (Introduction to *Trauma: Explorations in Memory*, 10)

Caruth's understanding of the (transgenerational) passing on of trauma leans especially on Shoshana Felman and Dori Laub's *Testimony: Crises of Witnessing in Literature, Psychoanalysis, and History* (New York: Routledge, 1992).

Monotheism, 173).[47] In the Ezra-tradition, legal observance was clearly meant to be repetitive (Freud would say obsessional) just as it was clearly meant to be transferred (as narrative, ritual, liturgy, theological doctrines, and moral guidelines) from one generation to the next (see Deuteronomy 6:4–9, and Nehemiah 8:1–8, for example). But, accepting Freud's notion that some aspect of this tradition needed to be unconscious before it could truly acquire the compulsive character typical of religious belief, we need finally to explain how the very public nature of Torah and its associated cultural practices could have "produce[d] such mighty effects" (130).

While we shall take up this topic in more detail in the following Coda, as a modest first-step into this thorny interpretive territory I would venture against Freud's own order that Judaic faith did not acquire its compulsive character as the result of the return of repressed memories in distorted form; obsession, that is, did not derive from what was first unconscious, at least not unconscious *content*. Rather, a psychical orientation or response became unconscious only after the content had first become a cultural obsession. In the postexilic period, Torah as both narrative (often re-rendered as recitation, including in the liturgical forms of prayer and hymn) and legal requirements (often in the form of specifically ritualized observances or prohibitions) became encoded in all forms of cultural behavior. In effect, the memic organization of postexilic culture made it impossible to render Jewish history simply as the past because the cultural obsession insisted that the past was ever-present. Constantly (re) translated into the terms laid out by Torah, the past came to function not just as something to be remembered but as memory itself (for example, in the proper form of prescribed behaviors: the order of language, the order of ritual which itself re-created normal as "sacred time"). Repeated over and over again, this memory could never simply be forgotten or even reduced to or organized as simple narrative memory.

To return to the link I just posited between trauma experienced at the collective cultural level and political subjugation (the situation of a colonized people), I would make two related observations. First, while I see no reason to believe that the political Unconscious of the colonized subject operates under the terms of the oedipal economy, that Unconscious is likely to be extremely

47 In a related context, Wieseltier comments that "the shocking thing about Biblical separation" as the foundation of the notion of holiness "is its specificity, which reaches its densest Biblical development in [the postexilic] Leviticus. The *pettiness of the priestly selections, its disturbing obsession with detail*, furnished a great polemical opportunity for the anticlericalism of the eighteen century" (33; my emphasis), a tradition from which much of Freud's perspective derives.

responsive to the constant sense of having lost something or that something has inexplicably gone missing or even that one's own continuing survival has mysteriously become a problem—so closer to the accident model of trauma than to the castration model. One or more of these feelings (and Freud's phrase "heritage of emotion" perfectly captures the collective and transgenerational aspect of such feelings) is likely to arise, and indeed to become even more urgent, in circumstances of helplessness, where something perceived as rightly belonging to the subject (not just territory but language, culture, self-determination, etc.) has been taken away by the Other simply because the Other is more powerful.[48] In colonial situations, this power differential is commonly experienced not just in direct violence but in other policing activities, ones that involve daily slights, insults, a constant if possibly low-level aggression and harassment; and, of course, overt violence as a method of subjugation itself can be either official (as in military actions of various kinds) or unofficial (e.g. beatings or sexual assault). As part of his effort to describe the impact of Roman colonization on the Jewish psyche in the time of Jesus (whose message about the "kingdom of God" might have been intended as a direct challenge to Roman rule), John Dominic Crossan observes that colonial situations often given rise to feelings of intense ambivalence in the colonized, a state of quasi-schizophrenia. "An occupied country," Crossan writes, "has, as it were, a multiple-personality disorder. One part of it must hate and despise the oppressor, but the other must envy and admire its superior power. And … if body is to society as microcosm to macrocosm, certain individuals may experience exactly the same split within themselves."[49] The split personality of the colonized subject, whether that subject is a single individual or the collective, undoubtedly promotes both external and internal aggression (in some instances of the latter even approaching a form of self-loathing).

48 Though hardly constituting proof, the following will, for now, have to suffice as limited evidence for my claim that this is not an uncommon response to colonization. Addressing what he calls the "fundamental theme" for contemporary African writers, Chinua Achebe wrote in 1964 that

"This theme … is that African people did not hear of culture for the first time from Europeans; that their societies were not mindless but frequently had a philosophy of great depth and value and beauty, that they had poetry and, above all, they had dignity. It is this dignity that many African people all but lost during the colonial period and it is this that they must now regain. The worst thing that can happen to a people is the loss of their dignity and self-respect. The writer's duty is to help them regain it by showing them in human terms what happened to them, what they lost." ("The Role of the Writer in a New Nation," in *African Writers on African Writing*, ed. G. D. Killam [Evanston, IL: Northwestern University Press, 1973], 8).

49 *Jesus: A Revolutionary Biography* (San Francisco: HarperSanFrancisco, 1989), 89.

My second observation, which I offer here as a very tentative attempt to establish the terms of a fuller argument, concerns the collective ritualization of symbolic identity, the way, for example, the past can be transformed into and so experienced not as the past to be commemorated but as a present to be (re)lived. I would like to suggest that transgenerational transmission of an unconscious attachment to unresolved traumatic experience is more likely to occur where, as in colonial situations, a constitutive *us vs. them* mentality arises. That is, what we might think of as the affective quality of the trauma, which might lead a later generation to experience the trauma of an earlier generation as its own lived reality, is more strongly informed and reinforced by the collective or socialized appeal to the unacceptable ongoing presence of a common (hated) group, the enemy Other.

In the context of understanding the history of any culture as the history of a trauma, Caruth argues that traumatic history entails "not only the passing on of a crisis but also the passing on of a survival that can only be possessed within a history larger than any single individual or any single generation."[50] What is transmitted as both crisis and survival, Walter Benn Michaels observes, "is not the normalizing knowledge of the horror but the horror itself."[51] But what precisely defines the horror or what Freud might have called the "kernel" of the trauma, especially as it can be passed on to one who was not originally present? To the extent Caruth understands the kernel as a constitutive absence or missing of some kind, we might say that, even for those who "come after" the origin of the trauma, what is absent or missed is the narrative structure providing the connective tissue between past and present. There is, in a sense, a gap in the people's history, a gap that cannot simply be filled by reality (or even memory) because such "filling in" would serve to normalize the traumatic situation itself, which is precisely what is unacceptable and so must be denied at all costs.

Even though their Persian overlords were hardly the taskmasters of Egypt, postexilic Judaean culture was forced to confront the reality of its political subjugation in the Promised Land itself. Undoubtedly, there was some local admiration for or even envy of Persian imperial power just as the later rule of the Greeks would prompt many Judaeans to willingly participate in the process of Hellenization. But to the extent the idea of being the chosen people, an idea created by Torah itself, still had a very special allure, Judaean culture survived in a state of contradiction: the lived reality of colonial domination, even

50 *Unclaimed Experience*, 71.

51 "'You who never was there': Slavery and the New Historicism, Deconstruction and the Holocaust," *Narrative* 4 (1996): 8.

if at times relatively benign, was at odds with the claim to be a holy nation, where "holy" meant especially "set apart from" (as in Exodus 19:6 and Leviticus 20:26). The Ezra-inspired (re)commitment to Torah gave (re)new(ed) emphasis to even as it defined the nature of holiness: to remain faithful to what set the (non)nation of Israel apart from the foreigners at once proclaimed the sign and so the ongoing fact of the people's chosenness (we are different from those who rule over us in our own land) and served as what Melford Spiro has called a "culturally constituted defense mechanism."[52] In his seminal study of the forms of Jewish memory, Yerushalmi makes three points that lend general support to Spiro's claim. First, that historiography in the modern sense was slow in developing in Jewish culture. Second, that the commemoration of the past served a deliberately memic function (the past was often seen as a kind of archetype, and it was typically retained through ritual and related liturgical practices that often made it virtually indistinguishable from the present). And third, to the extent Torah was the focus of memic commemoration, Jewish culture quite deliberately privileged a mythic narrative over history in broad terms and contemporary affairs more particularly.[53]

The replication, structured through Torah's memic capacity, of the assertion of being the chosen people of God, that is, could defend against the anxiety that the very status of Judaea as a minor province of a greater empire proved otherwise, that colonial subjugation was the hard reality and not an aberration. To tell the story of the origin of chosenness in the Torah narrative, a narrative that included the establishment of the Law that would be the very manifestation of the collective calling, was a way of proving that the calling had never truly fallen silent. For the Moses-Exodus account at the heart of Torah permitted the postexilic Judaeans to look forward with hope that another liberation and another national founding lay in their future. A (re)dedication to the conditions of the covenant, in short, would defend against the anxiety that chosenness, which had already failed, meant nothing by offering proof of chosenness, appearances to the contrary notwithstanding. Following Santner, we might think of the Torah-induced compulsion to repeat—both the obsessive revisiting of a past with its promises intact and the constant rehearsals in the form of ritual and liturgy—as the cultural (even cultic) site of the experience of excess of validity over meaning, an excess that subsequently drove "a desperate search for a meaning" in the very process of repetition. Within this framework,

52 "Religious Systems as Culturally Constituted Defense Mechanisms," in *Culture and Human Nature* (Chicago: University of Chicago Press, 1987), 145–60.

53 *Zakhor: Jewish History and Jewish Memory* (Seattle: University of Washington Press, 1982).

what Rosenzweig says of a single Jewish individual applies as well to postexilic Jewish experience as a whole: "something within ... is waiting."

Could any of this have happened if the exiled Judaeans had never returned from Babylon or if Ezra had not delivered the completed text of Torah to Jerusalem? What if the Persian empire had governed its provinces more in the Greek-style, that is, with an explicitly assimilationist orientation? What if Antiochus IV had succeeded in his Hellenization project? What if the Romans had never arrived in Judaea and Hasmonean Judah remained independent? If, if, if. As it turned out, the experiences of first, Israel (with Assyria) and then, Judah (with Babylon), followed eventually by the Judaean experiences of Persia, Greece, and Rome, set the stage for cultural reenactments in which the trauma of a conquered and subjugated people was never resolved. Torah was culturally established in this context as a response to a national crisis—the crisis of the nation itself. In some other history, it might have happened that Torah would eventually have lost its special status. But precisely because the pattern (conquest and destruction, subjugation, exile) was repeated, Torah continued to be accorded the memic status it first achieved during the Persian period. In short, Torah survived because it never ceased to be relevant. To put this another way, because postexilic Jews faced the crisis of incomprehensibility over and over again, were forced repeatedly to confront the pain of loss even as they found new ways to deny that very pain, they remained fixated to the trauma. At least as far as Jewish experience is concerned, this is the answer to Caruth's question: "What does it mean ... for history to be the history of a trauma?"[54] For the postexilic people of Israel, Torah at once revealed and concealed how the trauma at the heart of their history dispossessed them of their own origin story.

54 *Unclaimed Experience*, 15.

CODA 3

Fantasy and the Origin of the (Jewish) Subject

> It is a very remarkable thing that the *Unconscious* of one human being can react upon that of another, without passing through the Conscious. This deserves closer examination .... [B]ut, descriptively speaking, the fact in incontestable.
>
> —FREUD, "The Unconscious"

•••

> The confrontation between immature and helpless infants and the developed social life of their elders will ... always leave some residue of disturbance.
>
> —GAYLE RUBIN, "The Traffic in Women"

•••

> What haunts are not the dead, but the gaps left within us by the secrets of others.
>
> —NICOLAS ABRAHAM, "Notes on the Phantom"

In Coda 1, we saw that Freud failed to resolve the temporal structure of the foundational trauma he claimed resided at the origin of Jewish cultural identity because he could not locate in Jewish history the event that triggered the return of the repressed—what brought back, albeit in the distorted form of Yahwistic monotheism, the long-forgotten murder of the great father-imago, Moses. As an addendum to the exploration in Chapters 2 and 3 of the compulsive conviction underlying Judaic faith, I would now like to take up a related matter: how Freud's effort to locate the *mechanism* of the transmission of Jewish tradition in the discredited notion of phylogenetic inheritance—his infamous Lamarckism—inexplicably fails to consider his own better formulation of the problem of trauma's intergenerational transmission in the concept of fantasy. Just as important, in trying to locate what he refers to as the hypothetical

 | DOI:10.1163/9789004701663_008

bridge "between individual and mass psychology" (*Moses and Monotheism*, 128; German: "*haben wir die Kluft zwischen Individual- und Massenpsychologie überbrückt*" [16:207]), Freud does not avail himself of a different sort of meeting place between the one and the many, the single individual and the broader collective (an entire people) with which he would have been familiar from his own upbringing, the Jewish family. In what follows, then, I want to reflect on how a cultural trauma might have been transmitted across generations as Jewish tradition—replete with the compulsory force Freud theorized as driven by unconscious attachment—precisely to the extent a fantasy regarding the origin of Jewish identity could be passed down within the informal workings of familial life (workings not limited to the Jewish family but taking a very specific cultural or even ideological force within that context).

Although Freud himself has much of value to say on the topic of fantasy, my primary guide here will be Jean Laplanche and Jean-Bertrand Pontalis' 1964 essay, "Fantasme originaire, fantasmes des origins, origine du fantasme," translated into English in 1968 with the misleading title "Fantasy and the Origins of Sexuality."[1] Laplanche and Pontalis are certainly interested in the role played by fantasy in the origin of human sexuality and, indeed, the last section of the essay is almost exclusively focused on that issue. But the essay is concerned with fantasy much more broadly conceived and lists the fantasy associated with the origins of *sexuality*—"fantasies of seduction"—as just one of the three "original fantasies" (Freud's *Urphantasien*):

> In their content, … the original fantasies [primal scene, seduction, castration] … [all] relate to the origins. Like myths, they claim to provide a representation of, and a solution to, the major enigmas which confront the child. Whatever appears to the subject as something needing an explanation or theory is dramatized as a moment of emergence, the beginning of a history. Fantasies of origins: the primal scene pictures the origin of the individual; fantasies of seduction, the origin and upsurge of sexuality; fantasies of castration, the origin of the difference between the sexes. Their themes therefore display, with redoubled significance, that original fantasies justify their status of already being there. There is obvious convergence of theme, of structure, and no doubt also of function: … through the scenarios constructed by the varied quest for origins, we are offered the field of fantasy, the origin of the subject himself.[2]

1 "Fantasy and the Origins of Sexuality," *The International Journal of Psycho-analysis* 49 (1968): 1–18.

2 "Fantasy and the Origins of Sexuality," 11.

In what follows, I will set aside the fantasies of seduction and castration to focus on the fantasy of origins. Moreover, in taking up Laplanche and Pontalis' analysis of the role played by the fantasy of origins (the primal scene) in "the origin of the subject," I will give special attention to two crucial matters: first, to how the individual is never an isolated figure but is rather, as Jacques Lacan puts it, always already (de)constructed through its dispossession by an Other and second, to how such dispossession in the context of the familial life (a child whose subjectivity is formed through the constant pressure exerted by its engagement with earlier generations) can help us understand both the origin and the replication of the *Jewish* subject as it emerges in relation to fantasies peculiar to Jewish culture or, more narrowly even, to what in *Moses and Monotheism* Freud had called "the fateful content of the religious history of the Jews" (57).[3]

1

Laplanche and Pontalis begin their essay by observing that "from its earliest day, psychoanalysis has been concerned with the material of fantasy" where the "German '*Phantasie*' ... denote[s] ... not so much the faculty of imagining" as "the imaginary world" itself, "the patient's inner world of imagination." They go on to note that "it is difficult therefore to avoid defining this world in terms of what it is not, the world of reality."[4] Despite the fact that Freud himself referred to "the activity of '*fantasying*'" as a "species of thought-activity ... split off" and "kept free from reality testing"—in this context he also refers to "unconscious processes" defined by "their entire disregard of reality testing; they equate reality of thought with external reality" ("Formulations on the Two Principles of Mental Functioning," *SE*, 11:222, 225)—for Laplanche and Pontalis fantasy doesn't mean existing in the mind in opposition to what is objectively real (subjective and potentially illusory as opposed to having an actual material existence external to the mind). But neither is fantasy simply the product

3 Commenting on what he calls the "frustration inherent in the very discourse of the subject," Lacan glosses this frustration as the subject's inescapable grappling with "an ever-growing dispossession of ... being." He goes on to describe the burden of an incessant psychical "labor" in which the subject is compelled to "reconstruct this construct [its very being] *for another*," only to "find ... the fundamental alienation which made him construct it *like another one*, and which has always destined it to be stripped from him *by another*" (*The Language of the Self: The Function of Language in Psychoanalysis*, trans. Anthony Wilden [New York: Dell, 1968], 11).

4 "Fantasy and the Origins of Sexuality," 1.

of the mind's reworking of what is objectively real where that "real" is understood as having ontological and temporal priority over the thought-activity that is but reality's shadow.[5] Laplanche and Pontalis point out that Freud often has "recourse to the notion of 'psychical reality,'" and they appear to accept that, as Freud puts it in *The Interpretation of Dreams*, "*psychical* reality is a particular form of existence not to be confused with *material* reality" (*SE*, 5:620).[6] This phrasing didn't take its current form until the 1919 edition. In the 1909 edition, Freud had written that "psychical reality ... has more than one form of existence" (*SE*, 5:620n1). Laplanche and Pontalis note that "the successive reformulations of this principle in various editions"—other changes appear in 1914—"show both Freud's concern to define accurately the concept of psychical reality, and the difficulties he experienced in so doing." They add, however, that, "if Freud again and again loses the notion of psychical reality, ... the difficulty and ambiguity lie in the very nature of its relationship, to the real and to the imaginary, as is shown in the central domain of fantasy."[7] As an instance (perhaps the prime instance) of psychical reality, fantasy constitutes its own reality ("a particular form of existence"). The problem remains, however, of how to define this reality or to locate it within what Laplanche and Pontalis call "the domain of opposition between subjective and objective, between an inner world ... and an external world."[8]

Developing Freud's never fully organized thinking on the topic, Laplanche and Pontalis argue that fantasy is neither subjective nor objective; it is, rather, intersubjective. Freud himself, of course, had hypothesized that what in psychical reality transcended the historical life of the individual—what was antecedent to the individual's reality—was a "store of unconscious phantasies" ("From a Case of Paranoia," *SE*, 14:269) deriving from prehistoric truths and then passed on through a phylogenetic inheritance (the acquired characteristics or inherited memory traces of Lamarckism). By contrast, Laplanche and Pontalis understand the historicity of fantasy in different terms. They argue that if fantasy's residence "in history" yet "lies beyond the history of the [individual]

5 Freud, of course, always struggled with this distinction. As Laplanche and Pontalis remark, "at first he feels it almost his duty to show the patient what is under the counter" (2). But more broadly, Freud always sought as the external ground or origin of neurosis a precipitating event, the "there" of the neurosis that had a historical location of some kind, what he sometimes refers to as the "kernel of truth." Laplanche and Pontalis later point out that "the search for chronology, going backwards into time towards the first real, verifiable elements, is still the guiding principle of Freud's practice"; Freud, in short, "never entirely resigned himself to accepting [fantasies: e.g. the primal scene] as purely imaginary creations" (8).

6 "Fantasy and the Origins of Sexuality," 2.

7 "Fantasy and the Origins of Sexuality," 3, 3n5.

8 "Fantasy and the Origins of Sexuality," 2.

subject," fantasy possesses an historical aspect precisely as "a kind of language and a symbolic sequence."[9] Elaborating on the nature and function of this "kind of language" and in particular on its intersubjective dimension, Laplanche and Pontalis observe that in the domain of fantasy the "suspension of the reality of external events" is not "for the *benefit* of subjective reality"; rather, the suspension "creates a new field, that of verbalization, where the difference between the real and the imaginary may retain its value.... The homology between the analytic and the unconscious field, whose emergence it stimulates, is not due to their common subjectivity, but to the deep kinship between the unconscious and the field of speech. So it is not 'It is *you* who say so,' but 'It is you who *say* so.'" Nevertheless, the act of speaking (the *saying* so) cannot be fully separated from the subject-position of either the speaker (*you* who say so) or the listener (*I* who hear what you say) because, as Laplanche and Pontalis later remark, "the subject [of fantasy] is ... located in a structure of interrelationship." Returning to Lacan's notion of dispossession cited above, we might say that the experience of being dispossessed isn't simply the result of the fact that the Other imposes but that the Other speaks and the subject-in-formation hears. In that sense, as Laplanche and Pontalis comment, the field of verbalization that places this relationship "in history" has less to do with "a language system" than with "the complexities of a particular speech."[10]

Focusing on the listening side of the relationship (how the subject-in-formation is formed and informed by the Other's speaking), Laplanche and Pontalis note that, "in his first theoretical sketches on the subject of fantasy, Freud stresses ... the role of aural perception."[11] In a 1897 letter to Fliess, for example, Freud writes that "the origin of phantasies ... is things heard but only understood subsequently" (*Origins*, 201).[12] Elaborating on this claim in Draft L, he writes:

> Phantasies are psychical outworks constructed in order to bar the way to ... memories. At the same time, phantasies serve the purpose of refining the memories, of sublimating them. *They are built up out of things that*

9 "Fantasy and the Origins of Sexuality," 9–10. The full statement reads as follows: "The original fantasy is first and foremost a fantasy: it lies beyond the history of the subject but nevertheless in history: a kind of language and a symbolic sequence, but loaded with elements of imagination: a structure, but activated by contingent elements."

10 "Fantasy and the Origins of Sexuality," 3n6; 10n20.

11 "Fantasy and the Origins of Sexuality," 10.

12 We might note in the phrase "only understood subsequently" Freud is anticipating the concept of latency or deferred action (*Nachträglichkeit*) that he will later associate with the emergence of traumatic neurosis, a topic that is still central to his thinking in *Moses and Monotheism* (e.g. 82–130).

> *have been heard about and then subsequently turned to account*; thus *they combine things that have been experienced and things that have been heard about past events* (*from the history of parents and ancestors*) … They are related to things heard in the same way dreams are related to things seen. (*Origins*, 197–98; my emphases)

And then again in Draft M, he writes,

> *Phantasies arise from an unconscious combination of things experienced and heard,* constructed for particular purposes. These purposes aim at making inaccessible the memory from which symptoms have been generated or might be generated. Phantasies are constructed by a process of fusion and distortion … unconscious fictions which have not succumbed to defense. (*Origins*, 204; my emphasis)

He retains the concept in later writings. Commenting on the primal scene in "From a Case of Paranoia" (1914), he refers to the recollection of noises—here, the *sounds* of the parents' coitus rather than the sight of it—as "an indispensable part of the phantasy of listening" (SE, 14:269). And in *Moses and Monotheism*, he offers the general reflection that "thought-processes, and what may be analogous to them in the Id, are unconscious per se and obtain their entry into consciousness by their connection, via *the function of speech, with memory traces of perceptions through* touch and *ear*" (124; my emphases; original italics deleted). Remarking that "one must consider why such a privileged position was accorded [by Freud] to hearing," Laplanche and Pontalis "suggest there are two reasons." The first one "relates to the *sensorium* in question":

> hearing, when it occurs, breaks the continuity of an undifferentiated perceptual field [that is, it makes a distinction between the perceiver's experience and the source of that experience] and at the same time is a sign (the noise waited for and heard in the night) which puts the subject in the position of having to answer to something. To this extent the prototype of the signifier lies in the aural sphere, even if there are correspondences in the other registers.

But to the extent that, from a psychoanalytic perspective, the "complexities of a particular speech" are first and foremost what emerges in the speaking and listening characteristic of family life—what we might call familial discourse (Freud's "from the history of parents and ancestors")—the second reason for giving special attention to hearing's (aural perception's) role in the construction of fantasy may be even more important: "hearing is also … the history or legends of the parents, grandparents and the ancestors: the family *sounds* or *sayings*, this spoken or secret discourse going on prior to the subject's arrival, within which he must find his way."[13]

If, on the one hand, Laplanche and Pontalis' various phrases—"the noise … heard in the night," "the history or legends of the parents, grandparents, and the ancestors," "the family sounds or sayings," and "this spoken or secret discourse going on prior to the subject's arrival"—all help us conceptualize what they later describe as the situation of the "*dramatis personae*," who in fantasy "receive their notation from a family legend which is mutilated, disordered, and misunderstood," on the other hand the very notions of mutilated sayings, disordered familial history, and the overhearing of secrets (which may not even be fully understood) call attention to "the deep kinship between the unconscious and the field of speech."[14] More precisely, we can see how and why, as a field of intersubjective verbalization, the fantasy that gets established at the heart of familial discourse is marked by this kinship.

If we then coordinate the unconscious aspect of speech (the Other's speaking) with that aspect of listening (again, overhearing is perhaps a better term) that "puts the [hearing-]subject in the position of having to answer to something," we can understand that the intersubjective element of fantasy includes the hearing-subject's "answerability" to what is unconscious in the speaking-Other, or, to adapt a phrase from Eric Santner, the subject's answerability to the Other-with-an-unconscious. A major part of what the (hearing-) subject of fantasy is responsive to in familial discourse—the family's history and legends, sounds, sayings, and secrets that predate the subject's "arrival" on the scene—is the speaking-Other's own otherness to itself: for, as Santner adds, "what makes the Other *other* is not his or her spatial exteriority with respect to my being but the fact that he or she is *strange*, is a *stranger*, and not only to me but also to him- or herself, is the bearer of an internal alterity, an enigmatic density of desire."[15] Within this context, fantasy can be conceived as intersubjective precisely to the extent that it is takes root in the subject as the Other transmits what Laplanche elsewhere calls "enigmatic messages" that are retained in the subject's psyche as "unconscious residues."[16] "Transmitted,"

---

13 "Fantasy and the Origins of Sexuality," 10–11.

14 "Fantasy and the Origins of Sexuality," 13.

15 *On the Psychotheology of Everyday Life: Reflections on Freud and Rosenzweig* (Chicago: University of Chicago Press, 2001), 9.

16 *New Foundations for Psychoanalysis*, trans. David Macey (Oxford: Basil Blackwell, 1989), 130.

as Laplanche and Pontalis observe, "by the parental unconscious," a kind of "'foreign body'"—an enigmatic message or perhaps, more properly, an enigmatic signifier—is "brought to the subject, not by perception …, but by parental desire and its supporting fantasy."[17]

Building on Laplanche's reworking of the Freudian concept of seduction, Santner remarks in a related context that "the traumatic encounter with the dense, enigmatic presence of the Other's desire" is "constitutive of the inner strangeness we call the unconscious."[18] The subject (over)hearing what we might call the whispers of the family responds by way of echoing the Other's "own out-of-jointness," its own "'hindered' dimension," its own "internal alienness," and so "open[s itself] to the agitation and turbulence *immanent* to any construction of identity."[19] To put this another way, set in motion by the subject's experience of what Lacan calls an "ever-growing dispossession," fantasy emerges as the subject unwittingly comes to speak "like another one" in the shared language of desire. In short, faced with the Other's uncanny presence that conceals as much as it reveals (and conceals even from itself), the subject responds via repetition compulsion, a defense mechanism that yet reinforces and perpetuates precisely what is being defended against. The origin of fantasy would thus be a prime instance of what Santner calls "ibidity." As noted in Chapter 3, reworking Freud's foundational ego / id distinction, Santner observes that "the *libidinal* component of one's attachments to … symbolic identity must also be thought of as 'ibidinal'" in that it "calls forth a largely unconscious 'citation' of authority": prompted, invited, summoned, provoked by a "primordial *ex-citation*," the subject is "called out to engage in a repetitive and interminable citational praxis in relation to a source of authorization."[20] Especially for the child just learning to speak and thus exposed to the Other's enigmatic desire at a formative stage, the very capacity for verbalization acquires this ibidinal dimension: the Other's unconscious—its own fantasy, its own desire—takes root as "residues" within the developing psyche. The psychical reality (neither subjective nor objective) that thereby emerges

17 "Fantasy and the Origins of Sexuality," 10n20, 8n16. In *Totem and Taboo*, Freud had observed that "even the most ruthless suppression must leave room for the distorted surrogate impulses and for reactions resulting from them. If so, … we may safely assume that no generation is able to conceal any of its more important mental processes from its successor" (*SE*, 13:159).

18 *On the Psychotheology of Everyday Life*, 33–34; see Laplanche, *Essays on Otherness*, ed. John Fletcher (New York: Routledge, 1999), 128 and *passim*.

19 *On the Psychotheology of Everyday Life*, 7, 5.

20 *On the Psychotheology of Everyday Life*, 50.

is not simply in the form of fantasy but precisely the fantasy of the Other as transmitted, though perhaps in distorted or even mutilated form, across a generational divide.[21]

2

How then should we understand the role of fantasy in the origin of the *Jewish* subject especially as that subject's sense of its own origin—the fantasy construct of a peculiarly Jewish primal scene—predates even as it establishes the psychical framework for its encounter with Jewish tradition in the form of Torah (the main focus of Chapter 3)? We might first note that, as Laplanche and Pontalis recognize, in its historical situatedness fantasy structure (located in "a kind of language and a symbolic sequence") is "activated by *contingent* elements. As such it is characterized by certain traits which make it difficult to assimilate to a purely transcendental schema, even if it provides the possibility of experience."[22] In other words, while fantasy itself is a generalized human trait—the human psyche everywhere and at all times has the capacity for fantasizing—the link between fantasy and "the complexities of a particular speech" means that, while fantasy transcends the individual, there is no universal fantasy structure; fantasy, that is, arises in particular historical and cultural contexts.[23]

With this restriction in mind, we might consider the case of a hypothetical Jewish child during its formative years (for Freud always up to about age five,

21 In his summary of repetition compulsion as a "positive reaction" to trauma (in opposition to the "negative reaction" defined by inhibition or phobia), Freud associates repetition compulsion explicitly with "fixation to the trauma" (*Moses and Monotheism*, 95). But in the case of fantasy, the subject becomes fixated to the Other's trauma as that is communicated in the field of (unconscious) verbalization.

22 "Fantasy and the Origins of Sexuality," 10; my emphasis.

23 As an instance of what they mean by "contingent elements" in the origin of fantasy, Laplanche and Pontalis note, for example, that even in the case of the Oedipus complex, Freud's "generalized formulation ... cannot be taken in any formal sense: it describes a limited series of concrete positions with the inter-psychological field created by the father-mother-child triangle. From the point of view of structural anthropology, one might see this *as one of the forms* of the law governing human interchanges, a law which in other cultures might be incarnated in other persons and in other forms. The prohibitory function of the law might, for instance, be expressed by an agency other than the father" (10n20).

a period roughly coterminous with language-acquisition).[24] As it is learning to understand the familial language and to speak it, this child assimilates through the legends and history, the sayings, sounds, and secrets spoken or whispered by the members of earlier generations (parents and grandparents chief among these) the very mystery of Jewish answerability to God and in particular the incomprehensibility of Jewish identity in the wake of national loss and the concomitant recognition that God had failed to keep his promises. Jewish strangeness to itself thereby becomes for the child the precondition of the later and more formal (textualized, ritualized) acquisition of the memic replicator, Torah, that overlays the strangeness, at once deflecting and reinforcing it, providing answers (*we* failed God / *we* have been justly punished because we did not obey the Law) even as it provokes questions to be posed to the unanswering and unanswerable God.[25] If the members of earlier generations who speak of these matters experience an internal alienness in which, as Franz Rosenzweig puts it, "something within is [ever-after] waiting," the child who (over)hears at some level registers a before-time (what happened "prior to its

---

24 Reflecting back on his own earlier discoveries, Freud writes in Part III of *Moses and Monotheism*:

"The impression we experienced at an early age and forgot later, to which I have ascribed such great importance for the ætiology if the neuroses, are called traumata .... All these traumata belong to early childhood, the period up to about five years. *Impressions during the time when the child begins to speak are found to be especially interesting.* The period between two and four years is the most important. How soon after birth this sensitiveness to traumata begins we are not able to say. The experiences in question are as a rule entirely forgotten and remain inaccessible to memory. They belong to the period of infantile amnesia which is often interrupted by isolated fragmentary memories, the so-called "screen-memories." ... The traumata are either bodily experiences or perceptions, especially those heard or seen; that is to say, they are either experiences or impressions." (91, 93–94; my emphasis)

For Freud's emphasis on experiences happening at or near age five, see also "From the History of an Infantile Neurosis" (1918), *SE*, 17:109.

25 Freud's reflection on the role played by the Exodus story in the construction of Jewish identity is an especially apt statement of this strangeness:

"To achieve lasting psychical effect in a people it is obviously not sufficient to assure them that they were specially chosen by God. This assurance must be proved if they are to attach belief to it and draw their conclusions from that belief. In the religion of Moses the Exodus served as such a proof; God, or Moses in his name, did not tire of citing this proof of favor. The feast of the Passover was established to keep this event in mind, or, rather, an old feast was endowed with this memory. Yet it was only a memory. The Exodus itself belonged to a dim past. At the time the signs of God's favor were meager enough; the fate of the people of Israel would indicate rather his disfavor .... [T]he people of Israel, however, adhered to their God all the more devotedly the worse they were treated by him." (*Moses and Monotheism*, 142–43).

arrival") in relation to which its own present (and future) comes to be defined by an originary loss that does not even derive from its own direct experience.[26]

It is worth noting here the optimism of Rosenzweig's claim that, in "the moment of [this child'] second birth"—Freud might have thought of this moment as happening somewhere between age two and age four and certainly before age five—this child is not reborn "personally as an individual" but rather "is born a Jew" precisely through a discovery of its inseparable link to, and perhaps even its lived reenactment of, "the protohistory of [the] people's revelation."[27] No less optimistically but more cognizant of the stakes involved—the haunting of the Jewish psyche, we might say—Santner offers a related psychotheological perspective that is particularly applicable to the postexilic Unconscious at the heart of Jewish identity: "the possibility of a 'We,' of communality, is granted on the basis of the fact that every familiar is ultimately strange and that ... I am even in a crucial sense a stranger to myself."[28] As a corrective of sorts to Rosenzweig, Santner's comment permits us to see that to be "[re]born a Jew" via an encounter with "the protohistory of [the] people's revelation" means that the Jewish child entering the field of verbalization within the Jewish family is forever estranged from itself and will ever-after be compelled to replicate that self-estrangement.[29] Something within is indeed waiting: the uncanny presence inseparable from Jewish identity. Precisely because so deeply enmeshed in and inseparable from a culturally transmitted fantasy structure that fixes the origin of the people in what Freud had called "a traumatic experience" (*Moses and Monotheism*, 65), the God of Torah, the

26 Rosenzweig, *The Star of Redemption*, trans. William W. Hallo (New York: Holt, Rinehart and Winston, 1970), 404–05. Building on their claim that fantasies are "characterized by the absence of subjectivization"—if "the subject is present *in* the [fantasy-]scene" it is but "one character amongst many"—Laplanche and Pontalis observe that Freud himself understood fantasies as "dependent on" or even deriving from "earlier fantasy structures." In short, to the extent that, as Laplanche and Pontalis suggest, "the structure of deepest fantasy" is almost subjectless, this is in part because the subject does not truly create the fantasy (it does not belong exclusively to the subject). As they note earlier, in fantasy "the subject does not encounter the structure, but is carried along by it" (13–14, 10n20).

27 *Star of Redemption*, 396–97. Focusing explicitly on Jewish *male* identity, Rosenzweig adds that "the moment of his second birth ... must lie for him beyond the confines of his personality, before his own life. The rebirth of the Jew—and it is of him that we are here speaking—is not his personal one, but the transformation of his people for freedom in the divine covenant of revelation."

28 *On the Psychotheology of Everyday Life*, 6.

29 Laplanche and Pontalis venture that the Freudian *Urphantasien* (primal fantasies) mark "'inherited memory traces'" that "in turn provide support of individual fantasies" precisely to the extent Freud's notion of an individual's "pre-history ... can be located as a pre-structure ... *actualized and transmitted by the parental fantasies*" (17; my emphasis).

God whose choosing brought the people of Israel into existence as his chosen people, becomes, to borrow from Augustine's *Confessions*, that before which the Jewish subject becomes a problem to itself.[30]

If, as Laplanche and Pontalis argue in their elaboration of Freud's notion of *Urphantasien*, the three original fantasies together constitute the "the origin of the subject," that is because this "field of fantasy" creates for the emergent subject its various points of origin—as an individual, as a sexual being, as a gendered being. Without going into it in great detail, Laplanche and Pontalis associate these points of origin "with the concept of myth": for example, the fantasy of the child's seduction by the adult "would become the myth of the origin of sexuality." More broadly, in the mythic structure of fantasy the very concept of the point of origin is built into the fantasy: "The relationship of the myth to the time factor (the event) is present and, as it were embedded in the myth itself." This is so in part because the "myth (or fantasy) of the intrusion of the fantasy (or myth) into the subject ... cannot but occur to the organism, the little human being, at a point in time." But that time-factor then takes up a new place within the mythic construct of the fantasy: original fantasies "relate to the origins" through temporal projection backwards in time. For, as noted earlier, "like myths," original fantasies / fantasies of origin "claim to provide a representation of, and a solution to, the major enigmas which confront the child" through what Laplanche and Pontalis call a "postulate of retroactivity": "whatever appears to the subject as something needing an explanation or theory is dramatized as a moment of emergence, the beginning of a history."[31]

In simplest terms, then, fantasy takes up residence in the psyche—is preserved there—in the form of an origin story. Fantasy's psychical emergence in the form of an origin story (where the story is itself part of the fantasy) helps explain what Laplanche and Pontalis mean by their comment that "the subject can ... capture an unconscious fantasy ... in consciousness." Their subsequent observation that a psychical experience "close to the limits of the unconscious ... can pass from one side to the other" (that is, from unconscious to conscious thought-activity) helps us understand what it means to associate

30 Augustine, *Confessions*, Book 10: "But Thou, O Lord my God, hearken; behold, and see, and have mercy and heal me, Thou, in whose presence I have become a problem to myself; and that is my infirmity" (*Confessions*, trans. Edward B. Pusey [New York: Modern Library, 1999], 229). Santner observes of Torah's motivating impact that, first and foremost, "the force of the commandments derive ... from the fact that *they permeate the practices of everyday life* (rather than present a series of principles or theological doctrines about man, God, and world)." He adds that the commandments thereby "serve to sustain *the enigma of election* as a vital experience" (120; my emphases; original italics deleted).

31 "Fantasy and the Origins of Sexuality," 5, 11.

fantasy with mythic construction: in the form of myth, fantasy creates and then retains a narrative establishing an historical chronology. In short, fantasy takes the form of a story the subject constructs for itself regarding how the psychical reality of the fantasy came to be in the first place—its point of origin. As Laplanche and Pontalis remark, "the origin of the fantasy is integrated in the very structure of the original fantasy."[32]

Torah, of course, is precisely the origin story or foundation myth for the collective known as the Jewish people or the people of Israel. Within that conceptual framework we should then understand Torah in its capacity as memic replicator also in terms of fantasy structure and thus also as central to the "origin of the [Jewish] subject": the fantasy of origins that "pictures the origin of the individual" as the *Jewish* individual, Rosenzweig's second birth of the individual as a Jew and thus as an individual defined precisely in terms of the traumatic experience that gave and continues to give this group its distinctive identity. In very broad terms, as a "performative text," Torah is, as Robert Paul suggests, "a myth ... and as such ... does what myths do: it creates a cosmos within which a form of life takes place and acquires meaning for those under its influence." But more in line with Laplanche and Pontalis' understanding, Paul adds that Torah functions as a "dominant cultural symbol ... able to produce ... a fantasy ... that is motivationally powerful yet unconscious"; he argues more specifically that "the myth embedded in the Torah narrative, and the rituals and practices surrounding it, can be seen to mobilize the narcissism, aggression, envy, and ambition of each individual and then transform those impulses into the internal self-regulating agency through which each individual comes to experience the myth as true and its authority as ineluctable." Precisely because

32 "Fantasy and the Origins of Sexuality," 11n25, 12, 10. To take the example of the primal-scene fantasy (the "origin of the individual" as part of the broader foundation myth of "the origin of the subject"), Stanley Cavell suggests that the primal scene concerns not simply the origin "of the subject as an individual" but more precisely aims to answer "the question: Why of all the ones I might have been am I just this one and no other, given this world and no other, *possessed of exactly this mother and father*?" (*Disowning Knowledge in Seven Plays of Shakespeare* [Cambridge: Cambridge University Press, 2003], 187; my emphasis). The primal-scene fantasy then retroactively constructs the answer to that question: I was conceived by this particular mother and father at this particular time and place, an event that, paradoxically, I witnessed before I even existed (since I came into existence only as the result of my parents coming together at this particular time and place). Laplanche and Pontalis note in a related context that the original fantasies "are not only symbolic, but represent the insertion, mediated by the imagined scenario, of the most radically formative symbolism, into corporeal reality. The primal scene represents ... the conjunction of the biological fact of conception and birth with the symbolic act of filiation: it unites the 'savage act' of coitus and the existence of a mother-father-child triad" (11n23).

fantasy is intersubjective, however, Torah's function as memic replicator takes on that role within a peculiarly Jewish kind of fantasy structure. For, as Paul remarks in a passage we noted in Chapter 3, Torah aims to "produce … a community of individuals 'similar' to it and to each other, in the sense that they all, as individuals, embody the Torah by enacting the instructions within it." As the foundation myth of the Jewish people, Paul concludes "Torah not only enjoins those under its influence to practice the laws it gives but also insists repeatedly that it be transmitted across generations and that it itself be copied."[33]

Building on Laplanche's notion of the "implantation of enigmatic messages" from the Other that are retained as "unconscious residues" in the one receiving them, Santner argues in a way that matches Paul's understanding of the cultural situation of Torah that the "Other can be understood not only as another subject *but also as the symbolic tradition and order into which one was born*, which in turn, always includes traces of lost forms of life." He adds later that, "as another way of formulating Laplanche's fundamental thesis," we might say that "every induction into the domain of socio-symbolic relations is also … a seduction: one's solidarity with the spirit of one's family / community / institution is always in part sustained by the 'spirit world' of transgressive enjoyment structured in fantasy. The crucial point here" is that fantasy's centrality to the "governing rules of social relations is at least to some degree immanent to their effectivity."[34] It is precisely as an enigmatic message into which postexilic Jewish culture is seduced by Torah (a seduction that is then repeated within the discourse of the Jewish family in which many of the central practices of Torah have their primary location) that we might most fully appreciate Freud's

33 *Moses and Civilization: The Meaning Behind Freud's Myth* (New Haven: Yale University Press, 1996), 15, 171–72, 72, 187. Santner remarks in a related context that "one cannot … grasp the meaning of … Jewish election … in abstraction from the practices and experiences in which the concept has its life" (119).

34 *On the Psychotheology of Everyday Life*, 97, 102; my emphasis; original italics deleted. In a related conceptual context, offering a correction to Freud's Lamarckism, Paul adds that for

> "the "memory" produced by participating in [a] religious practice … [to] seem convincing, it must at some level correspond to fantasies, as well as to conflicts, impulses, anxieties, and defenses, generated by the interaction of an infant human with its nurturing environment …. In this way of understanding Freud, we see that the performance of religious practices creates, in the present, that sense of reality beyond any rational conviction with which a myth is experienced …. The myth gives shape to the individual fantasy, while the psychological energy of individuals is transformed through ritual symbolism into the fuel that animates the cultural symbol system." (174)

This intergenerational transmission of what Freud considered the "compulsive conviction" underlying Judaic faith is an instance of Santner's "ibidity": the child's "ex-citation"—the call to respond to the "cultural symbol system"—both replicates the system and repeats the dispossession that was its true origin.

comment in *Moses and Monotheism* that his struggle to understand "the problem of how and why the character of the Jewish people developed in the form it did ... haunted [him] like an unlaid ghost" (131–32).[35] For, as Cathy Caruth observes, "the peculiar temporality of trauma" includes the uncanny sense that "the past it foists upon one is not one's own." In a context in which Judaic monotheism, Jewish identity, and their shared commitment to the notion of divine election become intertwined in the aftermath of national loss, the people's very survival as a people takes on a fantasy structure in which their origin is forever-after inseparable from what Caruth aptly calls "a traumatic history that exceeds their grasp."[36]

---

35 We might take Freud's personal experience as a synecdoche Jewish culture as a whole, a culture bound to what Derrida refers to as an "hauntology": *Specters of Marx: The State of Debt, the Work of Mourning, and the New International*, trans. Peggy Kamuf (New York: Routledge, 1994), 10. For a related approach, see Nicolas Abraham, "Notes on the Phantom: A Complement to Freud's Metapsychology," in Nicolas Abraham and Maria Torok, *The Shell and the Kernel: Renewals of Psychoanalysis*, vol. 1, ed. and trans. Nicolas T. Rand (Chicago: University of Chicago Press, 1994), 171–76. Abraham writes, example, that as "a formation of the unconscious" whereby secret texts "are inscribed" within a child's unconscious, the phantom "passes ... from the parent's unconscious into the child's." He adds that "the presence of the phantom indicates the effects, on the descendants, of something that inflicted narcissistic injury or even catastrophe on the parents." And he concludes by observing that "it is crucial to emphasize that the words giving sustenance to the phantom return to haunt from the unconscious. *These are often the very words that rule an entire family's history*" (173–74, 176; my emphasis).

36 Caruth, *Unclaimed Experience: Trauma, Narrative, History* (Baltimore: Johns Hopkins University Press, 1996), 143n10 (original italics deleted), 67.

CHAPTER 4

"Stored like the fragments in an ark": Freud, Hamlet, and Filial Exodus

> If one leaves the tight world of one's ancestors, what replacements are made in the building of the soul? How are the crises of life marked: birth, marriage, death? How are the festivals managed? Men and women need ways of living within ethical frameworks, ways of passing on to their children their morality and their life-styles. What do we do—we who once thought only of abandoning the ways of our parents and parents' parents and gave no heed to the necessary replacements, substitutes we would need to make—what do we, in our empty apartments, what do we do to make the furniture and fabric for ourselves?
>
> —ANNE ROIPHE, *Generation without Memory*

•••

> The question of the archive remains the same: What comes first? Even better: Who comes first? And second?
>
> —JACQUES DERRIDA, *Archive Fever*

In *Love and Its Place in Nature*, Jonathan Lear remarks that "psychic health, Freud discovered, depends on abandoning the fantasy that one can be one's own child."[1] Freud himself gives this idea a more explicitly gendered context. In his "Contributions to the Psychology of Love," he writes that a son's ambivalence towards his father "make[s] him say: 'I want nothing from my father.' ... All his instincts ... find satisfaction in the single wish *to be his own father*" (*SE*, 11:172–73). As a starting point of this concluding chapter, I want to put this fantasy

1 *Love and its Place in Nature: A Philosophical Interpretation of Freudian Psychoanalysis* (New York: Farrar, Strauss, & Giroux, 1990), 4.

 | DOI:10.1163/9789004701663_009

into dialogue with an idea we encountered previously, what Lacan calls the "frustration inherent in the very discourse of the subject." Glossing this frustration as the subject's inescapable grappling with "an ever-growing dispossession of ... being," Lacan goes on to describe the burden of an incessant psychical "labor" in which the subject is compelled to "reconstruct this construct [its very being] *for another*," only to "find ... the fundamental alienation which made him construct it *like another one*, and which has always destined it to be stripped from him *by another*."[2] Read in relation to Lear's claim, Lacan's "discourse of the subject" might be taken to mean that the one whose child we are (whether that state is taken literally or figuratively) is capable of psychically dispossessing us by damaging or otherwise disabling our capacity to claim our lives as our own.[3]

In the face of this threat from the *(an)other*, the subject who would yet assert a claim of self-possession might need to take up the "burden" that Stanley Cavell locates at the heart of one of Freud's most cherished texts, Shakespeare's *Hamlet*: that "of proving that [one] exists, ... finding how to say, 'I am, I exist'; not ... to say it just once, but at every moment of your existence; to preserve your existence, *originate it*."[4] The central focus of this chapter is precisely the burden of this *saying*—the vexed effort to lay claim to oneself by a speaking of and for oneself—as evidenced in Freud's writing by way of Shakespeare's Hamlet, two sons struggling to free themselves from the paternal phantoms that would speak in their place.

1

First to Freud. How should we understand his experience of what we might call the burden of filiation? In a passage from his 1936 essay, "Disturbance

2 *The Language of the Self: The Function of Language in Psychoanalysis*, trans. Anthony Wilden (New York: Dell, 1968), 11.

3 We might compare Lacan's formulation to Paul Ricoeur's claim that Freud's writings constantly traverse "the crisis of the philosophy of the subject," a crisis defined primarily in terms an imposition of "the *dispossession of the subject* such as it appears primarily to itself in the form of consciousness." Ricoeur observes later that the "wounded *cogito* ... posits but *does not possess itself*" ("A Philosophical Interpretation of Freud," trans. Willis Domingo, in *The Conflict of Interpretations: Essays in Hermeneutics*, ed. Don Ihde [Evanston, IL: Northwestern University Press, 1974], 161, 173; my emphasis).

4 *Disowning Knowledge in Seven Plays of Shakespeare* (Cambridge: Cambridge University Press, 2003), 186–87; my emphasis.

of Memory on the Acropolis," he offers the following brief autobiographical reflection on his strained attempt to escape the shadow of his long-deceased father:

> It must be that some sense of guilt was attached to the satisfaction in having gone such a long way. There was something about it that was wrong, that from earliest times is forbidden. It was something to do with a child's criticism of his father, with the underevaluation which took the place of the overevaluation of earlier childhood. It seems as though the essence of success was to have got further than one's father, as though to excel one's father was still something forbidden. (*SE*, 22:247)

Freud goes on to point to a tension between "evidence of the son's superiority" and "a feeling of filial piety," a tension that had haunted him for forty years. In 1896 he had faced it in his dream of his father's funeral (*Origins*, 171); he had marked it mythologically in his reference in the *Interpretation of Dreams* (1900) to the triumph of Kronos and Zeus over their fathers (*SE*, 6:218, 218n1); and he had returned to the issue in "Mourning and Melancholia" (1915; published 1917) where, in anticipation of the 1936 passage, he had noted that even as "mourning impels the ego to give up the object by declaring the object to be dead, … the ego may enjoy in this the satisfaction of knowing itself … as *superior to the object*" (*SE*, 14:257; my emphasis). By 1936 he makes it clear that he is thinking precisely about the "son's superiority" over his father. The revelation of that superiority now becomes part of his own life. It is part of the story he tells about himself as he aims, to borrow from Cavell, to originate his own life.

Freud's grappling with the father-son agon should not, however, be reduced to the feeling of sexual rivalry experienced within the oedipal economy. On this point we might lean on Harold Bloom's insight that our own indebtedness to the Freudian conceptualization of the son's effort to disentangle himself from paternal authority—an effort that, following Freud's own phrasing, Bloom grounds in the son's "wish to be his own father"—"needs to be transformed, so as to place the emphasis less upon phallic fatherhood, and more upon *priority*."[5] Or, to reverse the idea, the son's anxiety-infused ambivalence in relation to the father has less to do with his fear of castration as Freud traditionally understood the resolution to the Oedipus complex than with the crisis of belatedness, what following a neologism of Jean Laplanche we might call

5 *The Anxiety of Influence: A Theory of Poetry* (New York: Oxford University Press, 1973), 64.

the son's experience of "afterwardsness."[6] Read in that context, the filial ambivalence on display in the 1936 passage might itself be conceived not as Freud's final statement on the matter but as the midpoint of a series of attempts in the last decade of his life to resolve a decades-long struggle with the ghost of Jacob Freud, a struggle culminating in the publication of *Moses and Monotheism* in the year of his death (1939).

As a way into Freud's own process of filial working-through, we might look to the year previous to the 1936 essay and in particular to a sentence Freud then added to his *Autobiographical Study* (first published in 1925): "My deep engrossment in the Bible story (almost as soon as I had learned the art of reading) had, as I recognized much later, an enduring effect upon the direction of my interest" (*SE*, 20:8). In his intellectual biography of Freud in the context of the writing of *Moses and Monotheism*, Yosef Hayim Yerushalmi suggests that among the reasons for this addition to a text originally published a full decade earlier was that Freud had recently completed a draft of *Moses and Monotheism* (1934), writing that may have led him to reassess the "enduring" role the Bible had served not just in the development of psychoanalysis but in his life more broadly. But Yerushalmi also claims that the writing of the draft served a deeper if unconscious purpose in Freud's life: his work on what would become *Moses and Monotheism* "represents, at last, a fulfillment of Jacob Freud's mandate or"—and here he borrows from Freud's own writing—"an example of 'deferred obedience.'"[7]

That "mandate," as Yerushalmi understands it, goes back to 1891, when, as a gift presented for his son's thirty-fifth birthday, Jacob Freud returned the Philippsohn Bible that he had first given the seven year-old Sigmund. Along with a new cover, Jacob added a Hebrew inscription that included the following:

> Son who is dear to me, Shelemoh. In the seventh in the days of the years of your life the Spirit of the Lord began to move you and spoke within you: Go, read in my Book that I have written and there will burst open for you the wellsprings of understanding, knowledge, and wisdom.... Since then the book has been stored like the fragments in an ark with me. For the day on which the years of your life were filled to five and thirty I have put upon it a cover of new skin and have called it: "Spring up, O well,

6 "Notes on Afterwardsness," in *Essays on Otherness*, ed. John Fletcher (New York: Routledge, 1999), 260–65.

7 *Freud's Moses: Judaism Terminable and Interminable* (New Haven: Yale University Press, 1991), 77. Although Freud employs the concept of deferred obedience many times in his writings, Yerushalmi explicitly mentions two passages from *Totem and Taboo* (*SE*, 13:143, 145).

> sing ye unto it!" And I have presented it to you as a memorial and as a reminder of love from your father.[8]

While Yerushalmi is most immediately intrigued by Freud's inexplicable denial of an ability to read Hebrew—"why ... did Jacob write this elaborate Hebrew inscription" if his son wouldn't be able to read it?—he is more broadly interested in Freud's return in the early 1930s to what the inscription had called "the Book of Books." That is, Yerushalmi understands the inscription as a paternal charge to the son to open himself to the "Spirit of the Lord" so as to let the words of the Bible speak "within" him as they had twenty-eight years earlier. In that context, coming as it does just one year after he had completed a draft of his study of Moses (a figure who, not coincidentally, Freud effectively understands as the great father of the Jews), Freud's declaration of his near lifelong, though previously unrecognized, "engrossment in the Bible story" marks the fulfillment of his obedience to his father's wishes that, in Yerushalmi's interpretation, he had deferred for some forty years.

To get a better understanding of how Freud might have experienced such deferred obedience even if unconsciously, we might focus on some of the key details of Jacob's inscription and in particular on how it encodes the father-son relationship within a biblical-covenantal setting. In broad terms, in the act of giving or giving *again*, Jacob (re)imposes on his beloved Sigmund his status as a son. The specific (re)gift explicitly reminds the now adult Sigmund of a time when he was a child and thus also of the necessary temporal relation: as father, Jacob necessarily comes before. But a more powerful locus of authority lurks within that priority. The gift of words comes in two forms that now merge in the physical book: the words the father writes to the son (the inscription) and the words that reside within and constitute the book itself, the Bible. To the extent the (words of the) human father become intermingled with the (words of the) father-god—who is, in typical biblical parlance, the god "of the fathers"[9]—the Spirit of the father-god speaking *within* the son cannot truly be refused: that Spirit's "I have written" takes precedence (authority and priority at once) over anything the son could say (or say of or for) himself. Although the gift is given as a "memorial" of paternal love, to the extent the

8 Qtd. / trans. Yerushalmi, 71; for original Hebrew, see 104.

9 Although there is no reason to believe that Freud would have been particularly sensitive to this idea, it is worth bearing in mind that the God of the Hebrew Bible is often less a father figure himself than the deity "of the fathers," a particularly common phrasing in the prophetic writings (but see also Genesis 26:23, 28:13, 31:5, 32:10, 46:1–3, 48:15–16, and Exodus 3:6); the phrase is still being used in New Testament texts: e.g. Acts 3:13. Surprisingly, the reference to God as "father" appears rather infrequently in the Hebrew Bible.

paternal word-giving aims precisely to remind the son of "the tablets in an ark" (the Ark of the Covenant made of acacia wood [Deuteronomy 10:3] strangely indistinguishable from some wooden chest or perhaps a bookcase where Jacob probably kept his beloved Sigmund's old Bible), what is remembered is not just love but also the demand to obey. That is, the gift is a memorial not just of the love of the father but also of the Law of the Father—the law of the father-god inscribed on stone tablets (metonymically, Torah as a whole) and the law of the fathers passed down over countless generations. That Jacob wants to give particular emphasis to the weight of tradition is evidenced by the fact that he dates the inscription with both the Gregorian year (1891) and the Jewish year (5651). The latter effectively declares the gift to be much older than the mere twenty-eight years between Freud's seventh and thirty-fifth birthdays.

In his meticulously crafted engagement with Yerushalmi's work, Jacques Derrida calls attention to another way in which Jacob Freud's words attempt to inscribe his son in and under the Law. Noting that the inscription's "very first sentence recalls, at least by figure, the circumcision of the father of psychoanalysis ('*in the seventh in the days* of the years *of your life*')," Derrida goes on to observe that Jacob's description of the rebinding of Sigmund's old Bible ("put upon it a cover of new skin") imagines the moment of circumcision as the first time his beloved son had the divine word (the Law, the covenant) imposed on him. But if the inscription "commemorates ... a circumcision," the very idea of a fatherly inscribing upon the body of the infant son—"what is written on the epidermis of a body proper"—also serves as a reminder of an "impression" more abstractly conceived: what Derrida calls "a dissymmetrical covenant without contract, ... to which Sigmund Shelomoh subscribed without even knowing how to sign—much less countersign—his name."[10] Perhaps

10 *Archive Fever: A Freudian Impression*, trans. Eric Prenowitz (Chicago: University of Chicago Press, 1995), 22, 20, 38; my emphasis. Because the Jewish son would typically be circumcised on the *eighth day* of his life, we may feel somewhat skeptical about Derrida's seeing a figure of circumcision in the phrase "in the *seventh in the days* of the years of your life." In an accompanying note, Derrida more cautiously poses his initial assertion as a question: "is it improper to read here an anniversary recall, by a father to a son, of circumcision?" Later he hedges in different way: Freud "can only say yes to this covenant into which he must enter one more time. Because he will have had to enter it, already, seven *or eight days* after his birth" (41; my emphasis). That said, Jacob's reference to his rebinding of the Bible as "put[ting] upon it a new skin" offers stronger evidence that he understands the gift in relation to circumcision as an act of initiation into the covenant. In this context, Michel de Certeau's reference to Jewish circumcision as the "law of inscription" is particularly apt: *The Writing of History*, trans. Tom Conley (New York: Columbia University Press, 1988), 341. He hopes that the return of his childhood Bible might spur the now adult Sigmund to reconsider his resistance to his Jewish heritage.

playing on the notion of the infant (*infans*) as a child not yet having the ability to speak, Derrida concludes that Jacob's 1891 writing repeats and renews the old inscription (the circumcision) even as it reenacts the earlier rendering of the son speechless: "under the new skin of the book that consigns the new skin, wounded and blessed, of a newborn, there resonated already the words intended for the newborn of a God speaking to him in him ('within you') even before he could speak, giving him to understand, to hear, in truth to read or decipher: 'Go, read my Book that I have written.'"[11]

As part of the melitzah on which the entire inscription is founded, Jacob Freud adapts that final sentence from a biblical source (Exodus 32:32). And from the perspective of the book that Freud himself had written by 1934 (the first draft of *Moses and Monotheism*), we might conclude, with Yerushalmi, that some forty-three years later he had fulfilled his father's mandate by dutifully returning to this sacred source—and specifically to Exodus as the foundation of the Moses story—and letting it speak, or speak again, "within" him. But if the writing of this draft was, as Yerushalmi imagines, an example of deferred obedience of the kind Freud himself had described in *Totem and Taboo* (the guilty son's effort to "to appease the [long-dead] father" [*SE*, 13:145]), we might also understand obedience as a symbolic (self-)silencing of the son who once again becomes the infant (the one who cannot speak). The words of the father that take precedence in both senses—and, in this instance, they are also the words of the father's god and thus of the father-god who is the god "of the fathers"—come down from the past to a Jewish son who cannot separate the divine law from the human father's loving request to heed it. What Derrida aptly calls "the paternal gesture" weighs down the son by rendering him passive in relation to what always already comes before, the father(-god)'s "I have written."[12]

Against Yerushalmi's reading, however, or perhaps simply as reminder that in his 1935 addition to the *Autobiographical Study* Freud had not yet had his final say, we might ask if the following year's "Disturbance of Memory on the Acropolis," does not reveal at least as much about his feelings towards the long-deceased Jacob. If in returning to his father's cherished "Book of Books" in his work on *Moses and Monotheism*, Freud might appear superficially to have played the dutiful son, does not the 1936 essay revise that image? Does it not suggest his need to seek ways to conquer the threat of chronic dispossession Lacan speaks of, a dispossession we might now understand as the discovery that, in the face of another's "I have written," one runs the risk of being

11 *Archive Fever*, 38.

12 *Archive Fever*, 39.

rendered eternally passive and *deferred*?[13] We might ask then if there are other ways that, in the last years of his life, Freud asserted his right and his capacity to speak against any (an)other who would speak in his place.

2

In a letter written the same year in which "Disturbance of Memory on the Acropolis" was published (1936), Freud refused the request of Arnold Zweig to be his authorized biographer:

> Only today … can I settle down to write you a letter, alarmed by the threat that you want to become my biographer—you, who have so much better and important things to do … I am too fond of you to permit such a thing. Anyone who writes a biography is committed to lies, concealments, hypocrisy, flattery, and even to hiding his own lack of understanding, for biographical truth does not exist … Truth is unobtainable, mankind does not deserve it, and in any case is not our Prince Hamlet right when he asks who would escape whipping were he used after his desert?[14]

Freud's reference here to *Hamlet* suggests that he recognizes in himself things that he might want to conceal, things that might not present him in a flattering light. He doesn't want to put his friend in a position of having to lie for the sake of his reputation. But given that in "Disturbance of Memory on the Acropolis" Freud showed himself more than willing to make public unflattering images of himself—things that, earlier in his life, he had wanted to conceal (his vexed feelings towards his father)—we might conclude that Freud simply doesn't want to assign the work of revelation to another. That is, it is not biography but autobiography that will be Freud's chosen vehicle for telling his life story. Freud, in short, must be his own author.

---

13 Robert Lippman has argued that as early as 1900 Freud had come to understand his "father problem"—"never [to] be his own person, never [to] govern his own life"—as inseparable from his fear that he would "forever be bound to the Law." Thus, his struggle to free himself from "submission to the Will of the Father" effectively conflated Jacob Freud with the biblical father-god. Lippman observes that Freud did not find it easy to shake his filial piety (both toward Jacob and toward Jacob's god): Lippman, "Freud's B'nai B'rith Dream: Having Lost His Way, His 'Brethren … Were Unkind and Scornful …,'" *The Psychoanalytic Review* 108 (2021): 246, 248.

14 *The Letters of Sigmund Freud and Arnold Zweig*, ed. Ernst L. Freud, trans. Elaine Robson-Scott and William Robson-Scott (New York: Harcourt, Brace & World, 1970), 127.

At a different level, Freud's reference to *Hamlet* to help him formulate a truth that moments before had been deemed "unobtainable" suggests that he understands storytelling rather than autobiography as the proper vehicle for revealing the truths that biography cannot. This is so, we might infer, because, in Freud's view, storytelling does not lie or conceal or flatter or hide its own lack of understanding. It is worth noting, then, that the story Freud suggests might more accurately tell the truth of his life is precisely Shakespeare's *Hamlet.*

In the very scene Freud alludes to, Hamlet himself locates the privilege of truth in the voice of the storyteller (or storytellers, for the dramatist in Shakespeare always recognizes his art as a collective act):

> Hamlet: Good my lord, will you see *the players* well bestow'd? Do you hear, let them be well us'd, for *they are the abstract and brief chroniclers of the time....*
> Polonius: My lord, I will use them according to their desert.
> Hamlet: God's bodykins, man, much better; use every man after his desert, and who shall escape whipping? (2.2.522–30; my emphasis)[15]

As if to prove this point, Hamlet will ask these "abstract and brief chroniclers of the time" to perform a play from which Hamlet hopes to recover truth that is unobtainable in other forms ("The Murder of Gonzago"). Such truth is available in the form of a play because, as Hamlet himself observes to the players, "the purpose of playing ... was and is ... to hold as 'twere the mirror up to nature" (3.2.20–22).

Yet in the end, Shakespeare cannot rely on "playing" (dramatic storytelling) for truth, at least not within the design of the story we know as *Hamlet*. For, in one of the most remarkable feats of stagecraft ever produced, Shakespeare's doubling of the actors' performance as both dumb-show and spoken drama has the effect of negating the mimetic truth of story in order to permit Hamlet to speak his own story, precisely autobiography. In other words, as the scene plays out, Hamlet cannot rely on mere story (the players' performances) to obtain truth. And the only truth he actually locates in the scene, despite what he may think, is what he wants or needs to reveal himself and reveal of himself. He must at all cost (and it truly comes at a cost since it is what gets him killed) be the author in and of this story.

15 Here and in what follows, quotations from Shakespeare's plays will be cited in the text by act, scene, and line number(s). Unless otherwise noted, they will be taken from *The Riverside Shakespeare*, 2nd ed., ed. G. Blakemore Evans, et al. (Boston: Houghton Mifflin, 1996).

My recognition that there is some strange relationship between the dumb-show and the spoken drama in 3.2 is hardly novel, but it does require some clarification. Consider, then, the relationships of the characters designated by the extended stage-direction of the dumb-show and how these relationships allegorize the story of *Hamlet*. A very basic summary would observe that the performers designated as the King and Queen within the dumb-show represent King Hamlet and Queen Gertrude and that the other character, the poisoner, represents Claudius. In fact, if the play had moved directly from the end of the dumb-show to Ophelia's line "The king [Claudius] rises" (3.2.265), and then to the subsequent action of the scene, we would have every reason to concur with Hamlet in this post-performance exchange with Horatio:

> Hamlet: O good Horatio, I'll take the ghost's word for a thousand pound. Didst perceive?
> Horatio: Very well, my lord.
> Hamlet: Upon the talk of the pois'ning?
> Horatio: I did very well note him. (3.2.286–90)

Nevertheless, despite Hamlet's excitement at the "probation" (to use Horatio's own earlier word in regard to the Ghost), Horatio himself is hardly giving a ringing endorsement of Hamlet's assessment that the Ghost has told the truth. For all Horatio says here is that he observed Claudius' behavior very closely (no doubt more closely than Hamlet himself who had actually entered into the performance). The key phrase is Hamlet's "upon the talk of the pois'ning" because "talk of" (as opposed to visualization of) draws attention precisely to the distinction Shakespeare himself has made by giving us two different versions of the performed play, the first mimed and the second with words. "*Talk* of the poisoning" can only refer to the second performance of the play and thus raises a vexed question: why didn't Hamlet or Horatio perceive anything about Claudius upon the initial *sight* of the poisoning (that is, when presented as part of the dumb-show)?[16]

Perception can change with performance, of course, but as far as we can tell from the text Claudius makes no response to the visualization of the murder

16 This is not the place to dwell on the larger implications of what the double performance might portend for the play as a whole. Suffice it to note that, taken to its logical conclusion, the relationship between the dumb-show and the spoken play suggests that Claudius did not murder his brother by pouring poison in his ear. This is essentially the point made by W. W. Greg in his essay "Hamlet's Hallucination" (*Modern Language Review* 12 [1917]: 393–421), perhaps the first sustained analysis of the complex relationship between the dumb-show and the spoken play.

in the dumb-show. What he does respond to—and what Hamlet misunderstands as the prompt for that response—is precisely the "talk" of poisoning. More precisely, Claudius responds to the very public accusation that Hamlet himself makes once he has given up his seat in the audience to become one of the actors (or at least the play's "Chorus," as Claudius has already intimated [3.2.245]): "'A poisons him i' th' garden for his estate. His name's Gonzago, the story is extant, and written in very choice Italian. You shall see anon how the murtherer gets the love of Gonzago's wife" (3.2.260–64). Even if Claudius had not murdered his brother, he could not simply sit still after such a charge, one obviously directed at him and, at least by suggestion, at Gertrude as well. But precisely because Hamlet has interfered in the plan to observe Claudius' response to the play, it is now impossible to know what he, Horatio, or anyone else has perceived: is it the effect of a guilty mind or the reaction of a king who has a proper respect for his and his wife's reputation?

That said, it is the fact of Hamlet's serving as Chorus that interests me precisely because, in joining into the play-within-the-play, he disrupts the players' ability to serve as the abstract and brief chroniclers of the time. This rejection of what Hamlet had previously endorsed, even celebrated, leads us to consider once again the relationships of the dramatic characters of the play-within-the-play and how these relationships allegorize the story of *Hamlet*. A very basic summary of the version with "talk" would observe that, rather than referring to relationships and events from the past (the backstory of *Hamlet*), the play-within-the-play has mysteriously morphed into an expression of Hamlet's own life and more specifically of his present feelings in relation to what he might do with or to others in the future. Indeed, as Freudian interpreters were among the first to appreciate, the identification of the murderer ("one Lucianus") as "*nephew* to the king" (3.2.244; my emphasis) completely reorients the "mirror" held "up to nature" (reflecting the past) in the dumb-show.[17] Through his interruption of the actors' performance, Hamlet as the real-life nephew to the king appears to be telling anyone who cares to listen that he intends to murder Claudius: "'A poisons him i' th' garden for his estate." It may be that it is this public threat (even more than a public accusation concerning a past crime) to which Claudius responds by rising and departing. For his part, Hamlet's

17 First suggested by Freud in *The Interpretation of Dreams*, this idea is treated at length in Ernest Jones' *Hamlet and Oedipus* (Garden City, NY: Doubleday, 1954). See also Lacan's "Desire and the Interpretation of Desire in *Hamlet*," trans. James Hulbert, in *Literature and Psychoanalysis: The Question of Reading Otherwise*, ed. Shoshana Felman (Baltimore: Johns Hopkins University Press, 1982), 11–52. And for a broad overview of oedipal readings of *Hamlet*, see Jean-Michael Rabaté, *The Cambridge Introduction of Literature and Psychoanalysis* (Cambridge: Cambridge University Press, 2014), 25–47.

own conduct in the scene returns us to Freud's choice of autobiography as the proper means of telling a life-story. For if Freud refuses Zweig's efforts to write the life of Freud because truth is not obtainable in *biographical* form, Hamlet himself rejects the efforts of his own era's chroniclers for a new text. And that text is precisely the life-story that only he can author.

At play's end, however, Hamlet appears to have changed his mind. For there he seems perfectly willing to consign his life-story to his friend Horatio, a willingness that bespeaks greater confidence than Freud had in Zweig or had in biography generally (Freud, of course, had written that "biographical truth does not exist"). Hamlet's charge to Horatio—"tell my story" (5.2.349)—might appear then to mark a full movement in the play from dramatic storytelling to autobiography to biography which, because it is to come as "story," returns us to where we began and so suggests that any of these modes can reveal truth.

Such optimism may be misplaced, however. Although Horatio is effectively assigned the role of Hamlet's biographer, it is not clear that Hamlet (or Shakespeare) actually imagines Horatio succeeding in this task. Indeed, it is impossible to say finally what story Horatio will be able to tell about Hamlet. What exactly does he know (and surely by this stage the audience knows more than he does)? While at play's end Hamlet entreats Horatio to speak *of* him rather than *to* him, we might wonder if the depiction of Horatio's failed effort to speak to the Ghost in the play's opening scene is intended in part to suggest that any post-play effort to tell the story of yet another person who exists beyond the grave is doomed to similar failure. Marcellus seems to believe that Horatio's speech will have special efficacy: "Thou art a scholar, speak to it, Horatio" (1.1.42). But the Ghost's very refusal to speak—a refusal to permit the words of another rendering him legible, we might say—may be Shakespeare's way of anticipating Hamlet's "the rest is silence" (5.2.358). For in that single, final line, Hamlet hints at secrets he has never revealed, a story he does not want told if that would require surrendering the truth of himself to another's telling. Like Freud, then, Hamlet will not let his biographer displace him as the author and authority of his own life.[18]

---

18 A refusal to let another control one's own narrative (an inner truth deliberately hidden away) is likewise suggested in Hamlet's exchange with Guildenstern after the performance of the play. This sentence—spoken by Hamlet to Guildenstern—particularly stands out: "You would play upon me, you would seem to know my stops, you would pluck out the heart of my mystery, you would sound me from my lowest note to the top of my compass; and there is much music, excellent voice, in this little organ, *yet cannot you make it speak*" (3.2.364–69; my emphasis).

3

At this point we might recall the words of Coriolanus: "I'll ... stand // As if a man were author of himself," a declaration then completed with, "And knew no other kin" (5.3.34–37). The claim to author oneself made precisely in the context of a refusal to recognize the bonds of kinship (as though that very recognition would interfere with self-authorship) might then also remind us that what Cavell calls Hamlet's special "burden"—"to say, 'I am, I exist'"—is taken up less in response to his authorized biographer, Horatio, than in response to a greater threat, that kinsman who would speak for him and perhaps even *within* him. In Hamlet's case, of course, as in Freud's, that person is the father.

Or perhaps more accurately, if we are thinking of a time after the death of Jacob Freud in 1896, for both Freud and Hamlet that person is a *revenant*, a word we might translate as ghost by which Freud glosses as "those we have lost [who] come back" (*Interpretation of Dreams*, SE, 5:486). In both cases, though in different ways, the *revenant* speaks. "A phantom speaks," Derrida notes and then asks, "What does this mean?"

> In the first place ... this means that without responding it disposes of a response, a bit like an answering machine whose voice outlives its moment of recording; you call, the person is dead, now, whether you know it or not, and the voice responds to you ... [I]t can give you instructions, make declarations to you, address your prayers, promises, injunctions.[19]

But for both Freud and Hamlet, the speaking is of another kind entirely. At one point in his musings, Derrida describes Yerushalmi's relation to Freud as akin to how Yerushalmi himself describes Freud's relation to Jacob Freud: he "'belatedly obeys the father,' whether he wants to or not ... *identifies with him while interiorizing him like a phantom who speaks in him* before him."[20] In short, Freud's phantom-father comes back, speaks within the haunted son, and compels—or at least tries to compel—filial obedience by demanding some identificatory interiorizing that precludes true self-possession.

If for Freud the paternal speaking in or within the son is most powerfully registered in the eternal precedence of the father(-god)'s "I have written," for Hamlet it is registered just after the father-phantom issues his final command to his son at the end of their Act 1 encounter: "Hamlet, remember me." Hamlet's

---

19 *Archive Fever*, 62–63.

20 *Archive Fever*, 61; my emphasis.

immediate acceptance of the charge reimagines it as an inscription that will thereafter dictate, even replace, his very thought:

> Remember thee!
> Yea, from the table of my memory
> I'll wipe away all trivial fond records,
> All saws of books, all forms, all pressures past
> That youth and observation copied there,
> And thy commandement all alone shall live
> Within the book and volume of my brain. (1.5.97–103)

Hamlet will grapple with this "commandement"—what we might call King Hamlet's private book of books—until the play's final scene.

Two brief examples of this grappling will have to suffice. Following along the interpretive path established by Cavell, Robert Watson has convincingly argued that, whether coming from the true ghost of his father or from his own needs and longings, revenge is represented in the plot of the play as a way by which the Ghost imposes—or Hamlet imposes upon himself—the necessity of sustaining his father's memory by acting as his father's surrogate. This is not just the fantasy that, as Watson notes of Fortinbras' quest, "the living child can repair the losses of the dead parent." Beyond that, the child comes to identify so completely with the dead parent that he loses all capacity for self-definition. Thus Hamlet's stirring proclamation at Ophelia's burial, "this is I, Hamlet the Dane!" (5.1.257–58) (a naming that conflates Hamlet with his dead father) is immediately followed by an even more powerful act of "sympathetic identification with a past life"—Hamlet's leaping into a grave (Ophelia's)—an act of identification that, as Watson argues, reveals itself as a kind of "demonic possession of the present."[21]

We should recognize, then, that the "I" in "This is I, Hamlet the Dane" is, at best, fluid. That this "I" refers not simply or exclusively to Prince Hamlet but is

21 *The Rest is Silence: Death as Annihilation in the English Renaissance* (Berkeley: University of California Press, 1994), 77–78. As Cavell similarly observes, "the Ghost asks initially for revenge for his murder, a task the son evidently accepts as his to perform ... But is this the son's business ...? Here the father asks the son to take the father's place, to make his life come out even for him, to set it right, so that he, the father, can rest in peace. It is a bequest of a beloved father that deprives the son of his identity" (188). In an 1897 letter to Wilhelm Fliess, Freud speculated that Hamlet's pathological drive to "bring ... down his punishment on himself" could be understood as marking an unconscious need to repeat his father's experience: "suffering the same fate as his father, being poisoned by the same rival" (*Origins*, 224).

rather some uncanny intermingling of two identities is borne out by a strange aspect of the initial exchange between the Prince and the Ghost:

> Ghost: Revenge his foul and most unnatural murder.
> Hamlet: Murder!
> Ghost: Murder most foul, as in the best it is,
> But this most foul, strange, and unnatural.
> Hamlet: Haste, haste me to know it, that with wings as swift
> As meditation or the thoughts of love
> May sweep to my revenge. (1.5.25–31)

Stephen Greenblatt has astutely observed of the final three lines that, in "urgently demand[ing] the information that will enable him immediately to heed" the call for revenge, Hamlet expresses a "desire for haste ... so intense that it erases the very person who does the desiring: the subject of the wish has literally vanished from the sentence."[22] That is, faced with the command of the dead father, the compulsion of filial duty is so powerful that it is grammatically registered in the very elision of the subject. That erased "I" of 1.5 rematerializes in the assertion "This is I, Hamlet the Dane!" But, as noted above, Hamlet's "I" in the burial scene of 5.1 appears less as *self*-assertion than as a kind of "demonic possession." The Ghost haunts him still.

Watson argues in relation to this scene that Hamlet's identification with his father "violat[es] a boundary between death and life that should be respected, for all our impulses to cross it."[23] But the necessary distinction between the living and the dead is, in Shakespeare's presentation, also the occasion in which an even more foundational, and more problematic, boundary between one's own life and the life of another is made manifest. Hamlet must come to recognize, as does Gertrude, that the ghost of the dead father cannot be seen, cannot be heard, that in the wake of such a death there is "nothing but ourselves" (3.4.133). To discover this for himself (something he is not yet able to do even as late as 5.1), Hamlet must lose his father; indeed, he must lose the very word "father."

22 *Hamlet in Purgatory* (Princeton: Princeton University Press, 2002), 207–08. Greenblatt grounds his assertion on the text of the Folio, which is the basis of the Norton edition, from which my own citation here comes. The slightly different wording in the 1604 Quarto, the basis of the Riverside version of this passage, does in fact supply the subject ("I") for the sentence.

23 *Rest is Silence*, 78.

The play's drive towards this moment is powerfully marked in its fullest expression of tragic *anagnorisis*:

> Horatio: If your mind dislike anything, obey it. I will forestall your repair hither, and say you are not fit.
> Hamlet: Not a whit, we defy augury. There is special providence in the fall of a sparrow. If it be now, 'tis not to come; if it be not to come, it will be now; if it be not now, yet it will come. The readiness is all. Since no man, of aught he leaves, knows what is't to leave betimes, let be. (5.2.217–24)

The rhetorical design of the passage forces us to conclude against our expectations that the "readiness" Hamlet's speaks of here refers to his own intimations of mortality rather than to his readiness to kill Claudius.[24] We are almost led to imagine that what he wants to "let be"—leave alone, untouched, unfulfilled—is precisely what we expect he should now, finally, be ready to do: avenge his father's murder.

As I have argued elsewhere, Hamlet's forgetting of the father's business is marked in the subtle deletion Shakespeare makes from the biblical source-text of this passage: "Are not two sparrows sold for a farthing, and one of them shall not fall on the ground without your Father? ... Fear ye not therefore, ye are of more value than many sparrows" (Matthew 10:29–31; 1599 Geneva text). Shakespeare here retains Matthew's core sentiment that every person, every moment, is uniquely special in the working out of God's inscrutable will. But even as this viewpoint depends on the comfort of faith in a beneficent God who loves us, Shakespeare chooses to leave out the very word Matthew employs to underwrite that faith: "father," or he in whose eyes and because of whom we have worth, even as what Hamlet's calls "providence" assigns us existence and a destiny. Without surrendering the notion that he might have a destiny, Hamlet surrenders the presence of the father (whether divine or human) as the source and ultimate purpose of that destiny.

Like Freud before him, then, Hamlet must refuse the paternal gesture not just of the father (the "commandement") but also of the father-god (the "I have written"). The speaking of the father that would render the son an infant once more must be resisted; both sons must "let be" the mandate by which a

24 In the interlineal comment in his published screenplay, Kenneth Branagh explicates this passage in a way that almost certainly matches our own intuitions, unexpected as these might be: Hamlet "has spoken with the heart-rending simplicity of a man who knows that he is going to die and probably very soon. He accepts the inevitability of it" (*Hamlet: Screenplay, Introduction, and Film Diary* [New York: Norton, 1996], 162).

phantom (a dead father) would, through a process of identificatory interiorizing, "speak in" them. For his part, Hamlet makes this refusal at the opening of the play's final scene. It is at the end of this scene, when his intuition of imminent death has proven true and his destiny is full upon him (he is dying from the poison on Laertes' sword), that he asks Horatio to tell his story. But it is not, we observe, the story of his murdered father as he might have expected from Act 1. Hamlet, we might say, only now realizes that his dramatic existence—the "tragedy of Hamlet"—traces out the story of the Prince, not the King, of Denmark. If in that realization this dutiful son of a loving father responds to the paternal gesture by refusing it, the tragic irony is that he can only take up the burden—to preserve *his* existence, to lay claim to his origin, in effect to become the author of his own life—when he reaches his end.

4

What then of Freud? Towards the close of *Moses and Monotheism*, Freud will reflect that his account of Moses, the figure he considers the great father of the Jews and thus the father of Jewish sons like Freud himself, had "haunted [him] like an unlaid ghost" (132). That said if, as Yerushalmi suggests, *Moses and Monotheism*, while not "merely ... psychological autobiography" (let alone "psychoanalytic confession"), might yet be understood as the "final chapter in a Freud's lifelong case history," there were earlier chapters that served to establish the storyline.[25] In Chapter 1, I noted some of the particular ways in which *Totem and Taboo* (1913) laid the conceptual groundwork for the idea that the slaying of the primal father was, from a psychoanalytic perspective, the originary act of human history.[26] If it marked deep filial hostility of the sons—the brother horde—toward the father, the murder also pointed toward a foundational ambivalence: the murdering sons both detested and identified with the father; they admired or even loved the father even as they longed to assume his primacy within the horde.[27]

---

25 Yerushalmi, *Freud's Moses*, 2.

26 So Freud writes: "The totem meal, which is perhaps mankind's earliest festival, would thus be a repetition and a commemoration of this memorable and criminal deed [slaying the primal father], which was the beginning of so many things—of social organization, or moral restrictions and of religion" (*SE*, 13:142). For Freud's notion of the human situation before the advent of this social order, see his description in *Totem and Taboo*, *SE*, 13:125–126; there he quotes from Darwin's 1871 *Descent of Man*.

27 For the full account, see *SE*, 13:140–46. As is his wont, Freud interprets the primal filial ambivalence in the context of the oedipal economy, and this despite the fact that his

In a sort of trial run for the new application he would make of it in *Moses and Monotheism*, Freud would at once personalize this theory and relate it more broadly to his Jewish heritage first in his 1914 essay "The Moses of Michelangelo" and then again in his preface to the 1930 Hebrew translation of *Totem and Taboo*. In the former, against the explicit account presented in Exodus 32, Freud reads Michelangelo's famed statue as depicting an angry Moses in the act of choosing not to shatter the stone tablets of the Law (or take other violent actions) in response to the Israelites' rebellion against his authority in their worship of the Golden Calf (*SE*, 13:224–25, 229–30).[28] If one might see in this radical revision of the biblical scene Freud's imagining of his (long deceased) father's acceptance of his own turning away from Judaism (if not from Jewishness itself), as part of the brief autobiographical introduction to the lengthy analysis of the statue, his account of his obsessive revisiting of the statue and its accusatory expression suggests that what he might have hoped to find in Jacob Freud's relenting forgiveness or at least resignation was yet tinged with the pangs of a guilty conscience:

> Another of these inscrutable and wonderful works of art is the marble statue of Moses, by Michelangelo, in the Church of S. Pietro in Vincoli … [N]o piece of statuary has ever made a stronger impression on me than this …. How often have I mounted the steep steps from the unlovely Corso Cavour to the lonely piazza where the deserted church stands, and have essayed to support the angry scorn of the hero's glance! Sometimes I have crept cautiously out of the half-gloom of the interior as though I myself belonged to the mob upon whom his eye is turned[.] (*SE*, 13:213)

In a way that might lead us to infer an ongoing experience of paternal reproach, Freud encounters this inanimate Moses as strangely alive: "I can recollect … when … during my first visits to San Pietro in Vincoli, I used to sit down in front of the statue in the expectation that I should now see how it would start up on its raised foot, dash the Tables of the Law to the ground and let fly its wrath" (13:220). And it is his feeling of being among "the mob upon whom his [Moses'] eye is turned"—a mob that, it is worth noting, is completely absent from the statue itself and thus only exists as a projection of Freud's mind—that moves

---

familial model of the primal horde gives no particularly privileged place to the mother: "All that we find there is a violent and jealous *father who keeps all the females for himself* and drives away his sons as they grow up" (*SE*, 13:141; my emphasis).

28 Exodus 32:19: "As soon as Moses … saw the calf and the dancing, he became enraged; and he hurled the tablets from his hands and shattered them at the foot of the mountain."

Freud, even haunts him in such a way that, to exorcise the ghost, he must return to view the statue over and over again. Over and over again, then, he unnervingly discovers himself as a member of a group that, because it "can hold fast no conviction, which has neither faith nor patience, and which rejoices when it has regained its illusory idols," has kindled the anger of Moses, the great father who now feels the urge to "annihilate" those who have renounced the very terms of the covenant he has been tasked with delivering to the people of Israel (13:213, 225). In short, the source of the statue's "powerful effect" (13:211) on Freud is the experience of being chastised by the father's withering gaze, as just one among the many apostates who, once liberated from Moses' authority, immediately disregards the very foundation of that authority, the divine word itself.

Yet the very fact that Freud can admire Michelangelo's "act of blasphemy" (13:230) in transforming the text of Exodus 32 simultaneously hints at Freud's own defiance of his father's attempts to impose on him the traditional biblical version of the story and thus Mosaic Law more broadly and thus also Judaism as a whole. In obsessively, repeatedly returning to the scene of the crime, as it were, he offers himself as a thoroughly modernized version of one of the murdering hordic sons recollecting the loved-and-despised father through the totem feast. As we noted in Chapter 1, drawing on his earlier description in *Totem and Taboo*, in *Moses and Monotheism* Freud would claim that through the primitive totem feast the sons would at once repent of the murder and symbolically reenact it, a duality that, as Freud put it, "retained the original ambivalency of feeling toward the father" (*Moses and Monotheism*, 104). First presenting his description of the totem meal in *Totem and Taboo*, Freud had written there that "totemic religion not only comprised expressions of remorse and attempts at atonement, it also served as a remembrance of the triumph over the father. Satisfaction over that triumph led to the institution of the memorial festival of the totem meal, *in which the restrictions of deferred obedience no longer held*. Thus it became the duty to repeat the crime of parricide again and again in the sacrifice of the totem animal" (*SE*, 13:145; my emphasis).[29] He then added as a more general conclusion based on the particulars of totemism that "we shall not be surprised to find that the element of filial rebelliousness also emerges, in the *later* products of religion, often in the strangest disguises and distortions." Freud's own obsessive revisiting of Michelangelo's statue might be understood as just such a "strange disguise" of his own filial rebelliousness, an otherwise inexplicable feeling that compelled him to "repeat

29 In *Moses and Monotheism*, Freud observes that the totem meal had both a "tender and adoring sense" and an "aggressive sense" (111).

the crime of parricide again and again." This repetition did not, of course, take the form of sacrificial meal; instead it took the distorted form of his own ritual, mounting and remounting "the steep steps from the unlovely Corso Cavour to the lonely piazza where the deserted church stands" and there to "essay ... to support the angry scorn of the hero's glance." In that self-essaying, Freud metonymically confronted the memory—and the impositions—of his own dead father in the form of the founder of Jacob Freud's religion, a religion that Freud's final (re)construction would present as having originated in a different sort of symbolic parricide, the murder of the great father of the Jews. But the notion that Moses had been murdered was a story for another time. In Freud's telling in 1914, whatever his sense of obligation to pay his respects to the paternal legacy in the form of Michelangelo's powerful image of Moses, in the end the father simply submits. For as Freud would have it, the Moses portrayed by the blasphemer Michelangelo does not act: he controls his wrath and thereby becomes passive in the face of his rebellious sons, the mob that has renounced the Law. In siding with the gentile Michelangelo's choice to "deviate ... from the text" in offering his "alteration" to the very "character of Moses" (*SE*, 13:232–33), Freud now offers a story different from what he would have inherited through Jewish tradition and so would have been bequeathed to him by his own father.

In *Moses and Monotheism* Freud will call this tradition—Judaism itself—the "Father religion" in contrast to Christianity as the "Son religion" (111). But perhaps more tellingly, in his preface to what was to have been the 1930 Hebrew translation of *Totem and Taboo* Freud will refer to Judaism as the "religion of his fathers" (German: *väterlich*[*en*] *Religion*), a group that, we would surmise, includes Jacob Freud. So he begins the preface:

> No reader [of the Hebrew version of] this book will find it easy to put himself in the emotional position of an author who is ignorant of the language of holy writ, who is completely estranged from the religion of his fathers—as well as from every other religion—and who cannot take a share in nationalist ideals, but who has never yet repudiated his people, who feels that he is in essential nature a Jew and who has no desire to alter that nature. If the question were put to him: "Since you have abandoned all these common characteristics of your countrymen, what is there left to you that is Jewish?" he would reply: "A very great deal, and probably its very essence." (*SE*, 13:xv)[30]

30 The preface was first published in German in 1934 (*Gesammelte Shriften*, 12 vols. [Vienna: Internationaler Psychoanalytischer Verlag, 1922–34], 12:385), perhaps not so coincidentally the same year in which Freud completed a draft of *Moses and Monotheism* (September,

The phrase "religion of his fathers" (or father[ly] religion), is a metonymy for Judaism, of course, but it also serves as a reminder of why Judaism is a part of Freud's life at all: it was the religion of his own father. But if, as he hints, the *väterlich*[*en*] *Religion* is still part of his own life because it was his father's before him, it is not simply something that belonged to and then ended with his father. In the first place, despite his overt estrangement from it, Jewish tradition is still a foundational element of his own personal-familial heritage from which he derives an essential if indefinable aspect of his own identity ("probably its very essence"). Beyond that more limited familial context, the openness of the German *väterlich*[*en*] (the plural of the English "religion of his *fathers*" perhaps captures this idea more effectively) takes us even further back in time to an inheritance that emanates from an ancient past and that has come down to Freud over countless generations. In *Moses and Monotheism*, Freud would mark the entailment of this inheritance in the new devotion to the canon of Hebrew Scripture in the aftermath of the Roman destruction of the Second Temple in 70 CE: "Immediately after the destruction of the Temple in Jerusalem by Titus, Rabbi Jochanan ben Sakkai asked for permission to open at Jabneh the first school for the study of the Torah. From now on, it was the Holy Book, and the study of it, that kept the scattered people together ... through two thousand years" (147). If, for Freud, this moment is the true origin of the "religion of the fathers"—a religion that ever-after would be centrally concerned with the meticulous observance of Mosaic law as the centerpiece of God's covenant with Israel—Freud's final major work strongly suggests that, while he continued to take a very obvious pride in this cultural-religious legacy, his "estranged" condition points to how he felt it as a weight from which he sought to unburden himself.

Jewish identity is, thus, for Freud something familiar yet strange, something whose "essence" he recognizes though he "cannot express clearly in words."[31] What Freud is unwittingly registering here, I would venture, is that the essential in his Jewish identity is what in it cannot be expressed precisely because its familiar inaccessibility *is* its essence: what it means to be Jewish (or at least

---

1934). We might even imagine that the 1930 preface to the translation of *Totem and Taboo* into "the language of holy writ" prompted Freud to revisit the book's argument in the more specific context of the origins on Hebrew monotheism. The Hebrew translation of *Totem and Taboo* was not actually published until 1939 (Jerusalem: Kirjeith Zefer), the same year in which the full text of *Moses and Monotheism* was published.

31 Six years later, Freud would still be making this claim: "the miraculous thing ...[that] makes the Jew" is nevertheless "inaccessible to analysis" (*Letters of Sigmund Freud*, ed. Ernst L. Freud, trans. Tania Stern and James Stern [New York: Basic Books, 1960], 428).

what it means, psychoanalytically, to be a Jewish son) is to experience the inaccessible origin that belongs elsewhere.

We might try to understand this elsewhere, this before-time, by briefly returning to the issue of circumcision and its privileged role in establishing (male) Jewish identity under what Genesis 17:11 calls "the sign of the covenant." Drawing on Franz Rosenzweig's 1930 *Star of Redemption*, Jacob Taubes observes that on the occasion of the circumcision a Jewish father prays, among other things, "that it may be vouchsafed him [the father] to bring him [the son] up to the Torah."[32] Reflecting more broadly on what he calls the Jewish "second birth," Rosenzweig writes of Jewish male identity that

> the moment of his second birth, of his rebirth, must lie for him beyond the confines of his personality, before his own life. The rebirth of the Jew—and it is of him that we are here speaking—is not his personal one, but the transformation of his people for freedom in the divine covenant of revelation. On that occasion the people experienced a second birth, and he in it, not he personally as an individual .... Henceforth, the individual is born a Jew. He no longer needs to become one in some decisive moment of his individual life .... [T]he Jew is relieved of becoming-Jew in the protohistory of his people's revelation.[33]

What we might say, then, is that, what comes to define the Jewish son on the eighth day after his birth is an inherited identity as a situation of self-estrangement, a situation in which identity is experienced not just through *what* his father bequeathed him—the inheritance the father entailed upon him (the *väterlich Religion* as "the protohistory of the people's revelation")—but also through the very fact that it was bequeathed to him by his father. This idea might then lead us to reformulate Freud's self-assessment in the 1930 preface: he cannot find words to express his own Jewishness (it remains inaccessible to him) because he is not as estranged from it as he believes. For the very metonymy he employs (Judaism as the religion of the fathers / the fatherly religion) suggests that he finds himself inescapably lodged within that very identity, what has come down as the weight of two thousand years of Jewish tradition.

---

32 Taubes, *The Political Theology of Paul*, trans. Dana Hollander (Stanford: Stanford University Press, 2004), 35; Taubes is quoting here from Rosenzweig's *The Star of Redemption*, trans. William W. Hallo (New York: Holt, Rinehart and Winston), 326.

33 *Star of Redemption*, 396–97.

5

While it is unlikely that he was consciously thinking in these terms, we might imagine that Freud's fear that his work on "the man Moses" would amount to little more that "an iron monument with feet of clay" (*Moses and Monotheism*, 17) hints that his aim was to produce his own version of Michelangelo's statue, a work of blasphemy that "deviated from the [biblical] text" in offering its "alteration" of the very "character of Moses" ("The Moses of Michelangelo," *SE*, 13:232–33). In *Moses and Monotheism*, Freud explicitly acknowledges that the historical foundation permitting him to see the work through to completion was the thesis put forward by Ernst Sellin in his 1922 *Mose und seine Bedeutung für die israelitisch-jüdishe Religionsgeschischte*: "in the book of the prophet Hosea [and other biblical writings and extra-biblical legends] unmistakable traces of a tradition to the effect that the founder of their religion, Moses, met a violent end in a rebellion of his stubborn and refractory people" (42). In both imposing Sellin's thesis of an ignominious death (a murder) on Michelangelo's very much alive Moses and re-rendering the statue's Moses as a father-figure ("an eminent father-substitute" [113; *Standard Edition*: "an outstanding father-figure," 23:89]), Freud was, of course, retelling the core psychoanalytic narrative in the guise of Jewish cultural history.

It is precisely in this context, as Eric Santner observes, that in *Moses and Monotheism* Freud presents Judaism as "the ultimate religion of the superego." Connecting the policing effect of this psychical agency to the formation of Jewish cultural identity in the wake of the (alleged) murder of Moses, Santner adds:

> One of the fundamental laws of psychic life as Freud understood it was that fathers rule not as real individuals but rather as symbolic agencies represented by their *name*. The name of the father is, furthermore, always the name of the *dead* father; the father who has been aggressively set apart, expelled into ... symbolic efficacy and transcendence ... The social bond contracted under the auspices of the paternal law is, in a word, sustained by some murderous betrayal; *Moses and Monotheism* attempts to locate and elaborate the structural necessity of that betrayal within the Jewish tradition.... [T]his, of course, is another way of saying that the paternal law—in this case the law given by Moses—is sustained by a dynamic of transgression and culpabilization, that is, by the superego. Our very obedience to the law testifies to the betrayal that sustains its efficacy. In the Freudian view, we are "in" a form of life, truly animated by its spirit, not so much when we agree with its basic rules, values, codes

> of conduct ... but rather when we are *haunted by its spirits*, so to speak, plagued at some level of our being by the immemorial transgression *structurally transmitted* by the form of life itself and the narrative, rituals, myths that lend it its symbolic consistency.[34]

As Freud understands it, the aggressive-turned-murderous ambivalence of the son(s) toward the father (in Moses' case, a father-substitute) becomes, as Taubes puts it, "even more deeply entangled in guilt not by way of the living father whom [the son(s)] wants to kill, but by way of the dead father" after the murder has taken place.[35] This guilt can never be completely separated from the sense of triumph over—or at least liberation from—the overbearing father, for, in exerting superegoic pressure in the form of juridical inscription, the law of the (now dead) father simultaneously compels submission and invites (even incites) transgression, a duality that at once expresses and sustains the original ambivalence towards what haunts the son(s) as impossible paternal demands. For Freud, the symbolic consistency of those demands in the interwoven forms of narrative, rituals, and myth is precisely what constitutes Judaism.

That said, Freud sees Jewish *identity* more specifically in terms of the "compulsive conviction" (108) of being ineluctably bound to the faith-practice. For, as we have seen in earlier chapters, from a psychoanalytic perspective Judaism is at its core an unconscious attachment to unresolved traumatic dispossession, an attachment then transmitted transgenerationally as akin to what he had referred to in *Totem and Taboo* as an "inherited psychical endowment" (*SE*, 13:31). This perspective helps explain Freud's infamous recourse in *Moses and Monotheism* to the discredited genetic theory of "soft inheritance" put forward by the French biologist Jean-Baptiste Lamarck (1744–1829), an issue we took up in Chapter 3. Yerushalmi speculates that "Freud's Jewishness ... played a role in his Lamarckian predilections": "I am not implying that Lamarckism is 'Jewish,'" Yerushalmi writes, but "rather have in mind its subjective dimension, the feeling harbored and expressed by committed and alienated modern Jews alike of the enormous weight ... of the Jewish past, whether it be felt as an anchor or a burden. Deconstructed into Jewish terms, what is Lamarckism if not the powerful feeling that, for better or worse, one cannot really cease being Jewish ... because *one's fate in being Jewish was determined along ago* by the Fathers."[36] In this sense, Judaism's own locating of its

34 *On the Psychotheology of Everyday Life: Reflections on Freud and Rosenzweig* (Chicago: University of Chicago Press, 2001), 104–06.

35 *Political Theology of Paul*, 89.

36 *Freud's Moses*, 31; my emphasis.

origin in the period of the patriarchs metonymically figures the immemorial nature of Jewish faith and collective identity. The time "of the fathers" is so distant that it can never be the subject of rational analysis. It is felt—and as feeling leaves an indelible mark on all who come after—but it is never truly understood. This mark is, we might say, literally inscribed on Jewish sons through circumcision, the "sign of the covenant" (Genesis 17:11). That is, Jewish sons carry on their bodies the mark of the father(s), the past itself and the collective identity that derives from that past.

Recalling here Rosenzweig's notion that "the Jew is relieved of becoming-Jew in the protohistory of his people's revelation," we might then understand how Freud's very grappling with Jewish protohistory—what was determined long ago by the Fathers—became a critical if not fully recognized factor in the development of his psychoanalytic project. Pursuing a line of thought similar to Lacan's notion of the subject's "ever-growing dispossession of ... being" in relation to the Other's priority, Santner observes in broad terms that "the subject of psychoanalysis ... begins not with biological life but rather where biological life is amplified and perturbed by the symbolic dimension of relationality at the very heart of which lie the problems of authority and authorization.... [W]e might say that the life that is of concern to psychoanalysis is ... life that has be *thrown by the enigma of its legitimacy*, the question of its place and authorization within a meaningful order." Returning to the notion of this "thrownness" later in his study, Santner draws on Jean Laplanche's related concepts of implantation and intromission, processes by which "enigmatic messages emanating from the Other" might create problematic authority structures within the Unconscious. Santner adds that "this Other can be understood not only as another subject but also as *the symbolic order into which one is born*, which in turn always includes traces of lost forms of life."[37] At the heart of *Moses and Monotheism* is precisely the "enigma of legitimacy" as experienced by the ambivalent son, Freud, whose own Jewish essence he could never fully explain. In effect, Freud encountered his own Jewish identity precisely as an Other in the sense of a symbolic order that "include[d] traces of lost forms of life," traces repetitively sustained in narrative, ritual and myth but residing unconsciously as a compulsive conviction. For one whose "fate in being Jewish was determined along ago by the Fathers," the priority of the father and of the father's religion—the religion of the fathers—always stumbled on Derrida's unanswerable questions I have cited in this chapter's second epigraph: "What comes first? Even better: Who comes first? And second?"[38]

37 *Psychotheology of Everyday Life*, 30, 97; my emphasis.

38 *Archive Fever*, 37.

Distinguishing implantation from intromission, Laplanche writes that "implantation is a process which is common, everyday, normal, or neurotic. Beside it, as its violent variant, a place must be given to *intromission*. While implantation allows the individual to take things up actively, at once translating and repressing, one must try to conceive of a process which blocks this, short circuits the differentiation of the agencies in the process of their formation, and puts into the interior an element resistant to all metabolization." Laplanche adds that some "process related to intromission ... has a role in the formation of the *superego*, a foreign body that cannot be metabolized."[39] In terms of this distinction, the compulsive aspect of Jewish identity should be understood as an instance of cultural intromission. Elsewhere reflecting on what form such compulsion might take, Laplanche comments that

> there are good reasons for looking very seriously into the notion that [Kant's] categorical imperative is born of the superego, and for dwelling on one specific aspect of it: categorical imperatives cannot be justified; they are certainly enigmatic in the same way that other adult messages are enigmatic; but not only are they unjustified, it is possible that they are unjustifiable, or in other words, non-metabolizable. This means that they cannot be diluted, and cannot be replaced by anything else. They exist, and they are immutable and cannot be symbolized. They resist the schema for the substitution of signifiers.[40]

In a related context, Michel de Certeau describes the core idea at work in *Moses and Monotheism* as the "tension .. elucidated as the very question of the 'I': the subject is fashioned through the experience of being both separable from and foiled by the other; he is divided by the prohibition that establishes the very transgression, and which institutes pleasure with a vital relation to lack and difference; he has no place of his own. But here everything takes place on the family scene. In such a unity of place, the son must—but never truly can—dislodge the father."[41] Without explicit reference to the compulsive conviction Freud locates in Jewish (un)consciousness, Santner remarks that "the deep sense of psychic rigidity or 'stuckness' that is of interest to psychoanalysis is, we might say, nothing but a persistence of this pulse of *meaningless yet valid* behavior that constitutes our unconscious *attachment* to as well as

39 *Essays on Otherness*, 136.

40 *New Foundations of Psychoanalysis*, trans. David Macey (Oxford: Basil Blackwell, 1989), 138–39.

41 *Writing of History*, 333.

our defense against the Other's 'exciting' secret or enigma. The fundamental problem for ... Freud ... is that of intervening into this rigidity, this pulse of undeadness, of releasing us from a repetition compulsion that permeates our being, that in some peculiar sense is *who we are*."[42] Reconceptualized in psychoanalytic terms, Gershom Scholem's description of Judaism as "a life lived in deferment" takes on a new perspective. If, as Scholem argues, "Jewish existence possesses a tension that never finds true release," it is precisely because tension is the central fact of that existence. The unconscious attachment to fantasy—the effort to reclaim what the mind never had to begin with—makes it impossible to claim the origin of Judaic faith as one's own and so renders an endpoint ever unreachable.[43]

As Freud put it in *Moses and Monotheism*, Moses "created the Jews" (136).[44] Freud clearly understood that the implications of this foundational claim were more far-reaching and potentially more disturbing than the seemingly more provocative one that Moses was actually an Egyptian. For if, in a traditional sense, Freud could readily accept that "the man Moses, the liberator of his people, ... gave them their religion and their laws" (3), more fundamentally Moses "stamped" the people with what was new to them (135), "forced" it all upon them (142), "burdened" (35) them with what was foreign, something new and difficult that came to them unbidden "from outside, from a great stranger" (63). If, as Freud would write to Zweig in 1934, the "the starting point of [his] work" on Moses was a simple question, "how the Jews have come to be what they are," on one level his answer was equally simple: "Moses made [the Jews] his people; they were his 'chosen people'" (*Moses and Monotheism*, 55).[45] But at a different level that answer misses Freud's own best point: from the moment of their beginning all the way to the present time, the chosen people were, in truth, the always already having been chosen people.

6

Yerushalmi remarks that even those he calls "psychological Jews" (among whose number he would certainly count Freud) grapple with the realization

---

42 *Psychotheology of Everyday Life*, 98.

43 Scholem, *The Messianic Idea in Judaism and Other Essays on Jewish Spirituality* (New York: Schocken Books, 1971), 35.

44 Freud had made this point several years earlier in letter to Zweig dated September 30, 1934: *Letters of Sigmund Freud and Arnold Zweig*, 91.

45 *Letters of Sigmund Freud and Arnold Zweig*, 91.

that "vital parts of their lives are still *determined by ancestral choices* they may no longer understand."[46] What could a Jewish son like Freud do in the face of these choices, the burden of a people's protohistory?[47] All he could do was refuse the act of choosing the great father ever-after imposed as Jewish tradition and to make a different choice instead. Marthe Robert gets to the crux of the issue in arguing that, "seized with a last stirring of revolt against the inexorable fatality of filiation, *Moses and Monotheism* Freud sought finally "to break the chain of generations and so free himself forever from all the fathers ... and ancestors." Freud's obsession with what Robert elsewhere calls "the old wound of Jewish existence" thus led him to invent a new genealogy in the figure of the Egyptian Moses. Most succinctly, he needed to discover (or invent) the Egyptian Moses—a non-Jewish father-figure—precisely to disavow the psychical inheritance of Jewishness itself, "his last protest and bulwark against the inevitable return of the fathers." What Freud sought at his life's end, Robert concludes, was "to be the son not of any man or country, but ... only of his life's work."[48]

Reflecting on Freud's personal investment in that work's final chapter, de Certeau argues that Freud's "writing begins with an exodus." But this is a leaving that, like Lot's wife from the destruction of Sodom and Gomorrah, cannot help but look back. While the "departure"—from the place of the father and of the religion of the fathers—might be "taken to be a liberation when it denies the debt" it owes to the past, de Certeau more accurately captures the rhetorical, emotional, and ethical complexity of Freud's work in remarking that "the text is born of a relation of departure and debt. Within identity, dispossession and membership create the rift from which writing is produced." Hereafter, "membership is expressed only through distance, through traveling farther and farther away from a ground of identity."[49] But to the extent *Moses*

46 *Freud's Moses*, 10; my emphasis.

47 Freud was not the only Jewish son whose ambivalence toward his father was caught up in and expressed through Judaism. In a 1921 critique of contemporary German-Jewish literature, Kafka had drawn as one of the key lessons of psychoanalysis "the observation that the father complex from which more than one Jew draws his spiritual nourishment relates not to the innocent father but to *the father's Judaism*. What most of those who began to write in German wanted was to break with Judaism, ... but their hind legs were bogged down *in their fathers' Judaism*, and their front legs could find no ground" (*Briefe, 1902–1924* [New York: Schocken Books, 1958], 337; my emphases).

48 *From Oedipus to Moses: Freud's Jewish Identity*, trans. Ralph Manheim (Garden City, NY: Anchor Books, 1976), 146, 166–67.

49 De Certeau adds that while, for Freud, "a name [Israel] still obliges," it "no longer provides the thing, this nurturing land.... The obligation to pay the debt, the refusal to abandon the name and the people ('Jerusalem, I shall not forget thee') and, hence, the impossibility

and Monotheism is still in some essential way concerned with the paradoxes of filiation, the very gesture of breaking away by which Freud creates the distance is yet tinged with loss.

Psychoanalysis, of course, had its beginning in mourning. In the Preface to the Second Edition of the *Interpretation of Dreams* (1909), Freud had written: "this book has a … further subjective significance for me personally—a significance which I only grasped after I had completed it. It was, I found, a portion of my own self-analysis, my reaction to my father's death—that is to say, to the most important event, the most poignant loss, of a man's life. Having discovered that this was so, I felt unable to obliterate the traces of the experience. (*SE*, 4:xxvi).[50] Directing special attention to his reaction to this "most poignant loss" later in that treatise, Freud recounts a dream he claims to have had on the night before the funeral (*SE*, 4:317–18). This recollection repeats even as it revises his description of the same dream ("a very pretty dream" he calls it) offered in a letter to Wilhelm Fliess roughly three weeks after Jacob Freud's death in 1896, a description that in this version sets the dream on the night *after* the funeral:

> I found myself in a shop where there was a notice up saying:
> You are requested
> to close your eyes.
> I recognized the place as the barber's to which I go every day. On the day of the funeral I was kept waiting, and therefore arrived at the house of mourning rather late. The family were displeased with me, because I had arranged for the funeral to be quiet and simple, which they later agreed was the best thing. They also took my lateness in rather bad part. The phrase on the notice-board has a double meaning. It means "one should do one's duty toward the dead" in two senses—an apology, as though I had not done my duty and my conduct needed overlooking, and the actual duty itself. The dream was thus an outlet for the feeling of self-reproach which a death generally leaves among the survivors. (*Origins*, 171)[51]

---

of not writing, are built over the dispossession of all 'genea-logical' language" (*Writing of History*, 318–19).

50 Robert has convincingly argued that it was the self-analysis initiated by the death of Jacob Freud that was the true foundation of psychoanalysis as both a content of ideas and a method of interpretation: see *From Oedipus to Moses*, 63–64, and 120–22.

51 The letter is dated November 11, 1896; Jacob Freud died on October 23rd.

More so than in the revised account in *The Interpretation of Dreams*, in the letter to Fliess Freud is clearly uneasy about acknowledging that his lateness in arriving at the funeral is the cause of the family's displeasure with him. But he does eventually get to a point where he interprets the notice as a reproach: "The phrase on the notice-board has a double meaning. It means 'one should do one's duty toward the dead' in two senses—an apology, as though I had not done my duty and my conduct needing overlooking and the actual duty itself." What Freud reluctantly reveals here is his lack of filial respect to the dead: he had come late to the house of mourning and had arranged for a funeral whose sparseness did not, as it does in the 1900 revision, accord with his father's preference. In the 1896 version, in fact, Freud interprets his dream's double meaning explicitly as an indication of emotional ambivalence: the "self-reproach which a death generally leaves among the survivors." But even this is a deflection of sorts. For what the failure of filial duty in coming late and in arranging such a "quiet and simple" ceremony points to is not simply survivor guilt but, more tellingly, Freud's uneasiness about admitting an insult to his father's memory, the source of which he cannot understand.

That said, it is worth noting that Freud introduces the dream with a loving tribute to his father: "[T]he old man's death affected me deeply. I valued him highly and understood him very well indeed, and with his peculiar mixture of deep wisdom and imaginative light-heartedness he meant a great deal in my life" (*Origins*, 170). But we should not be surprised. As Freud would draw out the notion theoretically in *Totem and Taboo*, (1913) and "Remembering, Repeating, and Working-Through" (1914) among other subsequent writings, mourning touches fundamentally upon what in "Mourning and Melancholia" (1915) he would call a "conflict due to ambivalence" (*SE*, 14:251). In his typically understated way, Freud describes this conflict as a "disturbance in self regard" or a feeling of "loss in regard to … [the] ego" (14:246–47). A person suffering pathological mourning (melancholia) "displays … an extraordinary diminution in his self-regard, an impoverishment of his ego on a grand scale"; or again, "the complex of melancholia behaves like an open wound … emptying the ego until it is totally impoverished" (14:246, 253). Although, as Freud will add, the one who mourns "cannot consciously perceive what he has lost" (14:245) in the love-object, this confusion appears to stem primarily from repressed resentment toward the one whose presence, even in death, can so impoverish—as he puts it so poetically, the point at which "the shadow of the [lost] object [falls] upon the ego" (14:249). Even as it is expressed most directly in terms of antagonism toward the self (feelings of self-reproach and unworthiness, self-criticism, even, finally, suicidal tendencies), the "conflict due to ambivalence" thus actually bespeaks a vexed relationship towards the deceased no matter how beloved at the conscious level.[52]

In 1896, when he came late to his father's funeral, Freud experienced even as he acted out just such a conflict: an unconscious insult to the memory of his beloved father. Generalizing on his experience almost two decades later, he will write at the close of "Mourning and Melancholia" that for the ego to work through grief requires that it sever its "attachment to the lost object"; at that point, Freud observes, "mourning impels the ego to give up the object by declaring the object to be dead and *offering the ego the inducement of continuing to live*" (*SE*, 14:257; my emphasis).[53] Cavell at once echoes and builds on Freud's claim in arguing that the "condition of this work is that you want to live"; as Cavell continues in a passage we noted previously, mourning entails finally the "burden of proving that [one] exists, ... finding how to say, 'I am, I exist'; not ... to say it just once, but at every moment of your existence; to preserve your existence, *originate it*."[54]

Two decades later, Freud is still grappling with this foundational idea. In the final section of *Moses and Monotheism* he writes that "ambivalency belongs to the essence of the father-son relationship" (172). Registering without endorsing Freud's claim that "the God of Israel was an unconscious projection of the retrieved memory of the Primeval Father," Yerushalmi yet acknowledges that Freud has a point as regards the biblical narrative: "the entire relationship between God and Man and especially between God and Israel" plays out on the terrain of "the tense agon of Father and son." But, citing a verse from the last of the Hebrew prophets—"He shall reconcile the heart of the fathers with sons and the heart of sons with their fathers" (Malachi 3:24)—Yerushalmi parts company with Freud on what this agon means for a true appreciation of Judaism and Jewish identity. "The difference," Yerushalmi comments, "lies not in the perception of past and present, but in the anticipation of a specific hope for the future." And "it is on the question of hope or hopelessness," Yerushalmi

52 In a draft of a letter to Fliess (dated May 31, 1897), for example, Freud writes that hostile impulses towards our parents (especially toward the parent of the same sex) "are repressed at periods in which pity for one's parents is active, at times of their illness or death. One of the manifestations of grief is then to reproach oneself for their death ... or to punish oneself ... by putting oneself into their position with an idea of retribution," an action Freud there terms "identification" (*Origins*, 207).

53 For one of Freud's earliest musings on the relation between mourning and that ambivalence deriving from fear of the dead's continuing claim upon the living, see *Totem and Taboo*, *SE*, 13:51–74.

54 *Disowning Knowledge*, 186–87; my emphasis; original italics deleted.

concludes, "even more that on God or godlessness, that [Freud's] teaching may be at its most un-Jewish."[55]

But did Freud lose hope or, more precisely, did he reject the possibility that the heart of the father and the heart of the son might be reconciled? Ambivalence cuts both ways, of course. If at some level in *Moses and Monotheism* Freud registered his resistance to the impositions of his father and of the religion of the father(s), he had, as he had told Fliess, loved "the old man"; he acknowledged and even revered Jacob Freud's "peculiar mixture of deep wisdom and imaginative light-heartedness."[56] And what did Freud believe about his father's feelings towards him? Did he imagine that Jacob was disappointed that his beloved son would not read the gift of the restored Book of Books as a faithful member of the covenantal people?

We earlier observed Freud's remark concerning his personal connection to Michelangelo's statue of Moses, his almost perverse reason for wanting to visit it again and again: "I can recollect [how] ... during my first visits to San Pietro in Vincoli, I used to sit down in front of the statue in the expectation that I should now see how it would start up on its raised foot, dash the Tables of the Law to the ground and let fly its wrath." But, Freud continues, "nothing of the kind happened. Instead, the stone image became more and more transfixed, an almost oppressively solemn calm emanated from it" (13:220). Freud's version of Michelangelo's Moses may not yet be the fully worked out father-figure he will become in *Moses and Monotheism*. But to the extent Freud's obsession with the statue might have derived from his feeling that he had betrayed his father's memory and his gift of the book—did he in fantasy see a wrathful Jacob Freud "dash[ing] the Tables of the Law to the ground" as a rebuke to his faithless son?—what he found instead was "solemn calm." As Freud reads Michelangelo's blasphemous (re)imagining of the Exodus 32,

> startled by the clamour of the people and the spectacle of the Golden Calf ... Moses desired to act, to spring up and take vengeance ...; but he has overcome the temptation ... Nor will he throw the Tables so that they will break on the stones, for it is on their especial account that he has controlled his anger; it was to preserve them that he kept his passion in

---

55 *Freud's Moses*, 95.

56 Ambivalence can take many forms. Otto Rank remarked, for example that "psychoanalysis is as conservative as it seems to be revolutionary, for its founder is a rebellious son who defends paternal authority, who, through fear of his own revolt as a son, took refuge in the security of the paternal role" (*Modern Education* [New York, 1932], qtd. in de Certeau, *Writing of History*, 352n46).

> check. In giving way to his rage and indignation, he had to neglect the Tables, and the hand which upheld them was withdrawn. They began to slide down and were in danger of being broken. This brought him to himself. He remembered his mission and for its sake renounced an indulgence of his feelings. ("The Moses of Michelangelo," *SE*, 13:224–25, 229–30)

For the Moses of Michelangelo of Freud, upholding the Law is the most important thing. And to fulfill that mission, Moses will not "take vengeance" no matter the pain he feels; for the sake of the Law and so also not to direct violence toward those who had chosen not to abide by it, he "renounce[s the] … indulgence of his feelings." In order to preserve the Law, to live by its spirit if not its letter, Moses (or Jacob) will respect the decision of those who turn their back on it to find some other way.

Even in the face of rebellion against the word of the god of the fathers, Michelangelo's Moses, Freud says, "will remain seated and still"; he will "control … his anger … [keep] his passion in check." Is this image meant as Freud's version of Malachi's prophecy of reconciliation, a reconciliation that, as Yerushalmi puts it, "posit[s] an ultimate resolution of the oedipal conflict between Israel and God … also on the level of the purely human"?[57] If the heart of the son was already reconciled with the father—"the old man's death affected me deeply. I valued him highly and understood him very well indeed, and … he meant a great deal in my life"—might Freud have also lived in hope that the heart of his father would be reconciled with his wayward son? If that was Freud's hope, then he must also have believed that his father's reconciliation would be marked by acceptance of his son's choice to live his own life, to find his own answers, to make (or discover) his own laws. But if the Jewish father and the Jewish son were to be reconciled as Malachi envisioned, from Freud's point of view that reconciliation would have to be on a foundation other than Judaism itself. Whatever Jacob Freud wished for his son in 1891, after 1896 if not before the book, the Law, the covenant, the God of Israel himself could not be what bound father and son together. For what was "stored like the fragments in an ark" within Freud himself would not be the words of the father or of the father's god who was the god of the fathers. Indeed, they could only be the words that he had spoken of and for himself.[58] Much like Hamlet

57 *Freud's Moses*, 95.

58 De Certeau remarks that Freud's relation to his past "prohibits him both from occupying a proper place, liberated from indebtedness in respect to the other's name, and from a loyalty incontestably identifying him with the Jewish … institution. In other words, for him

at the end of his play, then, in his (re)writing of the story of Moses Freud stands finally as a son unburdened by the (dead) father, a son who, through a process of working-through that necessitates a painful renunciation, would, in effect, give up the ghost. *Moses and Monotheism* is equivalent to Hamlet's "let be" at the end of the "providence in the fall of the sparrow" speech, the moment he acknowledges that, because the dead know nothing of what they leave behind, they cannot return from the undiscovered country to haunt the living. Both grieving sons choose finally to let the dead stay where they belong.

There is a distinction to be made here, of course, between merely forgetting the dead and, as Greenblatt has aptly observed of a key thematic in Shakespeare's play, "remembering [them] in the right way."[59] Remembering the dead in the right way ("normal" as opposed to "pathological mourning") at once feels the loss, pays its respects, and severs attachment to what will not return. This distinction is powerfully on display near the beginning of the final scene of *Hamlet* where Hamlet invokes his father one last time. Recounting his miraculous escape from his death-sentence while in route to England, Hamlet tells Horatio, "I had my father's signet ring in my purse" (5.2.49). For all its importance as a marker of royal status, the father's ring is also a memento or keepsake. At play's end, then, the son's relationship to the deceased father is represented precisely as a thing to be remembered and not re-lived, an objectified memory, we might say, a memory that marks the past as distant and different from the son's present. In this final memory of a beloved father, Hamlet relates to King Hamlet as someone to be mourned and not repeated, a father whose "rest" is, as Hamlet's own soon will be, nothing but "silence" (5.2.358).

And so too for Freud as he approached his death. His completion of *Moses and Monotheism* in 1939 permitted him to overcome his *revenant*, not Moses (who, Freud thought, centuries after having been murdered by his followers, returned as the god of Israel) but Jacob Freud, the figure who had died in 1896 and then as an "unlaid ghost" kept coming back. Of the father imago, Freud writes in Part III that "longing for the father ... lives in each of us from his childhood days," but he adds immediately that in legend this is "the same father whom the hero ... boasts of having overcome" (140). He had made a similar statement in Part I: "a hero is a man who stands up ... against his father and in the end victoriously overcomes him" (9). Freud could become just such a hero by renouncing the religion of his own father and so be (re)born once again, this time (his third birth?) by reversing the second birth that inscribed him, through circumcision,

as for the Egyptian Moses, a proper place or a proper name can no longer exist. In these two ways, the genealogical legend is broken" (336).

59 *Will in the World: How Shakespeare Became Shakespeare* (New York: Norton, 2004), 318.

under the sign of the covenant without his knowledge or consent.[60] But Freud will go even further in adding that, "at the dawn of [his] life," the true hero is the son "born against his father's will" (9). Like Hamlet, Freud could only be born against his father's will at the end of his life. It was with the publication of *Moses and Monotheism* in the year of his death—a death that, perhaps not coincidentally, took place in Shakespeare's own homeland—that Freud, like Hamlet before him, found a way to father himself.

60 De Certeau's makes the apt observation that, for Freud, Jewish tradition "reiterates what exists in the beginning ... the rejection of the founding father" (*Writing of History*, 325). Such a rejection is also a key element of the Egyptian history Freud aims to retell: in becoming Akhenaten, Amenhotep IV aimed among other things for "the erasure of the religion and the name of [his own] father," Amenhotep III.

CODA 4

"What heritage from this land": Freud in Exile

> There is nothing more genuinely Jewish than to inhabit a language of exile and to labor it from within, … turning it into more than just a grammatical language: making it a minor language … And yet … it is also a mother tongue, even though, as Rosenzweig says, it bears witness to the fact that "so far as his language is concerned, the Jew feels always he is in a foreign land."
>
> —GIORGIO AGAMBEN, *The Time That Remains*

•••

> Home is an inconclusive credential for a people known through legend and history for their wandering—to and from native terrain, or transient place of exile, or more recently, the sites of their murder. The wish of Jews to settle down in a place called home has been disrupted by repeated efforts of others to settle them elsewhere. The ultimate violation of this wish occurred during the Nazi era, when the German term *Umsiedlung* (change of home, resettlement) was used to describe the transports to the regions of Auschwitz and Treblinka.
>
> —LAWRENCE LANGER, *Landscapes of Jewish Experience*

•:

1

"What heritage remains for the sons," Michel de Certeau muses, Jewish sons of Jewish fathers, "unless it is … an exodus?"[1] That word, "exodus," a potent reminder of a shared place and a shared time and a shared story (Egypt, Sinai, and the wilderness under Moses' leadership, recounted through the final four books of Torah and then passed down for two thousand years or more), might

1 *The Writing of History*, trans. Tom Conley (New York: Columbia University Press, 1988), 344.

 | DOI:10.1163/9789004701663_010

in this new setting become a marker of a final separation. In the aftermath of his father's death and untethered from the weight of tradition (from his father's religion and so also from the religion of the fathers), Freud felt, as he had written to Fliess, "as if [he] had been torn up by the roots" (*Origins*, 170). Without roots, what foundation, what source of nourishment, what point of origin? De Certeau rightly says that Freud's 1896 dream on the night after his father's funeral was "a gesture of respect and of farewell," the beginning of "a voyage indissolubly linked to mourning."[2] Forty years later, as he completed *Moses and Monotheism*, his last major work, Freud still felt the loss and obligation, the debt and the departure at once.

Reflecting on a different voyage of mourning near the end of his life, Freud wrote in the second of this two prefatory notes to Part III of *Moses and Monotheism* (dated June 1938) that, "after the German invasion," and "in the certainty of persecution," he had been forced him to leave, "with many friends, the city which from early childhood, through seventy-eight years, had been a home" (69–70). He knew that he had gained something from the loss, for he "found the kindliest welcome in beautiful, free, generous England"; living there "a welcome guest," he was also "relieved from … oppression and happy that [he could] speak and write"—even, as he "almost said 'think'"—as he saw fit. In that setting, he finally "dared … to make public the last part of [his] essay" (70). He would come back to the circumstances of his departure from Vienna, his arrival in England, and his decision to complete his study in the opening of the second section of Part III, a section for which he provided the title "*Zusammenfassung und Wiederholung*." The *Standard Edition* translates the German as "Summary and Recapitulation" (*SE*, 23:103), and we might simply understand by the phrase that in what follows (Part III, section 2) Freud will review the material he had previously covered in Parts I and II. But *Wiederholung* might also be rendered as "repetition," and as repetition what he offers in his short introduction to the section more obviously returns to (reiterates) what he had already told his readers of how he had come to write what they were now reading: "Then in March 1938 came the unexpected German invasion. It forced me to leave my home, but it also freed me from the fear lest my publishing of the book might cause psychoanalysis to be forbidden in a country where its practice was still allowed. No sooner had I arrived in England than I found the temptation irresistible, and so I started to rewrite the third part of my essay" (132).

2 *Writing of History*, 321.

If in both statements Freud is superficially more concerned with explaining the existence and aim of his now completed study (with the addition of Part III), we might also give some attention to the repetition that, from the perspective of Freud's own life experience, any reader in 1939 or today might find even more compelling: "June 1938 … *after the German invasion* … in the certainty of persecution … *I left … home*" / "Then in March 1938 came *the unexpected German invasion.* It *forced me to leave my home.*" While the journey from his beloved Vienna to London encouraged and indeed enabled Freud to complete the project that was *Moses and Monotheism*, the voyage that speaks of a deeply felt loss ("I left, with many friends, the city which from early childhood … had been a home to me") might be understood as a different kind of repetition entirely.

Whether the old and dying Freud would have thought of his leaving Vienna as a traumatic experience, we might here return to Cathy Caruth's observation that "the peculiar temporality of trauma" includes "the sense that *the past it foists upon one is not one's own.*"[3] More specifically in relation to Freud, Caruth argues that his very writing of *Moses and Monotheism* should be understood as a kind of retelling of "the story of the Hebrews" and, as such, might at some level be viewed as an unconscious reenactment of the trauma that resides within that story. For, as she puts it, "the book itself, Freud seems to be telling us, is the site of a trauma; a trauma that … appears to be historically marked by the events that, Freud says, divide the book into two halves: first, the infiltration of Nazism into Austria, … and then the invasion of Austria by Germany, causing Freud to leave … The structure and history of the book, in its traumatic form … , thus mark it as the very bearer of a historical truth that is itself involved in the political entanglements of Jews and their persecutors." Caruth adds that "the trauma in Freud's text is first of all a trauma of leaving," an experience marked, as Caruth demonstrates, in Freud's repeated use—we might think of this as a neurotic repetition—of some form of the verb *verlassen* (to leave). Suggesting that Freud's trauma is registered in *Moses and Monotheism* less by his nod to the *Anschluss* ("German invasion") than by his short sentence "*verließ ich*" ("I left": *Moses and Monotheism*, 70; German text: 16:159), she then claims that Freud was in some mysterious way revisiting the very trauma he had explored in the text itself, the trauma at the heart of Jewish history. Consciously or not, Caruth argues, Freud aimed to "convey the impact of a history

3 *Unclaimed Experience: Trauma, Narrative, History* (Baltimore: Johns Hopkins University Press, 1996), 143n10.

precisely as what *cannot be grasped* about leaving."[4] It was, we might say, a trauma that was Freud's own and not his own simultaneously.

Caruth's elucidation of the terms of Freud's experience not just as a writer but as a Jewish writer in the 1930s is at once generally insightful and, more specifically, points to the possibility of a psychoanalytic inquiry into *Moses and Monotheism* that does not depend on rehearsing vague claims of Freud's own repressed oedipal inclinations.[5] That said, her argument yet strangely misses the mark in two key respects. First, as a relatively minor point, while traumatic experience might indeed be related to—might even have its origin in—something the mind finds incomprehensible at the moment of its encounter ("what cannot be grasped"), it can hardly be argued that Freud failed to grasp the reality of the situation, either the fact of his departure or its immediate cause. The "German invasion" led to his "certainty of persecution—now not only because of [his] work, but also because of [his] 'race'"—and in leaving (more precisely, escaping) Vienna for England he found that he could once again "speak and write ... [and] 'think'" "relieved from that oppression" (69–70). From this perspective, Caruth is seriously misrepresenting Freud in claiming that he is engaged in an "*unconscious* act of leaving" and that this very "unconsciousness ... bears the impact of history." It is unclear what is *unconscious* in Freud's experience or how it is expressed "in his own text" by "reference to his departure." And when she adds that the "full force" of the trauma's "historicity," a trauma "borne by an act of departure," is yet "in some sense absolutely opaque," it is equally unclear what she intends by that qualification: if it is only opaque *in some sense* it cannot be *absolutely* opaque.[6] In any event, the circumstances behind Freud's *verließ ich* (I left) are not at all opaque either to the reader or to Freud himself, and so whatever is traumatic in his situation does not easily fit within the interpretive framework Caruth provides.

The second, and more damaging, problem with Caruth's notion that Freud's text reenacts the traumatic (hi)story of the Hebrews is that, as we saw in Chapter 2, she doesn't appear to fully appreciate what made that (hi)story traumatic in the first place. For Caruth, "what cannot be grasped" in Freud's experience, the "history whose traces cannot be effaced" but which yet "haunts Freud like an unlaid ghost" is what Freud himself thought lay hidden at the origin of

4 *Unclaimed Experience*, 20–21.

5 For an example of this approach, all the more valuable because of its many genuine insights into Freud's personal and professional life, see Marthe Robert, *From Oedipus to Moses: Freud's Jewish Identity*, trans. Ralph Manheim (Garden City, NY: Anchor Books, 1976).

6 *Unclaimed Experience*, 22–23.

Jewish history: "Moses' murder, its effacement, and its unconscious repetition."[7] Since those are the explicit topics of *Moses and Monotheism*, it is simply impossible to know what Caruth means in suggesting that Freud himself repeats the cultural Ur-trauma by repressing or otherwise psychically disconnecting from it (effacing it or failing to grasp it except through the unconscious repetition of *Moses and Monotheism* itself). We noted in Chapter 2 that Caruth's insistence on making the murder of Moses the origin of the ongoing Jewish (and thus also of Freud's) trauma doesn't even do justice to, because not conceptually in accord with, her most compelling ways of formulating the issue:

1. "Freud implicitly and paradoxically connects the explanation of the Jews' persecution to their very liberation, the return from captivity to freedom" (12)
2. "... Freud's new understanding of the story of captivity, or exile, and return"; "the *Jews* ... become a true nation only in their act of leaving captivity ..." (13)
3. "the future is no longer continuous with the past but is united with it through a profound discontinuity ... the meaning of the Jewish past ... is a departure that is both a radical break and the establishment of a history" (14)
4. "in Freud's own theoretical explanation of trauma ... it is, finally, *the act of leaving* that constitutes its central and enigmatic core" (22)

As is evident, the very language Caruth regularly employs to describe the originary trauma of the people of Israel makes much more sense in the context of the exilic and postexilic period, that is, without any reference to the alleged murder of Moses. In fact, out of context, one might easily assume that in the passages just quoted Caruth is explicitly addressing the impact of the Babylonian Exile on Jewish culture. And that is precisely what she inexplicably misreads in Freud's personal history. For if, as she writes, "Freud's writing preserves history ... within the words of his leaving, words that do not simply refer" but also in some mysterious way "convey the impact of a history," it is by being forced into *de facto* exile because of persecution, persecution motivated by his Jewish heritage (his "race"), that Freud much more obviously repeats the story of his ancestors, the people of Judah who, more than two thousand years before, had similarly left the only home they had ever known, expecting never to return. For both ancient and modern Jews, it was, as Caruth observes—and here she is speaking more wisely than she knows—a "trauma ... borne by an

7 *Unclaimed Experience*, 20.

act of departure."[8] De Certeau captures this peculiar dynamic in remarking that "the Freudian theory of writing" underlying *Moses and Monotheism* "refers to the history which inverts the traditional myth: the destruction of the Temple and the loss of the identifying soil. This event was the impossible: a rupture of being that had been defined up until then by the relation between *the* land and the election. Hereafter the nation mourns." He concludes by observing that *Moses and Monotheism* effectively repeats the national experience: "The work has no hereditary soil. It is nomadic."[9] In short, whether Freud consciously grasped this fact or not, completed in the shadow of his own impending exile, *Moses and Monotheism* is fundamentally a work about the trauma of a lost home(land): *Heim / Heimat*.

As de Certeau's formulation should remind us, exile is one of the great themes of Torah, and, as we saw in Chapter 2, the idea frames the entire the Hebrew Bible: beginning with Adam and Eve's expulsion from their garden home and ending with Cyrus of Persia's edict, an invitation to the newly freed Judaeans to return to Judah (now Judea) from Babylon (in the final verse of the Hebrew Bible the returnees have not yet even started the journey home). And there are moments in the biblical narrative—Psalm 137 comes to mind immediately—that look back in longing on a lost homeland, a longing accompanied by a real fear of dying in exile. Freud's rueful remark in early 1938 to his son Ernst that "it is typically Jewish not to renounce anything and to replace what has been lost" might suggest that *he* could more easily give up or even renounce Vienna and replace it with "beautiful, free, generous England." But his public act of saying a final goodbye to his lifetime home is yet tinged with a note of melancholy.[10] More to the point, however driven by the unique circumstances of the 1930s, Freud's and his unnamed (undoubtedly Jewish) friends leaving home in response to Nazi persecution reenacts the forced departures that had haunted Jewish history ever since the Assyrian conquest of the northern kingdom of Israel in the late-eighth century BCE and the Babylonian conquest of the southern kingdom of Judah in the early-sixth century BCE. Freud and friends'

---

8 *Unclaimed Experience*, 21–22. It might be more accurate to say that Jewish history became traumatic in the vexed relationship (the gap) between two different departures: the departure from Egypt as liberation from foreign servitude and the subsequent departure from Judah in the wake of foreign conquest.

9 *Writing of History*, 318–19.

10 Letter to Ernst Freud (January 17, 1938), *Letters of Sigmund Freud*, ed. Ernst L. Freud, trans. Tania Stern and James Stern (New York: Basic Books, 1960), 440. In that same letter, Freud refers to sending along with the letter "an essay on Moses," undoubtedly the newly completed Part III. He adds with a touch of self-mockery that it is "one of [his] few recent works which may arouse general interest" even to the point of "be[ing] blown up into something sensational." As he accurately predicted, "Jewry will be very offended."

exile in all but name might be understood, then, as the memic replication of one of the central elements of the mythic narrative of the people of ancient Israel. If Freud in exile was unlike Adam and Eve in one crucial sense—he had been driven from his home for no fault of his own—he was yet like the primal parents in another sense: he would never return to the land his birth (he died in England on September 23, 1939). But even in this he was in good company: having departed his actual if not spiritual homeland (Egypt), the constantly journeying Moses had also died in a foreign land.[11]

Precisely because for Freud there was no coming back, if his experience of exile could be said to track the Bible's mythic construction of exile, then we must look to some other part of his journey from Austria to England for the sense of hope that in biblical narrative typically accompanies the time away from the homeland.[12] Caruth remarks that, to the extent a "traumatic structure" inhabits the "history of Jewish survival," it does so as at once "an endless crisis and the endless possibility of a new future."[13] But for aging Freud, already sick with the cancer that would kill him, there was little future left. So if "beautiful, free, generous England" was not going to be a home to return to at the end of his life (and unlike Jacob's and Joseph's his remains would stay where he had died), the hope he discovered or rediscovered in life abroad would need to be of a different order entirely. It is with a reflection on where Freud found that hope and how his assertion of it in the face of his own hardships replicates what he might have gathered from the biblical narrative that I now close.

2

In an understated and indirect way, Freud yet makes it quite clear where he had found that hope. As he wrote in the introduction to Part III, section 2, precisely by forcing the issue for Austrian Jews, the *Anschluss* "freed" Freud.

11 We might think of the Hebrew Bible's symbolic understanding of exile as "mythic" in the way Robert Paul describes "what myths do": "create … a cosmos within which a form of life takes place and acquires meaning for those under its influence." Paul adds that a "cultural myth obtains its energy from its correspondence with the deepest wishes, conflicts, and anxieties of the individuals under its sway. The individuals are themselves formed by the cultural myth in such a way that their inchoate impulses, fears, and fantasies are given a definite, publicly valorized shape and meaning" (*Moses and Civilization: The Meaning Behind Freud's Myth* [New Haven: Yale University Press, 1996], 15–16).

12 While, as noted, we expect no return to the garden for expelled Adam and Eve, the Hebrew Bible's more usual way of depicting situations of leaving home or living outside the (home)land—these invariably arise in the wake of a forced departure of some kind—almost always imagine the possibility of and often show an actual return.

13 *Unclaimed Experience*, 68.

What he adds immediately places this freedom in a very limited context: "the unexpected German invasion ... *freed me from the fear lest my publishing of the book might cause psychoanalysis to be forbidden* in a country where its practice was still allowed" (*Moses and Monotheism*, 132). Caruth completely misses the point in taking Freud at his word here: "leaving home, for Freud" represents, she writes, "the freedom to bring forth his book in England." Even if we acknowledge her subsequent elaboration—"the freedom, that is, to bring his voice to another place" and so "to bring forth his voice to others"—Caruth still sidesteps what Freud is plainly telling his readers: if the threat of Nazi persecution also frees him, that is because, as he had written in the second of his two prefatory notes, "in beautiful, *free* (German: *freien*), generous England," he will reclaim his own freedom, not just so that he might "dare .. to make public the last part of [his] essay," important as that was to him, but also, and more crucially, to be free from "oppression" (German: *Druck*; literally "pressure") so that he might speak and write and think (German: *reden, schreiben, denken*) in whatever way he chose (70). If Freud recognized that he was losing his home and homeland (*Heim*[*at*]) forever in his forced departure from Vienna, he also knew that he had gained something of inestimable worth.

The movement to freedom lies at the very beginning of the Exodus story, of course; the account comprises roughly the first third of the Book of Exodus. The very justification for the people of Israel agreeing to the terms of the Mosaic covenant, we are told over and over again, is that God had delivered them from "the house of bondage" that was Egypt.[14] Freedom, in short, was always understood as central to the cultural foundation myth with Moses' own heroic part in the myth defined less in terms of any revolutionary actions than in terms of his voicing the demand for freedom as a condition that had to be established prior to the emergence of the nation and even in advance of the formal ratification of the covenant with Yahweh.

Even prior to the people's deliverance, in more abstract terms freedom is portrayed as the condition prevailing at creation itself and, more significantly, as the underlying cause of humankind's original experience of exile, the loss of the paradisal home(land). Necessarily coming before the fateful choice made by Adam and Eve in Genesis 3, the prohibition against eating the fruit announced by God in the preceding chapter (2:16–17) establishes the very

14 See, for example, Exodus 13:3, Deuteronomy 5:6 and 6:12. For rich discussion of this revolutionary situation, see Michael Walzer, *Exodus and Revolution* (New York: Basic Books, 1985); for a more historically grounded discussion of the biblical account, see Jan Assmann, *The Invention of Religion: Faith and Covenant in the Book of Exodus*, trans. Robert Savage (Princeton: Princeton University Press, 2018), chs. 4–6.

possibility of making a choice at all and so also renders free will meaningful (fully operational, we might say): the freedom to choose to obey or not. Meir Sternberg's fine description of what he calls the Hebrew Bible's "ideological stakes" in its commitment to the narration of history as "linear progress" in time could just as easily apply just to the second story of creation (Genesis 2), which is in a very real sense the narrative origin of this commitment: "What hangs in the balance is nothing less than the foundations of Hebrew monotheism," foundations that show a productive tension between, on the one hand, "God's purposive control over developments in nature and society, with particular regard to Israel," and, on the other hand, "the relaxation of divine omnipotence in favor of humanity, free to make choices and, later, held accountable for the results."[15] Robert Alter similarly understands freedom so conceived as the heart of Judaism's monotheistic revolution the ethical philosophy of which is consistently and deliberately expressed through the formal rhetorical design of much of biblical narrative:

> Since art does not develop in a vacuum, the literary techniques of the Bible must be associated with the conception of human nature implicit in biblical monotheism: *every person is created by an all-seeing God but abandoned to his own unfathomable freedom, made in God's likeness as a matter of cosmogonic principle but almost never as a matter of accomplished ethical fact....* The purposeful selectivity of means, the repeatedly contrastive or comparative strategies used in the rendering of biblical characters, are in a sense dictated by the biblical view of mankind.[16]

Alter and Sternberg agree that there is a fundamental paradox in the biblical notion of human freedom: that freedom is real (there is, as Sternberg puts it, some "relaxation of divine omnipotence" that allows human beings to act

15 "Time and Space in Biblical (Hi)story Telling: The Grand Chronology," in *The Book and the Text: The Bible and Literary Theory*, ed. Regina M. Schwartz (Oxford: Basil Blackwell, 1990), 90.

16 *The Art of Biblical Narrative* (New York: Basic Books, 1981), 115; my emphasis. Earlier, Alter offered the following description:

"The key to these concerted means for the rendering of a narrative event in the Bible is the writer's desire to give each fictional situation, with minimal authorial intrusion, a marked thematic direction as well as moral-psychological depth.... *Every human agent must be allowed the freedom to struggle with his destiny through his own words and acts ....* The Hebrew narrator does not openly meddle with the personages he presents, just as *God creates in each human personality a fierce tangle of intentions, emotions, and calculations caught in a translucent net of language, which is left for the individual himself to sort out in the evanescence of a single lifetime.*" (86–87; my emphases)

independently of God), but it exists in a cosmos where God is yet "all-seeing"; thus, we can never quite comprehend how we can be truly free in a God-centered cosmos.[17] That said, the real issue isn't freedom simply for the sake of freedom. Rather, in our freedom to create—to create ourselves, our lives, the meaning of our existence—we are like God (made in the divine image). To be in God's image is a process that is coincident with living itself: as the Bible presents it, we are what we become through the moral choices made possible in freedom.

Whether or not he was even aware of just how biblical his final journey was (and we shall see in a moment that he made at least a rudimentary connection), Freud clearly understood freedom as something to be prized and so never to be taken for granted. In this recognition he had something in common with the Israelites in the wake of their deliverance from the "house of bondage": in much of the rest of Torah, even under Moses' leadership they would be forced to grapple with the consequences and burdens of their new freedom. But he was also akin to the post-exodus Israelites in that, in leaving the land of his birth with no expectation of return, he was choosing to accept those consequences and burdens as the cost of escaping oppression. For better or worse, biblically speaking to live in freedom is central to what it means to be human at all.

If in free England Freud felt he could speak and write and think without fear of censorship and ethnic persecution, he could cherish one other gift. Precisely because he knew the time that remained to him was short, to choose a life of freedom was also to choose, as he had written in a letter to his son Ernst just weeks before leaving Vienna, "to die in freedom." Freud's stoicism is balanced here with an almost playful awareness that in attaining this goal he would in some strange way be repeating the story of "Israel" himself: "I sometimes compare myself with the old Jacob who, when a very old man, was taken by his children to Egypt."[18] Despite writing to Ernst from his Viennese home at Bergasse 19, Freud would announce his coming death as though he had already

---

17 Alter observes that "the depth with which human nature is imagined in the Bible is a function of its being conceived as caught in a powerful interplay of this double dialectic between design and disorder, providence and freedom. The various biblical narratives in fact may be usefully seen as forming a spectrum between the opposing extremes of disorder and design" (33).

18 In immediately adding, "let us hope that it won't be followed by an exodus from Egypt," Freud reverses a key element of the biblical rendering: Egypt as the "house of bondage" becomes for Freud in 1938 "free England" while the Promised Land as the site of final liberation (the very goal of the biblical exodus) is reimagined as German-occupied Austria, the land of oppression to which Freud never wants to return: Letter to Ernst Freud (May

assumed his life in exile: in a letter otherwise written entirely in German, the phrase, "to die in freedom," was written in English. Freud's imagination of his final, defiant act of freedom, an act that could only be marked in the anticipatory declaration that he had lived a free man all the way to the end, would thus bear the mark of exile itself: four little words composed in the language of free England and not in his native language of oppressed Austria. But, as he also said in the letter, "compared to being liberated, nothing else is of any importance." And so in a way that would reenact the experience not so much of "the old Jacob" but, first, of Adam and Eve (expelled from Paradise because of their assertion of free will) and, then, of Moses (the great liberator himself), Freud could look forward to living the last days of his life in freedom only by accepting the necessity of leaving his *Heim(at)* to die in a foreign land. To borrow from Freud's great insight in *Beyond the Pleasure Principle* (1920), living as a free person would entail (at once including and bequeathing as both inheritance and burden) the chance to die on his own terms.[19]

As his own words attest, Freud was clearly both aware and self-aware of his circumstances. That said, we might yet follow Caruth, who herself follows Freud on this point, in maintaining that for an experience to be truly traumatic it must first exist in an unconscious state before it can acquire an "obsessive character" (*Moses and Monotheism*, 71, 130). Within that interpretive framework, we then must ask regarding Freud's obsession with freedom, an obsession that, however healthy, led him to repeat the exile of his ancestors, what

---

12, 1938) in *Letters of Sigmund Freud*, 442–43. For God's renaming of Jacob as "Israel," see Genesis 32:28 and 35:10.

19 While the context is completely different, Freud's precise way of describing the death drive is instructive:

"If we are to take it as a truth that knows no exception that everything living dies for internal reasons—becomes inorganic once again—then we shall be compelled to say that 'the aim of all life is death' … The attributes of life were at some time evoked in inanimate matter by the action of a force of whose nature we can form no conception.… The tension which then arose in what had hitherto been an inanimate substance endeavored to cancel itself out. In this way the first instinct came into being: the instinct to return to the inanimate state.… Seen in this light, the theoretical importance of the instincts of self-preservation, of self-assertion and of mastery greatly diminishes. They are *component instincts whose function is to assure that the organism shall follow its own path to death*, and to ward off any possible ways of returning to inorganic existence other than those which are immanent in the organism itself.… What we are left with is the fact that *the organism wishes to die only in its own fashion*." (*SE*, 18:38–39; my emphases; original italics deleted)

For a rich discussion of what Freud's theory of the "organism" means for the construction of human life, see Peter Brooks, "Freud's Masterplot," *Yale French Studies* (*Literature and Psychoanalysis: The Question of Reading Otherwise*) 55 / 56 (1977): 280–300.

was unconscious about it? To rephrase the issue in Caruth's terms, was there anything Freud could not grasp about his leaving? Or in what sense does an experience "borne by [Freud's] act of departure" deserve to be called a traumatic at all?

Elaborating on what he calls "the horror first confronted by the Jews," Slavoj Žižek argues that Judaism,

> in forcing us to face the abyss of the Other's desire (in the guise of an impenetrable God), in refusing to cover up this abyss with a determinate fantasmatic scenario, ... confronts us for the first time with the paradox of human freedom. There is no freedom outside the traumatic opacity of the Other's desire: freedom does not mean that I simply get rid of the Other's desire—I am, as it were, thrown into my freedom when I confront this opacity as such, deprived of the fantasmatic cover that tells me what the Other wants from me. In this difficult predicament, full of anxiety, when I know *that* the Other wants something from me, without knowing *what* this desire is, I am thrown back on myself, compelled to assume the risk of freely determining the coordinates of my desire.[20]

Žižek is wide of the mark in his corollary assertion that the traumatizing "secret to which the Jews remain faithful is the horror of the divine impotence." As we saw in Chapter 2 especially in relation to the Book of Job, it would be more accurate to say that the horror to which the Jews remain faithful is the biblical god's own lack of faithfulness: he is not impotent, he just doesn't care.[21] It is precisely in this context that Žižek is also wrong to suggest that Jewish culture "refus[ed] to cover up this abyss with a determinate fantasmatic scenario." For it was precisely the function of the Deuteronomistic History and certain other parts of the narrative (e.g. Daniel's apocalypticism) and of postexilic ritual and liturgy to create a "determinate fantasmatic scenario" that could "cover up this abyss": to explain, deflect, deny—for example, by assuming responsibility for the destruction of Judah and the loss of the Temple so that Yahweh would not need to held responsible. (This precisely the evasion—God would never punish the innocent—that the Book of Job then refuses.) But even if, as Freud imagines observant Jews of his own day echoing the banality of Job's

20 *The Puppet and the Dwarf: The Perverse Core of Christianity* (Cambridge, MA: MIT Press, 2003), 129.

21 Žižek is more to the point in subsequently remarking that Jewish experience is symbolic of "humanity as such, insofar as it was *abandoned by God*" (131; my emphasis; original italics deleted).

three friends, the people "deserved nothing better than to be punished by [God], because they did not observe the laws" (*Moses and Monotheism*, 173), that ethical consequence would merely beg the question: why did God impose the laws at all? More fundamentally even, why did God choose Abraham and his descendants in the first place? Why after ignoring their enslavement in Egypt for four-hundred years did he suddenly decide to call on Moses to begin the process of their deliverance? And for that matter, why did he not liberate other enslaved peoples (surely, he had an abundance of choices in the ancient world)? Why did he want his chosen people to become a mighty nation (what purpose would be served since great empires rose and fell with some regularity)? Why, having brought them to the summit of greatness under the Temple-building Solomon, did he permit foreign nations that did not recognize his authority (did not even acknowledge his existence) to lay waste to the kingdom established through the lineage of David, messianic sons of god? What did it mean be chosen, distinct, blessed, elect, the special favorite, bound through a covenant no other people had been offered or even knew to a god who found it an easy thing to turn his back when it suited his (inscrutable) purposes? Why, finally, stay faithful to a god who had made no sense in the beginning and had continued to make no sense over the long course of Jewish history (the rise of the Nazis just the most recent evidence of that fact)?

This is where Žižek's analysis shows its true insight. "Fac[ing] the abyss of the Other's desire ... in the guise of an impenetrable God," the chosen people were forced into the anxiety-riddled "predicament" of "know[ing] *that* the Other"—this impenetrable God—"want[ed] something ... without knowing *what* this desire [was]."[22] In Chapter 2, we examined in detail how this predicament is depicted in the Book of Job among other texts. Here are two other brief examples from the biblical narrative, both centrally concerned with exile or at least with the experience of being compelled by circumstances to live outside the homeland. The first, what we might take to be the chosen people's initial experience of exile, can be usefully contrasted to the circumstances of

22 We might relate Žižek's sense of this psychical dynamic to Jean Laplanche's concept of the implantation of "enigmatic messages" emanating from the Other, an issue we touched on earlier. Commenting on Laplanche, Eric Santner suggests that "this Other can be understood not only as another subject but also as the symbolic tradition and order into which one is born, which, in turn, always includes traces of lost forms of life" (*On the Psychotheology of Everyday Life: Reflections on Freud and Rosenzweig* [Chicago: University of Chicago Press, 2001], 97). We might then think of God's very act of choosing the people of Israel as his implantation of an enigmatic message which then created the Jewish subject and Jewish culture as a whole by fixing both within a "symbolic tradition" defined as much by absence ("traces of lost forms of life") as by presence.

an even earlier (non-Israelite) exile, Adam and Eve's expulsion from Paradise as the consequence of their disobedience. In Genesis 12, immediately upon receiving God's promise of the land of Canaan as the inheritance of his descendants (Genesis 12:7), Abram and Sarai are, through no fault of their own, forced by a famine to leave their new (home)land for Egypt (Genesis 12:10ff.). But it is unclear what the cause of the famine is (the narrative is notoriously silent on this matter). If God is the cause, then his very first act after establishing the covenant would be inexplicable: making the people of Israel's progenitors leave the very land that is so central to the covenant. If God is not the cause, then his very status as convenant-maker is called into question: there is no guarantee that he can actually fulfill his promises if he has no control over the random workings of the natural world. And if that is the case, it is unclear what the point of the covenant is: what can being chosen even mean in that context?

The second example comes from a passage we have had occasion to consider previously, the very last four verses of the Hebrew Bible:

> [20] Those who survived the sword [Nebuchadnezzar] exiled to Babylon, and they became his and his sons' servants till the rise of the Persian kingdom, [21] in fulfillment of the word of the LORD spoken by Jeremiah, until the land paid back its sabbaths; as long as it lay desolate it kept sabbath, till seventy years were completed. [22] And in the first year of King Cyrus of Persia, when the word of the LORD spoken by Jeremiah was fulfilled, the LORD roused the spirit of King Cyrus of Persia to issue a proclamation throughout his realm by word of mouth and in writing, as follows: [23] "Thus said King Cyrus of Persia: The LORD the God of Heaven has given me all the kingdoms of the earth, and has charged me with building Him a House in Jerusalem, which is in Judah. Any one of you of all His people, the LORD his God be with him and let him go up." (2 Chronicles 36:20–23)

While on the surface Cyrus' acts renew the promise of the Exodus—liberation from servitude and, in the wake of that liberation, a (future) return to the land God had given to Abraham's descendants as one of the terms of the covenant—the very fact that a foreign ruler is the immediate agent of history (however much Cyrus acts to fulfill "the word of the LORD spoken by Jeremiah") raises the strange possibility that God is not fully in charge.[23] (We might observe that

---

23 Sidestepping this very problem is undoubtedly a key reason that Deutero-Isaiah will refer to Cyrus as God's "anointed": Isaiah 45:1.

even the destination of the return is misstated: Judah has by this time in history become the Persian province of Yehud Medinata, and so the people would not truly be returning to reestablish the nation destroyed by Nebuchadnezzar's army.) Moreover, the fact that the Bible ends with the people liberated but still living outside the homeland appears intended to remind readers of the account of the death of Moses at the conclusion of Torah:

> [1] Moses went up from the steppes of Moab to Mount Nebo, to the summit of Pisgah, opposite Jericho, and the LORD showed him the whole land: Gilead as far as Dan; [2] all Naphtali; the land of Ephraim and Manasseh; the whole land of Judah as far as the Western Sea; [3] the Negeb; and the Plain—the Valley of Jericho, the city of palm trees—as far as Zoar. [4] And the LORD said to him, "This is the land of which I swore to Abraham, Isaac, and Jacob, 'I will assign it to your offspring.' I have let you see it with your own eyes, but you shall not cross there." [5] So Moses the servant of the LORD died there, in the land of Moab, at the command of the LORD.[6] He buried him in the valley in the land of Moab, near Beth Peor; and no one knows his burial place to this day. (Deuteronomy 34:1–6)

While for many reasons Moses' situation is unique, the fact that God's greatest prophet could not even experience the full promise of the covenant (indeed, was deliberately prevented from doing so) is a warning of sorts: not only are there no guarantees that the people living in Babylon will actually make it back to Judah / Judaea (they could very well end up with Moses' fate: the indignity of an unmarked grave), but even if they do the very repetition of servitude in Egypt in the experience of captivity in Babylon raises the specter of yet another repetition—untold exiles—in the future. That is, even if the exiles could reclaim the Promised Land (and there is little evidence of that), it is unclear if that would even matter in the long run. Finally and perhaps most intriguingly, we see that Cyrus' edict is an invitation to the exiles to return to Judah / Judaea and not a command. Thus, we might say that the Bible ends with the people facing a choice: to make, or not, a (freely chosen) commitment, to take, or not, a leap of faith in response to a situation that God may or may not control or even intend. So conceived, freedom, already wrapped up in the sense that exile is an ever-present possibility in Jewish experience, arises under the sign of uncertainty, not just the uncertainty of what the future has in store but also, and more threateningly, the uncertainty of what God really wants, what his full plan might be (assuming he even has one), and how much suffering his people might have to endure before the plan is completed. To return to Žižek, "freedom does not mean that I simply get rid of the

Other's desire"; rather, it means that, in response to the "traumatic opacity of the Other's [for the postexilic Judaeans, the impenetrable God's] desire," we are "thrown into … freedom." Under such terms (the postexilic condition), the covenantal people were compelled by the logic of their own national mythology to confront the horror of freedom—"compelled to assume the risk of freely determining the coordinates of [their own] desire"—where, by contrast, contemporary Greeks were forced by their mythology to confront the horror of its lack under the implacable rule of fate.

In so adapting Žižek's argument to the postexilic setting, we might say that, while a national trauma was the consequence of the Babylonian Exile, the real locus of the trauma (its "kernel" as Freud might have put it) is what the Exile called attention to, even culturally induced, in a new way: first, the opacity of God's desire—not just *what* he wanted but also *why* he chose Abraham's descendants as the vehicle of his desire's fulfillment—and second, freedom as the experience of the unresolved confrontation with that very opacity. To put this another way, the trauma resulting from exile transformed the preexilic idea of divine chosenness and its corresponding commitment to political and moral freedom into an unconscious attachment. In the postexilic world, freedom thus came to function for the Jews as the site of the national trauma and took on an unconscious dimension in precisely the terms Freud had gone looking for in his work on *Moses and Monotheism*: the compulsive conviction at the heart of Jewish culture. (We can imagine Freud speaking for all his people when he wrote to his son, "compared to being liberated, nothing else is of any importance.") Expressed as anxiety rather than, as Freud believed, repressed guilt for the murder of Moses, this conviction then produced as a cultural reaction formation the obsessive character of Judaic faith: rituals, liturgies, ceremonies, laws, a national narrative to be repeated over and over to defend against the freedom created by the doubt, questioning, uncertainty, and ultimately the sense of dispossession arising from the experience of exile. The notion that what Freud considered the obsessional element of Jewish culture is designed to defend against a collective dispossession is perhaps the best way to understand his statement about the historical origin of biblical tradition as we now have it: "The political misfortune of the nation taught them to appreciate the only possession they had retained, their written records, at its true value. Immediately after the destruction of the Temple in Jerusalem by Titus, Rabbi Jochanan ben Sakkai asked for permission to open at Jabneh the first school of the study of Torah. From now on, it was the Holy Book, and the study of it, that kept the scattered people together" (*Moses and Monotheism*, 147). More broadly, Freud saw in Jewish culture an "insatiable" need to "render their religious precepts ever and ever more strict, more exacting, but also more petty" (173). It was almost as though tradition, as it became increasingly ossified (a "fossil," as Freud put it [113]), marked its refusal to let go in ever more demanding ways precisely to stave off the anxiety that there was nothing to let go of.

We noted in Chapter 4 that, writing in his preface to a planned Hebrew translation of *Totem and Taboo* shortly before he began work in earnest on *Moses and Monotheism*, Freud mused that while he felt "estranged" from Judaism as a faith-practice he yet felt bound in some hard to define way to his Jewish heritage:

> No reader [of the Hebrew version of] this book will find it easy to put himself in the emotional position of an author who is ignorant of the language of holy writ, who is completely estranged from the religion of his fathers—as well as from every other religion—and who cannot take a share in nationalist ideals, but who has never yet repudiated his people, who feels that he is in essential nature a Jew and who has no desire to alter that nature. If the question were put to him: "Since you have abandoned all these common characteristics of your countrymen, what is there left to you that is Jewish?" he would reply: "A very great deal, and probably its very essence." (*SE*, 13:xv)

If what finally was "left to" Freud that was Jewish, what remained as the essence he could not define here in 1930 or even, years later, after he had "left" (*verließ ich*) for good, I would suggest that this essence was his very need, even a yearning, to live, and die, in freedom even if, to borrow the language of my first epigraph above, what made that freedom "genuinely Jewish" was its essential homelessness.[24] The avowedly non-Judaic Freud would still be *essentially* Jewish precisely to the extent that, through his quest to claim his people's heritage of freedom, a heritage itself constituted by what Eric Santner has aptly termed "the psychic registration of validity in excess of meaning," he would at the end of his life "inhabit a language of exile" by taking up his final residence "in a foreign land."[25] We might say that, as the locus of Jewish culture's compulsive character, validity in excess of meaning could be powerfully alluring for anyone born into the tradition, even for someone as estranged from it

24 The epigraph is from Giorgio Agamben, *The Time That Remains: A Commentary on the Letter to the Romans*, trans. Patricia Dailey (Stanford: Stanford University Press, 2005), 4–5. Agamben is quoting a line from Franz Rosenzweig's *The Star of Redemption*, trans. William W. Hallo (New York: Holt, Rinehart and Winston, 1970), 302.

25 Santner, *On the Psychotheology of Everyday Life*, 103.

of Freud claimed to be. It constituted the Jewish "essence," an essence that, though impossible to define, one could not easily escape. And Freud himself had no desire to escape it.

At the opening of Chapter 1, I cited a letter from Freud to Arnold Zweig (dated September 30, 1934) in which Freud writes: "The starting point of my work is familiar to you ... Faced with the new persecutions, one asks oneself again how the Jews have come to be what they are and why they have attracted this undying hatred."[26] I observed there that while this statement points to the escalating anti-Semitism of the early 1930s ("the new persecutions" / "this undying hatred") as the proper context for understanding Freud's decision to write a book about Moses, it is curious that, for Freud, the study's "starting point" had less to do with the underlying causes of anti-Semitism than with ethnic self-understanding—"how the Jews have come to be what *they are*" so as to attract persecution and hatred. While in the letter as later in *Moses and Monotheism* Freud showed that he understood quite well the ethnic bigotry motivating the Nazis—he knew that if he stayed in Vienna he would be persecuted because of his "race"—what he aimed for in reconstructing "the origin of monotheism among the Jews" (*Moses and Monotheism*, 81) was the "monotheistic idea" itself, an idea that, "treasured by them as their most precious possession," had also kept "this people alive by bestowing on them the pride of being the chosen people" (108).

Freud, of course, concluded that this pride was an aftereffect, formed as part of the reaction formation to the repressed, unresolved guilt for the murder of Moses which subsequently took the form of Judaic monotheism; that is, the repressed memory returned in the figure of the stern but nurturing father-god, Yahweh. Against this theory I have argued that chosenness, while still the psychical manifestation of what could not be consciously admitted, is best understood as a reaction formation not to the murder of Moses but to the Babylonian Exile, a founding violent event that called into question the very concept of national election that had firmly taken root in Judah by the late-seventh century BCE. Against the new reality of political subjugation and its attendant feelings of misery, suffering, doubt, and shock, the (re)formulation of a preexilic monotheism based on the concept of mutual loyalty (a treaty of sorts) could undo the psychical impact of the crisis by reimagining the conquered Judaeans as the universal god Yahweh's most treasured possession. But underlying the denial of the all but undeniable was the unnerving sense of freedom because of God's very absence in the time of national need. That freedom,

26 *Letters of Sigmund Freud and Arnold Zweig*, ed. Ernst L. Freud, trans. Elaine Robson-Scott and William Robson-Scott (New York, 1970), 91.

compelling because it left the people untethered from a past they could never quite surrender, created a feeling of cultural dislocation whose very emblem was the Exile they admitted even as they tried to explain it away. In short, after and in response to the Exile, the impossibility of knowing what God truly wanted forced the Jewish people to "confront ... the paradox of human freedom" even as they bound themselves ever tighter to subjection under Mosaic law in a futile attempt to disavow their very freedom. The Exile thereby transformed the vague idea of chosenness that had existed in preexilic Judah into a trauma by providing the idea with an unconscious dimension, what could only ever be acknowledged by being denied: we are free because the god we had always imagined in terms of absolute fidelity has been unfaithful or, worse, because he doesn't even exist. To put this another way, for postexilic Judaeans and modern Jews alike, the experience of being "thrown into freedom" was (and is) the result of and indeed inseparable from the trauma of their encounter not just with an impenetrable god but also, and perhaps more terrifyingly, with the incomprehensibility of their very existence as a people.

This, then, is the traumatic origin of the Jewish people that Freud went in search of but never quite found, the origin that his contemporary, Franz Rosenzweig, located at the heart of his own faith: "In Judaism, man is always somehow a survivor, an inner something, whose exterior was seized by the current of the world and carried off while he himself, what is left of him, remains standing on the shore. Something within him is waiting."[27] Inseparable from that waiting is the "horror first confronted by the Jews," the mystery of the excess of validity over meaning whereby, to draw on Alter once again, while "every person is created by an all-seeing God," we are yet each "abandoned to [our] own unfathomable freedom, made in God's likeness as a matter of cosmogonic principle but almost never as a matter of accomplished ethical fact." In his last effort to accomplish that "ethical fact" for himself, in order "to die in freedom," Freud chose exile.

If dying in freedom was more important for Freud than remaining in his homeland, we might then understand his final act of self-definition as echoing even as it clarified the ending of the Hebrew Bible. As we noted earlier, the final four verses of 2 Chronicles record Cyrus of Persia's liberation of the Judahites (soon to be Judaeans) living in captivity in Babylon followed by his invitation to them to return to Jerusalem and rebuild the Temple of Yahweh. Having written to Ernst before he had actually left Vienna, Freud was like the Judaeans of Cyrus' edict in anticipating rather than having completed a journey. In that

27 *Star of Redemption*, 404–05.

proleptic context, the assertion of freedom—of a will to freedom—must come before its destination: Freud must announce his determination to live and die in freedom, and the Judaeans must decide freely to respond to Cyrus' (which is perhaps also Yahweh's) invitation to set out once again. That said, for neither Freud nor the Judaeans) is the destination the homeland as they might have defined that: England may be beautiful, free, and generous, but it is not Freud's home; and for the Judaeans, Jerusalem is no longer even in the Promised Land because Judah is now a minor province of the Persian Empire. For both Freud and the Judaeans, then, living and dying in freedom is a separate question from having a claim on the territory in which one resides: one can be free without truly living in one's home(land) because freedom is a state of mind more than it is a national state.[28] Moreover, to the extent Freud's wish to die in freedom is communicated in a letter to his son, it is because Freud means to convey (in the literal sense of transporting) to Ernst the urgency of freedom, to transfer its value to the next generation. Such a transference is a hope for the future, but it is shared as both gift and burden: Jewish history had taught that freedom doesn't come easily and often doesn't come at all. And that is where the Hebrew Bible leaves its readers, with an ending that is also a beginning, a beginning that is also a departure. Starting once again, the Bible shows that freedom is less defined by a place than by a decision to answer a call to embark on a journey of hope, towards a future that hasn't been determined and offers no guarantees. At the end of his life, Freud had learned the lesson of his ancestors: freedom is a choice to take the risk to journey to a place of promise—for Freud a place to speak and write and think without fear of persecution—even it that place is not what the Bible would call the Promised Land.

---

28 Rosenzweig might be said to share this view. He had written in 1917 that "it is only by keeping their ties to the Diaspora that the Zionists will be forced to keep their eyes on *the goal, which is to become stateless inside time, and to remain nomads*" (qtd. in Stéphane Mosès, *System and Revelation: The Philosophy of Franz Rosenzweig*, trans. Catherine Tihanyi [Detroit: Wayne State University Press, 1992], 27; my emphasis). As Santner argues, Rosenzweig's commitment to the idea of the covenant and in particular to its notion of chosenness pushes back against the conceptualization of national identity embedded in the "nation-state." For Jewish culture, Rosenzweig imagines, instead, "a certain *rupture* with the time and space of ethnic and national histories" (114).

APPENDIX

Material Truth in *Moses and Monotheism*

> The question of the origin of monotheism among the Jews would thus remain unanswered or else one would have to be content with the current answer that it was the expression of their particular religious genius. We know that genius is incomprehensible and unaccountable and it should therefore not be called upon as an explanation until every other solution has failed.
>
> —FREUD, *Moses and Monotheism*

∵

At the very beginning of *Moses and Monotheism*, Freud endorses the traditional biblical account at least in broadest terms: "[T]he great majority of historians have expressed the opinion that Moses did live and that the exodus from Egypt, led by him, did in fact take place.... [T]he later history of Israel could not be understood if this were not admitted" (4).[1] Within this framework, lengthy sections of *Moses and Monotheism* (all of Part I, most of Part II, with summary statements in Part III) are taken up with Freud's speculative reconstruction of Jewish cultural history. He gives primary emphasis to that portion of the national past represented in the biblical narrative in the Books of Exodus and Numbers: the so-called sojourn in Egypt (with much attention to Moses' own birth and upbringing) followed by the people's departure from Egypt under Moses' leadership, an encounter with another people living in and near Midian (most importantly among them Moses' father-in-law, Jethro or Reuel), the theophany at Mount Sinai (including the law-giving and the story of the people's first rebellion in the story of the Golden Calf), and various other

1 Against Freud's working assumption, Jan Assmann observes that Moses is not a "figure of history": "No traces have ever been found of his historical existence. He grew and developed only as a figure of memory, absorbing and embodying all traditions that pertained to legislation, liberation, and monotheism" (*Moses the Egyptian: The Memory of Egypt in Western Monotheism* [Cambridge, MA: Harvard University Press, 1997], 23). Even Freud concedes of his own claim that Moses "was a historical person" and not merely a figure of legend that "we have no word of him except from the Holy Books and the written traditions of the Jews" (3–4).

 DOI:10.1163/9789004701663_011

moments where his "stubborn and unruly" (74) followers challenge the authority of Moses up to the time of his death recounted at the very conclusion of Torah (Deuteronomy 34).[2]

Moving backward and forward in time from the basic Exodus story, Freud occasionally makes short excursions into the patriarchal period preceding the sojourn (biblically recounted in the Book of Genesis) and the period of the conquest of Canaan that follows the death of Moses (biblically recounted in the Books of Joshua and Judges). While he has very little to say regarding either period, he accepts the basic biblical notion that a group that came to be known as the Jews migrated from Canaan to Egypt sometime before the period of the Exodus. He vaguely associates this collective with what history knows as the Hyksos, a Levantine people who first settled, or conquered, Lower Egypt in the seventeenth century BCE and then left, or were expelled, in the sixteenth century.[3] But he also believes that the biblical stories of the patriarchs most

2 With reference to this stage in their history, it would be more accurate to call the biblical people "Hebrews" or "Israelites" rather than, as Freud typically does, "Jews" (*die Juden*): 15, 18, 30, 32n, 33, 35, 37, 38–39, 43, 46, 55. That said, at one point, he refers to the people as the "immigrating Israelites" (56; German: *eingewanderten Israeliten* [16:147]). Still, the fact that Freud himself does not consistently make the distinction between Israelite and Jew (or Judaean) even as he fully grasps its historical basis is telling: without being explicit, he wants to insist on a very real transhistorical connection between those who left Egypt with Moses and Freud's own Jewish contemporaries.

3 This is all Freud has to say on this particular matter: "Perhaps [Moses] was at that time governor of that border province (Gosen [sic]) in which—perhaps already in the 'Hyksos period'—certain Semitic tribes had settled" (32). Scholars understand the Hyksos as a west-Semitic people who settled in (or invaded), attained cultural dominance (through conquest or not), and then, from their capital Avaris, ruled over parts but not all of Egypt for about a century in parallel with the native Egyptian sixteenth and seventeenth dynasties (the latter part of the Second Intermediate Period of pharaonic Egypt). The precise dates of the Hyksos reign are subject to debate, but it is generally agreed that it lasted approximately 110 years. Donald Redford, who follows scholarly consensus in referring to the Hyksos period as the Egyptian Fifteenth Dynasty, argues that it lasted 108 years, from 1668–1560 BCE. He also argues that the Hyksos most likely established themselves through military conquest rather than through a peaceful takeover although he acknowledges that the conquest theory is largely dependent on later accounts of Egyptians themselves who may have been influenced by subsequent invasions by Assyrians, Babylonians, and Persians: see "The Hyksos Invasion in History and Tradition," *Orientalia* 39 (1970): 1–51. More recently, Israel Finkelstein and Neil Asher Silberman have taken the opposite view: "the Hyksos 'invasion' was a gradual process of immigration from Canaan into Egypt" and thus most likely "a peaceful takeover of power" (*The Bible Unearthed: Archaeology's New Vision of Ancient Israel and the Origin of Its Sacred Texts* [New York: The Free Press, 2001], 55). For broad discussion, see John Van Seters, *The Hyksos: A New Investigation* (New Haven: Yale University Press, 1966); *The Hyksos: New Historical and Archaeological Perspectives*, ed. Eliezer D. Oren (Philadelphia: University of Pennsylvania Press, 1997); and Anna-Latifa Mourad, *Rise of the Hyksos: Egypt and the Levant*

likely originated with indigenous, non-Jewish pre-exodus Canaanites; in Freud's reconstruction, these stories were later adopted and adapted by the migrating or invading people of the Exodus—Egyptian-born "Jews" of the period of the conquest—in order to establish their own legitimacy in what was effectively a foreign land. He thus observes how a particular ideological purpose was served by "bringing the patriarchs" into the Exodus-Conquest account through the creation of a continuity between the Genesis stories and rest of the Hexateuch (Torah plus Joshua): "They [the patriarchs] had lived in Canaan [while the "Jewish invaders," of course, had not]; their memory [that is, the stories of the patriarchs] was connected with certain localities in that country. Possibly they themselves had been Canaanite heroes or local divinities whom the immigrating Israelites had adopted for their early history." Freud concludes that, by "evoking" the ancestry they shared with the native inhabitants they had either conquered or assimilated (Abraham was the great forefather of them all), the invaders established "proof, so to speak, of having been born and bred in the country, and denied *the odium that clings to an alien conqueror*" (56; emphasis added).

While Freud does allude from time to time to other periods and events in the national history (for example, "the destruction of the Temple, in 586 B.C., ... the Exile and ... the return" [51] and later "the destruction of the Temple in Jerusalem by Titus" [147]), most of his other "material" concerns focus on aspects of Jewish *religious* history.[4] At times this focus takes the form of vague speculation: for example, he describes "the Jews settled in Egypt" prior to the Exodus and even before encountering Moses as collectively practicing

from the Middle Kingdom to the Second Intermediate Period (London: Archaeopress Archaeology, 2015). For the expulsion of the Hyksos, see Donald B. Redford, *Egypt, Canaan, and Israel in Ancient Times* (Princeton: Princeton University Press, 1992), 125–29. At that point (ca. the mid-sixteenth century BCE), some part (perhaps even the majority) of the Hyksos population returned to the Levant. It is not clear if they returned to what they would have considered their ancestral homeland; nor is it clear if any part of the returnees settled in Canaan: for differing views, see Van Seters, 194, and Redford, *Egypt, Canaan, and Israel in Ancient Times*, 129. We might also note that some ancient writers saw a connection between the Hyksos and the people of Israel. Mistranslating the term from Manetho's third-century *Aegyptiaca* as "king-shepherds," Josephus, for example, identified the Hyksos with the biblical Hebrews: Josephus, *Against Apion, or on the Antiquity of the Jews*, in *Josephus*, trans. H. St. J. Thackery, 9 vols. (Cambridge, MA: Harvard University Press, 1961), 1:195.

4 Freud also has a general understanding of how at different times in its history the people of Israel came into conflict (typically on the losing side) with other nations. We have just noted one of the major events in an ongoing struggle with Rome ("the destruction of the Temple in Jerusalem by Titus"). Earlier, he referred almost in passing to "ever new tyrants ... who subjected and ill-treated [God's] people—the Assyrians, Babylonians, Persians" (79).

"some kind of religion" (18), which, given their status as immigrants (Freud's working assumption) we take to be a pre-Mosaic Canaanite religion, though perhaps not all that different from traditional Egyptian polytheism. On several occasions Freud refers to Mosaic tradition as the "religion [Moses] gave the Jewish people" (15 and *passim*). As we will consider in more detail below, one of the central claims of *Moses and Monotheism* is that, in its essentials, Mosaic / Judaic monotheism derives from—and so has its origin in—the core vision and values of the Egyptian religion of the god Aton (or Aten) as developed by the Pharaoh Amenhotep IV (Akhenaten); a supporter of Akhenaten's reforms, Moses subsequently brought Atonism to the Jews living in Egypt, and it was this people who, after leaving Egypt under Moses' leadership, became the foundation of people of Israel.[5] Built into that claim is Freud's corollary understanding of a long historical development: the religion of Moses only slowly took root in post-conquest Canaan, and even when it did the full emergence of what Freud calls "monotheism among the Jews" (81) was still centuries in the making.

As part of his interest in the long history (including the pre-history) of Judaism, Freud makes various mentions of doctrinal developments. For example, he entertains the possibility, even likelihood, that the earliest form of the Mosaic religion was not a "true monotheism" in that it did not "den[y] the character of God to other divinities" (61; see also 165). He also shows interest in historically situated religious groups (prophets and priests primarily) and the conflicting roles they played in promulgating Mosaic religion (more on those roles below). Above all, Freud takes a special interest in key moments in what we might call the compositional history of the Hebrew Bible. In very general terms, throughout *Moses and Monotheism* Freud demonstrates a more than adequate understanding of the basic truth of that history: the Hebrew Bible came into existence over many centuries and as the result of a complex, often inconsistent process of assembling, editing, revision, and addition, a process at the end of which a scattered collection of books or scrolls finally emerged as the Bible, a word that disguises the plural "the books" within its singular form.

In what remains of this Appendix, I will present in summary form Freud's own understanding of the material truth of Jewish history. The summary covers that history from the time preceding the Exodus up to the time shortly after the Roman destruction of the Second Temple (70 CE); and it gives special attention to what Freud calls "the origin of monotheism among the Jews" in the time-frame normally associated with the biblical account of the exodus

5 For Freud's basic reconstruction of this history, see *Moses and Monotheism*, 31–34, 43–49, and 72–74; see also 18, 21–26, and 61–62 for his understanding of the original Aton religion.

from Egypt and its immediate aftermath (the fourteenth century BCE). I will organize this summary as two distinct phases: "In Egypt" and "Out of Egypt." For each phase, I will both describe the basic facts—either as those would be accepted by modern historians or as Freud presented those facts as he understood them—and then offer some clarifying comments especially on how Freud interpreted or, just as often, misinterpreted the basic facts.

1 In Egypt

1.1 *Migration and Settlement*

A people hailing from the biblical Canaan or perhaps more broadly from somewhere in the Levant migrated to Egypt roughly between 1800 and 1600 BCE.[6] Once there, they settled in the northeastern delta region (the biblical Land of Goshen).

1.1.1 Comments

1. The tentative identification Freud makes between an immigrant population ("certain Semitic tribes") with "that border province (Gosen [sic])" (*Moses and Monotheism*, 32) is in general conformity with the biblical account of Israelite history in its late-patriarchal phase: Goshen is the region in which Jacob and sons are said to have settled after their journey to Egypt to escape the famine in Canaan (Genesis 45:10, 46:28–29, 34).

2. Against the explicit presentation of the biblical narrative, Freud never assumes these people were enslaved under pharaonic rule.

3. What Freud does quite bizarrely assume is that these "pre-Jews" as we might call them managed to exist in a sort of semi-autonomous ethnic enclave for the entirety of their time in Egypt, for Freud, following the biblical account, for four centuries or more. We've already noted Freud's assumption that this population maintained a shared identity through the practice of a religion: "the Jewish people in Egypt were certainly not without some kind of religion" (18). Of course, this religion could not have been Judaism, which, in Freud's view, only developed post-Exodus as a result of what Moses did (more on that below). But, in Freud's description, it does not appear to have been a traditional Egyptian religion let alone the new religion (the Aton religion of the

6 While this time-frame would overlap with the Hyksos period, groups from all over the Levant regularly migrated to Egypt, some groups as part of seasonal migrations related to herd-animals while other groups took up permanent residence. For broad summary, see Finkelstein and Silberman, 52–54.

heretic Pharaoh Amenhotep IV) that Moses would bring to them. In terms of the group's language, Freud interprets the reference in Exodus 4:10 to Moses being "slow of speech and slow of tongue" as an indicator of the challenge he faced as a native Egyptian in communicating with his new Jewish followers: "Moses spoke another language and was not able to communicate with his Semitic Neo-Egyptians without the help of an interpreter—at least not at the beginning of their intercourse" (38). Freud ventures this quite astonishing assumption—that Canaanite immigrants in Egypt ("Semitic Neo-Egyptians") had never learned to speak Egyptian even after having lived in the country for centuries—despite his later remark that the immigrants "had probably been in the country long enough to develop into a numerous people" (43). But this image of a established population is then countered by Freud's curious way of portraying the Jews in Egypt as more recent immigrants, ones not completely assimilated into Egyptian culture despite their long residence: from the Egyptian perspective, at least, they were "foreigners" (18); Freud twice refers to them as "Semitic tribes" (32, 74).

4. Modern archaeology has identified waves of Levantine migration to the northeastern delta region going back to 1800 or even earlier. It is quite possible that the rise of the previously mentioned Hyksos was facilitated, in part, by the fact that they simply assumed leadership over a large population of people with whom they shared an identifiable Levantine heritage.[7] But the Hyksos themselves appear to have ruled as self-styled Egyptians and not as foreigners: they adopted pharaonic customs and even paid special devotion to the Egyptian god, Seth, whom they equated with the Canaanite storm-god Ba'al.[8]

In any event, under the most likely cultural circumstances it is improbable that members of any immigrant group, Canaanite or otherwise, that had been settled in Egypt for as long as the Bible (and Freud himself) assumes it had

7 There is evidence, for example that, during the latter part of the Middle Kingdom, the northeast delta region saw several waves of immigrants from the Levant (Phoenicia, Palestine, and Syria); thus, the more salient feature of the period of Hyksos rule might be that, upon their arrival, they found that in many ways they had come among their own. In other words, it's possible that the presence of a sizable immigrant population from the Levant facilitated the Hyksos takeover of Egypt. For discussion, see Redford, *Egypt, Canaan, and Israel in Ancient Times*, 101); and Van Seters, 115–20 and 191–93.

8 In religious terms at least, Assmann views Hyksos rulers as essentially "in conformity with the religious obligations of traditional Egyptian pharaohs, whose role they assumed in the same way as did later foreign rulers of Egypt such as the Persians, the Macedonians, and the Romans." Even their special adherence to the cult of the Levantine deity Ba'al would not have seemed particularly foreign since, as Assmann adds, Ba'al was "a familiar figure for the Egyptians" (*Moses the Egyptian*, 24). For related perspective on Hyksos religious practices in Egypt, see Van Seters, ch. 12; and Redford *Egypt, Canaan, and Israel in Ancient Times*, 114–16).

been (four-hundred years or more) would not have understood themselves as Egyptians—speaking Egyptian, dressing as Egyptians, worshipping local Egyptian deities, etc.—even if the group maintained economic or other ties to its ancestral homeland.

1.2 *Egyptian Monotheism: Akhenaten's Atonism*

After and quite possibly as a response to the expulsion of the Hyksos in the middle of the sixteenth century, pharaohs of the Eighteenth Dynasty and throughout the period of the New Kingdom embarked on a project of empire-building that was new to Egyptian culture. From Freud's point of view, this change in Egypt's political situation is important primarily because of the corresponding transformation of Egyptian religion: in short, as he remarks, "In Egypt monotheism had grown … as an ancillary effect of imperialism; God was a reflection of a Pharaoh autocratically governing a great world Empire" (80). He elaborates in the opening of section of Part II of *Moses and Monotheism*:

> Political conditions in Egypt had about that time begun to exert a lasting influence on Egyptian religion. Through the victorious sword of the great conqueror Thothmes III Egypt had become a world power. Nubia in the south, Palestine, Syria, and part of Mesopotamia in the north had been added to the Empire. This imperialism was reflected in religion as universality and monotheism. Since Pharaoh's solicitude now extended beyond Egypt to Nubia and Syria, deity itself had to give up its national limitation, and the new god of the Egyptians had to become like Pharaoh—the unique and unlimited sovereign of the world known to the Egyptians. (22)

In that context, Freud subsequently observes that "possibly strengthened by suggestions from Asia, *there arose the idea of a universal god, Aton—no longer restricted to one people and one country*" (72; my emphasis). Because of Aton's centrality to Freud's understanding of Judaic monotheism, we might fill in some of the details of this new "universal god."

The reign of Amenhotep III as the ninth pharaoh of the Eighteenth Dynasty (ca. 1390–1350 BCE) was one of the high points of ancient Egyptian civilization in terms of prosperity, splendor, artistic achievement, and international prominence. Yet, while he was in many ways a traditional ruler of the New Kingdom, he appears to have promoted some rather unconventional ideas as regards established Egyptian religion observance. Despite the fact that his name calls attention to his bond to the god Amon or Amun (as in "Amon is satisfied"), Amenhotep III adopted the rather obscure, minor deity Aton, one of the aspects of the sun-god, as his personal deity.[9] This elevation may have had something to do with the imperial ideology that Freud refers to: what had started to develop earlier in the Eighteenth Dynasty as Egypt extended its authority beyond its traditional national boundaries to encompass regions to the south and the northeast. Zahi Hawass notes that while the notion of a reigning pharaoh's special connection to Aton was not entirely new—even as early as the Middle Kingdom Aton was understood as "the disk of the sun, with which the king merged at death"—the new prominence accorded this god may have been "linked specifically with maintenance of the empire, as the area over which, at least theoretically, the sun ruled. By associating himself with the visible disk of the sun, the king put himself symbolically over all the lands where it could be seen—all the known world."[10] That said, there is no evidence that Amenhotep III interfered with the cultic practices associated with Amon, nor is there reason to believe that he neglected his unique role in maintaining the central value of *Ma'at* (harmony and balance) through the ritual duties prescribed for any reigning pharaoh.

The same cannot be said for his son. Whatever ideas he might have inherited from his father or from earlier rulers of the Eighteenth Dynasty and whether his decision was motivated more by political concerns or by genuine theological commitments, Amenhotep IV quickly took his father's special fondness for Aton to unprecedented levels.[11] Here is Freud's own summary of this development:

---

9 Amon had risen to national importance only with the advent of the New Kingdom. Previously the patron deity of Thebes, he was fused with the sun-god, Re, and in that form his worship was extended throughout Egypt.

10 Zahi A. Hawass, *The Golden King: The World of Tutankhamun* (Washington, DC: National Geographic Society, 2006), 31. For related discussion, see Donald Redford, "Akhenaten: New Theories and Old Facts," *Bulletin of the American Schools of Oriental Research* 369 (2013): 11; and Jan Assmann, *From Akhenaten to Moses: Ancient Egypt and Religious Change* (New York: The American University in Cairo Press, 2014), 53–54.

11 While there is no reason to believe that Amenhotep IV's religious convictions were not genuine, his reign was marked by important corollary transformations of Egyptian political culture, most noticeably its increasing centralization of governance at the expense of local jurisdictions. Given that this centralization gave royal officials unprecedented control over the national treasure and produce, it's not inconceivable that political realignment was a major motive behind Akhenaten's religious reforms. Moreover, even those reforms had a decidedly political edge to them. As Redford notes, Akhenaten's creedal proclamations were more properly "a royal statement regarding the king's relationship with his father than a religion of the people. As such, it thrusts a teaching role upon the monarch in which he, as the sole individual privy to god's will, is obliged to make plain to the people the nature of god and the king's place in creation" (*Egypt, Canaan, and Israel in Ancient Times*, 379).

> [U]nder Amenhotep III … the worship of the sun-god was in the ascendant, … and in this Aton religion the young king [Amenhotep IV] had found a movement he had no need to create, but one which he could join.… In the two hymns to Aton which have been preserved to us through the inscriptions in the rock tombs and which were probably composed by him, he praises the sun as the creator and preserver of all living beings in and outside Egypt … [H]e worshipped the sun not as a material object, but as a symbol of a divine being whose energy was manifested in his rays. But we do scant justice to the king if we see in him only the adherent and protector of the Aton religion which had already existed before him. His activity was much more energetic. He added the something new that turned into monotheism the doctrine of a universal god: the quality of exclusiveness. In one of his hymns it is stated in so many words: "O Thou only God, there is no other God than Thou." (22–24)

As part of his promotion of the concept that Aton was "the universal God" and indeed "the *Only* God," (72), "the king changed his name … Instead of Amenhotep he called himself Ikhnaton [or Akhenaten]" (24).

1.2.1 Comments

1. While Freud remarks that in Akhenaten's vision we find "the first case in the history of mankind, and perhaps the purest, of a monotheistic religion" (72–73), Jan Assmann observes that, even before Akhenaten, a "latent monotheism [had] gained more and more momentum in the course of the New Kingdom" primarily as evidenced in its wisdom literature as opposed to cultic practice (though even in the latter a "henotheistic perspective start[ed] to affect certain domains of temple literature … especially hymns to Amun-Re"). Assmann adds that this general trend "became overwhelmingly manifest with the religious revolution of Akhenaten, who quite simply did away with the plurality of gods and abolished traditional religion altogether.… Akhenaten's revolution implemented the henotheistic perspective in terms of cult and religious institutions, turning the sun and creator god into the sole and only god, and denying the other gods any worship and even existence."[12]

---

12 *From Akhenaten to Moses*, 12–13. For broader discussion, see Donald B. Redford, *Akhenaten, the Heretic King* (Princeton: Princeton University Press, 1984); Erik Hornung, *Akhenaten and the Religion of Light*, trans. David Lorton (Ithaca: Cornell University Press, 1999); and James K. Hoffmeier, *Akhenaten and the Origins of Monotheism* (Oxford: Oxford University Press, 2015).

2. Freud's attempt to align Akhenaten's Atonism with Judaic monotheism seriously misrepresents the relationship between the two religions. In general terms, as Donald Redford comments, "before much of the archaeological evidence from Thebes and from Tell el-Amarna became available, wishful thinking sometimes turned Akhenaten into a humane teacher of the true God, a mentor of Moses, a Christlike figure, a philosopher before his time. But these imaginary creatures are now fading away as the historical reality gradually emerges. There is little or no evidence to support the notion that Akhenaten was a progenitor of the full-blown monotheism that we find in the Bible," which "had its own separate development—one that began more than half a millennium after the pharaoh's death."[13] More specifically, Freud's overstates what he believes are direct parallels or points of congruence between Atonism and Judaic monotheism. Freud gives special stress to his claim that certain key elements of the latter correspond to the novelties of Akhenaten's new religion; as we shall see in more detail in a moment, it is partly for that reason that he believes Judaic monotheism must have had its origin in Atonism (carried out of Egypt by the people of the Exodus to be established in Canaan as the religion of Israel). But, as Jan Assmann observes, Freud's case for the correspondence is weak:

Freud saw the common elements of the two religions in the following five points:

> both proclaim a strict monotheism, showing the most intransigent intolerance against traditional polytheism;
> both exclude magical rites and ceremonies;
> both are aniconic;
> both stress ethical requirements; and
> both discard any concept of a hereafter and of human immorality
>
> Today, one would perhaps agree with points one and three, but certainly not with two, four, or five. It is true that in the Amarna religion there is hardly any magic and very little ritual, whereas in the Mosaic religion there is a plethora of rites.[14] The stress on ethics in the Mosaic religion is obvious, but in Amarna, the ethical aspect of God is absent in the most striking manner. In Amarna, the traditional concept of a hereafter is discarded, replaced by a new one according to which the human

---

13 "The Monotheism of Akhenaten," in *Aspects of Monotheism: How God is One*, ed. Hershel Shanks and Jack Meinhardt (Washington, D.C.: Biblical Archaeology Society, 1997), 26.

14 Freud himself observes that the early Israelite priesthood promoted ceremonial and other ritual practices that were "at bottom only magic and black art, such as the old doctrine of Moses [derived from Egyptian Atonism] had unconditionally condemned?" (62–63).

> person lives on in the form of his *ba*, leaving the tomb during the day and entering it at night. Above all, however, Akhenaten's god is the sun and nothing but the sun, whereas the god of Moses is the liberator from Egyptian bondage, an actor in history. In fact, the two religions are worlds apart.[15]

Although Freud himself would come to precisely the opposite conclusion as he proceeded in Part II of *Moses and Monotheism*, his initial statement on the matter is much more accurate than he could have admitted: "I had hoped the suggestion that Moses was an Egyptian would prove enlightening and stimulating in many different respects. But our first deduction from this suggestion—that the new religion he gave the Jews was his own, the Egyptian one—has foundered on the difference—nay, the striking contrast—between the two religions" (20).

1.3 *The Fall of Akhenaten and the Emergence of (the Egyptian) Moses*

In the passage from *Moses and Monotheism* just quoted, Freud notes his "suggestion that Moses was an Egyptian" as a starting point for the broader claim that "the new religion he gave the Jews was his own, the Egyptian one"—and by "the Egyptian one" Freud explicitly means the Atonism established by Amenhotep IV as the Egyptian national religion. Before we consider Freud's understanding of Moses' role in transferring Egyptian Atonism to the people of the Exodus who would evolve into the people of Israel, we must first ask what happened to Atonism in Egypt itself.

The disruptive impact of Akhenaten's imposition of the Aton religion—what Jan Assmann has called the world's first "counter-religion"—on traditional Egyptian culture should not be underestimated.[16] As Freud himself comments:

> This king undertook to force upon his subjects a new religion, one contrary to their traditions and to all their familiar habits.... [R]eligious

15 *From Akhenaten to Moses*, 64; for related discussion, see Redford, *Egypt, Canaan, and Israel in Ancient Times*, 378–84. For Freud's detailed description of Atonism, see *Moses and Monotheism* 21–27.

16 For the notion of counter-religion, see Assmann, *Moses the Egyptian*, 3 and *passim*. Assmann notes that in the emergence of the Aton religion we witness "the first conflict between two fundamentally different and mutually exclusive religions in the recorded history of humankind ... this event is especially extraordinary because it took place within one society and did not involve any aggression from outside" (24).

intolerance, which was foreign to antiquity before this and for long after, was inevitably born with the belief in one God. (21)

[N]ot only from his name did he eliminate that of the hated god [Amon], but also from all inscriptions and even where he found it in his father's name, Amenhotep III.... The persecution by the king was directed foremost against Amon, but not against him alone. Everywhere in the Empire the temples were closed, the services forbidden, and the ecclesiastical property seized. Indeed, the king's zeal went so far as to cause inquiry to be made into the inscriptions on old monuments in order to efface the word "God" whenever it was used in the plural. (24–25)[17]

It is important to register that what Freud refers to here as Akhenaten's "persecution" was not simply a matter of the devotional system—the ending of services at the temples of the other gods, the desecration (if not precisely the mandated closing) of those temples, and thus the effective disbanding of their established priesthoods—or, more broadly, of the related ecclesiastical economy as temple income was increasingly diverted to the new cult. Even just in financial terms, Akhenaten's action in regards to traditional religious practice likely led to a massive contraction of Egypt's larger economy precisely because it was so dependent on activities related to temple-based devotion.[18] But because, as Assmann points out, Egyptian religious and socioeconomic culture were so intertwined, their shared transformation had more wide-ranging consequences. For together they were inseparable from a worldview that supported both an abstract sense of one's place and purpose in existence (a part of the reigning harmony of the cosmos) and the lived experience of a series of related cultural forms, customs, and habits that gave expression to, and located one's presence in, the daily or seasonal rhythms of such harmony. Thus to destroy the traditional religious infrastructure was to damage much of the spiritual sensibility at the foundation of Egyptian life more broadly.[19]

---

17 For related discussion, see Redford, "Akhenaten: New Theories and Old Facts," 13–16, 19, 23, 26.

18 This contraction might have been partly behind Egypt's short decline as an imperial power, though that decline may have been more directly the result of Akhenaten's personal lack of interest in foreign affairs, a matter of much scholarly debate. As Freud remarks, "the glorious Eighteenth Dynasty was extinguished; at the same time its conquests in Nubia and Asia were lost" (25–26). He will later note that Akhenaten "had estranged himself from his people" and "had let his world empire crumble" (32).

19 See *Moses the Egyptian*, 25–27; for related discussion, see Redford, "Akhenaten: New Theories and Old Facts," 26–27.

In this highly charged cultural environment, a counter-reaction was inevitable. While the reforms most immediately affected the priests of Amon who, not surprisingly, opposed the new regime in the strongest possible way, "it is not to be wondered at," Freud concludes, that Akhenaten's "orders produced a reaction of fanatical vengeance" not only "among the suppressed priests" but also among "the discontented people, a reaction that was able to find a free outlet after the king's death." His successor, Tutankhaton "was forced to return to Thebes" (the old capital) from the new capital Akhenaten had built (Akhetaton) and "to substitute Amon in his name for the god Aton [hence, the name with which he is now remembered: Tutankhamun]. Then there followed a period of anarchy until the general Haremhab succeeded ... in restoring order [in Freud's dating ca. 1315 BCE]. In this sad interregnum Egypt's old religions had been reinstated. The Aton religion was at and end" (25). In short, if Akhenaten had aimed to destroy the devotion to and even the memory of the traditional gods, the people's vengeance was as complete as it was swift: not only was his capital left in ruins and "his new religion swept way," but even "the memory of the heretic king [was] proscribed" (21). So subjected to "complete *damnatio memoriae*," the heretic king became, as Assmann notes, "a figure of history without memory."[20]

From Freud's point of view, it is at this stage that Moses—his *Egyptian* Moses—enters the picture:

> Let us assume that Moses was a noble and distinguished man, perhaps indeed a member of the royal house, as the myth has it. He must have been conscious of his great abilities, ambitious, and energetic; perhaps he saw himself in a dim future as the leader of his people, the governor of the Empire. In close contact with Pharaoh, he was a convinced adherent of the new religion, whose basic principles he fully understood and had made his own. With the king's death and the subsequent reaction he saw all his hopes and prospects destroyed. If he was not to recant the convictions dear to him, then Egypt had no more to give him; he had lost his native country. In this hour of need he found an unusual solution. The dreamer Ikhnaton [Akhenaten] had estranged himself from his

20 *From Akhenaten to Moses*, 61. Assmann elsewhere observes that "shortly after his death, [Akhenaten's] name was erased from the king-lists, his monuments were dismantled, his inscription and representations were destroyed, and almost every trace of his existence was obliterated.... Until his rediscovery in the nineteenth century, there was virtually no memory of Akhenaten" (*Moses the Egyptian*, 23). For Freud's own summary statement, see *Moses and Monotheism*, 73.

> people, had let his world empire crumble, Moses' active nature conceived the plan of founding a new empire, of finding a new people, to whom he could give the religion that Egypt disdained.... Perhaps he was at the time governor of that border province (Gosen [sic]) in which ... certain Semitic tribes had settled. These he chose to be his new people. (31–32)[21]

While, for Freud, Moses' identity as a born-and-bred Egyptian is important, what is more important is that this Prince of Egypt (a phrase often applied to Joseph as well based on Genesis 42:6) "was a convinced adherent of the new religion, whose basic principles he fully understood and had made his own." It is only in that context that Freud's other assumption could have any meaning: Moses would "give the religion that Egypt disdained"—Akhenaten's Atonism—"to the "Semitic tribes ... he chose to be his new people."

1.3.1 Comments

1. "Give" perhaps is not an adequate word for the process of cultural transference Freud imagines. Indeed, Moses' paired acts of "finding a new people" and then choosing them "to be his new people" appear mainly to have entailed his imposing upon a previously existing Egyptian-dwelling group (though perhaps ethnically undefined or at least disorganized in some sense) group traits, ideas, and practices they did not possess before: laws, rituals (circumcision, for example), and most of all the concept of a single god as this might have been part of the new Aton religion Moses had acquired from his mentor. Thus, at the opening of Part I Freud remarks that "the man Moses, the liberator of his people, ... gave them their religion and their laws" (3); and at the close of Part I he refers to "the legislation and religion [Moses] gave the Jewish people" (15). Moses, in short, "stamped" the people with what was new to them (135), "forced" it all upon them (142), "burdened" (35) them with what was foreign, something new and difficult that came to them unbidden "from outside, from a great stranger" (63).[22] If then Moses' imposition was the first movement toward the emergence of Jewish monotheism, Freud's understanding centers on a paradox: Moses established the very Jewishness of the already existing

21 Though always with the assumption that Moses was "a high official" in the Egyptian social order of the time, Freud is open to other possibilities regarding his original position: "If he were a priest, the thought of giving his people a new religion must have been near to his heart.... A prince of royal lineage might easily have been both: governor and priest. In the report of Flavius Josephus ..., Moses appears as an Egyptian field-marshal" (32n1).

22 Freud provides a concise overview at the beginning of Part III: 72–77.

Jewish people who, prior to Moses, could not possibly have been Jewish in any meaningful sense.[23]

2. Immediately following the long passage quoted above, Freud adds that, having "established relations" with the Egypt-dwelling Semitic tribes, Moses then "placed himself at their head, and directed the Exodus" (32). Throughout Part II especially, given his general understanding of what "really" happened, Freud not unreasonably tries to portray the experience of the Exodus as an actual historical event for some group that left Egypt under Moses' leadership. While as previously noted, Freud doesn't accept the biblical portrayal of an enslaved population (hence, there was no "liberation" as the Bible imagines), he is yet sensitive to the fact that it would not have been an easy thing for a large group simply to leave: Egypt had military means of keeping people "in" just as much as much as keeping people "out."[24] He thus takes a stab at how the people of the Exodus, whatever the actual headcount, managed to get away. Early in Part II he offers as broad context this account of the immediate aftermath of the death of Akhenaten:

> His end is wrapped in mystery. We learn of a few short-lived, shadowy successors in his own family. Already his son-in-law, Tutankhaton was forced to return to Thebes and to substitute Amon in his name for the god Aton. Then there followed a period of anarchy until the general Haremhab succeeded in 1350 B.C. in restoring order. The glorious Eighteenth Dynasty was extinguished; at the same time its conquests in Nubia and Asia were lost. In this sad interregnum, Egypt's old religions had been reinstated. The Aton religion was at an end, Ikhnaton's [Akhenaten's] capital lay destroyed and plundered, and his memory was scorned as a felon. (25–26)

Completing that paragraph that begins with "He established relations with them ...," Freud returns to this scenario later as a way of explaining how the Exodus was, in fact, simply an exodus: "In full contradistinction to the Biblical tradition we may suppose this Exodus to have passed off peacefully and

23 While throughout *Moses and Monotheism*, as previously noted, Freud consistently refers to the people of the Exodus as "Jews" or "the Jewish people," he also observes that what history proper would understand as the people of Israel did not truly come into existence until they had left Egypt: "... those who *later* [that is, post-Exodus] became the Jewish people" (43; my emphasis). In that context, it is not clear what Freud means when he subsequently claims that Moses "made [the Jewish people] his people."

24 For discussion of Egypt's control of its own borders during this period, see Finkelstein and Silberman, 58–61.

without pursuit. The authority of Moses made it possible, and *there was then no central power that could have prevented it.* According to our reconstruction the Exodus from Egypt would have taken place between 1358 and 1350 B.C.—that is to say, after the death of Ikhnaton [Akhenaten] and *before the restitution of the authority of the state* by Haremhab" (32–33; my emphases). He then makes a final reference to his theory that the Exodus was "facilitated by the anarchy prevailing in Egypt." Noting that "the kings of the Nineteenth Dynasty following Ikhnaton [Akhenaten] ruled the country with a strong hand," he concludes that "all conditions, internal and external, favoring the Exodus coincide only in the period immediately after the death of the heretic king" (36). Freud's account may be pure fiction, but it is at least carefully considered "historical fiction."

2 Out of Egypt

2.1 *The Murder of Moses*

In the wake of Akhenaten's death, according to Freud, Moses left Egypt with the Jewish population settled in Egypt and then "hallowed them by the custom of circumcision, gave them laws, and introduced them to the Aton religion, which the Egyptians had just discarded" (74). He dreamed that his new people would "be a better substitute for the Egyptians he left behind. He wished to make them a 'holy nation'" (33–34). But, stiff-necked as they were, these "culturally inferior immigrants" (18) (to be distinguished from Moses' own original Egyptian followers, the Levites) did not easily accept the yoke of the Aton-religion and especially its demands to renounce magic, anthropomorphic depictions of the gods, their cherished fertility and death cults, and perhaps most of all the hope of an afterlife (73 and *passim*). And so history partly repeated itself: "the Jewish people of Moses were quite as unable to bear such a highly spiritualized religion, to find in what it offered satisfaction for their needs, as were the Egyptians of the Eighteenth Dynasty. In both cases the same thing happened: those who felt themselves ... dispossessed, revolted and threw off the burden of a religion that had been forced on them." There was an important difference, however: "Moses met with the same fate as Ikhnaton [Akhenaten], the fate that awaits all enlightened despots.... But while the tame Egyptians waited until fate had removed the sacred person of their Pharaoh, the savage Semites took their destiny into their own hands and did away with the tyrant" (57–58). In short, "stubborn and unruly" as the Jewish people were "towards their lawgiver and leader," Moses, they "rebelled at last ... [and] killed him" (74).[25]

25 For Freud's full account of events leading to the murder of Moses, see 42–49.

2.1.1 Comments

1. Freud explicitly acknowledged that the historical foundation permitting him to see *Moses and Monotheism* through to completion was the thesis put forward by Ernst Sellin in 1922:

> In 1922 Ernst Sellin made a discovery of decisive importance. He found in the book of the Prophet Hosea ... unmistakable traces of a tradition to the effect that the founder of their religion, Moses, met a violent end in a rebellion of his stubborn and refractory people .... This tradition was not limited to Hosea; it recurs in the writings of most of the later Prophets; indeed, according to Sellin, it was the basis of all the later expectations of the Messiah. (42)

Freud would return to this idea at the end of the preface to Part III: without "Sellin's suggestion concerning Moses' end, the whole treatise would have to remain unwritten" (71). Freud had registered his concerns in a September 30, 1934 letter to Arnold Zweig: "The whole enterprise broke down in this third section, for it involved a theory of religion—certainly nothing new for me after *Totem and Taboo*, but something new and fundamental for the uninitiated .... [T]his work does not seem to me sufficiently substantiated."[26] That said, despite his stated concern that without Sellin's work his study would have no "secure foundation, like an iron monument with feet of clay" (17), Freud was at times explicitly cavalier about his lack of an historically-grounded methodology. As he would remark almost in passing toward the end of *Moses and Monotheism*, for example, "I am not an ethnologist, but a psychoanalyst. It was my good right to select from ethnological data what would serve me for my analytic work" (169). Earlier, Freud stated that, while he wanted to pose his interpretations "without contradicting the trustworthy results of historical research," he also aimed "to be independent of the historians in other respects and to blaze [his] own trail" (43).

2. And then the aftermath: "There came a time when the people regretted the murder of Moses and tried to forget it.... [T]he painful fact of his violent removal was ... successfully denied" (58–59). Because regret followed by denial is central to Freud's understanding of the "historical truth" of the "origin of monotheism among the Jews," I have addressed this part of the story already (see Chapter 1).

---

26 *Letters of Sigmund Freud and Arnold Zweig*, ed. Ernst L. Freud, trans. Elaine Robson-Scott and William Robson-Scott (New York: Harcourt, Brace & World, 1970), 92.

2.2 *After Moses: the Convergence of Two Peoples (and Two Gods) and the Conquest of Canaan*

As noted above, Freud follows the biblical account in depicting the people's eventual entrance into Canaan as at once a (Jewish) homecoming and an invasion. He can have it both ways because—and this is one of his most astonishing if unfounded claims—the Jews returning from Egypt *reunited* with relatives prior to the newly combined group's entrance into Canaan proper. There were, he thus asserts, "tribes who were the most nearly related to the Jews now leaving Egypt" who "lived south of Palestine" (33). Freud imagines an encounter between the two groups: "[T]he Neo-Egyptians, as I should like to call those who returned from Egypt in distinction to the other Jews, met with the blood relations" (46). From this encounter arose a unified people: they "were united in the people of Israel.... the different tribes were united into a nation" (60). It is in the context of this (re)unification of Jewish peoples outside of Canaan that the new people—the people of Israel—could reclaim the land of their common forefathers. And so he concludes that "the tribe returning from Egypt combined ... in the country between Egypt and Canaan with other related tribes that had been settled there for some time. [From] this union ... was born the people of Israel ... Thereupon the people felt strong enough to undertake the invasion of Canaan" (44–45).

Besides the political unification, the new collective was marked, and perhaps was even primarily constituted, by the "adoption of a new religion" that would thenceforth become the "common" cultural property of "all the tribes." This adoption "came about ... under the influence of the Midianites": "the Jewish tribes, who later became the people of Israel, ... took over the worship of the god Yahweh, probably from the Arabic tribe of Midianites who lived near by. Presumably other neighboring tribes were also followers of that God" (38–39).[27]

2.1.2 Comments

1. Freud's insistence on the role of Midian in establishing the religion of Yahweh is, of course, generally attested in the biblical narrative itself, especially through in the figure of Moses' father-in-law, the Midianite Jethro (or Reuel). While he is never described precisely as a priest of Yahweh (Exodus 2:16 and

27 Drawing on the work of Eduard Meyer and others, Freud tells us that "Yahweh was certainly a volcano-god" anthropomorphized as a "bloodthirsty demon who walks by night and shuns the light of day." But because "Egypt has no volcanoes and the mountains of the Sinai peninsula have never been volcanic"—whereas "volcanoes which may have been active up to a late period are found along the western border of Arabia"—he claims that "one of these [Arabian volcanic mountains] must have been the Sinai-Horeb which was believed to be Yahweh's abode" (39).

3:1 simply call him a "priest of Midian"—Freud will call him both a "Midianite priest" and a "priest of Yahweh" [39][28]), Yahweh first appears to Moses while he is tending Jethro's sheep; there he gives Moses a specific charge to assist in the liberation of God's people from Egyptian oppression (Exodus 3–4). After the Exodus, Jethro brings Moses' wife and children to Moses while the people are "encamped at the mountain of God" (18:5), which appears to have some connection to, if it cannot simply be equated with, Mount Sinai / Horeb. And it is there—wherever "there" is precisely—that Moses, having first received advice from Jethro about how to organize the people he now leads (Exodus 18:13–26), finally receives Yahweh's full revelation, the terms of what will serve as the foundation of the Mosaic covenant (Exodus 19–24).

2. The importance Freud ascribes to Jethro and Midian is generally in accord with what is commonly known as the Kenite Hypothesis. This theory draws together Jethro (Judges 1:16 identifies Moses' father-in-law as a Kenite), the land of Midian in which Jethro is said to reside and where Moses first meets him (Exodus 2:16–22), and Yahweh, whom Moses first encounters while tending Jethro's flock (Exodus 3).[29] Moreover, this theory, the basic terms of which Freud clearly accepts, essentially recognizes both that Yahweh was a Midianite deity and, as a corollary, that the deity who would become the god of Israel was not indigenous to Canaan and only entered into Canaanite culture at the time of the establishment of the nation of Israel.

3. At a purely speculative level, there is a certain narrative-historical logic to Freud's reconstruction at least in terms of how the Bible itself presents the trajectory of events. If an Egyptian group of some kind under the leadership of Moses left its country and eventually migrated to and settled in Canaan, within the framework of evidence provided by the biblical narrative that group stopped somewhere south of Canaan. If so, it is not impossible that they there interacted with an otherwise unknown priest of Midian named Jethro (Reuel), who was broadly associated, by geographical proximity if nothing else, with the worship of a mountain-dwelling deity who appears to have been known

---

28 While precisely what "priest of Midian" means is never fully articulated in the biblical account, it is worth observing that Jethro appears to have some familiarity with Yahweh not only in general terms but also, and more specifically, in the context of priestly ritual. In some ways his role as priest, marked particularly in a sacrificial feast at which Aaron is present, might be construed as the model for Aaron's own later priestly role and possibly even as a symbolic rendering of the origin of the cult of Yahweh among the Israelites: see Exodus 18:8–12.

29 For the Kenite Hypothesis, see Stephen L. Harris, *Understanding the Bible*, 8th ed. (New York: McGraw-Hill, 2011), 501; and Lawrence E. Stager, "Forging an Identity: The Emergence of Ancient Israel," in *The Oxford History of the Biblical World*, ed. Michael D. Coogan (New York: Oxford University Press, 1998), 142–49.

by the name Yahweh. This general scenario accords with the core biblical concept that Yahweh was unknown in Canaan—he was not part of the established Canaanite pantheon, the Elohim—prior to his being imported into Canaan and so into Israelite history by the migrating (or invading) people of the Exodus.[30]

4. Rather more infamously—and in this instance without the support of biblical scholarship—Freud takes the Bible's own identification of Moses as "son-in-law of the Midianite priest Jethro" (39) as a hint that there were two different people associated with the name Moses: "We cannot escape the impression that this Moses of Qadeš and Midian, to whom tradition could even ascribe the erection of a brazen serpent as a healing god, is quite a different person from the august Egyptian … who disclosed to his people a religion in which all magic and sorcery were most strictly abhorred. Our Egyptian Moses differs perhaps no less from the Midian Moses than the universal god Aton differed from the demon Yahweh on his divine mountain" (41–42).[31] So distinguished from the Egyptian leader of the Exodus, the Midianite Moses functions in Freud's reconstruction as the mediator between the Yahwistic priesthood of Midian and the (re)unified Jewish tribes who had come together just to the north of there at the oasis of Meribah-Qadeš (39).[32]

5. Freud actually shows little specific knowledge or interest in the conquest of Canaan itself either as fact or elaborate fiction. At one point he simply dismisses the very effort of historical reconstruction by observing that "everything connected with the settling of the Jewish people in Canaan is highly obscure and confused" (60). That said, he is in line with scholarly consensus in later adding that "the settling of the later Jewish people in Canaan was certainly not

30 As though acknowledging that he was not originally a Canaanite god, the Song of Deborah identifies Yahweh as coming from Seir and / or Edom (Judges 5:4).

31 Freud will observe subsequently "we know nothing personal … about this other [Midianite] Moses—he is entirely obscured by the first, the Egyptian Moses—except possibly from clues provided by the contradictions to be found in the Bible in the characterization of Moses. He is often enough described as masterful, hot-tempered, even violent [e.g. Exodus 32 and Numbers 20], and yet it is also said of him that he was the most patient and 'meek' of all men [e.g. Numbers 12:3]. It is clear that the latter qualities would have been of no use to the Egyptian Moses who planned such great and difficult projects for his people. Perhaps they belonged to the other, the Midianite. I think we are justified in separating the two persons from each other" (49).

32 Immediately before, Freud makes this link by arguing that the tribal (re)unification "did not take place in Egypt or at the foot of a mount in the Sinai peninsula, but in a place called Meribat-Qadeš [the biblical Kadesh or Kadesh-Barnea of Numbers 20, which itself might be linked to what Exodus 17 identifies as Meribah], an oasis … in the country south of Palestine." As previously noted, Freud goes on to observe that the Yahweh-worshipping "Midianites … lived near by" (38–39). He adds in a footnote that "the Biblical text retains certain passages telling us that Yahweh descended from Sinai to Meribat-Qadeš" (39n1).

a swiftly achieved conquest; it was rather a series of successive struggles and must have stretched over a longish period" (75).

2.2 *The Retention and Development of Mosaic Tradition: Priests, Prophets, and the Completion of the Hebrew Bible*

Commenting on the many "distorting tendencies" surrounding the memory of Moses scattered throughout the biblical narrative, Freud observes, as noted above, that the Mosaic tradition "did not achieve it effects immediately, but in a strangely indirect manner.... It took a long time, many centuries, to do so."[33] In the years after Moses' death and after the "Jewish people shook off" the political, religious, and moral vision Moses created and imposed on them, that vision "survived, obscured and distorted," along with the identity of Moses himself, only as "a sort of memory" (159). But, in terms of the material truth of Jewish history (the historical truth will be quite a different matter), how precisely did this memory survive?

We noted above that, among other aspects of Jewish religious history, Freud shows a real interest in certain historically situated religious groups, groups that, in their different ways, cultivated the Mosaic heritage among the post-conquest people of Israel. If some early version of monotheism first emerged in the cult of Yahweh established by the Temple priesthood and priests at other cultic sites, for Freud it was the preexilic prophets (Elijah, Isaiah, and Jeremiah especially) who truly championed and thus enabled the survival of the Mosaic tradition. Freud rises to otherwise unseen levels of admiration in his description of the key role of the prophets in retaining elements of the now vanished Mosaic Atonism. So he writes in Part III: "Monotheism had not taken root in Egypt, ... a failure [that] might have happened in Israel after the people had thrown off the inconvenient and pretentious religion imposed on them. From the mass of the Jewish people, however, there arose again and again men who lent new color to the fading tradition, renewed the admonishments

33 Among Freud's many statements on this issue we find the following:

"... the unmistakable signs of tendentious distortion and stratification accumulated through many centuries." (14)

"... this is the only way in which to treat material whose trustworthiness ... was seriously damaged by the influence of distorting influences." (30n1)

"... no historian can regard the Biblical account of Moses and the Exodus as other than pious myth, which transformed a remote tradition in the interest of its own tendencies. How the tradition originally ran we do not know. What the distorting tendencies were we should like to guess, but we are kept in the dark by our ignorance of historical events." (38)

and demands of Moses, and did not rest until the lost cause was once more regained" (141–42). He had waxed similarly poetical at the close of Part II: "There arose from the midst of the people an unending succession of men, not necessarily descended from Moses' people, but seized by the great and powerful tradition which had gradually grown in darkness, and *it was these men, the prophets, who sedulously preached the old Mosaic doctrine* ... The efforts of the Prophets met with enduring success; the doctrines with which they established the old belief became the permanent content of the Jewish religion" (63; my emphasis).

Mosaic tradition also meant the gradual emergence of religious laws (ceremonial regulations as well as ethical precepts) as these became central to the concept of the Mosaic covenant (whenever that was established). Although he is more than a bit vague about the process by which the laws were formulated, Freud remarks that over time Jewish "religious precepts [became] ever and ever more strict, more exacting, but also more petty" (173). He explicitly assigns the responsibility for this aspect of Jewish culture to the priesthood. While, he never puts the cultural work into any particular historical setting, Freud remarks that in the centuries that followed the exodus from Egypt "it had become the main task of the priests to develop and supervise the ritual." He goes on to observe that ideas or practices that initially only exist as "sparks" within a culture but which have for some time "quietly influenced beliefs and customs" may assume much greater cultural importance "under the influence of special events" until they break forth "more strongly and gain ... dominance with the broad mass of people" (62–64). This is an apt if unwitting description of the achievement of the postexilic theocracy regarding the establishment of Mosaic law as the centerpiece of Judaean culture.[34]

Moreover, Freud observes that, along with their prime role in the creation and maintenance of religious ritual, the priests also took on the task of "caring for the holy texts," a task which, over time, also meant "revising them in accordance with their [the priesthood's] purposes" (62). Those purposes were often advanced through the legitimation that came from grounding their own views on matters of contemporary cultural concern in an adaptive appropriation of the Moses-Exodus scriptural tradition. Freud gets at the basic issue in observing that

34 For broader discussion of the postexilic period of priestly rule and more specific discussion of the development of the (Mosaic) legal codes, see Michael Walzer, *In God's Shadow: Politics in the Hebrew Bible* (New Haven: Yale University Press, 2012), chs. 2 and 8.

> the priests in their rewriting of the Biblical text as we have it ascribe too much to Moses. Institutions as well as ritualistic rules undoubtedly belonging to later times are declared to be Mosaic laws, with the clear intention of enhancing their authority.... The priests, in the accounts they present, desired to establish a continuity between their own times and the Mosaic period. They attempted to deny ... the most striking feature of Jewish religious history: namely, that there was a gap between the Mosaic law-giving and the later Jewish tradition.... Their presentation denies this sequence of events with all the means in its power. (*Moses and Monotheism*, 81)

Although not overly concerned with when this priestly rewriting happened and what precisely prompted it, Freud shows reasonable familiarity with historically-informed biblical scholarship of his day in terms of the evidence of revision visible within the biblical narrative itself. For example, he summarizes and effectively endorses what is still a widely accepted view regarding the redactive process through which the five books of Torah were written and assembled into their final form, what is commonly known as the Graf-Wellhausen or Documentary Hypothesis:

> Let us begin by marking what critical research work on the Bible has to say about how ... the five Books of Moses ... came to be written. The oldest source is considered to be J, the Jahvistic [composed in the time of King David and probably in Judah] ... A little later ... comes the so-called Elohistic [E], belonging to the northern Kingdom. After the destruction of this Kingdom in 722 B.C., a Jewish priest combined portions of J and E and added his own contributions. His compilation is designated JE. In the seventh century Deuteronomy, the fifth book [D], was added ... In the time after the destruction of the Temple, in 586 B.C., during the Exile and after the return, is placed the rewriting called the Priestly Code [P]. (50–51)[35]

35 For opposing views about the continuing viability of the Documentary Hypothesis as a way of describing the composition of Torah, see Roger N. Whybray, *The Making of the Pentateuch: A Methodological Study* (Sheffield, England: JSOT Press, 1987); and Ernest Nicholson, *The Pentateuch in the Twentieth Century: The Legacy of Julius Wellhausen* (Oxford: Clarendon, 1998). Even many scholars who reject the specific formulations of the Documentary Hypothesis would yet agree that Torah and indeed almost all of the Bible (including the writings collected in the New Testament) are at their core palimpsests. There is a constant layering or stratification in which earlier writings still "bleed through" as it were.

Immediately adding of the Hebrew Bible as a whole that "the first century saw a definitive revision, and since then the work has not been materially altered," Freud later fills in some of the details of the work of completion and of its cultural impact: "The political misfortune of the nation taught them to appreciate the only possession they had retained, their written records, at its true value. Immediately after the destruction of the Temple in Jerusalem by Titus, Rabbi Jochanan ben Sakkai asked for permission to open at Jabneh the first school of the study of Torah. From now on, it was the Holy Book, and the study of it, that kept the scattered people together" (147).

2.2.1 Comments

There are many critical aspects of the Bible's compositional history that Freud either doesn't know or simply ignores as irrelevant to his concerns, Within the general time-frame of 650–400 BCE, two major gaps in Freud's reconstruction merit special comment.

1. First, while his summary of the Documentary Hypothesis demonstrates his grasp that Torah at least has a compositional history, Freud doesn't have any clear interpretive strategy for addressing how the perspectives of different time periods offer vastly different accounts of the national history even where later accounts essentially absorb earlier accounts. For example, in mentioning that Deuteronomy "was added" in the seventh century, he likely had at least a rudimentary understanding of the scholarly view that the book's primary association is with the court of the reformist King Josiah and was perhaps composed by the prophet Jeremiah or by a scribal tradition in which Jeremiah was a leading figure.[36] But he may not have fully grasped that Deuteronomy is associated with a broader tradition (the "Deuteronomistic History") that collected and reshaped some if not all of the biblical writings that had been composed prior to Josiah's reign.[37] In short, the fact that the core narrative in Torah was (re)fashioned from the perspective of that reign and so consistently

36 For the Bible's own account of the "discovery" of this book, which is comprised primarily of Moses' farewell sermons to the remnant of the people of the Exodus, see 2 Kings 22; for discussion of this moment in the narrative, see Harris, 112–13. For discussion of the origin and content of Deuteronomy more broadly, see Moshe Weinfield, "Deuteronomy, Book of," in *The Anchor Bible Dictionary*, vol. 2, ed. D. N. Freedman (New York: Doubleday 1992), 168–83; and the extensive commentary on the text provided by Ronald E. Clements in *The New Interpreter's Bible*, vol. 2 (Nashville: Abingdon Press, 1998), 271–538.

37 For discussion of the Deuteronomistic History, Martin Noth, *The Deuteronomistic History* (Sheffield, England: JSOT, 1981); Terence E. Fretheim, *The Deuteronomistic History* (Nashville: Abingdon Press, 1993); and Richard E. Friedman, *Who Wrote the Bible?* (New York: Harper & Row, 1987), chs. 4–6.

reflects the interests of Judah in the final years of its glory before the ancient kingdom of David was destroyed never figures into Freud's broader assessment of the Moses-Exodus story. We might contrast Freud's neglect with a more current view. Building on his general observation that "the event [of the Exodus] is supposed to have taken place in Egypt, yet Egyptian sources know it not," Redford notes more specifically that "a perusal of the bondage and Exodus narratives strains the imagination to elicit Egyptian background." While the narratives "might be explained" as the sort of work "indulged in by Israelite aliens living among Egyptians, or close enough to have limited and distorted knowledge of their customs," he concludes that nothing in the biblical account "suggests close familiarity with Egypt."[38]

2. Even if we accept that the core narrative (the nation's foundation myth or origin story) was created in the late-seventh century (mostly in tandem with the writing of Deuteronomy), the completion of the Hebrew Bible as a whole, as Freud himself points out, was a postexilic effort. Torah in particular, at least as we now have it, is primarily a postexilic work, though some of the writing and rewriting may have taken place during the Captivity. On the very specific question of Egyptian topographical references in the Exodus-account, for example, Redford observes that

> whoever supplied the geographical information that now adorns the story had no information earlier than the Saite period (seventh to sixth centuries B.C.) The eastern Delta and Sinai he describes are those of the 26th Dynasty kings and *the early Persian overlords*: his toponyms reflect the renewed interest in the eastern frontier evidenced for this period by fort building and canalization. He knows of 'Goshen' of the Qedarite Arabs, and a legendary 'Land of Ramesses.' He cannot locate the Egyptian court to anything but the largest and most famous city in his own day in the northeastern Delta, namely Tanis, the royal residence from about 1070 to 725 B.C. .... In short, with respect to the geography of the Exodus, *the post-Exilic compiler of the present Biblical version* had no genuinely ancient details. He felt constrained to supply them from the Egypt of his own day and, significantly perhaps, cited several places where Asiatic

38 *Egypt, Canaan, and Israel in Ancient Times*, 408, 410, 411–12. For broad discussion of the central role played by the court of Josiah in creating what we might call the first full draft of Torah, at the heart of which is the Moses-Exodus story, see Finkelstein and Silberman, Prologue and ch. 11.

> elements and especially Judaean mercenaries resided *in the sixth and fifth centuries*.[39]

More broadly, whatever first draft of Torah existed at the court of Josiah was reworked as a response to the Babylonian Captivity, a major event that elicits only a few scattered mentions in *Moses and Monotheism*.[40]

In sum, while he knows that the Bible as a collection of writings has its own history, Freud has no way of taking its full history into account without undermining the story of an Egyptian Moses and his Aton-religion that he sees as the foundation of "the origin of monotheism among the Jews." In this context we might repurpose the very comment Freud makes regarding the priestly redactors: "[his] presentation denies [much of the actual historical] sequence of events with all the means in [his] power." In Part II Freud remarks that "Eduard Meyer says, it is true, that he never doubted there was a kernel of ... truth in the story of bondage in Egypt and the catastrophe of the Egyptians, but evidently he does not know where that recognized fact belongs and what to do with it" (40). We might turn this statement around and apply it to *Moses and Monotheism*: Freud is aware that the Bible evolved over a long period of time and thus as a response to very different events; he simply "does not know ... what to do with" the very facts he recognized because he has no way of sustaining his own (psychoanalytic) narrative unless he can retain something much closer to the biblical version of the events, at least in terms of a basic dating, narrative chronology, and setting. In short, maintaining the Moses-Exodus Ur-story as grounded in events of the fourteenth century BCE (the biblical version) is crucial to what he thinks is most important about the story: its historical, which is to say psychoanalytic, truth. The exploration of that truth has been the central focus of the main body of this study.

---

39 *Egypt, Canaan, and Israel in Ancient Times*, 409–10; my emphases.

40 Freud not only refers to the general role of the priesthood in creating and preserving the texts that were eventually assembled as the Hebrew Bible, but he also mentions the particular roles played by Ezra and Nehemiah: "about eight hundred years had elapsed between the Exodus and the fixation of the Biblical text by Ezra and Nehemiah" (57). It would be more accurate to understand Ezra and Nehemiah's role less in terms of the "fixation of the [entire] Biblical text" than in terms of the "fixation" of Torah: as the biblical account tells us, Ezra (assisted by Nehemiah) brought the completed Torah from Persia to Jerusalem (most likely in the mid- to late-fifth century BCE) and had it read aloud in its entirety to the assembled people (see Nehemiah 8:1–8). Freud's lack of appreciation of the full meaning of Ezra's critical role in the creation of the Mosaic tradition is telling.

Bibliography

Abraham, Nicolas. "Notes on the Phantom: A Complement to Freud's Metapsychology." In Nicolas Abraham and Maria Torok, *The Shell and the Kernel: Renewals of Psychoanalysis*, vol. 1. Ed. and trans. Nicolas T. Rand. Chicago: University of Chicago Press, 1994. 171–76.

Achebe, Chinua. "The Role of the Writer in a New Nation." In *African Writers on African Writing*. Ed. G. D. Killam. Evanston, IL: Northwestern University Press, 1973. 7–13.

Agamben, Giorgio. *Homo Sacer: Sovereign Power and Bare Life*. Trans. Daniel Heller-Roazen. Stanford: Stanford University Press, 1998.

Agamben, Giorgio. *The Time That Remains: A Commentary on the Letter to the Romans*. Trans. Patricia Dailey. Stanford: Stanford University Press, 2005.

Alter, Robert. *The Art of Biblical Narrative*. New York: Basic Books, 1981.

Alter, Robert. *The Art of Biblical Poetry*. New York: Basic Books, 1985.

Armstrong, Karen. *A History of God: The 4000-Year Old Quest of Judaism, Christianity, and Islam*. New York: Ballantine Books, 1993.

Assmann, Jan. *Moses the Egyptian: The Memory of Egypt in Western Monotheism*. Cambridge, MA: Harvard University Press, 1997.

Assmann, Jan. *Of God and Gods: Egypt, Israel, and the Rise of Monotheism*. Madison, WI: University of Wisconsin Press, 2008.

Assmann, Jan. *Cultural Memory and Early Civilization: Writing, Remembrance, and Political Imagination*. Cambridge: Cambridge University Press, 2011.

Assmann, Jan. *From Akhenaten to Moses: Ancient Egypt and Religious Change*. New York: The American University in Cairo Press 2014.

Assmann, Jan. *The Invention of Religion: Faith and Covenant in the Book of Exodus*. Trans. Robert Savage. Princeton: Princeton University Press, 2018.

Augustine. *Confessions*. Trans. Edward B. Pusey. New York: Modern Library, 1999.

Badiou, Alain. *Saint Paul: The Foundation of Universalism*. Trans. Ray Brassier. Stanford: Stanford University Press, 2003.

Badiou, Alain. *Being and Event*. Trans. Oliver Feltham. London: Bloomsbury Academic, 2013.

Barnaby, Andrew. *Coming Too Late: Reflections on Freud and Belatedness*. Albany: SUNY Press, 2017.

Bellamy, Elizabeth, J. "From Ficino to Freud: Egyptian / Greek / Jew in Cultural History." In *Repossessions: Psychoanalysis and the Phantasms of Early Modern Culture*. Ed. Timothy Murray and Alan K. Smith. Minneapolis: University of Minnesota Press, 1998. 23–46.

Bertman, Stephen. *Cultural Amnesia: America's Future and the Crisis of Memory*. Westport, Conn.: Praeger, 2000.

Bhabha, Homi K. *The Location of Culture*. New York: Routlege, 1994.

Bloom, Harold. *The Anxiety of Influence: A Theory of Poetry*. New York: Oxford University Press, 1973.

Borg, Marcus, and John Dominic Crossan. *The First Paul: Reclaiming the Radical Visionary Behind the Church's Conservative Icon*. New York: HarperOne, 2009.

Branagh, Kenneth. *Hamlet: Screenplay, Introduction, and Film Diary*. New York: Norton, 1996.

Brooks, Peter. "Freud's Masterplot," *Yale French Studies* (*Literature and Psychoanalysis: The Question of Reading Otherwise*) 55 / 56 (1977): 280–300.

Caruth, Cathy. Ed. *Trauma: Explorations in Memory*. Baltimore: Johns Hopkins University Press, 1995.

Caruth, Cathy. *Unclaimed Experience: Trauma, Narrative, and History*. Baltimore: Johns Hopkins University Press, 1996.

Cavell, Stanley. *This New Yet Unapproachable America: Lectures after Emerson after Wittgenstein*. Albuquerque: Living Batch Press, 1989.

Cavell, Stanley. *Disowning Knowledge in Seven Plays of Shakespeare*. Cambridge: Cambridge University Press, 2003.

Clements, Ronald E. "Comments on Deuteronomy." In *The New Interpreter's Bible*, vol. 2. Nashville: Abingdon Press, 1998. 271–538.

Crossan, John Dominic. *Jesus: A Revolutionary Biography*. San Francisco: HarperSanFrancisco, 1989.

De Certeau, Michel. *The Writing of History*. Trans. Tom Conley. New York: Columbia University Press, 1988.

Derrida, Jacques. *Specters of Marx: The State of Debt, the Work of Mourning, and the New International*. Trans. Peggy Kamuf. New York: Routledge, 1994.

Derrida, Jacques. *Archive Fever: A Freudian Impression*. Trans. Eric Prenowitz. Chicago. University of Chicago Press, 1995.

Durkheim, Émile. *The Elementary Forms of Religious Life*. Trans. Joseph Ward Swain. London: George Allen & Unwin, 1915.

Durrant, Sam. *Postcolonial Narrative and the Work of Mourning*. Albany: SUNY Press, 2004.

Edelheit, Henry. "On the Biology of Language: Darwinian / Lamarckian Homology in Human Inheritance (with some thoughts about the Lamarckism of Freud)." In *Psychoanalysis and Language* (Psychiatry and the Humanities, v. 3). New Haven: Yale University Press, 1978. 45–74.

Ehrman, Bart D., ed. *The Apostolic Fathers*. Trans. Bart D. Ehrman. 2 vols. Cambridge, MA: Harvard University Press, 2003.

Erikson, Kai. "Notes on Trauma and Community." In *Trauma: Explorations in Memory*. Ed. Cathy Caruth. Baltimore: Johns Hopkins University Press, 1995. 183–99.

Felman, Shoshana, and Dori Laub. *Testimony: Crises of Witnessing in Literature. Psychoanalysis, and History*. New York: Routledge, 1992.

Finkelstein, Israel, and Neil Asher Silberman. *The Bible Unearthed: Archaeology's New Vision of Ancient Israel and the Origin of Its Sacred Texts*. New York: The Free Press, 2001.

Fredman, Ruth Gruber. *The Passover Seder: Afikoman in Exile*. Philadelphia: University of Pennsylvania Press, 1981.

Fretheim, Terence E. *The Deuteronomistic History*. Nashville: Abingdon Press, 1993.

Freud, Sigmund. *Gesammelte Shriften*. 12 vols. Vienna: Internationaler Psychoanalytischer Verlag, 1922–34.

Freud, Sigmund. *Aus den Anfängen der Psychoanalyse: Briefe an Wilhelm Fliess, Abhandlungen und Notizen aus den Jahren 1887–1902*. London: Imago Publishing, 1950.

Freud, Sigmund. *Standard Edition of the Complete Psychological Works of Sigmund Freud*. Ed. and trans. James Strachey, et al. 24 vols. London: Hogarth Press, 1953–74.

Freud, Sigmund. *The Origins of Psycho-Analysis: Letters to Wilhelm Fliess, Drafts and Notes, 1887–1902*. Ed. Marie Bonaparte, Anna Freud, and Ernst Kris. Trans. Eric Mosbacher and James Strachey. New York: Basic Books, 1954.

Freud, Sigmund. *Moses and Monotheism*. Trans. Katherine Jones. New York: Vintage, 1954.

Freud, Sigmund. *Letters of Sigmund Freud*. Ed. Ernst L. Freud. Trans. Tania Stern and James Stern. New York: Basic Books, 1960.

Freud, Sigmund. *Gesammelte Werke*. 18 vol. Ed. Marie Bonaparte, Anna Freud, et al. Frankfurt am Main: S. Fischer, 1968–78.

Freud, Sigmund. "Overview of the Transference Neuroses." In *A Phylogenetic Fantasy: Overview of the Transference Neuroses*. Ed. Ilse Grubitch-Simitis. Trans. Axel Hoffer and Peter T. Hoffer. Cambridge, MA: Harvard University Press, 1987. 5–20.

Freud, Sigmund, and Arnold Zweig. *The Letters of Sigmund Freud and Arnold Zweig*. Ed. Ernst L. Freud. Trans. Elaine Robson-Scott and William Robson-Scott. New York: Harcourt, Brace & World, 1970.

Friedman, Richard E. *Who Wrote the Bible?* New York: Harper & Row, 1987.

Geertz, Clifford. *The Interpretation of Cultures: Selected Essays*. New York: Basic Books, 1973.

Greenblatt, Stephen. *Hamlet in Purgatory*. Princeton: Princeton University Press, 2002.

Greenblatt, Stephen. *Will in the World: How Shakespeare Became Shakespeare*. New York: Norton, 2004.

Greg, W. W. "Hamlet's Hallucination." *Modern Language Review* 12 (1917): 393–421.

Harris, Stephen L. *Understanding the Bible*, 8th ed. New York: McGraw-Hill, 2011.

Hawass, Zahi A. *The Golden King: The World of Tutankhamun*. Washington, DC: National Geographic Society, 2006.

Hirsch, Marianne. *The Generation of Postmemory: Writing and Visual Culture After the Holocaust*. New York: Columbia University Press, 2012.

Hoffmeier, James K. *Akhenaten and the Origins of Monotheism*. Oxford: Oxford University Press, 2015.

Hornung, Erik. *Akhenaten and the Religion of Light*. Trans. David Lorton. Ithaca: Cornell University Press, 1999.

Jones, Ernest. *Hamlet and Oedipus*. Garden City, NY: Doubleday, 1954.

Josephus. *Against Apion, or On the Antiquity of the Jews*. In *Josephus*. Trans. H. St. J. Thackery, 9 vols. Cambridge, MA: Harvard University Press, 1961. 1:161–411.

Kafka, Franz. *Briefe, 1902–1924*. New York: Schocken Books, 1958.

Khanna, Ranjana. *Dark Continents: Psychoanalysis and Colonialism*. Durham, NC: Duke University Press, 2003.

Lacan, Jacques. *The Language of the Self: The Function of Language in Psychoanalysis*. Trans. Anthony Wilden. New York: Delta Books, 1968.

Lacan, Jacques. "Desire and the Interpretation of Desire in *Hamlet*." Trans. James Hulbert. In *Literature and Psychoanalysis: The Question of Reading Otherwise*. Ed. Shoshana Felman. Baltimore: Johns Hopkins University Press, 1982. 11–52.

LaCapra, Dominick. *Representing the Holocaust: History, Theory, Trauma*. Ithaca: Cornell University Press, 1994.

LaCapra, Dominick. *Writing History, Writing Trauma*. Baltimore: Johns Hopkins University Press, 2001.

Langer, Lawrence L. *Landscapes of Jewish Experience: Paintings by Samuel Bak*. Boston: Pucker Gallery in association with Brandeis University Press, 1997.

Laplanche, Jean. *Life and Death in Psychoanalysis*. Trans. Jeffrey Mehlman. Baltimore: Johns Hopkins University Press, 1976.

Laplanche, Jean. *New Foundations for Psychoanalysis*. Trans. David Macey. Oxford: Basil Blackwell, 1989.

Laplanche, Jean. *Essays on Otherness*. Ed. John Fletcher. New York: Routledge, 1999.

Laplanche, Jean, and Jean-Bertrand Pontalis. "Fantasy and the Origins of Sexuality." *The International Journal of Psycho-analysis* 49 (1968): 1–18.

Laplanche, Jean, and Jean-Bertrand Pontalis. *The Language of Psycho-analysis*. Trans. Donald Nicholson-Smith. New York: Norton, 1974.

Lear, Jonathan. *Love and its Place in Nature: A Philosophical Interpretation of Freudian Psychoanalysis*. New York: Farrar, Strauss, & Giroux, 1990.

Leys, Ruth. *Trauma: A Genealogy*. Chicago: University of Chicago Press, 2000.

Lippman, Robert. "Freud's B'nai B'rith Dream: Having Lost His Way, His 'Brethren ... Were Unkind and Scornful ...'" *The Psychoanalytic Review* 108 (2021): 243–50.

Michaels, Walter Benn. "'You who never was there': Slavery and the New Historicism, Deconstruction and the Holocaust." *Narrative* 4 (1996): 1–16.

Mosès, Stéphane. *System and Revelation: The Philosophy of Franz Rosenzweig*. Trans. Catherine Tihanyi. Detroit: Wayne State University Press, 1992.

Mourad, Anna-Latifa. *Rise of the Hyksos: Egypt and the Levant from the Middle Kingdom to the Second Intermediate Period*. London: Archaeopress Archaeology, 2015.

Nicholson, Ernest. *The Pentateuch in the Twentieth Century: The Legacy of Julius Wellhausen*. Oxford: Clarendon, 1998.

Nietzsche, Friedrich. *The Birth of Tragedy: Out of the Spirit of Music*. Ed. Michael Tanner. Trans. Shaun Whiteside. London: Penguin Books, 1993.

Noth, Martin. *The Deuteronomistic History*. Sheffield, England: JSOT, 1981.

Oren, Eliezer D., ed. *The Hyksos: New Historical and Archaeological Perspectives*. Philadelphia: University of Pennsylvania Press, 1997.

Paul, Robert. *Moses and Civilization: The Meaning Behind Freud's Myth*. New Haven: Yale University Press, 1996.

Rabaté, Jean-Michael. *The Cambridge Introduction of Literature and Psychoanalysis*. Cambridge: Cambridge University Press, 2014.

Redford, Donald B. "The Hyksos Invasion in History and Tradition." *Orientalia* 39 (1970): 1–51.

Redford, Donald B. *Akhenaten, the Heretic King*. Princeton: Princeton University Press, 1984.

Redford, Donald B. *Egypt, Canaan, and Israel in Ancient Times*. Princeton, NJ: Princeton University Press, 1992.

Redford, Donald B. "The Monotheism of Akhenaten." In *Aspects of Monotheism: How God is One*. Ed. Hershel Shanks and Jack Meinhardt. Washington, D.C.: Biblical Archaeology Society, 1997. 11–26.

Redford, Donald B. "Akhenaten: New Theories and Old Facts." *Bulletin of the American Schools of Oriental Research* 369 (2013): 9–34.

Ricoeur, Paul. *The Conflict of Interpretations: Essays in Hermeneutics*. Ed. Don Ihde. Evanston, IL: Northwestern University Press, 1974.

Robert, Marthe. *From Oedipus to Moses: Freud's Jewish Identity*. Trans. Ralph Manheim. Garden City, NY: Anchor Books, 1976.

Roiphe, Anne. *Generation Without Memory: A Jewish Journey in Christian America*. New York: Linden Press / Simon & Schuster, 1981.

Rosenberg, David. *The Book of J*. New York: Vintage, 1990.

Rosenzweig, Franz. *The Star of Redemption*. Trans. William W. Hallo. New York: Holt, Rinehart and Winston, 1970.

Santner, Eric L. *On the Psychotheology of Everyday Life: Reflections on Freud and Rosenzweig*. Chicago: University of Chicago Press, 2001.

Scholem, Gershom. *The Messianic Idea in Judaism and Other Essays in Jewish Spirituality*. New York: Schocken Books, 1971.

Schwartz, Regina, M. *The Curse of Cain: The Violent Legacy of Monotheism*. Chicago: University of Chicago Press, 1997.

Sellin, Ernst. *Mose und seine Bedeutung für die israelitisch-jüdishe Religionsgeschischte*. Leipzig: A. Deichert, 1922.

Shakespeare, William. *The Riverside Shakespeare*, 2nd ed. Ed. G. Blakemore Evans et al. Boston: Houghton Mifflin, 1997.

Shakespeare, William. *The Norton Shakespeare*. Ed. Stephen Greenblatt et al. New York: W. W. Norton, 1997.

Spiro, Melford E. *Culture and Human Nature: Theoretical Papers of Melford E. Spiro*. Ed. Benjamin Kilborne and L.L. Langness. Chicago: University of Chicago Press, 1987.

Stager, Lawrence E. "Forging an Identity: The Emergence of Ancient Israel." In *The Oxford History of the Biblical World*. Ed. Michael D. Coogan. New York: Oxford University Press, 1998. 142–49.

Sternberg, Meir. "Time and Space in Biblical (Hi)story Telling: The Grand Chronology." In *The Book and the Text: The Bible and Literary Theory*. Ed. Regina M. Schwartz. Oxford: Basil Blackwell, 1990. 80–145.

Sulloway, Frank J. *Freud, Biologist of the Mind: Beyond the Psychoanalytic Legend*. New York: Basic Books, 1979.

Tal, Kali. *Worlds of Hurt: Reading the Literatures of Trauma*. Cambridge: Cambridge University Press, 1996.

Tanakh: A New Translation of the Holy Scriptures According to the Traditional Hebrew Text. New York: The Jewish Publication Society, 1985.

Taubes, Jacob. *The Political Theology of Paul*. Trans. Dana Hollander. Stanford: Stanford University Press, 2004.

Van der Kolk, Bessel, and Onno van der Hart. "The Intrusive Past: The Flexibility of Memory and the Engraving of Trauma." In *Trauma: Explorations in Memory*. Ed. Cathy Caruth. Baltimore: Johns Hopkins University Press, 1995. 158–82.

Van Seters, John. *The Hyksos: A New Investigation*. New Haven: Yale University Press, 1966.

Walzer, Michael. *Exodus and Revolution*. New York: Basic Books, 1985.

Walzer, Michael. *In God's Shadow: Politics in the Hebrew Bible*. New Haven: Yale University Press, 2012.

Watson, Robert. *The Rest is Silence: Death as Annihilation in the English Renaissance*. Berkeley: University of California Press, 1994.

Weinfield, Moshe. "Deuteronomy, Book of." In *The Anchor Bible Dictionary*, vol. 2. Ed. D. N. Freedman. New York: Doubleday 1992. 168–83.

Whybray, Roger N. *The Making of the Pentateuch: A Methodological Study*. Sheffield, England: JSOT Press, 1987.

Wieseltier, Leon. "Leviticus." In *Congregation: Contemporary Writers Read the Jewish Bible*. Ed. David Rosenberg. New York: Harcourt Brace Jovanovich, 1987. 27–38.

Wright, Lawrence. "Letter from Jerusalem: Forcing the End." *The New Yorker*, July 20, 1998: 42–53.

Yerushalmi, Yosef Hayim. *Zakhor: Jewish History and Jewish Memory*. Seattle: University of Washington Press, 1982.

Yerushalmi, Yosef Hayim. *Freud's Moses: Judaism Terminable and Interminable*. New Haven: Yale University Press, 1991.

Young, Kay, and Jeffrey L. Saver. "The Neurology of Narrative." *Substance* 30 (2001): 72–84.

Žižek, Slavoj. *The Puppet and the Dwarf: The Perverse Core of Christianity*. Cambridge, MA: MIT Press, 2003.

Index

www.ingramcontent.com/pod-product-compliance
Lightning Source LLC
Chambersburg PA
CBHW071247230926
51849CB00001B/261
* 9 7 8 9 0 0 4 7 0 1 0 8 3 *